Gower Handbook of Internal Communication

To Bev, for driving me

Gower Handbook of Internal Communication

Second Edition

Edited by
MARC WRIGHT

GOWER

Published by
Gower Publishing Limited
Wey Court East
Union Road
Farnham
Surrey, GU9 7PT
England

Ashgate Publishing Company
Suite 420
101 Cherry Street
Burlington,
VT 05401-4405
USA

www.gowerpublishing.com

British Library Cataloguing in Publication Data
Gower handbook of internal communication. -- 2nd ed.
1. Communication in personnel management. 2. Communication in management. 3. Communication in organizations.
I. Handbook of internal communication II. Wright, Marc.
658.4'5-dc22

ISBN-13: 9780566086892

Library of Congress Cataloging-in-Publication Data
Gower handbook of internal communication / edited by Marc Wright. -- 2nd ed.
p. cm.
Includes bibliographical references and index.
ISBN 978-0-566-08689-2 (hardcover) -- ISBN 978-0-7546-9097-9 (ebook)
1. Communication in personnel management. 2. Communication in management.
I. Wright, Marc.

HF5549.5.C6G69 2009
658.4'5--dc22

2009012106

Mixed Sources
Product group from well-managed forests and other controlled sources
www.fsc.org Cert no. SA-COC-1565
© 1996 Forest Stewardship Council
FSC

Printed and bound in Great Britain by
MPG Books Ltd, Bodmin, Cornwall.

Contents

List of Figures

List of Tables

About the Editor

Marc Wright MA. Oxon. has spent 25 years in corporate communications. He was the Creative Director and Chairman of two agencies – Crown Business Communications and MCA Live – where he designed and produced internal communication programmes for governments and corporations including British Airways, BT, Vodafone, American Express, ICI and Tetra Pak.

He wrote and directed the BBC TV series, *20 Steps to Better Management – the Drama*. He is a former Chairman of the International Visual Communication Association and has been voted into the Top 10 speakers on corporate communications worldwide by the International Association of Business Communicators. He is the publisher of the knowledge site www.simpy-communicate.com, which is read by 16,000 communicators each month.

About the Contributors

The internal communications community is a relatively small and supportive bunch. I am hugely indebted to the contributors to this book. Some are long-standing acquaintances yet many I found for the first time through the wiki we used to find and develop the content. I am glad to say that as a result many have become close friends.

I am particularly indebted to Ike Levick who, as well as contributing an article herself, edited Bill Quirke's chapter on Leadership and Engagement. Another special mention goes to Fiona Robertson for her clear and incisive chapters in Part II.

Caisa Alpsten

Caisa Alpsten is founder and Head of Vinco in Scandinavia (www.vinco.se). She has extensive experience in strategic internal communication and communicating change, both as communication manager and as consultant/advisor for big Nordic and international companies within the oil and energy sector, banking, consumer trade and public sector.

Lindsay Uittenbogaard

Lindsay Uittenbogaard moved into organisational communication from a general management career 10 years ago. Since then, she has worked with clients such as Shell, Petroleum Development Oman and Unilever. She is currently the Communication Manager for T-Systems exclusively on the Shell Global account. Lindsay is also VP Professional Development for the Dutch branch of the IABC and has won awards for her work in business and corporate film production. She shares her approach and more articles at www.lindsaybogaard.co.uk.

Ian Buckingham

Ian Buckingham is the founder of the Bring Yourself 2 Work Fellowship (www.by2w.co.uk), a close-knit group of organisations representing the communication agency, arts in business, design and advertising and skills development worlds. He was formerly the founding MD of Interbrand Inside and Partner at Smythe Dorward Lambert and is a widely published author with works including *Brand Engagement – How Employees Make or Break Brands* (Palgrave Macmillan 2007) and *Brand Champions* (due 2009).

Sue Dewhurst

Sue Dewhurst is Managing Director of The SD Group, a company specialising in professional development for internal communicators and communication-related training, coaching and toolkits for leaders, line managers and project teams. She led in-house teams at organisations such as the UK Post Office and Barclays Bank before starting her consulting career.

Ruth Findlay

Ruth Findlay has over a decade of experience working at a senior level in internal communications. She has worked for the Japanese Government and Bank of Scotland and was a Non-Executive Director of Carnegie College. She currently leads the internal communications function for the diverse and forward thinking Scottish Water. She is a member of the Chartered Institute of Public Relations and was one of the first UK practitioners of Appreciative Inquiry. She has won many awards for her innovative approach to communications projects and channels.

Liam FitzPatrick

Liam FitzPatrick is a consultant and specialist in professional development for internal communicators. Liam has helped organisations as diverse as American Airlines, BP, The House of Commons, Marconi, Maersk and the UK Government.

Nicky Flook

Nicky Flook is the founder of Mandarin Kite (www.mandarin-kite.com), an innovative communications consultancy, whose award-winning change campaigns are known as much for their bottom-line financial returns as for their 'laugh out loud' fun. Nicky is a passionate advocate of new and interesting ways to communicate. As well as the interactive StoryMat©, she has developed the ground-breaking RumourMill© – helping clients tap into the power of informal networks. Mandarin Kite's clients include B&Q, Compass Group, Fat Face, and GAP.

Joanna Goodrick

Joanna Goodrick is a specialist in communications and change management with a specific focus on information technology, working for Napp Pharmaceuticals in the UK. She is also experienced in managing information technology change across different European cultures. Joanna has previously worked in policy and strategy publications and corporate communications for the International Telecommunication Union – a UN agency based in Switzerland.

Jacqui Hitt

Jacqui Hitt is founder of JMH, an independent consultancy specialising in communication, engagement and change. Over the last 18 years, she has worked in the UK, Europe, US and Asia helping organisations engage their people around important business issues using a blend of communication, coaching, dialogue, psychology and learning-based approaches.

Kelly Kass

Before entering the world of corporate video and internal communication, Kelly Kass worked in television production as a coordinator for CBS and Lifetime TV, followed by a 6-year stint at a major New York City production company. She has also worked as a journalist for several New York area newspapers and even dabbled in live radio news. When she's not writing, blogging and editing for simply-communicate.com, Kelly also works as a video producer for corporate and charity organisations.

Kevin Keohane

Kevin Keohane is currently Global Head of Brand and Employee Engagement for Publicis, the world's 4th largest media group, which includes Saatchi & Saatchi, Leo Burnett, Zenith Optimedia and Publicis Consultants. With more than 15 years' experience in business communication, Kevin is an accredited business communicator. In addition to his core expertise in brand management, employee engagement, marketing and PR, he also has 5-years experience in HR and organisational development. He was instrumental in creating the Intranet Benchmarking Forum (IBF) and founded the UK Usability Professionals' Association. He holds an MA in Social Science and is a graduate of the Georgetown Institute on Political Journalism. His most recent work includes developing global employer brands for BP and The Coca-Cola Company. His blog, 'Death to Internal Marketing' can be found at www.kevinkeohane.com.

Mike Klein

Mike Klein is EMEA Communications Lead for the Tartan programme at Cargill, based in Mechelen in Belgium. Prior to joining Cargill in his first inhouse role, Mike was an internal communications consultant on a wide range of major change initiatives and programmes, including EasyJet's acquisition of Go Airlines, Cable & Wireless' launch of Digital Cable Television in the UK, and the US Department of Transportation's COMPASS program. Prior to receiving his MBA at London Business School in 1998, Mike managed political campaigns in 14 US states. He has also published an internal communications blog, CommsOffensive325.

Ike Levick

Ike Levick (nee Veeneklaas) joined Salt & Shein, the Australian recruitment firm specialising in corporate affairs and communication roles, to focus on agency and consultancy clients and candidates. She is passionate about people, internal and external communication. With almost 15 years of experience spanning consultancy and in-house roles, she has worked for ABN AMRO (Australia and New Zealand), Impact Employee Communications (Sydney) communications and brand engagement consultancy Banner McBride (London) and Shreeveport Management Consultancy (London)

Ulla Mogestad

Ulla Mogestad is Vinco's specialist in communicating change. She is an experienced advisor to leaders and communicators. Her background in international consultancies like Carta and Booz-Allen & Hamilton, includes more than 15 years of accomplishments in the field of change management for many big Nordic and global companies. She has also written books about change management. Among others *Make Change Work, a practical guide for communicating change*, published by Ericsson Company 2000.

Paul Miller

Paul Miller is a partner at Bring Yourself 2 Work and a former England gymnast, coach, performing artist, writer, coach, trainer, consultant and facilitator. As well as writing extensively for business journals, he has a number of BBC plays and two West End shows to his name.

Paul Miller

Paul Miller is a business and social entrepreneur and a key figure in the development of the modern information workplace. He is best known as Chief Executive Officer and Founder of The Empowerment Company Limited and as CEO and Founder of the Intranet Benchmarking Forum (IBF). Paul established IBF in 2002, and today it has more than 100 member organisations around the world. It is widely acknowledged that IBF has set the industry standards for intranet and portal performance.

Paul spent his early career as a national newspaper journalist. In 1990, he launched *WAVE* magazine, covering new thinking in the arts, business and technology, and a forerunner of *Fast Company* and *Wired*. Paul went on to become one of the pioneers of the new discipline of employee communication. In 1992, he set up The Empowerment Group, a niche consultancy focused on helping global blue-chip organisations communicate change. He called on his experiences to write the best-selling knowledge-management handbook *Mobilising the Power of What You Know* (Random House, 1998). Paul is also Executive Producer of My Green Film, the global green corporate film festival and CEO of the Internet Benchmarking Group (IBG).

Yang-May Ooi

Yang-May Ooi is the Online Editor for THFC Space at The Housing Finance Corporation (www.thfcorp.com) where she is also the Security Portfolio Manager. In a personal capacity, she is a writer and also blogs on cross-cultural topics and social media at Fusion View (www.fusionview.co.uk). Her book, *International Communications Strategy: Developments in Cross-Cultural Communications, PR and Social Media* (co-authored with Silvia Cambie) is published by Kogan Page in July 2009.

Jonathan Priest

Jonathan Priest is a creative writer specialising in corporate communication and training and can be found at www.creative-writer.com. His scriptwriting activities have been rewarded with 45 international awards. Jonathan was recently made a Fellow of the International Visual Communication Association (IVCA) to reflect his career-long contribution to professional business communication.

Bill Quirke

Bill Quirke is MD of Synopsis – www.synopsisonline.com – an internal communication consultancy whose clients include AstraZeneca, Vodafone, Intel, Shell, BBC, Diageo, UBS Group, Pfizer, Rolls-Royce, Unilever and Whitbread. He is the author of *Making the Connections – Using Internal Communication to Turn Strategy into Action* (Gower 2008) and *Communicating Corporate Change* (McGraw Hill, 1995).

Fiona Robertson

With over 20 years' work in media, Fiona is an experienced producer of live events, focusing predominantly on the areas of engagement, change and internal communication. Building on her degree in Philosophy and Psychology, she delivers corporate programmes aimed at individuals which then generate profound shifts at an organisational level. Fiona also writes web content, speeches and scripts and was the original Editor of simply-communicate.com. In this role, she helped to design the site's structure, commissioned over 1,000 articles on internal communication and wrote approximately 150 of its key features and templates. Fiona can be contacted at fiona@fionarobertson.co.uk.

Hilary Scarlett

Hilary Scarlett's work has spanned Europe, the US and Asia and concentrates on the development of people-focused change management programmes and employee communication. She is a director of Scarlett Associates, www.scarlettassoc.com, whose clients include Virgin Atlantic Airways, The Natural History Museum, Deutsche Bank, EDF Energy, the COI and the NSPCC. She holds an MA in Modern and Medieval Languages and Oriental Studies from King's College, Cambridge University.

Ingrid Selene

Ingrid Selene is a Principal with Aon Consulting and has executive responsibility for Aon Consulting, Australia's human capital practice. Her responsibilities include Aon's communication consulting practice in Australia which specialises in employee and superannuation/pension fund communications. Her career also encompasses strategic management consulting and market research, as well as various board positions in the not-for- profit sector. Ingrid is a frequent presenter at conferences on the topics of strategic communication and human capital risk.

Euan Semple

Euan Semple is a speaker and consultant on introducing social media into large organisations including BP, Nokia and The World Health Organisation. Euan pioneered the use of weblogs, wikis and online forums while at the BBC and his work there continues to enable staff to work more effectively and more collaboratively across the entire organisation. www.euansemple.com

Lee Smith

Lee Smith is an award winning communicator and one of the UK's leading bloggers on internal communication.

In 2006, he co-founded the UK-based internal communication agency, Gatehouse (www.gatehousegroup.co.uk), which provides employee engagement and behavioural change advice and consultancy to organisations ranging from large corporates through to the government sector and charities. He holds an M.Sc. in Corporate Communication & Reputation Management and is a Fellow of the Chartered Institute of Public Relations.

Lindsay Uittenbogaard

Lindsay Uittenbogaard moved into organisational communication from a general management career 10 years ago. Since then, she has worked with clients such as Shell, Petroleum Development Oman and Unilever. She is currently the Communication Manager for T-Systems exclusively on the Shell Global account. Lindsay is also VP Professional Development for the Dutch branch of the IABC and has won awards for her work in business and corporate film production. She shares her approach and more articles at www.lindsaybogaard.co.uk.

Susan Walker

Susan Walker's background is in the field of internal communication and staff research. Her experience with internal communication roles includes United Biscuits and Thomson Holidays. She is an Accredited Business Communicator (IABC) and a Fellow of Communicators in Business and the RSA. Susan headed MORI's HR and communication research practice before launching her own business specialising in communication and engagement measurement. The main focus for her work is developing practical action orientated management information from internal research data to contribute towards business success. www.commevaluation.com

Patrick Williams

Patrick Williams is a Senior Consultant with Ragan Communications (www.Ragan.com). The author of several books on employee communication, Patrick has designed and taught face-to-face communication programs for Allstate, Comcast, Motorola, Quaker-Tropicana-Gatorade, Eli Lilly and hundreds of others.

Simon Wright

Simon Wright has specialised in marketing and communications for almost 20 years with the past 10 years focused on internal communications. In 2006,

Simon co-founded the internal communications agency, Gatehouse (www.gatehousegroup.co.uk), which specialises in providing employee engagement and behavioural change advice and consultancy to organisations ranging from large corporates through to the government sector and charities.

Introduction

J Edgar Hoover was famous and feared throughout his reign at the FBI for his rigorous attention to detail. There is a story that revolves around him taking a holiday. He was going through his papers on the eve of departure when he came across a report from a junior agent which caught his eye. The layout failed to match his exacting requirements and sure enough when he took a ruler and measured the columns his wrote in disgust 'watch the borders' down the side of the offending page, threw it in his outbox and headed off for a fortnight's break.

On his return he was alarmed to find FBI HQ on red alert. All leave had been cancelled and staff were running around in a state of near panic. Hoover called his senior managers into his office and demanded to know why the entire FBI had been mobilised during the dog days of a hot August.

'Well sir,' replied a minion, 'you didn't stipulate which borders. So we had to deploy men to cover both Canada and Mexico.'

The story may be apocryphal but a Chairman of BT (British Telecom) once confided to me that he had to be very careful about making any casual remarks in large meetings. 'I'd say something in passing and the next fortnight a two inch thick report would thump onto my desk. Hundreds of man hours had been wasted on analysing a problem that was of no interest or use to our business.'

That's the trouble with communication in large organisations. Leaders are treated like medieval monarchs – their every utterance considered to be a jewel of wisdom of the highest order. Yet most CEOs did not get to the top of the organisation because their wit surpassed that of Oscar Wilde nor did their insights put Galileo in the shade. Most got to where they are through hard work, native cunning and hoarding information as power. Yet once they achieve top dog status we ordain them with the Wisdom of Solomon and hang on their every word. Indeed internal and corporate communication during the latter half of the twentieth century became the last bastion of feudalism in the developed world. In some companies it still is.

The dilemma is that top-down communication only works when the leaders know something that the followers want to hear. In the 1950s and 1960s there was enough growth to keep them in this Delphic position. In the 1970s the cracks began to appear as a new generation of managers appeared who were not conditioned by the Second World War. In the 1980s and 1990s senior managers moved from telling instructions to selling them – much to the benefit of the nascent video and event production companies who were employed to sugar the pill of coercion with lashings of razzmatazz entertainment. But none of us knew back then how many of our colleagues ignored the internal newsletter, trashed the company magazine, avoided our team briefings and washed away the memory of the CEO's keynote speech in conference bars.

Sure we had people who could interview and measure, but it was a brave head of corporate communication who admitted to the Board that employees were ignoring them. The message would go out to whoever was in charge of the corporate towers of Babel: SOS – 'Send Out Stuff' and more trees would be pulped and more TV presenters autocued to cascade the company view. We conformed because deep down we knew that it didn't really matter if staff could not recite the company's Vision, Mission and Values when the senior management couldn't either.

And then this meteorite hit the communication world called the Internet. Rather inconveniently its internal manifestation, the intranet, does not lie – or rather the analytical data behind it cannot be ignored. Only when the facts revealed that less than 5 per cent of our colleagues were reading anything coming through our internal channels were our worst fears confirmed. The audience are in control. In fact they always have been; they just didn't let us in on the secret.

So where does that leave the communications executive or manager who picks up this book looking for advice, tips and techniques for making communication more effective in their organisation? If top-down messages no longer work from California to Cardiff is there any useful role for the message carrier? This book sets out to answer that question.

Of course there are times in any organisation's life when your colleagues will crave instruction. During a merger or takeover, downsizing or office move people will be knocking on your door for information. Your intranet hits will go through the roof and your newsstands will be plucked empty the instant the information you hold has an effect on the lives of others. But these periods are few and far between. Most professional communicators experience them once a decade unless they are very unlucky. For at times of crisis and real change senior management stop talking just when staff start listening and you are left exposed, a sole player standing on an empty stage with no lines.

You'll find plenty of advice in here on how to communicate the basics – the *what, why* and *how* of communication. But the world has moved on and if you want to raise your influence in the organisation then it is probably the rest of this handbook that you'll find more useful. Here you will learn how to facilitate rather than lecture; inspire conversation rather than kill it; help managers to communicate rather than manage communication.

This handbook is for communicators working in the connected world. It does not contain all the answers, but it is a response to the biggest questions. Each week we track the articles and advice that are most downloaded from our site www.simply-communicate.com. At the time of writing there are more than a thousand articles online attracting some 16,000 visitors each month. This book is a response to the top 5–10 per cent of questions we have been asked over the past couple of years. In that respect the content has been selected by people like you rather than an editor like me. I am only too aware that each day the questions will shift, change and mature. So use this handbook as an anchor, a checklist to ensure that you are up-to-date. But to stay truly current please interrogate the site – and if we haven't answered your question, then tell us and we'll respond.

After all, the biggest message contained in these pages is that in the world of internal communication it's the audience who call the shots.

Marc Wright
London

PART I

The Fundamentals of Internal Communication

1

Measurement

by Susan Walker

Measurement is not just an optional extra for communicators, but an essential part of their professional toolkit. It has been seen sometimes as a threat (Will they cut my budget? Will they cut me?). However it can be an exciting opportunity to evaluate, guide and direct communication initiatives and investment.

The advent of easy to use, do-it-yourself online surveys puts the facility to research and measure employee experiences, opinions and attitudes in the hands of functions and individuals in the organisation.

On one hand, this has the advantage of enabling you to keep in touch quickly and simply. On the other, it can lead to a multitude of unregulated surveys with decisions made on unreliable results. Moreover, the advent of social media encourages people to comment and give opinions quickly and easily. This type of feedback is useful, but remember, it may not be representative of your whole audience.

This chapter outlines what you need to know about measurement to advise colleagues, carry out your own surveys or commission research from external professionals.

Effective measurement has two essential steps: getting the basics right and developing a strategic approach. Before we move on to these, the fundamental question you need to ask is: 'Why are we embarking on this measurement?' If you don't answer this basic question appropriately, then the rest of the process will not succeed. This may seem too elementary to mention, but it is surprising how many research projects start without clear, stated and achievable objectives.

The initial rationale for measurement may include:

- the strategy/values of the organisation: knowledge/commitment;

- understanding of and involvement with a new initiative;
- the communication role of the line manager/supervisor;
- visibility and image of senior management;
- channel access, usage and effectiveness;
- accessibility, tone and honesty/openness of organisational information;
- upward communication – whether a listening process is in place and how well it works;
- lateral communication – sharing best practice and exchange of knowledge across the organization.

A good way to define objectives is to envisage the end of the process: What information do you want to see in the results? How will the information be used? Will it be used at all?

Don't jump into measurement – take a long, hard look at the water before leaping in. Consult others – function heads, line managers and senior management. What feedback would they find useful to help improve communication?

And do not make the mistake of considering the information channels in isolation. The only way you will be able to assess communication effectiveness is by looking at the media (channels such as the intranet, briefing meetings and publications), the messages (organisational strategy, objectives, values and employee feedback) and meaning (understanding, commitment, involvement and how this might influence behaviours).

Stage 1: The Basics of Measurement

The basics may sometimes seem tedious and even petty and unnecessary. But these are the essential firm building foundations to produce reliable, constructive information. Aspects such as methodology, sampling, statistical reliability, objective questionnaire design and coverage all need to be considered. These will not be separate issues but all are interrelated so they will need to be taken into account together before you make any decisions.

METHODOLOGY

The first step is to consider the outcomes needed. Will a qualitative approach involving focus groups and interviews or quantitative, questionnaire-based research best meet your needs?

Both have their advantages and disadvantages.

Qualitative research is likely to be on a smaller scale and therefore less intrusive for the organisation. It will:

- give faster feedback, provide understanding and insight;
- be able to probe, question and challenge;
- adapt for different functions/levels of employees;
- be well suited to more sensitive topics.

But it will not:

- give hard numbers;
- provide data for future tracking of trends;
- provide information by employee roles or functions;
- enable analysis to reveal key drivers of good communication.

Quantitative research on the other hand will provide:

- firm figures and reliable data;
- a base for tracking any changes in the future;
- comparisons with normative data;

- detailed results by demographics, functions, locations and so on.

But it may not answer all the questions in depth, or explain the reasons behind employee views and opinions.

The two approaches are not necessarily mutually exclusive – both are needed for the full picture. Focus groups sometimes precede the questionnaire design stage to help develop the questionnaire. They can also be used effectively after the quantitative stage to explore the issues raised and gain fuller understanding of the research outcomes.

Qualitative research has a place as a stand-alone project, especially if the topic is sensitive, or if new initiatives are tested or input sought to develop solutions.

Quantitative options

If questionnaire-based research is selected as the most effective approach for your measurement objectives then there will be more options you need to consider, such as the research medium:

Telephone: a short questionnaire delivered via a telephone interview is a good, quick choice to follow an event or a new initiative. However, the time and cost of a telephone approach means it is not suitable for large numbers of respondents.

Face-to-face: as with the telephone interviews, a face-to-face questionnaire can be useful for a short, sharp survey in which respondents are interviewed personally.

Postal: questionnaires can be circulated with reply-paid envelopes to encourage respondents to post them back when completed.

Group self-completion: employees are gathered together in groups and given the questionnaire to fill in there and then. This methodology is most appropriate in a manufacturing or similar work environments where the response rate for a postal survey may be low.

Online: this is becoming the preferred approach as it gives people the chance to complete a questionnaire online which is fast, convenient and cheaper to distribute and analyse. Typically a link is sent out to employees that leads to an electronic questionnaire for them to fill in online.

Sample or census

You will also need to decide whether to sample a proportion of employees or invite all to participate. With any organisation employing under about 5,000, the most sensible method will probably be a business-wide census. Larger organisations may wish to consider a sampling approach depending on a number of issues:

- For some methodologies (postal, for example) a sample will be less costly (saving print and postage.) However, there is much less investment difference between a sample and census for an electronic survey.
- A sample tends to get a lower response rate as communication campaigns/follow-up reminders (see below) cannot be publicised to all employees.
- What are your measurement objectives? If the intention is to provide management information by all units then a census may be more appropriate so results can go back to line managers. If the feedback is needed only at corporate level, then a sample may be sufficient to provide the top line data required.
- How big should a sample be? Again, there is no easy answer as this depends on the measurement objectives. You will need to build up your sample from the required result outputs (what level of detail will you want to report on) with statistical reliability in mind.

Statistical reliability

The subject of statistics may sound boring but is an essential part of the measurement process to gain reliable, robust data. When reporting around election time, the media often refers to plus or minus 3 per cent reliability on a sample of 1,000. This means that a survey result of, say, 70 per cent who express a certain opinion, could be either 3 per cent higher or lower than the reported figure. Sometimes the media ignores this rule of statistical reliability and reports a difference of 1 per cent which is meaningless. When considering the size of your sample, you may find the following web link useful in assessing the reliability of the numbers: http://www.surveysystem.com/sscalc.htm.

You will need to take this into account when deciding the size of your sample. The employee groups that you want to look at will need to be sufficiently large to give reliable data – that is data on which you can rely to give a dependable, representative view of your audience's opinions which you will need for effective decision making.

QUESTIONNAIRE DESIGN

Another essential to gain reliable measurement is a relevant, objective questionnaire. When developing the content of your questionnaire, it is valuable to consider the information which will be needed for assessing and prioritising communication. There is little point in asking a question which cannot result in action. So, if there is no chance that the quarterly publication will be published more frequently, a question about frequency of publication is pointless.

However, if a more general question about timeliness of information shows this to be an issue, there may be a number of ways this can be addressed: for example, the use of 'standard' questions about the level and credibility of information, information sources, opportunities for upward and sideways communication. There will also be questions specific to your organisation such as new initiatives, values and mission statements. Here you may want to look at awareness, understanding, involvement and support.

The questionnaire needs to be interesting to complete otherwise people may give up half way through so a variety of question types can be used rather than a long list of agree/disagree statements. It can be tempting to ask for 'yes'/ 'no' answers for simplicity. But a balanced scale – usually five points, with the midpoint neither positive nor negative – is essential.

There is also a school of thought that dismisses the midpoint as the 'easy option' which should not be included otherwise people will choose this rather than think through their answer. However, this is an important group. If they have no strong views either way then – as 'fence sitters' – there is more potential to move their views into the positive group as they are not actively negative and are still waiting to make up their minds.

In addition to the pre-coded questions, open questions can be included which invite people to respond spontaneously in their own words. Beware of including too many; these questions will require coding into response categories.

How long should be questionnaire be?

You should consider questionnaire length from the perspective of the time taken to complete the questionnaire – between 8 to 20 minutes depending on the audience. Managers and staff in professional roles, for example, may take the 20 minutes needed – others may get bored after 10 minutes and fail to complete the questionnaire. Remember to factor in the level of literacy of the group for whom you are designing the questionnaire.

Before you go live, you will need to test the questionnaire by asking several employee groups to complete the draft. This will reveal the length of time it takes to fill in, its relevance and ease of comprehension. Here you would be looking at whether the topics are within the experience of the employees and if the language is understandable to them. Some of the questions may be couched in a way that is open to misinterpretation or full of 'management speak' so your test is an opportunity to get the questionnaire right before circulating to all.

DEMOGRAPHICS

One section of the questionnaire will ask about the profile of respondents. Too much detail may produce piles of computer tables without adding useful information to the final findings. This is especially true of communication surveys where it may not be possible to respond to individual groups of employees. Location, employee level and service length are usually included in the profile. Employees can be concerned about the privacy of their individual responses and concerned about cross-analysis that could identify them so only essential personal details should be included.

The Market Research Society best practice guide recommends that no group smaller than 10 should be analysed separately to ensure that the views of individuals/small groups are protected from identification.

STIMULATING RESPONSE RATES

The challenge for both postal and online surveys is how to gain the highest possible response rate. Typically a communication survey which tends to focus on communication media and messages gains a lower level of response than a full employee survey which covers aspects such as reward, recognition, training, career opportunities etc.

The type of audience is an influence: for part-timers in the retail sector the response rate may be around 30 per cent while this might treble for a manager survey (assuming that full-time managers feel more ownership and commitment to their organisation than part-time employees). The main stimulus in maximising the response rate is the belief on the part of the respondent that action will follow based on the results. So a communication from senior management giving a commitment to take the findings seriously will assist in attracting responses. Allowing respondents 2 weeks to complete the questionnaire generally gives those who are on holiday the opportunity to respond. A reminder at an appropriate time prior to the deadline usually helps raise the response rate.

Stage 2: Measurement Strategy

At the same time as you establish the basics to create a firm foundation, you need to consider the strategy behind the measurement project. This should include:

Communication: you need to develop a communication programme at an early stage to give information about the purpose of the research, its timetable, proposed feedback process and commitment to action. This programme can help raise the response rate and make the measurement programme a part of the planning process.

Linking with the business: a measurement programme should link communication with the business. In order to do this, you'll need to review organisational aspects such as:

- the vision and values of the organization;
- strategy and future plans;
- image among external audiences such as customers;
- dashboard or similar organisational performance management tools;

- other organisational research which may already exist;
- relevant business measures in place.

Just to take one practical example, where customer data exists, their reactions/opinions to aspects of service can be compared to those of employees, especially front-line people. This can reveal any gaps in understanding to help align the behaviours of employees to expectations of customers.

In this way the measurement programme can form a real part of the business instead of being just an 'add on' of 'nice to know' information. When the measurement links with the business, the outputs can be developed into specific action plans.

FEEDBACK AT ALL LEVELS

It is never too early to consider the feedback process. When the research is complete, the first level output will be the overall results with the total score for the whole organisation. This will be of general interest and useful for planning at corporate level where issues may encompass all parts of the company. This information may be used by the leadership team and the communication manager/department.

Next will be the results by the relevant group such as department, location, job level and so on. It is often at this level that the real value of the measurement lies. If some of the questions cover aspects within the remit of the departmental manager – team meetings for example – then it will be useful to provide the relevant information to them so they can address any issues raised. In the same way, there may be information helpful for the IT function, if users are reporting difficulty navigating a site, for instance.

INSIGHTS

Some insights can be gained from the basic data, but matching data from the communication survey against other sources of data can provide greater depth and understanding. For example, the value of team meetings can be gauged by looking at the statistics of those people who attend and those who do not attend and comparing this with the survey results on the level of understanding of organisational strategy.

One case study example in a large retail company showed that around half regularly attended team meetings while the other half did not. So when the views of those who attended the team meetings were examined, they found that those who had the opportunity to attend were five times more likely to understand organisational objectives than those who did not participate in team meetings. This suggests a correlation between attending team meetings and understanding strategy, a powerful tool to persuade line managers of their value.

Another example of a potentially useful comparison of data involves matching those people who trust their organisation and believe the information they receive against the various information sources. This will reveal the most trusted sources of information, both formal and informal.

COMMUNICATION RETURN ON INVESTMENT

How can the value of internal communication be proved to the organisation? A number of published studies already reveal a link between business success and communication.

Here are just a few examples, A study by the International Association of Business Communicators (IABC) found that high performing companies have a formal communication strategy (51 per cent versus 40 per cent of non-high performers) and 72 per cent of employees understand organisational goals (versus 57 per cent). In a similar vein, *The Sunday Times* Best Company to Work shows that for the past 3 years the best 50 have returned 3.6 per cent compared with 15 per cent decline in the FTSE. And investors have earned 12.1 per cent (compounded annual return) versus 5.8 per cent decline overall. Watson Wyatt reported that companies in which employees understand the goals of their organisation have 29 per cent greater shareholder return.[1]

While this is interesting and useful to report to senior management, it is much more difficult to assess any link between good communication and business success within individual organisations. A host of factors can influence commercial success and profitability which makes it hard to isolate the impact of good communication.

One solution is to take an aspect of success that can be tracked over time – a customer service project, economy drive or other specific initiative where

1 Watson Wyatt Annual Employee Engagement Report, www.watsonwyatt.com

a communication campaign can play a significant role. By identifying any improvements or savings achieved as a result of the campaign (minus campaign communication costs), a figure for return on investment can be estimated.

PERSPECTIVE

Comparisons against normative data – that is the average scores from other organisations – can give additional perspective to the results. Some of these 'average' scores are not high in themselves; this may provide comfort in knowing other organisations have similar communication problems to your own. However, such scores should not be viewed as 'targets' in themselves, especially where organisations are aiming to be best in their field rather than simply average.

ACTION POINTS

Any action points arising from a survey need to be practical and attainable with a clear assignment of responsibilities. In many cases, the internal communication team may be responsible for given actions while others may be the responsibility of functions such as customer service, IT or training. Some action plans may only be achieved with the active input of senior management and line managers.

HOW SUCCESSFUL HAS YOUR MEASUREMENT PROGRAMME BEEN?

Changes in behaviours may be apparent. But to measure any alteration in views and attitudes a follow-up survey will be needed. This will show any changes and enable you to assess the success of any action programme put in place based on the baseline feedback from the first survey.

How often should this tracking survey take place? The right frequency has no definitive answer. When change is fast (for example, when a transformation programme is being put in place), every few months could be the most effective frequency. But with a large, static organization, where action will be slower to assess and implement, every 2 years may be sufficient.

Whatever action plans are put in place, it will be vital to inform your audience that the measurement programme has listened to their views and – where possible – taken them into account when developing new programmes and initiatives. All too often this vital step is overlooked. In communication terms, it shows that the organisation is listening and will also encourage people to participate next time around when they see that their opinions have helped shaped internal communication for the future.

2

Creating an Internal Communication Strategy

by Marc Wright and Fiona Robertson

Introduction

Building a communication plan for your company or organisation can appear a daunting task. Where to start – and how to make it relevant to the needs of your organisation? This chapter helps you avoid your communications strategy gathering dust in forgotten drawers of the executive suite. It explores five distinct aspects of communication strategy:

1. Strategy;
2. Structure;
3. Systems;
4. Standards;
5. Skills.

Strategy

Your communication strategy must start with your business strategy. The trouble is, few businesses are able to describe their real business strategy overtly. So how do you marry your communication plan to a business plan, if no one above you can tell you what the business plan looks like?

This should not be a frustration to you; very few businesses have a CEO with a clearly articulated vision. This is because few people in life have a clearly articulated vision; mostly, we are driven by the first four of Maslow's Hierarchy of Needs: creating security for ourselves, keeping the threats to our safety at bay, companionship, self-esteem and so on. Few of us have a guiding principle beyond making a success of ourselves and our companies.

However, every business does have a covert, unexpressed business strategy and it should not take rocket science to discover it; to do so, look at:

- Where is your company spending the big bucks?
- What type of attitude gets rewarded and promoted?
- What keeps the CEO awake at night?

By going round the functional heads of the organisation and doing your own audit of what is going on, you become proactive rather than reactive. This will raise your profile and credibility among the senior team, as well as establishing communication as a strategic business tool.

Creating a communication strategy is all about making the covert, hidden business strategy open and engaging for your staff and colleagues. And to do that, you need to ask yourself another question:

- What are your people thinking?

COMPANY SPENDING

This is the easiest part of the strategy to deduce. Study the finance director's budget for the present and coming year and see where the board are investing. That huge IT project may be low on your list of communication priorities; it's astonishingly boring, is owned elsewhere in the company and the benefits are unclear and long term. Think again; go and interrogate the IT Director, talk to the IT suppliers, find out from HR the plan for training and implementation.

And look at any unusual investment plans – new buildings, possible acquisitions, new advertising campaigns. In short, if the board have committed money to it, then you need to have it in your communication plan.

Become conversant in how to read a balance sheet. And try to take a number of bearings on any piece of information. As well as your senior management, talk to industry analysts and stockbrokers about your company and the competition. Do you have a strong balance sheet and a war chest for future expansion? Is your stock price under pressure and the quarterly earnings short of target? This hard financial data will tell you more about your company's strategy than any vision statement.

WHO GETS PROMOTED?

Look at the recent promotions and hirings at a senior level in your company. These are significant decisions by the executive team and will tell you a great deal about the organisation's current character.

If you use a psychometric such as the Myers Briggs to establish what personality types are being favoured in these hirings, this can offer the strongest indicator of your organisation's personality. Are the senior team a broad mixture of introverts and extroverts, sensing or intuitive, feeling or thinking, judging or perceiving types? Or do they conform to a particular type? And does that type conform to an industry type or do you stand out from the competition? A bank that recruits senior candidates who are extrovert, intuitive, feeling and perceiving is going against the grain of most financial institutions, which will have a definite effect on its business strategy.

If, however, your organisation is hiring people who resemble the industry norm, then this speaks volumes about the covert business strategy: more of the same, steady as she goes...what Jim Collins identifies as the Flywheel Effect.[1]

ASK THE CEO

Make an appointment, or better – a series of appointments – with your CEO, where you can follow your agenda rather than theirs. The quality of your communication strategy will depend on the quality of the relationship you have with your ultimate boss.

Many CEOs do find it quite lonely at the top and have few people they can spend time with, reflecting on the broader direction of the business. Go to the meeting with some communication models that you can talk through (see below), and listen carefully to their language; to what they talk about first and

1 *Good to Great* by Jim Collins, New York: Harper Collins, 2001.

what they ignore altogether. Aim to distinguish between an issue that is front of mind because it came up 5 minutes before you met, and their longer-term goals.

Try questions such as:

- 'If we didn't invest in Project X, what would happen?'
- 'What other organisations or CEOs do you admire?'
- 'What business theories/books do you find attractive?'
- 'What keeps you awake at night?'
- 'What do you want our staff to think and feel about working for this organisation?'
- 'If you didn't do this job, what would you most want to do?'
- 'Describe something that happened in the past that gave you the most satisfaction from this job.'

MEASUREMENT AND RESEARCH

When you have gathered your data, remember that it is not your job to decide on whether a particular strategy is good, bad, desirable or otherwise. Your job is to create a communication strategy that matches the business strategy. This means that, whatever the true, covert business strategy of your organisation is, your mission is to make that overt, understandable and attractive to as many of your staff and stakeholders as possible.

The next step in building your communication strategy is to establish people's level of awareness and their attitude to things that are really important to your business. Track your employee attitude surveys for the past 3 years and look at any significant changes. Gather as much desk research as possible and – if it does not exist – commission it.

Use an external agency to design and conduct your employee attitude survey – but make sure that the company you use has expertise in Internal Communication and not just HR practices. An external agency will be able to benchmark your scores against industry norms, or you can use the reports published by companies such as Ragan, Melcrum and Sinickas, or trade associations such as IABC, CiB and the IVCA.

CREATING YOUR COMMUNICATION STRATEGY

Once you have established your company's real, covert business strategy, and established where your staff and colleagues are in terms of their understanding and feelings toward the company, you can now build your communication strategy.

We have worked with companies in Europe and the US and have found three main strategies for Internal Communication that are commonly developed within organisations:

1. information openness;
2. the supportive climate;
3. performance-based communication.

Information openness

This is a tried-and-tested strategy based on Jack Gibb's work on five managerial information-sharing practices. Implemented fully, it can be a very powerful approach to internal communication as it focuses on demystifying and clarifying information around the organisation. However, it does encourage a centrist approach to communication: a telling to the many of what has been decided by the few.

As organisations have become more transparent with their information, this approach may become less relevant. The information that a company really needs to survive and thrive can often come from sideways and bottom-up ideas – particularly from customers and the marketplace. If, as a communicator, your strategy keeps you in the corporate centre, dishing out company wisdom from on high, you run the danger of becoming irrelevant to the operational parts of the business and your strategy will fail.

The supportive climate

This is why many companies adopt a different internal communication strategy, which focuses on the managers throughout a business and helps them change the climate in an organisation. What does this mean? Well, just as a parent or a teacher can make a trip or a lesson interesting, inspiring or depressing, depending on their mood, so a manager has the greatest effect on the many micro-climates around your business. They can encourage teamwork or stifle innovation, all depending on:

- what they say;
- what they do;
- how they look.

What managers say, the language they use, the inflection they put into their voices, affects the way they think, as well as the way those around them respond. A simple change in vocabulary, repeated consistently and at length, can change an organisation's view of itself; for instance, the term New Labour revolutionised what the UK Labour Party stood for and lead them to election success.

What managers actually do confirms what they believe. It is their actions, decisions and what they choose not to do that are the little moments of truth which set the micro-climate. The role of the communication professional within the strategy is to support other managers to be better communicators, rather than trying to do all the communications yourself. Roland Draughon of Gavin Hodges describes this kind of communication strategy as a targeted communication process. Such a strategy can be viewed as happening and succeeding when the message sent is:

- the message received;
- the message responded to (feedback from receivers);
- influencing the target audience;
- making the target audience exhibit the desired behaviour(s);
- making the target audience take the desired action(s).

What is really powerful about climate control is that it can be taught. Managers are often unaware that they create the office environment within which they work. A boss who comes in very early in the morning may just want to clear their emails before the first meeting but actually they are creating a culture of early-starting. Staff will start to learn unwritten rules about when is the 'right' time to get in of a morning.

The manager who regularly brings their team together to celebrate individual achievement will encourage peer recognition. A manager who displays their anger can create a climate of fear, while the manager who hardly shows any emotion at all will create a climate of non-engagement and indifference.

By training managers in understanding climate control, you can make a huge difference in opening up communication channels and engaging staff. Of course, a manager is influenced by the way their own boss behaves so climate control needs to be understood and managed at the top. It's a double-sided strategy: encourage the behaviours you want at the micro- and the macro-level at the same time.

Performance-based communication

The third strategy, and the most recent to appear, is performance-based communication. Building on the work of Gibb and D'Aprix, Jim Shaffer argues for the communication department to take on a completely new role his book *The Leadership Solution: Say It Do It*.[2] He claims,

> *'The Communication Department knows no function.'*

That is to say, communication does not belong to any one function in the business but to all of them. Consequently, the strategy of the communication department should be to go out into the business and find areas in the operation that will benefit from better communication; and, having identified these areas, to introduce better communication practices alongside these particular elements of the business.

This is a very useful approach if you find yourself with limited resources and if your department is undervalued. (The two facts are often not unrelated.)

Performance-based communication, as the name suggests, involves concentrating on the elements of communication that are shown to be most effective. This means that it is far better to succeed in a small project than to

2 *The Leadership Solution: Say It Do It* by Jim Shaffer, New York: McGraw Hill, 2000.

fail across the board. Understanding what works implies using measurement systems to find out what staff actually value of the communication you put out. If you can show that the quarterly magazine is being ignored, then bin it and use the money to make a difference in a carefully defined project in a distinct part of the business instead.

Once you achieve success with one of the operational barons and can prove the value of your intervention, just watch your budget and your influence grow as you get called in by other parts of the operation.

Structure

FUNCTIONAL LOCATION

Unless you are setting up your team from scratch, where you are based and to whom you report are probably fixed. However, you still need to know how to balance your communication team, depending on where you sit in the corporate hierarchy, whether it's in corporate, marketing or HR. These reporting lines can strongly influence the type of internal communication capability that you have, and it is helpful to understand the strengths and weaknesses of each position.

The corporate communicator

Corporate internal communications have the advantage of a close link to the CEO and the levers of power but tend to focus on top-down messages and 'sending out stuff'.

Advantages:

- you are closer to the seat of power;
- you have status from having the ear of the boss;
- it's easier to coordinate internal and external communication.

Disadvantages:

- operational managers can distrust or undervalue your work;

- you can become remote and irrelevant from day-to-day business;
- you may become closely associated with a senior executive who will eventually leave.

How to balance your role:

- Imagine for a second that the world does not revolve around the corporate centre but, like Copernicus, you have discovered that this is an illusion and that similarly to those other planets called sales, operations, manufacturing, logistics and so on, you all travel in complex orbits around the customer.
- Now try imagining what life might be like on planet sales.
- Review the last 3 months of communication you and your team have been sending out to this planet.
- Then go and walk about planet sales asking people what they thought of your newsletter, or the management conference, or the last video.
- Move your desk to this planet for a month.
- Prepare and send out a piece of internal communication either exclusively for or exclusively from this planet, and then gauge the result.
- When the month is up, choose another planet and move in there for a month.
- Carry on doing the same work, and attending the same senior meetings, but become a nomad. Don't ask for permission – just do it. And, as you camp out on each of these different planets, use the opportunity to build on the communication tools you find there.

After 6 months, you will have developed a completely new view of your universe, a view that not only puts the corporate centre in its right perspective but also teaches you the subtle relationships and interdependencies of the different functions and departments in your company.

The marketing communicator

A marketing-based team will tend to favour internal marketing techniques, which use the tools of advertising to get staff to buy into new ideas and messages. Budgets tend to be spent on high-profile videos and live events.

Advantages:

- you are surrounded by people who understand the power of good communication, design and how to use media;
- there is more money around (you just have to find ways of tapping it);
- it's fast paced;
- it's brand-focused;
- you are closer to the customer.

Disadvantages:

- external communication is given more money, attention and status;
- strategies are short term and your boss is more likely to be impatient for results;
- focus is on 'products' such as videos, brochures, websites, rather than people's attitudes and developments.

How to balance your role:

- Use the language of marketing to present your boss with a proposal for an internal marketing programme with the promise that it will improve customer service – which will increase customer brand loyalty, giving higher levels of repeat purchasing and hence greater sales.

- Then go to the HR department and sell the same programme to them, stressing how it will help with their organisational development programme. This will give you the best of both worlds (and budgets) to create an integrated communication programme across the whole organisation.

The HR communicator

HR-owned departments tend to have a more involving approach They are interested in how communications can help develop staff and reinforce key performance indicators, and improve employee engagement levels.

Advantages:

- there are some key HR models that can be used to improve your internal communication;
- your boss is a specialist who will respect your own specialism;
- HR professionals are capable of taking a longer view.

Disadvantages:

- HR does not carry as much clout or kudos as other departments;
- decision making can be slow;
- budgets for non-training initiatives can be small and vulnerable to cuts;
- HR is the default home for internal communications and there is more support and expertise for IC from this sector than any other.

How to balance your role:

- stand out from the crowd by being an excellent communicator yourself. Brush up your presentation skills; write better emails and newsletters;

- develop an internal advertising campaign to market and communicate what HR is doing throughout the organisation . This will have two beneficial effects:
  - your HR colleagues will rise to the challenge and become the dynamic, go-ahead, engaged bunch of people that you say they are;
  - and other functions will be queuing up to have you on their side to promote themselves internally;
- use this strategy to create a network of champions for internal communication throughout your organisation; they represent a virtual team which will increase your influence and capability.

TEAM LOCATIONS

A key decision that should come out of your communication strategy is where your team should live and work. If you are uncertain of your company culture, just look at where the communications team is based. If they are all based in head office, then you tend towards a command-and-control culture; if they are dispersed around the regions, then yours is more of a distributed or matrix culture.

- By putting your communications team into the heart of the business's operating units, you will produce communication that is more closely tailored to the needs of your different populations and, in return, you will receive more accurate feedback on what people are actually thinking.
- If you centralise your team, you will get greater consistency of top-down messages, less duplication of effort and some cost savings.
- If you run your teams from virtual bases – especially if they're working from home – you will encourage communication systems biased towards email and your intranet.

How to balance your location(s):

- Use your own team to pioneer new ways of working, such as blogs, wikis and webinars, to roadtest the productivity of these new and virtual methods.

- Find ways to work smarter (rather than harder) by mastering the technology of remote working; use meetings sparingly and keep everyone in touch with each other with regular updates via the intranet or your own blog.

- Surround yourself with the best quality suppliers and consultants you can afford.

CAREER PATHS

Is your communications team made up of dedicated professionals who will spend their entire careers in communication roles, or do you use it as a development opportunity for general management?

Do you recruit new team members on experience and skills, or do you 'grow your own'? How do you reward your internal communications team: is there a glass ceiling or is there a career path to the board?

These characteristics will have a marked impact on the type and effectiveness of communication in your company. The 'video girl' or the 'newsletter writer' can become great repositories of knowledge about the stories and personalities around the organisation. They know who to interview in order to bring a particular issue to life or demonstrate best practice. But are they able to turn that knowledge into competitive advantage for your organisation? Not as long as you keep them in a process-orientated role. For instance, many communication departments have someone assigned to keeping everyone to brand guidelines; the infamous Brand Police. Consider whether their time might not be better used responding to the changing needs of the brand as it is used throughout the organisation, for instance in creating a toolkit to help departments structure their own intranets. Help develop them into internal consultants who will add real value, with measurable outcomes.

How to develop career paths:

- Join the International Association of Business Communicators and enrol in their professional qualification of Accredited Business Communicator (ABC). For more information see their website: www.iabc.com.

- Attend at least one conference a year on internal communications – and send your staff on training workshops.

- Encourage your staff to take sabbaticals in other parts of your organisation, and even within your supplier base. Six months with an agency can develop a team member dramatically, and agencies will often leap at the benefit of building longer-lasting relationships.

BUDGET

The structure of your department will be determined by budget.

Spending on internal communication per head is increasing faster than any other functional budget. There are a number of drivers at work here. Companies are becoming more knowledge-dependent, and so need communication systems that keep everyone up-to-date. Generation Y employees are less respectful of hierarchy and expect to be listened to more. Employee engagement is one of the few differentiators that lead to better customer service, and good communication is a foundation of engagement.

So how do you convince your boss to open the purse strings?

How to secure an appropriate budget

- Build support at board level for internal communication by allying your projects to the big money investments going on in your organisation. If the company is obsessing with quality issues then find out all you can about the subject and propose programmes that communicate 'zero defects' or 'kaizan' or whatever aspect of quality your senior management are interested in.

- Look very closely at where you are spending money. Do some research and find out if the newsletter you have been publishing for years is actually read by your colleagues. If it isn't close it and with the money you free up, choose a particular small-scale internal communications project that will give you a quick-win in terms of savings or greater productivity.

- Use this evidence to launch two more projects, and build from there.

- Fight for a training budget for your staff and then demonstrate how it has saved money on hiring external resource.

Systems

There are a wide variety of systems – or technology and processes – that you can use for internal communications. These have grown dramatically in recent years, thanks to the rise of the Internet. Some you can control, some you can't – but all should be recognised in an internal communication plan.

We have grouped them here in chronological order, starting with the traditional, through media-based tools to web-enabled. We then address the thorny question of which communication channels to use and why.

TRADITIONAL SYSTEMS

Newsletters

Newsletters and magazines have fallen in popularity in recent years, in most cases simply because you can make a good financial case – saving ten of thousands of pounds or dollars – by moving them online. But the printed medium still has a valuable role to play. They score particularly well as a 'read-on-the-way-home' medium and they are particularly useful for staff who are may not have access to your network during the working day.

If many of your staff commute to work by bus or train, then a magazine or newsletter which they can pick up as they leave their office is still a valuable option; provided, of course, the content is targeted, of interest and well written.

Noticeboards

Posters and noticeboards are the traditional media of the internal communicator and have fallen out of fashion. They are difficult to control, and much ephemeral information is better communicated online.

It astonishes us just how much redundant information – such as posters for programmes that are long over – remain stapled and curling on the bottom of notice boards.

Don't feel you are limited to just the noticeboards that many people have programmed themselves to ignore. Use the inside and outside of elevator doors, where you have a captive audience. Alternatively, if you can make the business case for the expenditure, you may choose to replace your noticeboards with plasma screens which display information more attractively and give you more control. From a central location you can change the messages and content with a simple file download.

Team meetings

Face-to-face meetings are one of the most popular forms of communication, particularly when held regularly and with small groups. Human beings are social animals and we like to interact with our peers.

The quality and effectiveness of this media is driven by the person who is holding the meeting. Make it your job to provide them with the training, support and materials to run effective team meetings.

Team meetings are the simplest of communication media, but the hardest to get right – and the stakes are high for your organisation's productivity. The consultant TJ Larkin in his *Communicating Change: Winning Employee Support for New Business Goals*[3] argues strongly that team leader meetings are the most powerful form of employee communication – more effective than senior management town hall meetings or roadshows.

If you do nothing else, develop a strategy to evaluate the current strengths and weaknesses of team meetings in your company and build a programme to support and improve this vital communication channel.

Live events

Live events have the advantage of getting people together in one place and one time to focus on a particular series of messages. In our attention deficit society it is probably the only system you will run where you have such a strong control on the environment, the messages, the behaviour of management and the assessment of feedback from audiences.

Live events are also the most expensive, high-profile and time-consuming medium in internal communications.

---

3 *Communicating Change: Winning Employee Support for New Business Goals* by TJ Larkin, New York: McGraw Hill, 1994.

MEDIA-BASED SYSTEMS

Videos

Video is a powerful tool that many communication managers use to boost and enhance their communication programmes. This is because videos give a consistent message and enable you to communicate emotional issues as well as merely information.

Traditional corporate video is an essentially passive medium; your audience need to want to watch them for them to be effective. To make a video compelling to watch requires great skill, good subjects and significant investment.

Some organisations have adopted a policy of providing cheap, domestic video cameras to staff and allowing them to tell their own stories and messages from around the company. The result, properly managed, can be liberating for organisations. Communication on this basis becomes no longer the sole domain of top-down, one-to-many communication, so you may wish to consider initiatives such as the democratic use of video cameras around an organisation in your communication plan.

These forms of democratic and universal communication can be particularly valuable if your organisation is large and distributed. Featuring people's stories from around the country or globe will do more to spread knowledge and best practice than any amount of emails or reports.

Plasma displays

Plasma screens – large, bright, flat TV screens, have come down in price and are now becoming accessible to corporate communicators' budgets. They enable you to replace static notice boards with screens, which are considerably more versatile and effective in getting broadcast messages across. But beware – they are not just a channel for communication but also a public advertisement of how well you are doing your job as a communicator. Using the same revolving PowerPoint slides about the company barbecue day after day will make your colleagues wonder what you do to earn your salary.

Telephone conferencing

If your organisation is multi-national or geographically-spread, then you may rely heavily on telephone conferencing. It's relatively cheap, easy to set up and saves on travelling time. However, it is a medium with major drawbacks.

Telephone conferencing cuts out all the visual clues that are key to good communication. On a telephone conference, you cannot pick up the nuances of irony, humour and, most importantly, dissent since you cannot see the colleague in Mexico shaking their head, or the team member in France who does not say a thing because others more senior are on the line.

Some judicial training is helpful for anyone who does much telephone conferencing, and it is essential for managers who chair such meetings.

Video conferencing

Video conferencing brings in the visual dimension – it can be amazing to put a face to the name you have been talking to for months. In time, this system will become submerged into web-conferencing, with small video cameras on PCs, which offers both a cheaper solution and means that participants do not have to leave their desks.

Training does exist for video-conferencing but currently there is little help on how to come across well on webcams using VOIP channels like Skype. The important aspect is not so much mastering the technical side of these meetings but understanding what effect your image is having on the person at the other end. For example, think about your background; does a messy office cubicle give the image you want to convey?

Phone

It seems strange to include the phone as a system in communication but its role is changing with the rise of email and i-messaging. We heard a senior communicator at Yahoo say that when she got a phone call, it was a real event because phone calls have become a rarity.

For younger generations, a telephone conversation is no longer the primary communication vehicle in companies.

Email

The moment you send an email, you lose control of who will see it and how it will be interpreted. An ill-conceived email, written in the heat of the moment, could one day be used in a court of law to prove malice, incompetence or shady dealings.

Your communication plan can help establish the rules of email etiquette in your company so everyone can sleep easy about the thousands of emails they send each year.

Texting

Texting is another medium that is specific to younger generations. It appeals strongly to the under 25s in your company, particularly in the UK – although texting is not widely available or practised in the US. Texting has become the default medium for sharing less significant news such as: 'I'm running late for a meeting.' However texting remains a less satisfactory medium for communicating more complex or emotional issues.

Radio broadcasting

This is a system that is used in some retail stores and factories, where a consistent message can be sent to staff in their working environment via a DJ or through recorded interviews and announcements, interspersed between music. It's a little too 'Big Brother' for most communicators' tastes.

Business television

Business TV is a costly medium that has to be managed very carefully to succeed. It is a push medium – sending out messages to an audience whether they are interested or not. The danger of Business TV is that whilst senior managers may love it as a platform for pushing out messages, actual viewing figures can be disappointingly low. Business TV succeeds best in an environment where the audience can interact with the material and messages, and where programmes can be targeted to specific audiences. The cost per head is prohibitive compared to web-based alternatives.

Phone broadcasts

This is the medium involving pre-recorded features or interviews that are sent down the line. Staff call up an identified number and listen to the message at work or home. This medium is being superseded by intranet sound files and podcasting.

WEB-ENABLED SYSTEMS

Intranet sites

Anyone developing a communication plan needs to think very long and hard about intranets as a system of communication. Intranets are far more than a communication medium; in some companies, they are the company. Ethan McCarty is Chief Editor of IBM's w3 intranet and he explains that some IBM employees in a 30-year career may never meet face-to-face with some of their co-workers. In the not-too-distant future, the intranet is where we will all go to get most of our daily work done. This means that the intranet is not a system purely for the communication department – it belongs to the whole organisation.

The role of the communications department is to operate as a publisher, setting the standards and structure of the intranet, but allowing the rest of the organisation – the subject experts – to write, edit and monitor the content.

Consequently the investment in your intranet and your intranet strategy is something that will eventually be discussed and owned at board level – it's that important – more important possibly than the bricks and mortar that make up the physical buildings and work environment you inhabit. An effective intranet is one that allows staff to do their job as quickly as possible – whether it's filling in expenses, dealing with a supplier or managing a project online. They are hard to get right as few companies are prepared to invest the time and money that have made consumer Internet sites such as Amazon and eBay so easy to use. Gerry McGovern – an intranet expert from Ireland – (see www.customercarewords.com) recommends that the best way to manage an intranet is to work out the top ten things that people come to your site to do and then make them as user-friendly and efficient as possible, If you can get the top three right then you are doing well!

Web-streaming

As band capacity on networks increases, we will be seeing more and more capturing of information and its dissemination via web-streaming. The big change here has come with remote hosting sites such as YouTube that allow you to store and access video material for free on the web. You can even make your material password-protected so that it's only viewable by those with access or you can talk nicely to your IT colleagues about setting up one on your intranet platform. The issue with video on the net is that it's pretty much uncontrollable. If someone wants to post your corporate video there is nothing you can do to stop them – just make sure you only make good ones!

With the next generation of mobile phones, the dissemination of video files will happen anywhere and anytime in your organisation. Anything, from a senior management briefing to a complaining customer, can be captured and sent anywhere, inside or outside your organisation. Microsoft already run a system called Academy Mobile whereby video podcasts are made available to all sales staff through their mobiles. Web streaming can be an enormous source of good in communication terms; it also means that all spoken presentations have the potential of becoming public property and being sent round the world.

The technology is only just starting but your communication plan will benefit from anticipating this huge step change.

Blogs

Blog is short for web-log – a log that anyone can write and publish online. The clever bit is that blogs are interactive. They invite others to respond and comment on what they have just read. It's like a cross between an email and a webpage – a medium for one person to talk to many, but with the many having the opportunity to answer back.

A blog differs from a message board or a chat room in that it is driven by the thoughts and writings of the blogger. Other people can respond to the blog and post their own views online – but these are tributaries off the main stream; the reader will always return to the blogger's column.

But defining a blog on the basis of its technical features is like describing *Pride and Prejudice* as a medium-sized book with stiff covers. The technology is irrelevant; what is important is what you do with your blogs, and how they fit into your communication mix.

Wikis

A wiki is a web application that allows users to add content, as on an Internet forum, but also allows anyone to edit the content. The term 'wiki' also refers to the collaborative software used to create such a website. A defining characteristic of wiki technology is the ease with which pages can be created and updated. Generally, there is no review before modifications are accepted. Most wikis are open to the general public without the need to register a user account. But the technology is also being adopted within companies where private wiki servers require user authentication. Here, the prime use is to capture knowledge about products, services and customers within an organisation. It is a powerful system because it is run by the staff themselves and pushes the communication down to the person with the greatest knowledge and expertise. But beware, while the software is generally cheap and accessible, the amount of time your staff could end up investing in creating and capturing knowledge will be immense.

RSS

Really Simple Syndication (RSS) is a system which enables you to include other people's content on your own intranet. Obvious examples are news headlines and stock market prices. The advantages to you are that you can just set up the RSS feed and your intranet will be updated automatically. It is essential that you monitor your RSS feeds regularly as the system updates automatically; you have no filter to stop information that's inappropriate. RSS also means that your colleagues can now decide which information they want to have drawn to their desktops, a process that gives them unprecedented power over internal communications. Thus an engineer could end up only reading blogs and articles that appeal to their interests – and your centrally produced communications will never touch their desktop.

Podcasts

Podcasting is a method of publishing audio broadcasts via the Internet, allowing users to subscribe to a feed of new files (usually MP3s).

The technology became popular with the automatic downloading of audio onto portable players or personal computers. 'Podcasting' is a portmanteau word that combines the words 'broadcasting' and 'iPod.' The term can be misleading since neither podcasting nor listening to podcasts requires an iPod or any portable music player.

Podcasting enables you or anyone in your organisation to create self-published, syndicated 'radio shows' and gives broadcast radio programs a new distribution method.

Listeners may subscribe to feeds using 'podcatching' software (a type of aggregator), which periodically checks for and downloads new content automatically.

The advantage of podcasting, from an internal communications perspective, is that your audience can choose to listen to the broadcast at any time they want, either in the office or on the move. It's the only communication medium people can use effectively while they are doing something else like walking the car or driving to work.

I-messaging

Instant messaging requires the use of a client program that hooks up to an instant messaging service. It differs from email in that conversations are then able to happen in real time. Most services offer a 'presence awareness' feature, indicating whether people on one's list of contacts are currently online and available to chat. This may be called a 'buddy list'. In instant messaging programs, the other party in the conversation generally only sees each line of text right after a new line is started. Instant messaging applications may also include the ability to post an *away* message, the equivalent of the message on a telephone answering machine.

The appeal of instant messaging in the office is that it is silent and enables an employee to have a private conversation with a colleague or friend. Such systems are taking over from email as a way of collaborating and getting an instant response to a query. They are also used for gossip! The key issue around i-messaging is that the message is rarely recorded and therefore there is no formal paper trail of the conversation. In hi-tech companies, staff can regularly be found to be i-messaging during a meeting – even during a face-to-face conversation. You may have protocols about the use of i-messaging but its use is really down to the individual. If they have access to the Internet, then they can i-message whomever and whenever they want.

VOIP

Voice-Over Internet Protocol (VOIP) is simply an alternative way of routing phone calls. VOIP is a piece of software that gives you free telephone calls over the Internet. All you need is a broadband connection and a headset – any headset that connects to your sound and microphone ports on your PC or laptop.

Thanks to the technology you now have a hi-fi alternative to bunching around the teleconference starfish and paying the phone company a small fortune for a 1-hour meeting with individuals around the world. And because VOIP can take a video signal along with the audio it has opened up video-conferencing to a mass market.

Web meetings

Collaboration software is now becoming available that supports the total management and conduct of meetings over the Internet, providing structure to increase their effectiveness and avoiding the costs and time of travel.

Web meetings or Webinars are appropriate for two types of meeting:

1. presentation-style (one-to-many) meetings; and
2. agenda-driven (many-to-many) types of communication.

Webinars are a time-efficient way of disseminating detailed, instructional messages to colleagues in remote sites without them having to leave their desks. All that is required is that they log on and listen to (and watch) a subject expert present on a particular issue. They may ask any questions of the expert and generally contribute to the meeting. You can also download a webinar after the event and watch it in your own time. This communication system lends itself well to distance training. These systems have been developed by the large software companies and will be eventually bundled with other desktop applications. This means that, one day, the IT department could present you with a default choice of which system you have in the company. It is therefore worth learning more about these systems so that you are in a position to influence any IT purchasing decisions to get the one that suits and integrates best with your business.

COMMUNICATION CHANNELS

How should you structure your communications? Do you use a single channel approach, with communications coming down from the top? Or delivered exclusively through managers and supervisors at team meetings – side-to-side, via intranet; or bottom-up, from staff to managers? Or do you combine a number of these channels?

There has long been a debate in internal communications about the benefits of communicating exclusively through line managers. It goes back to some flawed research in the 1980s that 'proved' that staff preferred to get their news from their immediate supervisor. It's true that people welcome the personal touch from someone they know and trust, and who will listen to what they say. But, although communicating through line managers is a powerful channel, you run big risks if you use this method alone.

In every other sphere of communication, politics, entertainment or education, we see audiences reaching out to both their local communities and national leaders. We read about our local councillors and listen to them at meetings but we also want to hear what presidents and prime ministers have to say on a particular subject; we love to hear our local bands but still buy the CDs of international chart toppers; we listen to our tutors and teachers but buy the books, or pay to listen live to the gurus in our favourite subjects. The point is the human mind needs different reference points in order to come to a conclusion. Just as sailors take three bearings to work out their position, we want to hear the views of people at different levels in the workplace in order to make up our minds on the key issues.

There was a time when the supervisor was king because there were no other communication channels. This model continued throughout the twentieth century with the hegemony of the foreman and office manager. But, as all the web-enabled enthuse, that model is now broken and it's never going to come back. Whatever your supervisor says will be undermined by access to the other sources of information available from in or outside the company, at the click of a mouse.

Human interaction in small groups is the most effective way for people to communicate, *providing* that the person who is leading that group is a competent communicator – and therein lies the rub. A sizeable slice of supervisors hate the communication side of their job; they are uncomfortable in the facilitation role, and no amount of training is going to substantially change that. By putting all your resources in this channel, you risk, at best, boring a third of your staff and, at worst, alienating them completely.

Standards

As the communicator's role has moved from doing the communication for managers to helping managers to communicate, the establishment of standards has become more important.

It's your job to help the organisation agree on certain consistent behaviours.

There are three categories of standard that you can usefully apply to your communication plan:

1. how you look;
2. what you say;
3. how you behave.

HOW YOU LOOK

You will be familiar with the first of these standards already. Think about how you use the company brand in internal communication – is it subject to same standards that are applied to external communication? At the risk of being seen as a member of the brand police, you could ensure that wherever the company brand or brands appear, they do adhere to brand guidelines.

The next standard you can influence is how your people look. Staff take their cue from supervisors and line managers who, in turn, take their cue from senior management. (It is an interesting tribal phenomenon – most famously evident at IBM during its blue suit period of the 1970s and 1980s.) So what your presenters wear at a management conference, town hall event or in that latest video will have an impact on how the rest of the organisation will dress.

Therefore, have a definite standard in mind when you put your CEO on stage. If they insist on a pin-striped suit and braces, then this will be the fashion around the management corridors for years to come. If, like Alan Leighton, Chairman of Royal Mail and Selfridges, they are only ever photographed in an open-neck shirt, then that is what will become acceptable – from postmen to accountants – in those organisations.

The next question is the appearance of your work environment. You may not consider this within the control of internal communications but you can influence it positively:

- make the posters you put up in your reception and corridors as innovative and creative as your external advertising;
- use tray mats in your canteen to tell stories about individual successes;
- use banners and pop-up stands to promote any company initiative, new campaign or the charity you sponsor;
- most of all, create space so that people can influence how their area looks;
- encourage the creation of a team spirit by helping people brand their own area. You might start with your own unit by dusting off those old awards and putting them where everyone can see, or set up a large board with examples of communication that you are particularly proud of.

WHAT YOU SAY

The way we talk affects and determines the way we think. So the language we use around an organisation has a crucial effect on the way the company thinks and the way in which everyone approaches projects and challenges.

A simple negative example is that of swearing. In newspaper offices around the world, the colourful nature of the expletives creates a culture that is macho, tough and confrontational. And these standards are self-reinforcing as newcomers arrive and adopt the same language in order to fit in.

But is the language conducive to the work at hand? And when the language gets formalised in emails sent by managers, then you could be limiting the potential of your staff, as more delicate and sensitive users of language withdraw into themselves or just leave.

In companies that are failing, negative words start to seep like cancer into the everyday talk of the company. Before you know it, you are talking yourselves into a spiral of corporate depression.

How do you change language? By changing the language of your senior team in meetings; bringing them up-to-date with what is and isn't acceptable language through scriptwriting and the judicious use of advice and direction. Once managers start dropping the language of the past, others will soon follow:

- Instead of talking about what's bad and what's going to get worse, start using positive language about what's good and what could be better.

- Keep it simple. Try to get the bureaucratic out of the instructions that people bump into as they go about their working day.

  The Americans do this better than Europeans. Where the Brits put up notices saying, 'Do not deposit inflammable materials adjacent to machinery' the equivalent American sign will say, 'No Trash!'

- On the back of those little paper tents that people write their names on in meetings, print the simple instruction, 'Think!' Not a bad instruction for anyone about to open their mouth in a meeting.

- Set the standards for writing on your intranet. There are commercially available courses on advanced writing and editing – Ragan's Advanced Writing & Editing is particularly popular.

- And remember that writing for the web is different from writing for the page so you will benefit from creating a style guideline for everyone to look at before they start writing. Gerry McGovern's *Killer Web Content*[4] is worth considering.

4 *Killer Web Content* by Gerry McGovern, London: A&C Black, 2006.

- Combine this with a template for layout, style and metadata to get a more consistent look for your intranet. This screengrab from American Electric Power (Figure 2.1) is an award-winning example of a well-designed intranet.

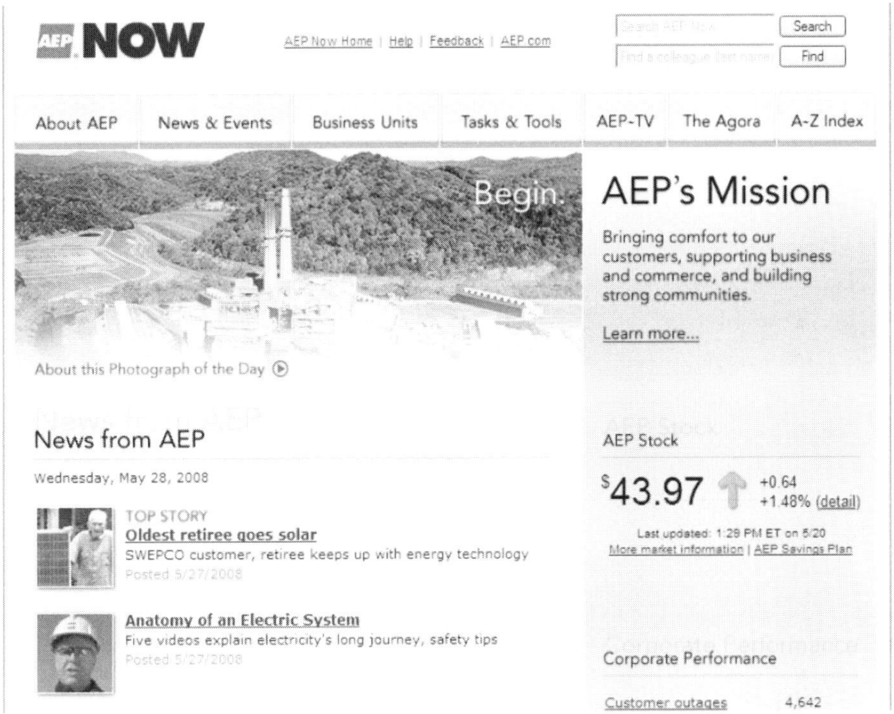

Figure 2.1 An award-winning intranet

HOW YOU BEHAVE

The third area of standards is how you behave. What senior managers do is far more eloquent than what they say. The finance director who preaches financial rectitude and then gets caught fiddling their expenses; the HR director who espouses equality and then gets mad when someone parks their car in their privileged space; the communication director who does not reply to emails; these behaviours are the true setters of the climate within your office, your building and your organisation.

Now it's fine for managers to smoke openly in a cigarette company, for staff to dress provocatively in a fashion house and for troops to get aggressive on manoeuvres; as long as that is the culture that you want to cultivate in your organisation. But if you are in the middle of a values programme to shift the climate from authoritarian to innovative, then by changing some high-profile behaviours, you will get there a lot quicker.

Be aware, though, that merely setting standards will make little difference in your company. Standards only become standards when they are adopted by managers and staff. Start by identifying the changes that you believe will be easiest to make and that will have the biggest impact and make sure that you pick the battles that you know you can win.

It's better to have a few embedded standards around the organisation than dozens enshrined in a manual that no one opens. The most important and hardest standard to establish is that you are the company's expert and a leading authority on internal communication.

Skills

There is not room here to outline the many courses you can follow to develop your skills or those of your staff and your colleagues throughout your organisation. There is a richness of training courses available from specialist communication publishers, such as Ragan (ww.ragan.com), Melcrum (www.melcrum.com) and of course www.simply-communicate.com as well as the two trade associations, IABC (www.iabc.com) and CiB (www.cib.uk.com).

If you really want to become top of the class in communications, then enrol on the IABC's accreditation qualification and become an ABC (Accredited Business Communicator). Academic courses in the UK are centred at the Kingston Business School, Kingston University where they teach an excellent Diploma in Internal Communication Management and Bournemouth University where they offer an MA in Corporate Communication.

If you don't have time to go on an academic course, Sue Dewhurst and Liam FitzPatrick have put together a competency framework which outlines the skills you might think of applying to yourself and your team. You can read about it in the next chapter.

3

What Makes a Competent Communicator?

by Sue Dewhurst and Liam FitzPatrick

Over the last decade employers have changed how they think about internal communication; they don't just want their staff to be aware or informed, they want people to be involved and engaged. And getting them there calls for a new type of professional – the expert advisor who can make sure communication is central to the organisation's mission and not incidental to it.

This chapter looks at the competencies this new breed of communicator needs.

There is no single model for the perfect internal communicator. Every organisation has its own problems, a different history, a distinct culture and a unique workforce. A model that works for one company may well fail miserably in another, even if they are in the same industry and their two operations look similar.

With this in mind, this chapter assumes you will want to develop a model of desired skills, knowledge and experience that suits your particular organisation. We have pulled together the core components in such a way that you can create the blend that works for you but, at the same time, those central building blocks should be recognisable and applicable across industries, countries and sectors.

Competencies: Our Definition

Since we will use the word 'competencies' frequently, it's worth defining what we mean by it. *Competencies* are the characteristics – the skills, knowledge and experience – that drive outstanding performance in a role. They describe the behaviours we would expect to see from someone carrying out their role to a highly effective standard.

This means when we talk about a 'competent communicator', we are describing someone who has the right competencies to operate as a highly effective professional, performing their role in an outstanding way.

Understanding What Makes a Competent Communicator

We started thinking about competencies some years ago when we were part of a working group sponsored by several professional associations in the UK. We came together because we wanted to define a common competency framework, which defined what 'good' looked like, gave internal communications practitioners a framework for their professional development and brought clarity to recruitment and to career planning. With colleagues in our associations we came up with a basic framework to inform thinking across the profession.

In 2007 we carried out an international research project to learn from practitioners themselves the competencies they needed to operate successfully. We ran an online survey and we followed up with interviews and research groups.

Using the Competency Framework to Guide Your Development

The competency framework is set out in full below. To use it to provide a tailored framework for your own role and a guide for your development, follow these three simple steps:

1. Reflect on what your organisation needs from you and how you can add the most value and then decide which competencies you need to perform your role effectively.

2. Assess yourself against these competencies and identify the gaps between where you are now and where you need to be.

3. Put together a personal development plan, which sets out how you will fill the gaps.

Step 1: Use the Framework to Put Together Your Individual Competency Model

Figure 3.1 lists the twelve core competencies in our framework and gives a simple definition for each. The fuller descriptions will help you establish where specific skills or behaviours fit. The competencies are specific to internal communicators. Your organisation probably already has a model for general management competencies, such as team leadership or time management.

Competency	Definition
Building effective relationships	Developing and maintaining relationships that inspire trust and respect. Building a network and being able to influence others to make things happen.
Business focus	Having a clear understanding of the business issues and using communication to help solve organisational problems and achieve organisational objectives.
Consulting and coaching	Recommending appropriate solutions to customers; helping others to make informed decisions; building people's communications competence.
Cross functional awareness	Understanding the different contributions from other disciplines and working with colleagues from across the organisation to achieve better results.
Craft (writing and design)	Using and developing the right mix of practical communication abilities (for example, writing and design management) to hold the confidence of peers and colleagues.
Developing other communicators	Helping other communicators build their communications competence and develop their careers.
Innovation and creativity	Looking for new ways of working, exploring best practice and delivering original and imaginative approaches to communication problems.
Listening	Conducting research and managing mechanisms for gathering feedback and employee reaction.
Making it happen	Turning plans into successfully implemented actions.
Planning	Planning communication programmes and operations, evaluating results.
Specialist	Having specific subject matter expertise in a specialist area.
Vision and standards	Defining or applying a consistent approach to communication and maintaining professional and ethical standards.

Figure 3.1 The twelve core competencies

Full descriptions of the competencies are set out at the end of this chapter. They include three separate levels:

- Level 1 – Basic;

- Level 2 – Intermediate;
- Level 3 – Advanced.

In each case, we describe the behaviours you would typically expect to see from somebody operating at each level.

When building the framework start by deciding which competencies are relevant to your role and then, which level is appropriate for each competency. The aim is explicitly not to aim to climb to 'advanced' at every level. Just look what is needed to perform the role well. For example, the 'advanced' level in the *Listening* competency describes someone who is probably a highly skilled researcher – a talent relatively few organisations need.

Finally, use the 'time focus' column to set out which competencies may be called into use more or less often than others. This column essentially asks, 'What do you expect to spend most of your time doing?'

By the end of this process you should have as sheet of paper that looks something like Figure 3.2 opposite.

Step 2: Assess Where You are Now

There is a wealth of advice available on competency testing and we won't try to reproduce it here. We recommend asking a colleague or your manager to help you make an assessment of your current position. If you assess yourself, you may miss important development needs or, if you're having a bad month, underestimate some of your core strengths!

Step 3: Compile Your Personal Development Plan

The final step is to decide how you will fill the gaps between where you need to be to perform your role to a highly effective standard, and where you have established you are now. Again, we recommend talking this through with your manager or a trusted HR colleague, who can discuss the learning and development options available to you.

Job Role: Internal Communications Business Partner			
Competencies			
	Description	*Time focus*	*Current level*
Building effective relationships	*Level 3 – Advanced*	High	
Business focus	*Level 2 – Intermediate*	High	
Consulting and coaching	*Level 2 – Intermediate*	Medium	
Cross functional awareness	*Level 3 – Advanced*	Medium	
Craft (writing and design)	*Level 2 – Intermediate*	Low	
Developing other communicators	*Level 1 – Basic*	Low	
Innovation and creativity	*Level 2 – Intermediate*	Medium	
Listening	*Level 2 – Intermediate*	High	
Making it happen	*Level 2 – Intermediate*	High	
Planning	*Level 2 – Intermediate*	High	
Specialist	*Level 1 – Basic*	Low	
Vision and standards	*Level 2 – Intermediate*	Low	

Figure 3.2 Example of a completed competencies table

In Summary

There is no one model of the perfect internal communications professional. The key is to understand what's important to your organisation, how you can add the most value to the business, and what competencies you need to enable you to fulfil this role outstandingly well.

Treat the competencies set out here as a set of mix and match building blocks enabling you to set out a clear and comprehensive definition of the skills, knowledge and experience you need. Read through the behaviours to understand what you could expect a knowledgeable, experienced professional to be doing routinely in relation to each competency.

These competencies are not founded on our personal opinions. They are based on the views of people working in our industry all over the world. Based on all their combined experience and observations, these are the foundations needed by today's professional internal communicator.

Appendix: The Competencies

Competency:	Building Effective Relationships
Definition: Developing and maintaining relationships that inspire trust and respect. Building a network and being able to influence others to make things happen.	
Typical Behaviours	
Ineffective behaviours	• Focuses purely on achieving own objectives. Fails to consider, or inappropriately ignores, other people's views. • Relies on force or hierarchy to push initiatives through. • Fails to engage or influence key stakeholders resulting in the failure to implement planned activities. • Afraid to ask questions or challenge decisions. • Being right matters more than getting the best result.
Level 1 – Basic	• Identifies individuals or groups that can help or prevent things happening and finds ways to work well with them. • Appears confident and comfortable working with people at all levels. • Respects and values other people's views. Tries to understand what's important to them. • Listens carefully, asking questions to aid understanding and clarification. • Seeks and uses feedback from clients. • Does what they say they will.
Level 2 – Intermediate	• Takes a structured approach to identifying their stakeholders and understanding their relative influence and importance to making things happen. • Builds a wide and effective network across their business area and invests time in cultivating relationships. • Seeks to understand and respect even the most difficult clients. • Can adapt their style to quickly inspire trust and respect from clients and colleagues at all levels. • Involves others in decision making and planning as appropriate to make sure activities happen as planned. • Stands up for their views without damaging relationships. Manages any conflict effectively.
Level 3 – Advanced	• Is a trusted and respected advisor to the most senior leaders. • Works well with colleagues at all levels. • Uses influence successfully to shape the strategic communications and business agenda. • Not easily intimidated but knows where to compromise. • Able to negotiate conflicting requirements from different stakeholders to build a coherent plan which is accepted by all. • Helps others to resolve conflicts or difficult issues. • Builds a strong network of relationships that can survive a change of direction, reporting lines or personalities. • Develops external relationships that enhance their knowledge and bring best practice into the organisation.

Competency:	Business Focus
Definition: Having a clear understanding of the business issues and using communication to help solve organisational problems and achieve organisational objectives.	
Typical Behaviours	
Ineffective behaviours	• Does not make the link between communication activity and the business/organisational context. • Lacks understanding of their business area, its structure or its operations. • Has insufficient understanding of their core audiences. • Shows a poor grasp of the business priorities or challenges in conversations with leaders and clients.
Level 1 – Basic	• Has a sound basic understanding of their area's structure, purpose, products/services, priorities and key measures. • Makes an effort to understand their audiences, potentially through work shadowing or visiting different locations. • Thinks about and clarifies the business purpose of the communication activities they work on. Asks 'why?' • Understands how their personal objectives relate back to the business objectives for their area.
Level 2 – Intermediate	• Demonstrates a good understanding of their area's business strategy, targets and performance and uses it to shape communication strategies, plans and materials. • Anticipates future developments or issues and is proactive about discussing how communication can help. • Challenges where they are asked to undertake activity with no clear business purpose, or which seems to work against stated business direction. • Regularly spends time with their core audiences to maintain their audience understanding. • Can discuss business issues credibly with leaders and clients. • Can identify the key issues from an annual report or set of financial results.
Level 3 – Advanced	• Seen as a credible business person, who uses their communications expertise to help solve business problems. • Talks the language of business with stakeholders, rather than the language of communication. • Able to analyse complex business challenges and scenarios and formulate communication solutions. • Maintains a good understanding of audience needs and issues, either through personal contact or through the communications network. • Earns communication a seat at the top table and is seen as having an important contribution to make to business planning. • Routinely sought for advice about potential issues and complex scenarios at an early stage. • Financially literate. Understands and can debate financial measures, plans and performance.

Competency:	Consulting and Coaching
Definition: Recommending appropriate solutions to customers; helping others to make informed decisions; building people's communications competence	
Typical Behaviours	
Ineffective behaviours	• Constantly carries out tactical activity themselves, rather than helping others to do it when appropriate. • Does not recognise or respond to opportunities to consult or coach. • Does not understand what coaching really means. Confuses it with telling, advising or giving feedback. • Fails to listen effectively to clients or customers. • Does not clarify expectations. • Afraid to challenge or question decisions and assumptions.
Level 1 – Basic	• Uses effective questioning and listening techniques to take a clear brief from clients or customers. • Sets clear expectations about their own role. • Provides sound advice about potential communications solutions. • Negotiates with clients to help them choose the most appropriate solution. • Can give basic advice and tips to help customers improve competence in specific scenarios (for example, giving a presentation, holding a team meeting) or direct them to appropriate resources.
Level 2 – Intermediate	• Listens carefully to client or customer briefs, using questions to clarify understanding. Challenges the brief where appropriate to explore alternative communications solutions. • Is relied upon to provide sound communications advice and expertise and recommend appropriate solutions. • Is not afraid to say what people may not want to hear, and stands their ground when challenged. • Anticipates and prepares for questions or objections. • Sets expectations about their own role. Makes appropriate judgments about where they can add most value and where others are best placed to own actions and deliverables. • Has basic coaching skills and can coach line managers and customers to improve their communications competence in specific scenarios. • Gives feedback constructively and confidently when asked.
Level 3 – Advanced	• Helps colleagues/clients explore their wider business needs and explores options in anticipation of a discussion about communications solutions. • Quickly analyses complex scenarios to determine where communication can add value and recommend appropriate solutions and options. • Can present their case objectively and authoritatively. • Has well-developed coaching skills and the confidence to use them. • Identifies and takes opportunities to coach senior leaders and project managers to enhance their skills and improve performance. • Trusted and respected as a coach at a senior level. • Able to flex their style between directing, advising and coaching and identify which technique will be most appropriate in the circumstances.

Competency:	Cross Functional Awareness
Definition: Understanding the different contributions from other disciplines and working with colleagues from across the organisation to achieve better results.	
Typical Behaviours	
Ineffective behaviours	• Adopts an insular approach to internal communication and fails to make connections with the work of other departments. • Appreciates the needs of too few departments or may attend to the needs of one group or department to the exclusion of others.
Level 1 – Basic	• Understands the role of other departments and how internal communications helps them achieve their differing objectives.
Level 2 – Intermediate	• Understands relevant elements of law (including financial reporting rules) and local employment practice and the constraints they place on internal communications. • Can identify the implications for other functions from communication initiatives. • Can advise other functions or departments on communications issues.
Level 3 – Advanced	• Seen as a trusted advisor by leaders in other professionals and is involved at an early stage in projects. • Keeps abreast of developments in HR, marketing, the law and areas of practice relevant to their organisation.

Competency:	Craft (Writing and Design)
Definition: Using and developing the right mix of practical communication abilities (such as writing or design management) to hold the confidence of peers and colleagues.	
Typical Behaviours	
Ineffective behaviours	• Writes material that is inappropriate or unappealing for its audience. • Cannot brief or supervise a designer. • Produces or sanctions work which breaks identity standards, contains grammatical errors or is poorly designed or delivered. • Is not trusted by managers to deliver any communication activity without highly detailed supervision. • Clients and colleagues use other suppliers for skilled tasks which should be done by this person.
Level 1 – Basic	• Writes simple items in a way that is engaging, grammatically correct and appropriate to the audience. • Can correct other people's writing. • Appreciates and follows visual identity principles. • Understands how to work with external suppliers and can prepare a simple brief. • Is trusted by managers and colleagues to deliver activities reliably. • Copes well working on a number of different tasks – sometimes with conflicting deadlines.
Level 2 – Intermediate	• Writes in a variety of styles for a variety of formats in a way that is engaging, grammatically correct and appropriate. • Can ghost-write for senior leaders in a way that captures their personality and spirit. • Can supervise specialists in different media (for example, web layout, print design or photography). • Can quickly and sensitively subedit other people's writing for a variety of formats. • Is a reliable project manager, directing the work of other people and suppliers to deliver projects on time and to budget.
Level 3 – Advanced	• Writes and coaches less experienced communicators in writing in a variety of styles for a variety of formats in a way that is engaging, grammatically correct and appropriate. • Coaches other communicators in other practical areas where they are particularly skilled (such as design management). • Defines and develops basic standards for practical skills in the team.

Competency:	Developing Other Communicators
Definition: Helping other communicators build their communications competence and develop their careers.	
Typical Behaviours	
Ineffective behaviours	• Does not allocate time or budget to development activity • Fails to give feedback on performance. • Blocks access to development activity. • More interested in keeping individuals in convenient roles than helping them develop their career.
Level 1 – Basic	• Helps non-professional communicators such as communications champions develop basic skills and knowledge. • Invests time in helping them to build a network and share plans, ideas and best practice. • Commissions or delivers simple development interventions, for example, training days. • Provides templates, toolkits and resources to help build competence. • Supports colleagues with their development needs.
Level 2 – Intermediate	• Supports direct reports in planning their personal and professional development. • Understands the organisation's performance management process and their role within it. • Sets clear development objectives based on business needs and people's personal aspirations. • Coaches team members to enhance performance and build competence, giving constructive feedback as appropriate. • Develops improvement plans to support team members where performance is below acceptable standards. • Recognises and publicises good work. • Shares interesting and challenging tasks where there is a genuine development opportunity for colleagues. • Understands the range of development options available and the strengths and weaknesses of each.
Level 3 – Advanced	• Champions the development agenda within the team. • Allocates time and budget for team development activity. • Clearly defines the competences needed to operate successfully. • Chooses different approaches to development (ranging from coaching through to training) to achieve business results. • Ensures the team is kept up to date with best practice, new thinking and industry developments. • Supports sensible risk-taking in the interests of learning and is supportive if people make mistakes. • Develops the internal communications network, building capability and facilitating the sharing of knowledge, ideas and best practice across the team. • Ensures work is allocated with development in mind. • Is a highly skilled facilitator and coach.

Competency:	Innovation and Creativity
Definition: Looking for new ways of working, exploring best practice and delivering original and imaginative approaches to communication problems.	
Typical Behaviours	
Ineffective behaviours	• Consistently repeats old routines without taking account of changing circumstances or needs. • Produces dull or unengaging materials. • Lacks curiosity about best practice from inside or outside their organisation. • Discourages others from exploring new ideas.
Level 1 – Basic	• Actively looks for ways to improve work processes and makes practical suggestions. • Looks for imaginative solutions to communication problems and ensures solution is fit for purpose. • Reads professional literature and is curious about how other communicators tackle similar issues.
Level 2 – Intermediate	• Initiates and develops new processes that work. • Is normally successful at presenting ideas and communications in a fresh and compelling way. • Advises on where to find ideas on good practice in their area (from inside and outside their organisation).
Level 3 – Advanced	• Initiates and develops new ways of working which will still be in use after they have moved on. • Is recognised inside and outside their organisation for extending established practice and developing fresh thinking. • Supports and encourages colleagues to generate new ideas or adapt existing ones in order to produce strong communications. • Looks outside internal communication for inspiration.

Competency:	Listening
Definition: Conducting research and managing mechanisms for gathering feedback and employee reaction.	
Typical Behaviours	
Ineffective behaviours	• Is not interested in gathering employee feedback and does not see its place in communications planning. • Presents their own views (or views of colleagues) as representative of wider employee opinion. • Accepts other people's claims about employee attitudes or experience without checking the facts. • Does not anticipate employee reaction to events or news or provide timely mechanisms to gather such feedback.
Level 1 – Basic	• Includes simple research or listening exercises in the planning and evaluation of communication activity. • Has basic network of contacts around the organisation which can be used as a simple sounding board. • Can present intelligence in a persuasive and credible way. • Supports other professionals in the conduct of focus groups (either as a scribe, logistics specialist or secondary facilitator). • Understands the legal framework surrounding consultation and information sharing in the territories where they operate – knows when to seek specialist help.
Level 2 – Intermediate	• Makes choices about research methodologies based on communication and business need. • Manages focus groups and depth interviews, including the selection of a representative and credible sample frame, the preparation of topic guides and the creation of reports. • Produces simple surveys which are credible to both managers and employees. • Manages stakeholders' sensitivities which arise when a study is proposed or designed or when results are delivered. • Presents findings and recommendations persuasively. • Reflects research in communication plans. • Ensures that communications are compliant with legal obligations to consult or inform. • Supports specialist colleagues in the smooth running of employee consultation groups or councils. • Has a robust informal network of contacts around the business which is used for ad hoc intelligence gathering.
Level 3 – Advanced	• Advises others on their research needs. • Builds management respect for data gathered and it's use in shaping communications decisions. • Manages research contractors. • Understands different approaches to analysis and knows when to apply statistical tools. • Designs and leads programmes of qualitative research. • Coaches others in facilitation for qualitative research. • Presents findings and recommendations persuasively. • Contributes to professional good practice.

Competency:	Making it Happen
Definition: Turning plans into successfully implemented actions.	
Typical Behaviours	
Ineffective behaviours	• Is not trusted by others to deliver activities as planned. • Develops impractical or unworkable action plans. • Does not keep to budgets/deadlines. • Fails to recognise the local implications of activities. • Lacks attention to detail. • Panics – and panics others around them. • Is easily frustrated or diverted.
Level 1 – Basic	• Can be relied upon to organise simple activities such as conference calls, open forums, mass email distributions or executive visits, efficiently and effectively. • Appears calm and capable, giving an image of confidence. • Knows the right people, resources and processes to make things happen. • Anticipates potential questions or issues and ensures all angles are covered. • Keeps team members and other stakeholders informed. • Delivers on time and within budget. • Safe pair of hands is probably far too subjective. • Finds ways around obstacles with supervision.
Level 2 – Intermediate	• Successfully organises larger events or initiatives such as management conferences or roadshows. • Able to juggle a number of tasks and prioritise effort. • Produces comprehensive project plans. • Makes effective use of systems to store and organise information. • Forms effective working relationships with suppliers. • Negotiates competitive rates, possibly working with the supply chain function. • Deals calmly and efficiently with queries, requests and changes. • Handles poor service or unreasonable requests firmly but pleasantly. Stands their ground. • Is a calm and capable presence 'on the ground'. • Always overcomes obstacles or problems calmly without damaging relationships unnecessarily.
Level 3 – Advanced	• Organises complex initiatives or events, potentially involving large budgets and multiple locations. • Manages multiple suppliers efficiently and effectively, involving the supply chain function as appropriate. • A good programme manager – coordinates complex programmes, tracks progress, identifies and manages issues and risks. • Identifies and builds relationships with key stakeholders, keeping them informed about progress and maintaining their confidence. • Anticipates potential problems and produces contingency plans. • Knows the project plan inside out and can act as an information hub, directing action as appropriate. • Inspires trust and confidence.

Competency:	Planning
Definition: Planning communications programmes and operations, evaluating results.	
Typical Behaviours	
Ineffective behaviours	• Develops activities in a haphazard manner without due regard to resources, timescales or clarity of objectives. • Does not objectively evaluate communication programmes. Uses their own subjective judgement.
Level 1 – Basic	• Plans simple projects involving relatively few stakeholders and requiring simple deliverables. • Follows a simple planning model in all activities which sets out clear objectives, timescales and resource needs. • Understands the strengths and uses of different channels and can choose between them. • Tracks, as a minimum, whether communications reach intended audiences. • Is aware of other communications activity which is due to take place in their work area (using formal and informal means). • Learns from mistakes or experience.
Level 2 – Intermediate	• Develops complex plans for projects or divisions which include multiple stakeholders, uncertainty and risk. • Always plans work and includes audience segmentation, definition of messages and channel selection as well as making clear links back to business objectives. • Understands the different needs of change and business as usual communication plans. • Applies a methodical approach to crisis communication. • Ensures that channels are always fit for purpose and identifies improvements where necessary. • Can explain planning choices and options to stakeholders. • Has mechanisms in place to alert them to communication or other activity which might conflict or clash with their own plans. • Evaluates individual projects and whole programmes based on whether audiences understand messages. • Delivers projects or activities within defined resources. • Reflects learning from evaluation in evolving plans. • Understands, and can advise when to use, the most recently available tools, including the social media range.
Level 3 – Advanced	• Defines communications planning standards for their organisation. • Oversees the coordination of multiple programmes and manages complex organisational, cultural or operational change programmes. • Anticipates and mitigates crises (have to say that otherwise it looks like saying 'I told you so' is the competency!). • Ensures that there is a suite of channels available in their organisation to meet needs. • Keeps up to date with recent technological developments and can advise on when new solutions are appropriate for the organisation. • Establishes and maintains a framework for the coordination of plans to avoid overload, confusion or insistency. • Oversees budgets to assure value for money and the effective use of resources. • Is accountable for business results (rather than simply communications outcomes).

Competency:	Specialist
Definition: Having specific subject matter expertise in a specialist area. NB. Organisations should add in the skills, knowledge and behaviour appropriate to the nature of the specific role concerned.	
Typical Behaviours	
Ineffective behaviours	• Does not have the specialist knowledge or expertise needed to perform their role. • Is not trusted by other team members to provide a high quality service or give good advice. • Has little or no knowledge of best practice, new techniques or current thinking in their specialist area.
Level 1 – Basic	• Has the specialist knowledge, skills and experience needed to carry out their role with minimum supervision. • Is trusted by other team members or customers to provide a good quality of service or give sound advice in their specialist area.
Level 2 – Intermediate	• Is respected as an internal expert in their subject area. • Is deferred to as the natural spokesperson/advisor in conversations about their subject area. • Has a good awareness of best practice and current thinking in their subject area and suggests ways of using it within the organisation.
Level 3 – Advanced	• Is known throughout the industry as a subject matter expert. • Wins awards/has case studies published for their work. • Ensures the organisation has access to the very latest best practice and new techniques. Constantly seeks ways to apply the thinking.

Competency:	Vision and Standards
Definition: Defining or applying a consistent approach to communication and maintaining professional and ethical standards.	
Typical Behaviours	
Ineffective behaviours	• Produces communications without any overarching goals on a purely ad hoc basis. • Is unaware of (or ignores) rules and standards for communication or visual identity. • Communicates information which is dishonest or misleading either deliberately or without care. • Does not apply consistent ethical standards appropriate to national or organisational expectations. • Can be pressured into issuing communications that are inappropriate for the audience, channel or situation.
Level 1 – Basic	• Understands their organisation's standards around communications and visual identity. • Can articulate clearly role which internal communications plays in their workplace. • Maintains agreed standards for individual channels by not using them for inappropriate messages or compromising on quality. • Takes responsibility for the quality of their own communication. • Conforms to expected ethical standards and behaviours. • Where necessary, sets out simple standards for the team as a whole.
Level 2 – Intermediate	• Helps define quality and operational standards for communication in their organisation. • Coaches colleagues in correct standards and values. • Takes responsibility for ensuring the quality of communication and channels in their team. • Develops with local managers a sustainable vision for the role that communication is expected to deliver in their areas.
Level 3 – Advanced	• Defines a sustainable overall vision for the role of internal communication and wins senior management support for that vision. • Is consistent in their pursuit of that vision. • Defines quality standards of internal communications. • Accepts accountability for the quality of communications and channels in their organisation, but articulates clearly where the role of the internal communications function ends and the role of a line manager beings. • Models ethical behaviour within their organisation.

4

Connecting with the Unconnected

by Ruth Findlay

Introduction

It seems we can't open a magazine or book on internal communications without reading about the headlong advance of social media and online communications. Whilst these areas are very exciting, and as communicators we do need to make sure we move with the times, we mustn't forget that many of us work with or in companies where there are many 'unconnected' employees. Most professional communicators now agree on two fundamental principles – that communications should be an engaging, iterative flow, not solely 'tell and sell' (though there is at times a place for that), and secondly that within any employee group there are subdivisions and subcultures and the communicator needs to use a variety of communication media to do their job. Developing engaging and innovative ways of communicating with the 'unconnected' within any given employee group presents its own challenges which we are going to examine in this chapter.

Who are the unconnected? We use this term to describe those who do not have the same opportunities for access to information resources as most desk-bound employees. There are three main reasons for this – access, training or education. It could be that they don't have access to online media because of the nature of their work – they may work 'direct to site' in manual jobs, for example, and never actually enter an office or defined place of work. It could be that they have online access to company systems but are technophobic or may never have been given the appropriate computer skills training. For others, their educational background means their reading and writing level may inhibit their ability to respond easily to online or traditional print media.

How is the environment of the unconnected employee changing? Even in companies where there are employees who are remote workers, manual workers or workers who are geographically dispersed in some way, the impetus for communicating with this audience is changing. Today's companies want, and need, to be much smarter about how they relate to employees. They might be doing this simply to increase opportunities for communicating with their people, to facilitate change more easily, to reduce paper-based processes (self-service HR via the intranet for instance) or to gather customer and process data in the field. Employees themselves may be 'unconnected' at work but, increasingly, not at home, where their families are surfing the net, reading blogs or getting involved in online social networking sites. They may have a digital television and digital camera and are experiencing the interactive revolution at first hand. These environmental changes have one of two effects – either they alienate the employee who feels that technology is passing them by, or they raise the employee's expectations that they should have access to such technologies at work. In any case they do not want to feel 'left out of the loop' at work.

In most organisations there is no such thing as parity of information sharing through communication channels, however hard internal communicators try. This is because communication relies essentially on human interaction; the skills and ability of the person delivering a message or the fact of the recipient being interested/engaged enough to receive, understand and engage with the message. In companies with a large 'unconnected' demographic we often find an acute split between information elitism and information poverty. In many cases we find that there is a large proportion of the employee demographic who receive internal TV, radio, intranet, newspaper/magazine, briefings and have regular access to employee events. And there are other parts of the demographic who receive only some, or occasionally, none of these channels. The concern in this is that these people are often 'at the coal face' – making or building or packing the product, or fixing the pipe or the cable out in the field. They are often the human face of the company, and the quality of their work is what the customer directly sees. If these employees don't know what's going on in the company, why changes are being introduced, or indeed are denied a channel to give feedback and suggest improvements, then the company is taking operational and reputational risks.

In this chapter we're going to explore a systematic approach to finding out who your unconnected audience are, and the best ways to engage with them. A useful model (see Figure 4.1) sets out the three steps for connecting with the unconnected: situational analysis, organisational strategic context and, finally, taking action. At the end of the chapter there is a case study from Scottish Water called 'Making the Connections' – an award-winning project which brought fresh ideas and imagination to engaging the 'unconnected' employee group.

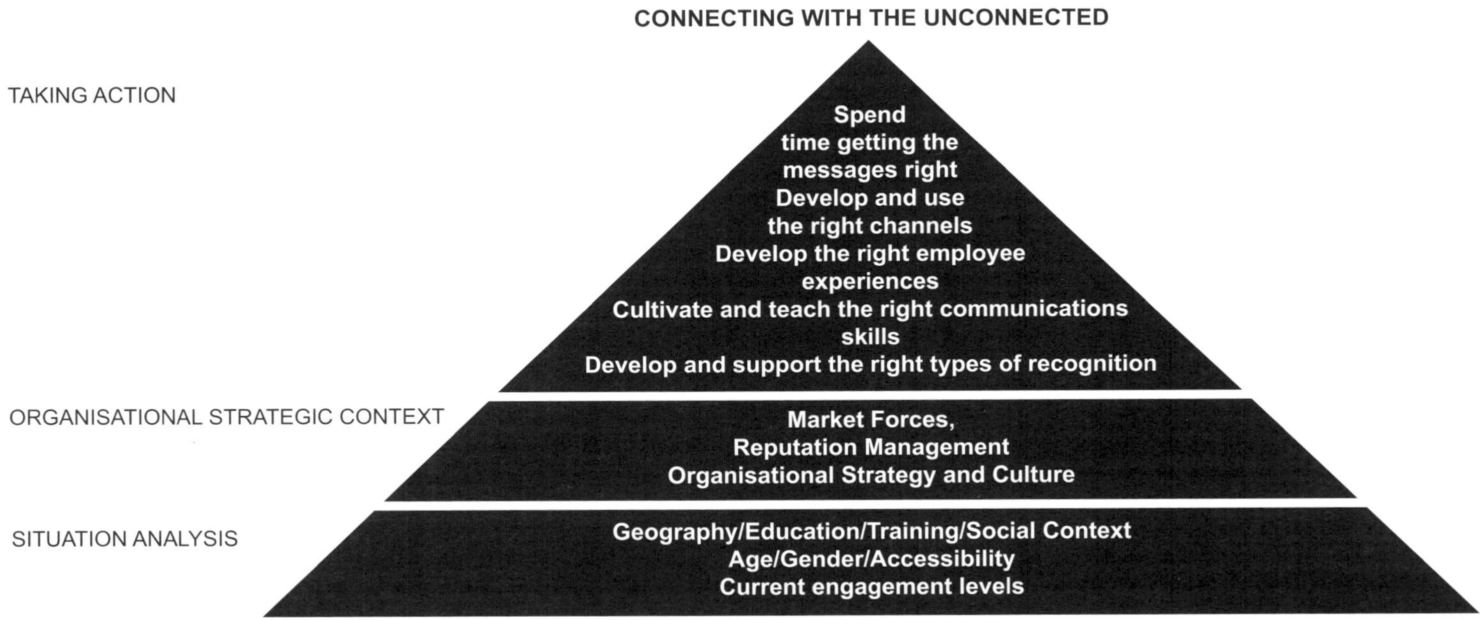
CONNECTING WITH THE UNCONNECTED
TAKING ACTION
Spend
time getting the
messages right
Develop and use
the right channels
Develop the right employee
experiences
Cultivate and teach the right communications
skills
Develop and support the right types of recognition
ORGANISATIONAL STRATEGIC CONTEXT
Market Forces,
Reputation Management
Organisational Strategy and Culture
SITUATION ANALYSIS
Geography/Education/Training/Social Context
Age/Gender/Accessibility
Current engagement levels

Figure 4.1 A model for getting connected

Situational Analysis

Knowing where you're starting from and who you're dealing with.

GEOGRAPHY

Employees are often based in many different locations, and geography can be one of the biggest influencing factors in the levels of connectivity an employee experiences. As communications professionals there are a number of ways we can get to grips with the geographic breakdown of the employee base. One way is to work with the HR function to gain access to the current HR information system. In many instances this will give you details of the employees' main work base and whether the employee is a remote, direct to site or lone worker. This is unlikely to tell you what systems or channels they have access to, but you at least you will be able to see where the unconnected groups are sited. If your organisation is unionised, it's important to build a good working relationship with employee and union representatives. There is a mutual shared benefit in communicating effectively with all groups of employees and often union officials are extremely knowledgeable about where employees are based and the types of sites in which they work.

EDUCATION/TRAINING

If you have an organisational learning and development department within your company you can work with them to find employee information such as educational level, results of training needs analysis and personal training records. Keep a record of the training subjects which are most popular, any educational issues, such as whether there are employees who have reading or writing or learning difficulties, and which training methods have worked particularly well (whether on the job, practical, classroom or coaching/mentoring). This will give you an idea of how the employees prefer to learn and engage with new ideas or information – use this information to inform your approach to engaging the unconnected employee group.

SOCIAL CONTEXT

The social context in which employees operate is harder to quantify, but you can get a feel for it by using networks and contacts within the employee base to assess how the unconnected group is broken down. You may want to conduct an informal survey. What publications do they read? What television programmes do they enjoy? What are their interests outside work and how do they spend their time? Do they listen to radio, and if so, which station?

AGE/GENDER/ACCESSIBILITY

Your organisation's HR system is also likely to be able to provide a reasonably thorough breakdown of employee demographic factors such as age, gender and accessibility. Study these breakdowns – what do they tell you about the unconnected audience? Is it mostly male or female? Which age groups are you communicating to? These statistics will help you think through the type of communication and channels which might work with your audience. Such classic segmentation analysis allows you to tailor your messages appropriately.

CURRENT ENGAGEMENT LEVELS

Finally, assess the current engagement levels among your unconnected audience. A source for this can be existing employee surveys and anecdotal feedback from managers, team leaders and union representatives. By engagement levels we mean an assessment of contributing factors, possibly including levels of commitment to the organisation, satisfaction with 'basics' such as terms and conditions, and other factors such as levels of satisfaction with recognition. Try to assess whether engagement levels are constant across the demographic (this is unlikely) or whether there are variations from geographical area to area or age group to age group, for example.

Pulling all this demographic information together takes a lot of time and effort up front, but it is a worthwhile exercise in really getting to grips with your unconnected audience; their needs, likes, dislikes and expectations.

The Organisational Strategic Context

Once you have gathered enough demographic information to give you a clearer picture of your unconnected audience, you can start to assess their communication needs within the context of your organisational strategy. You will need to satisfy the answers to some fundamental questions: What are the market forces in your industry? What are the strategic imperatives for your organisation? What's the brand strategy? What is the current culture of your organisation and how might it need to change?

MARKET FORCES

Take a look at the external environment in which your company operates. This is the environment your unconnected audience lives in, reads about in newspapers and talks about with friends and colleagues. External forces such as political pressures, economical/financial changes, legal changes, competitive changes (new/emerging/existing entrants to market), environmental changes and technological advances have a significant impact on the nature of the audience, and the ways in which you could or should communicate with them. For example, competitive changes may mean that the unconnected audience has to change the way they work, either because they need to work faster, and more efficiently to sell more products than a new competitor, or because the service they provide to the customer is changing in line with what competitors are offering. Your communications to the unconnected audience need to take into account what is changing in the way this audience works. If market forces are leading your company to produce new products then you need to plan for that within your communications.

REPUTATION MANAGEMENT

Reputation management is about considering the reputational environment of your organisation within which employees operate. What does it mean personally for employees that they work for your organization? How might they be judged by others when they reveal who employs them? Are employees working for an organisation they can be proud of? How does your 'unconnected' employee base understand the corporate brand and its values? Would they be able to describe what the organisation stands for? A particular employee may drive a branded vehicle for work or perhaps they work in a remote location. That employee is the living embodiment of the marketing strategy and brand for everyone in the local community. It really doesn't matter how great your marketing strategy is on paper; if that employee doesn't live the brand and company values in the way they act and behave, the strategy is pointless. Your communications with the unconnected audience need to reflect your brand and organisational values. This is what employees will engage with.

You will also need to understand your crisis management and emergency stakeholder procedures. Unfortunately the unconnected employee can be the last to know about emergencies and crises as they occur, because of the difficulty in getting urgent information to them. It's best to draw up a plan, in conjunction with your emergency planning team, for how you will approach communication with different groups of unconnected employees in the event of such emergencies.

ORGANISATIONAL STRATEGY

Consider your organisation's operational strategy. Identify the main components of the strategy and how communications approaches might deliver these. For example, does your operational strategy have a focus on environmental or sustainability issues? This will impact both on some of your key messages to your 'unconnected' groups and also how you get those messages out there. There's no advantage in mailing out glossy magazines to all employees when your corporate strategy is trying to emphasise sustainability.

CULTURE

Your own communications team or your HR function may have carried out a formal culture analysis on your organisation. Whilst there are no 'right' or 'wrong' cultures, it is useful to have a clear understanding of accepted behaviours and norms so that you can learn how to engage with the employee audience. A culture analysis can include such information as social rituals, hierarchies, leadership styles and business language – the outputs can be a useful tool for analysing the types of communications activities and channels which might attract and engage the unconnected audience. What is the prevailing culture within the 'unconnected' group? Do they predominantly like traditional styles of communications? Are they hierarchical, formal or progressive? Do they enjoy team working or lone working and what is the most common reporting style and why? In what ways does the culture need to change?

TAKING ACTION

Messages

Spend time getting the messages right – use the knowledge you've gained on organisational, operational and brand strategy to develop messages which are aligned to your organisation's goals. For example, if part of your organisational strategy is to reduce operating costs then your messages should at least reflect this (with the most basic practical examples of how to reduce costs written large) and you should ensure that your communication channels are, and are seen to be, value for money. Plan your messages carefully so that they are pitched at the right level for the 'unconnected' audience to make sense of and understand in a personal context, and include the 'what's in it for me?'.

Channels

Develop and use the right channels – you will probably need to use a mix of channels across various unconnected groups. Break down the appropriateness of each channel according to your demographic analysis and the organisations strategic imperatives. Scottish Water introduced a fortnightly radio-style programme accessed by mobile phone, as many of their most unconnected employees were remote workers who did not have a base or access to a computer. They did however do a lot of driving and enjoyed listening to the radio. The radio news programme was therefore accessible via mobile phone from the van. Each programme has two hosts and is professionally produced to sound like a traditional news bulletin on a radio station. This regular programme receives a host of listeners from the more hard-to-reach audience groups, and employees can leave feedback or comments at the end of each broadcast. The facility also gives the organisation the ability to record and broadcast 'special bulletins' for urgent announcements or emergency information. These specials are quick and easy to record and employees can be alerted to their release via text message, allowing early notification of emergency information, even for the most 'unconnected' employee. For publications use your social and demographic information to assess what style of resource you need, for example, a stylish magazine or a tabloid-style newspaper.

Experiences

Develop the right employee experiences – the case study within this chapter on Scottish Water's award winning 'Making the Connections' programme is a good example of how to use your knowledge of your employee base to design the right communication experiences for employees. Employee events and communications activities are an important part of the range of communications channels, but will only be useful and engaging if delivered with professionalism, creativity and energy.

Skills

Cultivate and teach the right communications skills – in some cases the managers or team leaders of groups of unconnected employees have been promoted to these roles on the basis of technical ability or merit, whether they are good communicators or not. If this is the case in your organisation, think about what kinds of communications skills might be required in order to give these managers and team leaders the support required to deliver your communications channels and messages. If, for example, you want to roll out team discussion or briefing sessions, either face to face, or by phone, and you want it to be delivered by managers, then you must support them with appropriate communication skills training. They may need support with presentation skills, facilitation skills or interpersonal skills. Research suggests that most employees want to receive important information from their line manager – in which case you need to make sure the managers are equipped to make the communication clear and meaningful.

Recognition

Develop and support the right types of recognition – how will you recognise and reward good communication within your organisation? How will you know who are the local heroes of your unconnected audience? The culture of some organisations is such that peer recommendation and nomination can work well. For some, managerial recommendation works whilst for others, customer feedback or the more formal performance review system provides you with information on who's doing well, and why. You will need to assess your strategy, employee survey outputs and your culture web in order to decide on what type of recognition might be best received. Some organisations have recognition schemes, others have awards ceremonies, others still, use their performance management structure to reward the right behaviours. Your organisational culture will dictate what works.

It's true that you need to try to engage with your entire employee base, but some audiences are easier to get to than others. By ensuring the remote worker, the customer-facing employee, the homeworker or the shop floor worker has effective opportunities to understand the organisation and the part they play in driving it forward, you can greatly improve engagement levels, customer service and customer perception, potentially lower sickness and attrition levels and, ultimately, improve performance and enhance value. You'll also make yourself critical to your organisation in the process.

Case Study: Scottish Water, 'Making the Connections'

Scottish Water is the only publicly owned water company in the UK, providing water and waste water services across Scotland. It was set up in 2002 with almost 6,000 employees, formed of three previously separate Scottish water companies, and was set a massive challenge to improve customer service and reduce operating costs by 40 per cent over a 4-year period. Two years into this programme of change it became apparent that the organisation's ability to drive out costs was slowing down. This was primarily because the focus needed to shift from driving down costs in specific business units to making end-to-end processes across the whole organisation more cost efficient. Employee surveys were also spelling it out loud and clear, namely that employees didn't feel 'connected' up – that they did not or could not understand the remit of others outside their own team, and didn't understand the impact of their actions on others. This wasn't helped by the fact that many of the then 5,500 employee base were based remotely and had little or no access to traditional communications channels. Scottish Water had a huge challenge to communicate to these 'unconnected' groups.

The board and directors of Scottish Water realised the need for decisive action and agreed to invest in an innovative programme of change in order to help employees become better connected. The change programme became known as 'Making the Connections'. It went on to win numerous awards, including the CiB Gold Award for Best Internal Communications Project. The objectives were simple:

- To help people understand why their job was important to the business and to the strategy.
- To help employees understand how they connected with others in the organization.
- To bring a sense of pride and ownership to making change happen.
- To encourage learning and communication in a fun and innovative way.

Central to the success of the programme was that it was run collaboratively – reflecting the message of the programme itself. Two main teams led the project group – internal communications and organisational development. Critically, the project group was also made up of trade union representatives, interested employees and sponsoring senior managers. The make-up of the project group was crucial in gaining a sense of the social context for the change programme. Having a range of employees in the group also helped to 'ground' the elements of the programme in events and activities which would genuinely appeal to the audience. There was a strict reporting mechanism within the project team, so that others could see what had been achieved, what was planned and how resources were being spent. Clarity and openness around these points was important for fostering a sense of 'shared ownership' about the programme.

The programme had three key phases which ran over a 6-month period:

1. An event for leaders within the business to gain their buy-in and feedback and support to the process of making connections.

2. Team sessions called 'mapping sessions' where teams began to think about who they connected with and how those relationships worked and could be improved.

3. A series of experiential employee events specifically aimed at the more 'unconnected' employees where the learning experience was driven by existing knowledge of the demographic breakdown of this segment of the audience base.

LEADERSHIP EVENT

The leadership event was held off-site and was facilitated by managers themselves, an important part of the ownership process. With a geographically dispersed audience base, it was important to get leaders on board who could go back to their various regions and drive and support the programme and its messages. At the event, the importance of needing to 'make connections' was explained in the context of the organisation strategy, and leaders were given an opportunity to experience the mapping sessions and learn about the approach to the employee events. Leaders were taken through a number of high octane experiences and the outputs were made into useful booklets full of ideas called 'tools and techniques for making the connections' which were distributed to all leaders after the event. The experience was high energy, fun, professional and celebratory in feel. It encouraged the most senior management population in Scottish Water to see the importance of 'connections' and gained their buy-in for the roll-out of the remainder of the programme throughout the organisation. It also started to create a buzz around the programme and it came to be seen as a desirable and positive project to be associated with.

MAPPING SESSIONS

The project group decided to hold team sessions which would allow employees to think about and discuss connections with and between themselves and other teams. The project group drew on demographic information about the employee base to develop team mapping sessions. The employee base demographics suggested teams would respond to experiential learning activities, particularly using discussion and visual-based media. Learning charts had been used successfully before and were ideal for this purpose. Each team was given one giant laminated 'map'. On one side were islands depicting the 'directorates' of the business and the islands around these became the business units (see Figure 4.2). Teams were required to draw lines and links between their own team on the map and five other areas they currently connected with and did not connect with. Then they were asked to describe the nature of these connections – did they work well, could they be improved, and if so, how?

Each team mapping session lasted about 1 hour and was facilitated by the team manager. The outputs consisted of a set of actions team members agreed to take to improve or set up connections with other parts of Scottish Water. This exercise encouraged Scottish Water employees to start thinking about the nature of their connections within their day-to-day work, and was excellent preparation for the employee events which took place about a month later. On completion of the mapping session many employees had identified parts of the organisation they wanted to know more about. The employee events would help them do just that.

EMPLOYEE EVENTS

Using demographic analysis, input from employees and unions, and feedback from the senior managers, the project team devised a series of employee events which would appeal to a wide range of employees, but in particular the 'unconnected' group. The objective was to really engage employees in the messages of making the connections, to enable them to meet each other, understand a bit about where the organisation was going, and of course, to have fun. The project team was keen to steer clear of 'tell and sell' type corporate events. They knew that many of their more remote or field workers did not like

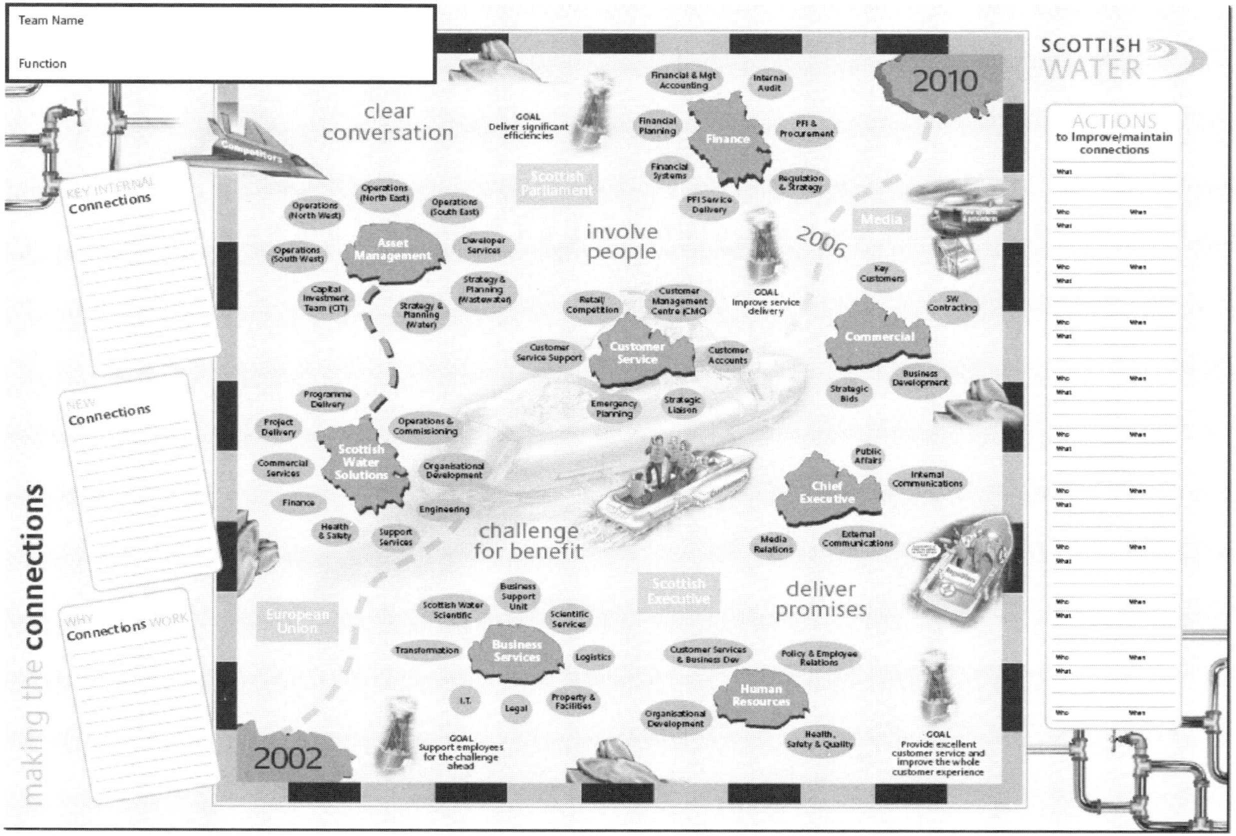

Figure 4.2 An example learning chart

traditional conference style events, nor large amounts of listening or reading, nor lots of corporate content. In addition they knew that their target segment led full social lives – attending community events, auctions, farmer's markets, fairs, sports events and so on at weekends and holidays. This was the type of event their audience was used to and valued. The project team therefore decided to use this format for the employee events and the 'funfair' idea was born. Twenty different areas of the business, from waste water treatment, to finance, to the contact centre and the laboratories had 'stalls' at the fun fair, each manned by enthusiastic employees. The 'stallholders' job was to communicate what their area did in a fun and enjoyable way, while engaging the employees at the event to talk about how they might be connected with their area, and how they could work together. There were activities at each stall to appeal to each different learning type – visual, taste, physical and touch. The atmosphere at each event was deliberately hyped – full of music, laughter and fun much like a traditional funfair. Prizes were awarded to those who managed to visit all 20 stalls and complete the activities on offer.

The funfair toured Scotland from North to South so that employees could attend a session close to them. They were highly successful, not just because they were managed and run 'in-house' (therefore had full employee ownership – over 200 employees were responsible for running each event), but because they also tapped into the project team's knowledge of the 'unconnected' employee base, their likes and dislikes and information/learning needs. An employee did not have to be well versed on corporate strategy to be able to understand the goals of the event, they did not even feel like they were directly 'learning' as they participated. The events did not feel like a typical corporate event at all. The feedback was enormously positive: almost 100 per cent said they enjoyed the day and that they felt committed to improving their connections at work.

Scottish Water did go on to beat its target of reducing operating costs by over 40 per cent in 4 years, and is now working on delivering against another set of challenging targets to be delivered by 2010. Levels of employee engagement have also increased dramatically since 2002.

5

Recognising and Rewarding Employees

by Ike Levick

> *'There's a revolution going on in today's workplaces. Workers want respect … Most important, they want to be appreciated when they do a good job.'*
>
> Nelson and Spitzer[1]

It doesn't matter in which industry you specialise or operate. Most leading organisations will tell you that attracting and retaining the best people requires more than a fancy job title and competitive pay package.

In Australia and New Zealand, the investment banking industry is extremely competitive and growing rapidly. Headhunters, competitors and clients regularly approach employees with interesting employment opportunities. In response, ABN AMRO Australia and New Zealand have introduced a range of initiatives in recent years to ensure our bank is a great place to work.

Initiatives include:

- A programme that matches employee donations to an employee-selected list of charities – dollar for dollar, and with tax benefits;

- Leveraging interesting and unusual sponsorships to the benefit of employees, such as our sponsorship of the Australian Chamber Orchestra and the possibility to meet the Artistic Director and

---

1 *The 1001 Rewards and Recognition Fieldbook: The Complete Guide* by Bob Nelson and Dean R. Spitzer, New York: Workman Publishing, 2003.

Leader of the Orchestra, attend rehearsals 'behind the scenes', concerts and more;

- Offering employees a substantial, capped annual refund for monies spent on a variety of pursuits outside work;

- Most recently with the growing interest in climate change, we have introduced a recurring campaign to help employees calculate and minimise their carbon footprint through buying carbon credits at special wholesale rates.

This chapter focuses on yet another initiative aimed at making ABN AMRO Australia and New Zealand great places to work: the Triple A Awards programme. Designed and launched in-house in 2003, this tailor-made programme encourages peers and local management to openly recognise those individuals and teams who make lasting contributions to the company's success. In doing so, we don't only identify and promote a sense of goodwill and pride; we are also able to share success stories around the organisation in Australia and the rest of ABN AMRO globally and spread great ideas around so others can learn from them. In addition, the programme is designed to embrace front, middle and back office employees in an effort to generate a sense of unity across the various business areas.

We believe it is this type of initiative that can give employers an edge in their employees' mind, especially when they are weighing up the pros and cons of changing jobs. It's what can make your company the more meaningful one to work for.

Background

So, why bother with an internal reward and recognition programme?

The idea of having an internal, company-wide awards programme started in exactly the right place – with the local management team. By late 2002, it was agreed that a formal mechanism to recognise people who made exceptional contributions towards ABN AMRO's success in Australia and New Zealand was required. In addition, the management team wanted actively to encourage and celebrate the behaviours, actions and thoughts required to achieve our business goal at that time – to be a Top 3 bank in the markets in which we operate. The local marketing communications team was tasked with exploring the idea further and making it happen.

After careful consideration by the marketing communications team, a programme was created to meet the management team's objectives outlined above, and also:

- encourage employees to celebrate outstanding contributions to teamwork, transactions, cross-business unit working, efficiency gains and innovation – all recognised as the desired behaviours to be a Top 3 bank;
- increase employee understanding of ABN AMRO's local operations, what we stand for and how we are different;
- increase awareness of the four global corporate values – teamwork, respect, integrity and professionalism;
- communicate the importance of our brand and what the company aspires to be;
- make people feel a sense of pride in working for ABN AMRO.

Ultimately, we also hoped that the programme would strengthen our general reputation through positive word of mouth and more specifically, our status as a preferred Employer of Choice within the Australian Financial Services industry.

The Communications Strategy: Who, What, Why, When, With (How Much)?

As part of a large global company, it was necessary to complete a communications strategy that clearly showed our objectives and how we would launch and run the new programme. This proved to be an exciting challenge to overcome as it encouraged us to think through how we were going to implement the complete programme. Essentially, the strategy outlined how we would develop strong, inter-linked internal communication activities and provided a picture of the expected costs. We also demonstrated how we would maximise employee acceptance amongst all ABN AMRO employees located in Australia and New Zealand.

The communications strategy was also a great tool to demonstrate to local management how we had interpreted their awards idea and converted this into a tangible, effective communication campaign.

As part of developing the Communication Strategy we learned about the value of:

- Involvement: involving your employees in your communications strategy from an early stage encourages buy-in and interest.
- Interviews: conducting short informal interviews with different people (natural enthusiasts and cynics) can help identify what will make the programme a success and you can incorporate this into your strategy.
- A well-argued business case: carefully comparing the pros and cons of investing time, money and effort in running an internal reward and recognition programme against other solutions, and considering what the consequences would be if the programme was not introduced, will provide the basis of a robust business case.

Measurement: Keeping an Eye on the Ball

It is important to make sure that the programme is meeting its objectives and staying on track.

In addition to meeting the objectives stated earlier, we felt that success could be demonstrated by achieving the following results:

- CEO and management committee endorsement and ownership, which would look like personalised emails encouraging involvement, 'walking the talk' and valued participation in the judging process;
- between five and 10 completed, quality Nomination Forms for each award;

- participation from a range of employees, located in every city in which we are located;
- a strong library of winning examples that might be used for internal marketing purposes (and external, if appropriate);
- if the programme was perceived as the basis for a new annual tradition throughout ABN AMRO Australia and New Zealand;
- a measurable contribution towards the company's desired positioning as 'a great company to work for';
- a demonstrable increased sense of enthusiasm in the workplace.

Award Categories: What Behaviour are You Recognising?

Nothing is set in stone. When creating award categories, be flexible and accommodate changes to reflect trends, market conditions and management opinion. In ABN AMRO's case, the four award categories that were launched in 2003 have since been tweaked and grown to five award categories, ensuring that the programme remains relevant at all times and truly reflects our desired business behaviours. For example, an early category, which rewarded effective cost control, has since evolved to include recognition of sustainable business practices to more accurately reflect where we are headed as a business.

The key lessons we learned when creating award categories were:

1. The importance of value: thinking about your corporate values and how these can be incorporated into the programme categories will help you identify and exploit every opportunity to bring your brand to life!

2. The need to reward each category of employee: remembering to include categories for each target audience (front, middle *and* back office) as well as teams and/or individuals, according to the make-up of your business, will help ensure your awards are truly inclusive.

Nomination Process: Obtaining Enough Information for Judging Purposes with Minimum Effort

We felt it was important to create a nomination process that enabled both individuals and team representatives to complete nominations. Keep this in mind when creating the checkboxes on your nomination form to help people realise that they are not expected to nominate themselves (even though this is possible) but rather nominate their colleagues. Since the launch 5 years ago, we have found that the majority of nominations are made by someone nominating someone else or their own or another team.

In the first 2 years, we used hardcopy forms that could be downloaded from the intranet or requested from the team. This evolved to include an online nomination form, accessible through the local intranet, to reflect changes in employee preferences as well as a more paper-conscious working environment. In 2007, the majority of employees used the online version.

To indicate that you appreciate the effort people have gone to in completing a nomination, acknowledge receipt of nominations with a quick courtesy email. In our case, we used a dedicated Triple A Award Lotus Notes email address to further raise awareness of the programme's existence and branding.

The key lessons we learned when designing the nomination process were:

1. Brevity: ensuring it does not take more than 30 minutes to complete a form will encourage the maximum number of people to participate.

2. Word limits: establishing word limits of, for example, 250 words per criteria encourages nominators to articulate clearly why they think their nomination should win and provides judges with entries that are undemanding to read and understand.

3. Prompts: when the time comes for nominations, creating a list of which projects, deals and people you think should be nominated will help prompt nominations. To do this search the local intranet for good news stories, research press releases, review emails and ask business managers and the CEO/senior managers for suggestions. Armed with this information, actively encourage people to make nominations. If necessary, offer your assistance in putting together

first drafts for their review, making the nomination process as easy and painless as possible. The more nominations you help generate, the more nominations you will end up receiving and the more people you can recognise.

Rules and Conditions: Keeping it Fair

Making sure you end up comparing 'apples with apples' requires clear rules and conditions. It is also important to create the right feeling around the company – one of *in*clusion rather than *ex*clusion. For example, one of the Triple A Award programme award categories is the Deal of the Year Award. To make sure everyone was on a level playing field, we asked nominators to include only those projects and mandates which were successfully closed within a time period by a certain date. This practice was familiar to our bankers, as external industry awards use similar policies.

Something else to think about when developing rules and conditions is employee eligibility. For example, we articulated that all full- and part-time employees were able to participate. However, for one of the awards – the individual CEO's Living the Values Award – it was decided that senior executives would not be eligible in case this sent the wrong message to employees.

Rules can be developed easily in response to the kind of questions you think employees are most likely to ask:

- Timescales: for example, when did the work in question need to be completed by? What are the award deadlines? When will judging take place and winners be announced?

- Prizes: what will people win, above and beyond being recognised by management and peers?

- Eligibility: who is eligible and who is entitled to make nominations? Can people make more than one nomination in general or per category?

- Nomination formats: what format are nominations to be made in? What can people submit? Is additional supporting documentation/ material acceptable? If so, how much and what type (for example, press release, colleague or client feedback)? Are people disadvantaged if they do not include additional material?

- Award categories: may people submit the same nomination more than once (for example, for different award categories)?

- Winners: can there be more than one winner per award category?

The rules and conditions should also outline whether you intend to share the content received via the nominations in any way. For example, do you intend to use content for internal and/or external marketing purposes of success stories? If so, the nomination form and related communication materials should clearly alert nominators that by submitting an application, they are thereby giving the marketing communications team permission to use its content to spread great ideas and good news, such as through newsletter articles, websites, roadshows and so on.

The key lessons when developing the rules and conditions were:

- Concision: keeping your rules and conditions to one page ensures employees will read them.

- Communication: considering how your rules and conditions will be communicated enables you to get maximum exposure for the awards. To encourage virtual communication, think about using the intranet to host these and other key documents and information.

- Consistency: ensuring your rules and conditions filter through all communications, particularly the nomination form and judging guidelines, will guarantee a perception of fairness.

- Clear and consistent sources of advice: using the rules and conditions to develop a FAQ document will allow you to anticipate as many queries in advance as possible. Remember to update both when reviewing key communication tools each year, as dates and details will change.

Judging: Keeping it Simple but Effective

At ABN AMRO we formed an annual judging panel made up of the entire senior management team, an HR and a communications team representative. Each year, judges are allocated to judge those awards where there will be the least likelihood of bias or prejudice (for example, the head of equities helped to judge the Sustainable Business Award in 2007).

Keeping the judging panel informed with the right amount of information at the right time is very important for ensuring their involvement. Briefing packs should be emailed out to every judge at least 48 hours prior to the judging meeting, which typically takes up to 1 hour. Materials included the judging criteria, examples of what the judges should be looking for, copies of the nominations and a judging score card using the Likert Scale (or similar methodology) which allows judges to measure the extent to which each of the different award criteria were met. As the communications team representative, it is essential that you have an opinion on all the nominations and their merit in case the judges have not had the time to read all of the nominations and you are required to play a hands-on role.

Key lessons learned from designing the judging process were:

- Additional prizes: deciding – in advance of the judging – whether you will allow for a 'highly commended' category in addition to the 'winners' category, will enable you to recognise a wider range of nominees. But you will also need to consider whether having a highly commended winner devalues the award. If it involves further trophies and prizes, a second category may exceed your original budget.

- Employee reaction: considering what the employee reactions may be to the winner/s, will help avoid the risk that people may feel left out. Try to avoid being too one city/country-centric, for example

- Timing: some judging outcomes depend on the results of who has won the other awards, to ensure the final award winners represent a good majority of the business. To ensure that instant decisions can be made, consider having one overall judging meeting to consider all award nominations at the same time. We will be testing this approach in 2008, again with an HR and communications representative in attendance.

Launch: Capturing Employees' Hearts and Minds

To make sure all related communication is immediately recognisable, create a brand for the programme that reflects its name and spirit. Once we had decided on The Triple A Awards, we commissioned an external designer to come up with a unique logo, using the colour yellow to signify innovation and positive energy. This logo has remained unchanged since the launch 5 years ago, giving a sense of continuity and longevity.

We also found it helpful to work with natural communication champions throughout the business – such as the business managers of the business units, enthusiasts and people we knew could lead by example. This strategy helped ensure a widespread impact at the launch. It was these same people we used to test different communication tools such as the nomination forms and FAQs as we originally designed and later tweaked the programme. Since launch, we have continued working with natural champions to ensure a solid response to the programme each year.

During the first year of the launch, we asked randomly selected, but enthusiastic, employees to become involved in the development of the brochure. By creating our own photography style guide and distributing disposable cameras to key business contacts, we encouraged colleagues to contribute photos of peers 'at work' and 'at play' for inclusion in the Polaroid-style visuals in the brochure. This early involvement created a wonderful sense of unity across the business and also meant people had some fun. We made sure in advance that the quality of the disposable camera pictures would create reasonable pictures for the final brochure. Copies of some of the pictures were sent around the business as keepsakes and thank you's. We also used the photos for the Triple A Awards intranet site. If you feature employees in this way, remember to ask for their permission first (this does not typically cause a problem) before you use their picture. And be mindful of the people who may be in the process of changing roles. For example, we found that one of the people on the brochure's front cover was soon relocated to the ABN AMRO London office. Fortunately people felt the brochure was a nice reminder of her, rather than feeling that her picture gave a sense that the programme was behind the times.

Key lessons learned when launching the programme were:

- Sustainability: keeping in mind that it is not just the initial launch you need to consider. You will need to think about exciting and enthusing employees during each year of the programme. One way to generate interest is the way in which you communicate the awards' key dates. For example, in our second year every employee received a postcard desk drop with key information on it

- Confidence: involving employees by asking them to share their opinions and thoughts during quiet times in their day will often generate some excellent ideas.

Naming Competition: Involving Employees Early On

It is important to involve employees at an early stage. We used a brightly coloured fluorescent green desk drop (to stand out from all the other paper on employees' desks!), to communicate the programme's objectives briefly and invited employees to christen the new programme. This communication process created early employee awareness and generated a sense of excitement and fun. Whilst it's not essential to have a naming competition, we found it helped increase acceptance of the new initiative.

We included some naming criteria with the desk drop to guide people's ideas in a common direction. We asked them to choose a name that is:

- easy to remember;
- aspirational;
- timeless (and one that won't date or become irrelevant to local employees);
- reflects our culture and values (including our Australian/New Zealand roots);
- meaningful to ABN AMRO employees.

We had an excellent response rate (one in every seven people throughout Australia and New Zealand responded). Eight people won a bottle of French champagne, along with the reward of seeing their suggestions up in lights in the coming months. The Triple A Awards name (Figure 5.1) worked for several reasons: it is a well-recognised high industry ranking, used by rating agencies to assess the likelihood of credit default; and it stood for **A**BN **A**MRO **A**ustralasia.

Figure 5.1 The Triple A Awards logo

In addition, the three AAAs can be used as an acronym for the actions required to win an award – Asking the right questions, Applying yourself and Achieving success.

Key lessons we learned when designing the naming competition were:

- Choice of media: taking time to consider which media to use in today's work environment will help give your message more impact. For example, would an online mechanism prove more effective than a hardcopy desk drop?

- Naming criteria: careful definition of the naming criteria will provide clear guidance about the objectives and purpose of the programme and manage employee expectations.

CEO Endorsement: Flagging that this Matters to Senior Management

We felt it was important to indicate to employees that this programme was of personal interest to our CEO and his team. Thanks to a clear endorsement from the top team, employees took notice and realised that this programme would be and still is an opportunity to be recognised by members of the senior team.

Ideas for showing CEO endorsement include (also see Table 5.1 at the end of this chapter for more information):

- Face-to-face launch at large employee gatherings: in ABN AMRO's case this was the half-yearly staff update, a forum designed for top-down face-to-face communication. In addition, every year we remind the CEO and his team to encourage (and suggest) nominations during the nomination period.

- Paper communication: we followed the face-to-face launch with a brochure desk drop, containing a personal foreword by the CEO. In subsequent years, we have opted to use screen savers and posters in the lift wells.

- Online: each year, we include a CEO or COO introduction on the Triple A Awards intranet site and often make sure a launch or nomination completion email is sent by the CEO.

Key lessons we learned from this process were:

- Opportunity spotting: remembering that there are both formal and informal opportunities for the CEO to encourage uptake of the programme, which will ensure the greatest possible impact from their support.

- CEO involvement: asking the CEO for nomination ideas and using this when approaching people to make nominations (for example, the CEO thinks that XYZ is an exceptional project to include in the ABC award category…) helps encourage employees to get involved.

Maintaining Momentum: Sharing the Good News

Recognition can begin as soon as all nominations have been received. It is important to start spreading the good news of who has been nominated early. This is a delicate communication challenge – involving emailing all employees or posting the news on the intranet – as inevitably you *also* expose who has not been nominated. There is no real way to overcome this, other than making sure that for those nominations that have been completed, the team nominations have been double and triple checked with the nominators (see the lessons learned section).

Once judging decisions have been made, communicating the winners (and highly commended winners, if applicable) is the next communication milestone. In our case, the management team are the first to find out who the winners are. For the wider internal audience, we reveal who the award winners are at the company-wide staff updates, which are held soon after judging is completed. The results are communicated following the business performance results in the style of the Hollywood Oscars: A quick reminder of the award category and what it is designed to recognise, who judged it, who was nominated and who won, and why. To raise the profiles of individual senior managers, we ask one judge from each award category to present the results (this means that they will require speaker notes and slides). This also gives the presentation process some momentum and variety.

Once your immediate target audience is informed of the nominees and winners, you can spread the good news further afield. For example, develop stories for the global intranet, internal newsletters, emails to other communication colleagues and more. If you are successful, you will be asked to advise on award programmes in other countries or be paid the ultimate compliment of your award programme being copied elsewhere!

Key lessons we learned from maintaining momentum were:

1. Early start: starting the recognition process early creates a sense of 'feel good'.

2. Wider recognition: if the number of nominees and winners make it feasible, writing letters to all of the winners as well as everyone who was nominated to explain the reasons for their nomination and/or award, allows you to give maximum recognition to all the employees. You can cc direct line managers and heads of business units to further spread the word about excellent employee performance. Bear in mind that whilst this sounds like a simple communication exercise, it can be tricky as many people are nominated for more than one award and you can end up writing many hundreds of letters, many of which need to be customised, and this can take several days. However, is a very worthwhile exercise.

Conclusions

TEAM MAKE-UP AND SIZE

We have learned several lessons over the last 5 years. Of these, probably the most difficult challenge was and continues to be the size of teams in team nominations, such as for our Deal of the Year category. We found that front office employees tend to overlook back and middle office employees when making team nominations. In reality, many people play an instrumental role in making projects and deals happen. Who should you include in a team nomination? Just the key people, everyone involved (which could mean up to 50 people in some cases) or should you impose an artificial limit of, say, 15 people? In 2008 we will be limiting the number of team members for the first time, to highlight those people who truly went above and beyond the call of duty.

In previous years we invited nominators to reconsider their team nominations, to ensure that everyone was included. We also sent emails to the heads of service functions to give them the chance to suggest the names of people who may not have been originally included. Although this has meant that we have ended up with some very large teams, it has also meant that everyone is recognised, which was one of the original objectives of the programme.

THE PRIZES

Hand-in-hand with team size comes the value of individual prizes. Beyond the honour of being recognised, what is considered to be a worthy prize? Do you want to leverage external sponsorships, give gift vouchers, restaurant vouchers or use corporate frequent flying points? This will depend on the culture of your organisation and the budget of the programme.

Also, does each award carry the same prize? For example, in ABN AMRO's case, winners of the Living the Values Award receive a more valuable individual prize than the other categories because the winner is considered a true role model for individual behaviour.

We review the prizes, trophies and certificates each year to ensure we continue to reward employees appropriately and meet their expectations and reinforce the values behind the programme while acting in a sustainable manner.

AFTER WORD

The Triple A Awards programme was designed to be flexible. In its fifth and most recent year, we decided to increase the frequency of employee recognition from every year to every month. To achieve this without causing confusion, it was decided to introduce a new, standalone award known as The Way We Work Award. This award is designed to recognise and reward one individual – also nominated by colleagues – to win an instant cash prize every month for best living the corporate values. The communications team manages the process and the CEO decides on the winner and sends a results email to all employees each month. At the end of the year, all winners of this monthly award are automatically shortlisted for the Triple A Awards' CEO's Living the Values Award category.

The key benefit of introducing this second award initiative is that it highlights individual actions every month, helping people understand how they can best live the corporate values. It also generates pride and a sense of accomplishment. Since its introduction, people no longer need to make separate nominations for the CEO's Living the Values Award, thereby simplifying the nomination process.

Communication Tools Summary

All communication should be clearly branded with the programme's name. Consistency is key. All communication tools should also comply with any internal brand guidelines, so that the company brand is heightened rather than diffused. Remember, employees do not necessarily expect flashy or expensive forms of communication. In fact, in some cases this can disengage and anger employees as it is perceived as a waste of money. Be careful when creating communication tools to keep these factors in mind. Table 5.1 shows some of the tools used by ABN AMRO Australia and New Zealand over the last 5 years.

Key lessons we learned when developing the overall communication mix were:

- Cost/benefit: when considering what communication tool to use, weighing up the amount of time required to complete the communication activities against the benefit they will have will help you ensure the biggest impact for the least effort.

Table 5.1 Communication tools summary

Purpose	Electronic	Paper	Face-to-face
Raise awareness	Screen saver/wall paper with key dates 'Crawling' message on the intranet homepage with reminders Customised email signature for everyone in the communications team during nomination period	Competition desk drop Postcard desk drop (created by designer) Posters in lift wells/ kitchens	Staff update to 'inform the troops'
Create understanding	Dedicated intranet with rules and conditions Nomination form (word and online versions) FAQ Overview of the awards process and key milestones, copy of the brochure (PDF version), and so on. Branded Lotus Notes email address to receive nominations, take questions, send nomination receipts and make key announcements/ reminders	Brochure, acting as a 'one stop shop' containing all the information needed to feel inspired to nominate, with pointers to more sources. The content was written to ensure a long shelf life (created by designer)	Team meetings – ask business managers to mention the awards and provide updates
Encourage acceptance	Nomination form Share winning stories on the dedicated intranet site	Nomination forms could be downloaded from the intranet and completed in hardcopy too	
Generate excitement	Company-wide email informing everyone of who has been nominated for an award (once all team sizes/names have been double checked) Update intranet with all names	Letter sent to each individual informing them that they have been nominated (or email); a copy of this letter could be sent to the line manager and business unit head Individual certificates given to all winners and highly commended	Judging outcome: winners not announced until the half year staff update to encourage attendance and facilitate peer recognition All winners' names appear on a Triple A Award board, strategically located in each office

- Print deadlines: if you are using printed communication, remembering that there are print deadlines you will need to meet *and* that the content may not last much beyond 6–12 months will help expensive and embarrassing mistakes. However, printed communication is stylish and can be very effective if used sparingly.

6

Communication at the Coalface

by Lindsay Uittenbogaard

This chapter identifies a gap in the way organisations typically approach internal communication. It explores why the gap exists and what it means for organisations that ignore it. Some common sense approaches to bridge this 'gap' are outlined and some views on it have been canvassed from practitioners in different corners of the communication world and included below.

To provide a context for this gap, here are some questions:

- Do you think the hard part of business is strategy implementation?
- Do you think communication has an important role to play in strategy implementation?
- Do you support the premise that everyone in an organisation is a communicator?
- Do you think most employees could be better communicators?

If your answers to all these questions is *yes*, then you may agree with the following statement:

> *Employees need guidance, tools and learning and support in the area of communication if they are to realise their objectives as efficiently and as effectively as possible.*

While Internal Communicators play an increasingly valuable role in the areas of leadership communication, aligning employee with strategy, and in facilitating the sharing of key content, they generally spend little or no time supporting front-line employees in the communication challenges that these employees face as part of their daily jobs. This shortcoming diminishes the organisation's ability to implement strategy because it creates abundant opportunity for communication breakdown and misunderstandings which, in turn, wastes many man-hours, reduces employee efficiency, performance, motivation and results.

What Kind of Communication Requirements are Employees Typically Faced With?

Business is far more complex than it ever used to be; the increasing pace and range of new legislation, developing professional practice and the rapid evolution of organisational structures and requirements all require ongoing attention. Consequently, front-line employees find themselves collaborating with a far wider and more diverse group of stakeholders than before. More importantly, the skills these people are expected to use are more sophisticated than they used to be. Since email, the Internet and other virtual connecting technologies took off in the 1990's, the task of connecting with others has become increasingly dynamic and complex. The reasons to interact, who we interact with, how we do it and how fast we can deliver through these interactions is dependent on our communication capability. Today's employees need to be outstanding communicators to deliver to their objectives and yet it is very rare for employers to provide support, learning and development on the communication skills they need to enable great performance.

What Kind of Communication Challenges do Employees Face?

When it comes to organisational communication, there are only two main issues:

- *disconnects:* (where a message should have been shared in an appropriate way, at the right time and place but wasn't);
- *misunderstandings:* (where the message was shared but wasn't received as intended, for whatever reason).

But how does this play out into specific challenges?

CASE STUDY

A 2007 study of over 100 IT project managers in a major European energy company found that there were four key communication challenges at the root of many project failures. These failures (otherwise known as 'escalations') occur when a project does not run to plan and results in some kind of unexpected cost, delay or an increase requirement for resources. When this happens, the situation is escalated to leaders whose role is to explore what went wrong and how it can be fixed. Two of the most common escalations were:

Sharing meaning effectively: misunderstandings arose because parties simply did not successfully communicate shared understanding. A word or phrase is so frequently used in one part of an organisation that an extended meaning is attributed to it. This extended meaning, which is taken for granted by one group, is nevertheless unknown in another part of the same organisation. Take, for instance, the phrase 'refer it to the steering committee'. In team 'A' this simply implies that a project decision will be made at a higher level of authority. In team 'B', it implies that delays will be incurred as further viewpoints are sought.

Creating and using a communication plan: in many of the IT projects researched, the project managers were reluctant to create and use a communication plan. In some cases this was due to the lack of availability of a practical communication planning template. On closer inspection, a stark contrast between the purpose of a project plan and that of a communication plan was throwing people off. A project plan is designed to dictate the chain of events. In fact, the more rigorous the project plan and the better the project manager, the more likely the plan will play out as designed. The name of the game in project management is 'deliver to plan' and IT project managers are rigorously trained to use their approved plan as a bible. In communication however, the plan needs to be much more reactive:

- based on feedback from activity 1, you may change activity 2;
- based on reactions to messages with stakeholder x you may amend them to work better with stakeholder y;
- in the event of an unexpected result, a whole new set of communication activities may be suitable.

The differences between how a project plan and a communication plan need to be handled are significant. However, IT project managers were invariably not trained to use a communication plan, despite its relevance to the success of their work.

What Kind of Communication Activities are Employees Involved In?

Once again, the example in the major European energy company illustrates the gap that exists between the need for guidance, tools and skill-building for employees on how they can communicate more effectively as part of their roles and the provision they currently receive. In bridging this gap, you need to forget communication being about the 'what' and think of it as being more as being about the 'how'. Imagine communication activities as simply being about anything that involves the preparation and sharing of meaning with others On this basis, employees regularly engage in a variety of activities in the course of their work (see Figure 6.1).

What Kind of Support Can an Organisation Offer to Bridge this Gap?

Firstly, people with power inside organisations need to recognise the extent to which this issue is affecting performance and in what ways it is damaging the organisation.

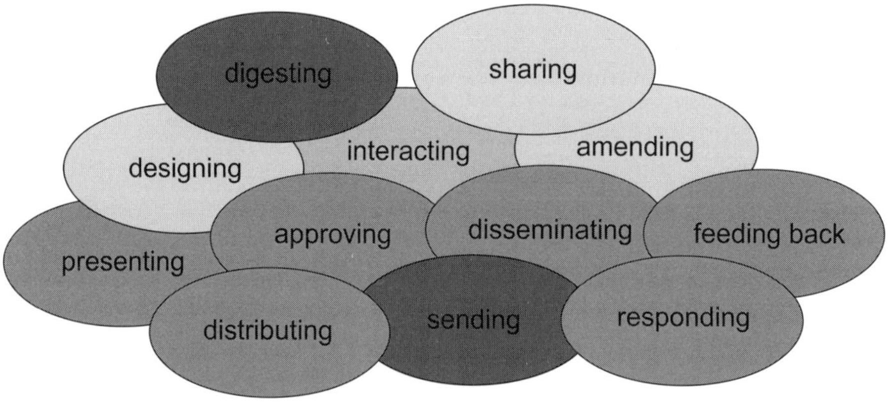

Figure 6.1 What is communication?

Ask yourself or some of your employees some of these questions to find out how much good communication is being sacrificed to get things done faster (but arguably, less effectively):

- Have you ever seen someone tick the communication box on their work by posting up a new intranet page and hoping the right people see it?
- Have you ever wondered if an important conversation might have had a different outcome if only the people involved had better dialogue skills?
- Do you find yourself working on emails while in teleconferences and not really knowing if everyone on the call ended up on the same page?
- Is it so frustrating for your team to work with others with different cultures that you end up avoiding spoken contact and hoping everything works out in the end?
- Do you tune out of presentations to think about pressing work issues because the slides didn't engage you?
- Do you wonder if anyone would actually notice if the end results were better because all your project stakeholders were fully on board, instead of just noticing that it took longer for you to get there with stakeholders that weren't fully on board?
- Have you found yourself deleting emails from people in your organisation because you just do not have time to reply?

What are the issues, precisely? How much is systemic; about, for example, having the right training, systems, reward structures and resources available for people to use? How much comes down to individual skills and behaviours of employees themselves?

There are three parts to this answer and the most obvious involves **learning:**

1. *Learning for leaders:* leaders play a major part in driving good organisational communication practice, not least because *'at least*

65 per cent of how employees make sense of their world at work is driven by observing their bosses.' (Ed Schein, MIT). Leaders have the power to determine direction and strategy, motivate and inspire, and determine behavioural habits within their organisations purely through examples set by their own actions.

2. *Learning for employees:* mistakes, rework and non-productive efforts not only cost time and money but are disappointing for those involved and can damage relationships and morale. Employees may well be familiar with the mantra *'communicate, communicate, communicate!'* But what does that really mean? How can people inside an organisation connect with their colleagues and leaders across different locations, cultures and disciplines? This is a learning proposition.

3. *Systemic support:* this is about having the right encouragement and support, knowledge sharing systems, reward structures and resources available for employees to use.

The learning content includes developing awareness about what communication actually is, how powerful it can be, how relevant it is to all of us, and how specific communication challenges can be overcome. Further content encompasses:

People

- dialogue;
- group dialogue;
- team dynamics and processes;
- connecting cross-team;
- cross-cultural communication;
- managing meetings and events;
- change and engagement;

- understanding people and diversity;
- stakeholder analysis and audience segmentation;
- self-awareness: say/do;
- values and ethics;
- behaviours as message senders and receivers;
- resources and support.

People using media

- virtual working;
- using social media;
- choosing media;
- using media;
- resources and support.

Other

- recognition and reward;
- structures and frameworks;
- provision of resources.

Be aware: tailoring communication is important. Employees will have very different communication challenges, depending on their seniority, discipline or function and on the culture of the organisation they work in. 'Difficulty overcoming silo boundaries' will demand a totally different solution from 'difficulty connecting with a specific leader', for example. A tailored learning package involving interviews up front should identify those challenges and help you build a relevant and effective learning experience around them.

The second element of employee support is *resource awareness*. To what extent do your employees know the answers to these questions? This is a communication exercise in itself.

SERVICES: How can I access translation, copywriting or visual design services?

CONSULTANCY SUPPORT: What do I do if I need dedicated communication resources for my project?

TOOLS: What tools are out there to help me put together a communication plan or undertake other communication tasks?

TACTICS: Where can I get advice on best practice – for example, how can I ensure my stakeholders are up to date with developments from my project when they're busy with other priorities? How can I use communication channels to communicate with lots of people at once? How can I convert stakeholder hostility into support, or how can I improve the effectiveness of communication within my project team?

LEARNING: What courses are available to help me improve myself as a communicator – either inside the company or as recommended external training? Where can I find them.

The third part involves the availability of on-demand *coaching*. Each communication situation is a unique opportunity for an experienced and creative communication response. Even seasoned corporate veterans need objective advice to get the best results.

And the final element around supporting employees to be effective communicators is about *recognition*. If leaders recognise that communication is important – that communication is a competence – and if they reward good communication performance, then the quality of communication will improve. From formal recognition schemes to a quick one-to-one phrase acknowledging effort and giving praise – any kind of feedback that recognises, endorses and rewards at the same time is important.

Why Does this Gap Exist?

Communicators want to *own* what they're doing to be able to show they add value and they want this value to be significant. During the 1990's internal communicators were sick of being labelled as the people who 'did' newsletters and websites. Internal communication is potentially a very powerful business tool. Intent on their objective of achieving the status of valuable contributors, internal communicators have carved out a role for themselves as being 'strategic business partners' whilst sidelining crucial requirements from deeper in their organisations.

- Communicators are responding to demand. Employees don't always know they can be more efficient and effective by improving the ways in which they communicate. Internal communicators are not anxious to spend time creating demand for skills training nor are they always in the best position to do so.

- Communicators are responding to the requirements of their sponsors. If employees aren't demanding help and if leaders can't feel the pain points around communication, then communication roles and responsibilities will focus on the perceived current and real requirements of the business.

- Communicators aren't trained to enable others to be better communicators. Arguably, improving the communication performance of others is a different role from that of the more traditional communicator.

Communication is usually the means to an end, it is rarely the objective of a piece of work. The statement 'we need to upgrade a system with a supplier' inevitably carries the subtext 'we need to work on the same page as our supplier on liaising effectively around the system upgrade'. The focus is on the system upgrade, not on the process of communicating.

- Admitting that you need help in doing your job can feel like you're admitting you can't do your job properly; this is not a natural flag for people to wave.

- Communication is rather like swimming. Most people can swim – why would you need help to improve when you can already stay afloat?

- Just as it's easy to think you know how to communicate, it's also easy to think you know what communication is. For example, thinking of communication as being about the company newsletter, the website or visual design is a strong diversion from thinking around improving communication.

Recognising poor communication and knowing what to do about such instances is a skill in itself. If poor communication is not identified, there is no demand for change.

- Communication impacts different people at different levels, working on different subjects in different ways. Leaders may perceive the problem several layers lower in the organisation (or won't consider them significant enough to deal with), so rarely allocate budget to fix something that doesn't seem to be broken.

- 'Fixing' poor communication is not really possible. It's not that simple. There is never a 100 per cent solution. You can't 'fix' communication but you can facilitate moving things to a more advantageous state. Managers understandably shy away from this kind of woolliness.

- Poor communication is almost invisible and very difficult to measure. How do you know if a stakeholder group could have been engaged in a better way if no one complains? How do you know if efforts spent on improving 'connectivity' between your stakeholders worked if you can't prove what didn't connect as a result of the work? Take for example, the poorly skilled project manager. Who can say that if they had been more communication savvy the project would have taken 2 months less to deliver; or their poor communication practices cost the project an extra $78,000?

What is the Cost to Employees of Poor Communication?

If you could count the 'micro' instances of poor communication that occur with employees every day and add up the effects, the results would be staggering. The cost of poor communication, inefficiencies, performance losses and frustration is extremely high. Measurement of this can be very difficult and depends on exactly what intervention or response is being applied to each circumstance.

A research report from the International Association of Business Communication Research Foundation[1] identified the four critical challenges faced by communicators worldwide and involved extensive research: literature reviews, analyses of IABC Gold Quill Award winners, interviews with 22 communicators on three continents, and an online survey completed by 472 organisations from four continents. The challenges identified in the report were:

- Motivating employees to align with the business strategy – creating a line of sight between employees and the organisational strategy.
- Leadership and management communication – educating and engaging leaders and managers in their role in employee communication (this was further clarified as meaning that leaders throughout the organisation need to communicate and engage their employees in the business strategy and visibly demonstrate what it looks like).
- Managing information overload – breaking through the communication 'clutter'.
- Measuring the return on investment of internal communication – linking communication to business results.

The common theme within these challenges is that the main objective of every one of them is communication. And yet the report doesn't mention the importance of improving communication when it plays a parallel role in the achievement of other people's objectives.

Similarly, one of the companies listed in the Fortune 500 states that the mission of their global internal and management communication is to, 'Help achieve sustained business success by leveraging internal communications and relationships to positively influence employee engagement.'

The question posed against that here is then: why is the internal communication mission focused solely on the engagement of employees, when

1 International Association of Business Communication Research Foundation, *Best Practices in Meeting the Top Employee Communication Challenges of the 21st Century*, (2005). Sponsored by and Conducted by Right Management Consultants.

communication is fundamentally about interactions between people at all levels?

The author contacted various communication specialists in different industries and from different parts of the world to get their perspectives too:

Susan Dorflinger is the Director of Global Employee Marketing at GE Real Estate based in Connecticut. She suggests that the transference of communication expertise occurs incidentally if professional communicators work effectively with leaders and managers in the cascade and realisation of business strategy:

- *By holding manager communication workshops with those individuals who manage people, the communication executive can review the fundamentals of communication, while outlining how and why it's the manager's job for being accountable for the translation of business messages.*

- *By defining communication as a process where information is given to a person or group of people to achieve a shared understanding, managers leave knowing that communication is not a tactical event or a vehicle, such as email.*

- *By sharing simple examples of communication planning and providing assessment worksheets to help the managers answer the ever-important question on employee's minds: 'What does this mean to me?' ensures that managers can take responsibility for communication.*

- *By working one-on-one in developing communication action plans for the managers to execute; managers are drawn to seeing that two-way interaction establishes them as great communicators.*

- *By supplementing the workshops with monthly email messages to managers on topics ranging from business updates to leadership and communication tips builds on the foundation for further development of expertise.*

- *With a little energy and plenty of enthusiasm for results, the communication executive in any organisation can directly influence the notion that everyone is responsible for communication – the trick is in redefining communication and making use of the word effective.*

Rob Briggs is the Senior Manager, Communications for RBC Wealth Management – British Isles, based in London and Jersey. He sees that communicators can help others in the organisation by moulding and shaping the inevitable flow of information:

- *Yes, I can identify with the premise as I recognise some of the symptoms. It's a challenge and it's about pushing back on our own idle assumptions about what communications actually is. Communication goes on around us all the time – the best we can do is a bit of traffic planning – we do not and cannot control the fact that information flows, nor can we control the enormity of its power. We can (and should) help people in business to mould and shape that flow, and (to mix metaphors) to carve a diamond from that jet-black coal you're mining.*

- *I'd consider looking at ways in which two-way conversations can be facilitated, rather that providing top-down tools. Poor communication can be seriously costly. A lack of understanding or awareness of societal expectations (implicit and explicit) can result in such significant brand damage that the firm goes out of business. The more usual tools we see are process inefficiencies coupled with significant employee attraction and retention issues.*

- *Since the advent of email, and short-term pressures of shareholder demands for constant growth, managers have lost sight of their primary role – to set information in context for employees. The simple coping skills equation sums up the core of our dilemma succinctly: too much information* x *not enough time = information ignored.*

David Murray is the former editor of the *Journal of Employee Communication Management* with Ragan Communications, provider of a forum and resources for an online community of communicators. He concurs that the 'coalface gap' exists and describes his understanding around why it's there:

- *'Yes, I agree that most communication and arguably the most crucial communication happens down, through and all over the organisation. And yes: to the extent that professional communicators can help non-communication managers and others do a better job, they can wield a powerful and useful influence in the organisation. That said, a number of practical problems get in the way:*

1. *Communicators have limited budgets and time, both of which can be consumed VERY QUICKLY as they consult with or train non-communication managers in the organisation.*

2. *Communicators are trained in mass communication, but not necessarily in interpersonal communication (which is why communication departments themselves are not always managed particularly well).*

3. *Non-communication managers aren't necessarily receptive to the help of the 'PR person' in managing their departments.*

- *In short, the theory is spot on, but the practice is problematic and so many communicators conclude that the best thing they can do is focus on the 'big' official and unofficial company-wide communication and hope to set a consistent tone that helps everyone else in the organisation do a better job of communicating.*

Mia Shaw is Mercer's Corporate Communication Manager for Australia and New Zealand. She articulates the main purpose of communication as she sees it, and how the 'coalface' issue fits within that:

- *I do identify with the perspective raised in your chapter, however I don't necessarily agree with all of the issues raised. Communicators in organisations face many challenges – the biggest is getting the communication and engagement balance right to meet the needs of the organisation and its people. All employees within the organisation are communicators; however some employees have more of a prominent role than others, for example, senior leaders.*

- *It is the role of senior leaders within the organisation to clearly and openly articulate business strategy – what it means for the organisation, how the organisation will achieve it, what success looks like and the role employees play in that process – and other key initiatives to employees so they are willing and motivated to go above and beyond their job requirements. If the internal communication team has the right people and structure in place it can work with those teams and/or employees to address some of the issues raised in your chapter. Communicators should be working with employees at all levels to provide advice and address issues or gaps at a strategic business and a local business/team level to avoid the cost of poor communication.*

- *Mercer's What's Working*[2] *study in 2006 found that engaged employees who are inspired by leadership, guided by management, equipped with the right tools and managed by the right systems and processes deliver superior performance and business success. By regularly 'pulse checking' employees within the organisation and sharing this information with senior leaders/management helps communicators understand the issues and to stay one step ahead. Most importantly, it ensures the organisation develops solutions that address communication and engagement issues to ensure its employees, and ultimately the organisation, is performing at its optimal level.*

In contrast, **Prof. Dr. Siegfried Schmidt** is an internationally recognised communication researcher. He was keynote speaker at the Philosophy of Communication Conference in the UK in 2007 and his comment on the 'gap' from the academic perspective is sharply objective:

- *Fundamentally, the concept of communication in business is still seen as modelling the exchange of information, which is misleading. Today's research insights from psychology, the cognitive sciences and communication theory understand that when people receive messages they don't copy and save them to their brains, or paste them to others, they interpret them in their own closed cognitive system, which is where meaning is formed. A message is simply a collection of letters, symbols, images and signals, which are interpreted in very different ways by different people.*

- *Ultimately therefore, truly effective communication depends on having the knowledge, interest, intentions, emotions, moral orientations or values of all parties involved, harmonised as far as possible. This starting point enables a mutual trust upon which a shared appreciation of the meaning behind the communication message can be genuinely achieved. The success of such a procedure depends upon the willingness of all partners to replace thinking in terms of hierarchies and power relations with thinking in terms of partnership, respect and cooperation.*

---

2 Mercer, *What's Working?* (2006), www.mercer.com.

- *Building awareness and skills around this approach with communication practitioners as well as with their partners (employees themselves) is an essential first step.*

Conclusions

Fraser Likely of Likely Communication Strategies in Canada recently described his perceptions of the role of the internal communicator in an edition of Melcrum's Strategic Communication Management:[3]

> *'From what Melcrum employees and those involved with other enterprises and professional associations write about, speak about and discuss online, there appear to be four roles:*
>
> 1. *Communicator (content; delivery; technology; audience and so on).*
> 2. *Change agent (culture; internal branding; engagement; change management programs; ad so on).*
> 3. *Head trainer (improving C-suite and middle manager communication capabilities).*
> 4. *Performance consultant (operation performance improved through work-level communication).*
>
> *These are very rough percentages, but I'd say those in internal/ organisational communication see communicator as 75 per cent of their role, change agent as 15 per cent, head trainer as 7 per cent, and performance consultant as 3 per cent.'*

Redressing those proportions to put more emphasis on the 'head trainer' and 'performance consultant' roles is the key to closing the 'coalface communication' gap. This approach has already been documented by Marc Wright, who outlines Jim Shaffer's thinking on performance-based communication in Module 1 of Simply Communicate's[4] Communication Plan Toolkit on Strategy. In it, he says:

3 Melcrum, *Strategic Communication Management*, www.melcrum.com.
4 *Module 1 of Simply Communicate's Communication Plan Toolkit on Strategy*, www.simply-communicate.com.

'Building on the work of Gibb and D'Aprix, Jim Shaffer argues for the communication department to take on a completely new role. He claims, 'The communication department knows no function.' That is to say, it does not belong to any one function in the business but to all of them. Consequently, the strategy of the communication department should be to go out into the business and find areas in the operation that will benefit from better communication; and, having identified these areas, to introduce better communication practices alongside these particular elements of the business.'

Effective communication between people can improve efficiency (as fewer disconnects and misunderstandings speed up the shared understanding people have around achieving a shared goal). It can increase performance as improved communication frees up innovation, ameliorates the quality of decision making and altogether drives more effective outcomes.

Central to the 'gap' are two very separate areas of communication, which are being confused with each other. These areas are:

1. motivating employees to deliver the business strategy (largely through disseminating content about what that strategy is); and

2. developing the communication capabilities of employees (through improving not content but communication process and skills).

People communicate with other people dozens – perhaps hundreds – of times every day, and the word 'communicate' means something specific to everyone based on their experiences and environments. It is easy therefore, for even 'professional communicators' inside organisations to mix up communication content and process, because in practice the two are interdependent.

Moreover, ideas about the role of communication are determined not by what the subject of communication has to offer but by what budget holders are prepared to commission. This is predicated by the return on investment that those budget holders can perceive. It's unfortunate that the benefits of 'coalface communication' are difficult to measure. Evidence of value from communication done by employees can only be indirect, that is, via customer satisfaction ratings, opinion surveys, or outcome and performance indicators.

This leaves us with the believers and the non-believers. There are sponsors who believe from a common sense point of view, that by improving the skills and means by which their employees communicate, their business results will improve. And they have the freedom and willingness to make investments based on this alone. At the other end of the spectrum there are those who only want to focus on activities that they can prove will make a difference: using hard interventions to get hard results.

Hopefully, managing from a common sense standpoint – and not relying on data to justify activities that don't fit that mould – will become more fashionable. After all, in the spirit of good communication, healthy relationships between leaders and their team members is about the development of mutual trust and the freeing of talents so that exceptional rewards can be gained.

PART II

Classic Models for Communication

There are some psychological and HR models that you may find useful in your work as an internal communicator. These are among the most popular articles that are downloaded from our site www.simply-communicate.com, and I often find them quoted at conferences. I am indebted to Fiona Robertson who made a study of the top seven and rendered them simple and accessible in this next section:

1. Maslow's Hierarchy of Needs.
2. The Change Curve.
3. Management Theories X, Y and Z.
4. Johari Window.
5. McClelland's Needs-Based Model of Motivation.
6. Herzberg's Two-Factor Theory.
7. Mayo's Hawthorne Study.

7

Maslow's Hierarchy of Needs

by Fiona Robertson

Abraham Maslow is regarded as one of the founding fathers of the humanist approach to management due to his lifelong study of motivational psychology. In 1943, he wrote a seminal paper in which he identified five basic types of human need, all of which act as drivers of behaviour. Each person's personal circumstances will naturally force them to focus on their immediate needs and it is these requirements that are the basis of human motivation. What was particularly significant about Maslow's theory was that he ranked these in a hierarchy, stating that the basest needs in the pyramid (see Figure 7.1) had to be satisfied before an individual could progress to focusing on needs of the next type.

The structure of the needs hierarchy, in sequence, is as follows:

1. Physiological needs: these cover the function, comfort and maintenance of the body at its most basic level: our primitive survival requirements of air, food, drink, heat, shelter, sleep, light, water, health, and so on.

2. Safety needs: safety refers not just to our own physical safety and protection from harm but also to our continued well-being. This level therefore covers our financial security (employment, pension, savings) as well as insurance, access to medical help, law and order, limits, stability – all the infrastructure that keeps us secure.

3. Belonging needs: these refer to our various needs for human contact: family, friends, relationships, love, acceptance, teams, a social life and society generally.

4. Esteem needs: these recognise the need for status, power, prestige, acknowledgement, respect, responsibility, mastery or dominance

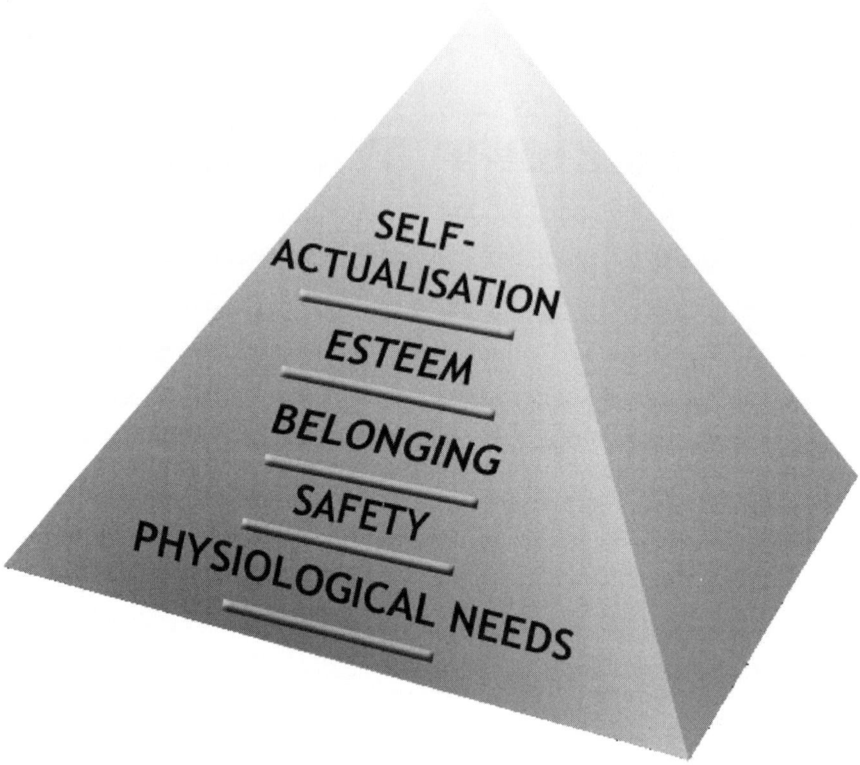

Figure 7.1 Maslow's Hierarchy of Needs

– the sort of attributes that can elevate individuals in some way, giving them a higher position within a social group.

5. Self-actualisation needs: the final set of needs deals with each person's desire to become the best that they can be through personal growth and by achieving their potential; to be fulfilled by living out their individual destinies.

During the course of his life, Maslow continued to refine this basic model and either he (or unattributed colleagues) added an additional three stages to the hierarchy:

- the need for knowledge and thinking (cognition);
- the need to appreciate and enjoy beauty (aesthetics); and

- the need to selflessly help others (transcendence).

However, for the purposes of applying the model to internal communication practice, Maslow's original five-stage hypothesis is ideal for understanding human motivation since his ideas remain just as valid today as when they were first presented over 60 years ago.

The key to understanding this model of human behaviour is to accept that a person will always focus on their most basic needs first. Only when these are being satisfied will a person then turn their attention to the next level of requirement. So to give an example, someone with a good job, a decent income and a supportive network of friends will probably be concerned with their perceived status within the company they work for or amongst their peer group. They may want more recognition for their work and will consequently find a better job title more motivating than a pay rise; they may seek fresh challenges or wish to learn new skills. It's safe to say that they won't be worried about having a roof over their head or where their next meal is coming from – unless they lose their job, their house, their health or some other driver further down the scale.

If this should happen, then immediately their focus will be shifted to their more fundamental requirements. To illustrate further, someone facing heart surgery doesn't think twice about how well they've mastered their job (Esteem); their attention is preoccupied with their health (Physiology). Therefore, only once any threat to a person's basic needs has been eliminated can they begin to focus on their higher needs for relationships, self-esteem and their aspirations for fulfilment.

At this point we need to introduce a broad difference between deficiency needs (physiological, safety, belonging and esteem requirements) and growth needs (Self-Actualisation):

- Deficiency needs are basic requirements that need to be met and neutralised. In addressing these drives, they become eliminated so deficiency needs cease to be motivators of behaviour.

- Growth needs, however, are enduring drivers; they can never be wholly satisfied or neutralised because, in achieving them, a person will invariably extend their ambitions to some greater project or higher goal so they remain permanent sources of motivation.

As Maslow put it, 'A musician must make music, the artist must paint, a poet must write, if he is to be ultimately at peace with himself. What a man can be, he must be.' (*Motivation and Personality*, 1954).[1]

Maslow's Hierarchy has helped businesses to shape the modern working environment by addressing as many of an individual's basic needs as possible.

- there are prescribed working hours and meal breaks to allow their physiological needs to be met;
- there are laws governing an individual's safety at work, and procedures to give their behaviour boundaries and structure;
- companies now organise social gatherings to help foster a sense of belonging, while employees are often grouped into working teams to give a sense of family;
- regular employee assessments mean that a person's achievements can be tracked and recognised, fuelling their sense of self-esteem;
- finally, their self-actualisation is also deemed vital since a person's opportunities for growth (through training and acquiring new skills) may influence how long they decide to stay with a company or how engaged they feel by their work.

Maslow's concept of self-actualisation is of direct relevance to organisations today. The current focus in internal communication on employee engagement and its links to customer satisfaction and increased productivity can all be traced back to Maslow. He foresaw an individual's need to strive for self-actualisation, to find meaning and purpose in all that they do – not just in their home lives but at work as well – and that self-actualisation was a powerfully motivating driver within all staff, not just within management. At no time has this been more important than today with Generation Y entering the workplace.

Those companies who achieve high employee satisfaction scores are those that care about their people: they listen to their opinions (Esteem and Belonging), they act on their concerns (Safety and Physiology) and they focus not only on their training and career development but on their personal growth as well (Self-Actualisation).

1 *Motivation and Personality* by Abraham Maslow, 1954.

To quote Businessballs.com:

> *The best modern employers and organisations are beginning to learn that sustainable success is built on a serious and compassionate commitment to helping people identify, pursue and reach their own personal unique potential.*

However, the drivers in the Hierarchy have far-reaching applications for entities such as businesses as well as for individuals. These motivational factors can be related to departments, business streams and whole sectors of industry just as effectively as they can to people.

For example, if a department is in organisational disarray and isn't meeting its targets (that is, it lacks structure at the safety level), then trying to motivate its workers with recognition and rewards (Esteem drivers) will be ineffectual. The workforce will probably be more concerned with salary payments and, ultimately, their job security so inducements to motivation must be pitched at the appropriate level if they are to hit home and have the desired effect.

Self-actualised Employees

However, where all other things are equal between two employers – for example, rates of pay, good working conditions and an attractive career progression – the company that can appeal to an individual's sense of self-actualisation is the one that will achieve higher levels of dedication, esprit de corps and productivity. This goes some way to explaining why nurses work long hours for relatively low pay.

To give another illustration, let's say there are two mechanics: one works for Ferrari and the other works at Ford. They both earn the same amount but the Ferrari mechanic's dedication to their job is higher because working for the Ferrari brand fulfils their aspirations. In their mind, Ferrari makes the best engines so they are working with the best there is; they are therefore the best engineer that they can be so they are self-actualised.

This stream of thinking leads into the role of brand ambassador programmes, which are used to engineer the highest level of Maslow's hierarchy into the way people think about their jobs as well as their personal life. As a consequence, the purpose of an engagement programme should be to align more closely the aspirations of individual employees with their respective notions of self-actualisation.

8

The Change Curve

by Marc Wright

Originally developed by Kubler-Ross, the Change Curve (Figure 8.1) is a model that explains the grieving process. However, it is has been adopted as a means of getting staff through a period of major change, whether it be a restructuring or the result of a merger or acquisition.

The Change Curve describes the stages anyone must go through when faced with a change in their lives. From grieving for a loved one to changing an IT system, people have to experience the same three stages of personal development (albeit in markedly different timescales) in order to move on. These stages describe nine states of emotion:

- Stage 1: Shock, Denial, Numbness;
- Stage 2: Fear, Anger, Depression;
- Stage 3: Understanding, Acceptance, Moving On.

In this chapter, these three stages are applied to the communication process to show how you can help staff get through Stage 2 more quickly – the stage that can cost your organisation its productivity, people and profits, and which could undermine your organisation's business mission and derail its strategy.

Stage 1: Shock, Denial, Numbness

Major changes in organisations are usually the result of mergers and acquisitions or restructurings. During these periods, communication has an important role to play in achieving the objectives of the change.

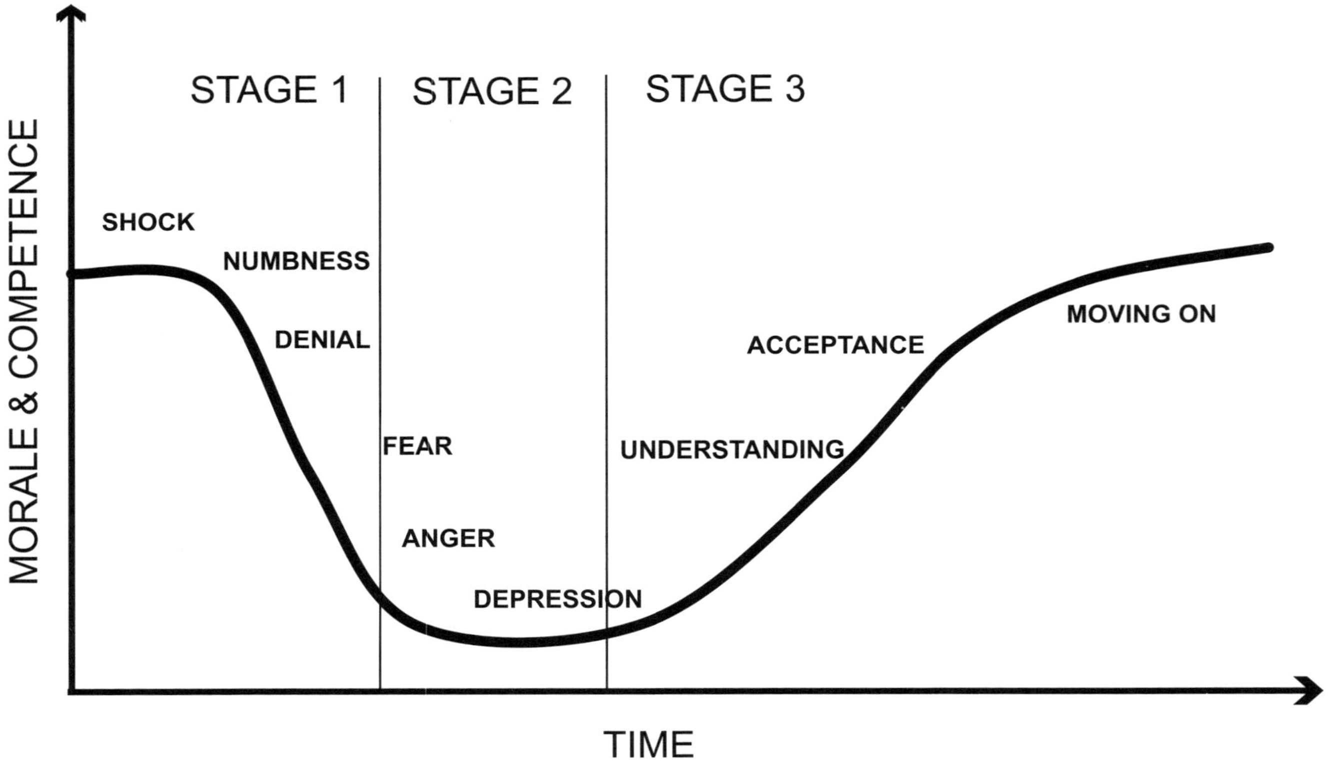

Figure 8.1 The Change Curve

In this first stage, many staff will be aware something is up: they will have heard rumours or read the leaks in newspapers. This means they will be in a state of fear, uncertainty and doubt. So, when an announcement actually happens, there is often a sense of excitement and relief, for example, 'Now we actually know it is true.' But for those who were not expecting any change, the natural result is shock.

In communication terms, all this starts around 'announcement day': the day on which you coordinate all messages around the big news and the moment when a communication plan kicks in.

Draw up a grid for all your staff and segment it by region, level of seniority or function, depending on how people will be affected by the news. You should notify everyone within a 24-hour period in order to avoid damage through the rumour mill and to prevent appearing callous or even incompetent.

Use the channel and media most appropriate to each part of your segmented audience. If you are talking to a subsidiary company that will be unaffected by the changes, then an email from the CEO may be sufficient and timely. But for anyone whose job is, or could be, affected by the change, you will need to supplement an email with some face-to-face communication, either with their line manager or at an all-staff meeting.

Try to think of all the ramifications that might result from an announcement. Closing a factory or call centre is of greatest concern to those people who work there. But it is also of concern to every other factory or division, whose first reaction will be to wonder whether they will be the next to go. Announcements require careful planning on your part in order to deliver a consistent message that balances people's concerns with the positive future your CEO wants to project. Understand the 5/95 Split. Five per cent of staff (that is, the leaders) will be well through the change curve by announcement day while 95 per cent will be just entering the rollercoaster of the Change Curve. Be sensitive to the 95 per cent and frame your messages accordingly while at the same time temper your senior management team's exuberance.

Coordinate with your external communications division so that staff inside the company hear the news before the Press does, even if it's just 30 minutes earlier. The point is – tell them first. Senior and middle managers, who are not in-the-know, should be told before their staff hears anything – either the day before or at a meeting which precedes the all-staff announcement.

Prepare a comprehensive list of Frequently Asked Questions (FAQs) and post it on your intranet so that managers have a consistent source of information to hand, when asked for details. If you don't post a list of FAQs and review it daily, managers will make things up and get themselves (and you) into trouble later.

Do not expect much feedback from staff on announcement day. Relief that they know what is happening will quickly move to shock as people realise nothing will be the same again. The denial stage will then kick in: people are aware of news of the changes but they carry on behaving as though nothing has happened.

Remember: the questions you do get from staff and management on announcement day may be muted or irrelevant. People will need to internalise the news, discuss it among their peers and work out the implications for themselves. Often senior management can misread this quietness on the part of staff and congratulate themselves too early on the lack of negative response. During this phase, many people will appear numb and unforthcoming so communication will not flow easily within large groups. Therefore, work with HR to arrange one-to-one interviews for those most affected by the change.

And remember – the information given at these interviews is not as important as the way you express it so show sympathy and reflect the concerns of your staff.

Stage 2: Fear, Anger, Depression

This is the most dangerous period of the Change Cycle since it's the time that will cost your organisation its morale, productivity, sales and profits. The longer your staff are in this depressive stage of the cycle, the greater the chances are that your change programme will fail, just as business performance also starts to suffer.

The cure is to create a vision of the future that staff can buy into, while making them feel comfortable about their place in the new order of things. Maslow's Hierarchy of Needs shows us people won't be interested in the lofty goals of an organisation if they are unsure how much they will be paid, where they will work and who they will report to. These more basic needs must be fulfilled before staff can move on. This is where HR has the biggest job:

negotiating with unions and conducting one-to-one interviews with staff who will lose their jobs or move to a new position or location.

A major challenge for communication managers during Stage 2 is the lack of detail that they are able to communicate. Much of the restructuring will still be undecided; and change teams will be recruited from the very staff who are still in the depressive stage of the Change Curve. As a professional communicator, your job is to 'talk about talking'. Tell people what is certain and what is still undecided but do not speculate about the future. Instead, describe the process – talk about the timetable for future announcements and the principles that management has agreed – notably, that staff will be consulted at every stage and that they will be treated in a set and fair manner.

During this period focus on the survivors. These people are your company's future and they will probably have to work harder once any redundancies have taken effect. Therefore, engage them and make them feel appreciated so as to avoid 'survivors' syndrome', where people quit the company mentally but stay on the payroll.

Also, make change champions of the people you most want to keep. By giving people a role in developing their own futures, staff will move onto Stage 3 that much quicker.

Stage 3: Understanding, Acceptance, Moving on

During a change programme, CEOs are often keen to call the staff together for a motivating event, so that the company can celebrate its new future. Try to resist staging any such events while the majority of your staff are still in Stages 1 or 2 of the Change Cycle, even though the board are well into Stage 3. Wait until the majority of middle management has reached Stage 3, then hold a management event for them to ensure they are all through the dip and looking forward to a brighter future.

For the rest of the staff, get the major negotiations out of the way and ensure that staff are in the bargaining stage – where they have started to understand and accept their place in the new order. Once they've reached this point, it will be time to plan a communication programme that paints the future vision and gets staff bought into the new business strategy.

Make the emerging new leaders of the business both visible and human, otherwise they might be seen as hatchet men, simply put in place to drive through further cuts. Explain the external factors that caused the change and create a credible story around the new business strategy.

Stage 3 is as critical to get right as Stages 1 and 2. If you don't get people to accept the company's new structure and mission, they will continue to cling to the past. This is particularly true of mergers, where people can continue to live the brand and values of the old company – sometimes years after a merger has happened. It can be useful to have a celebration or create a memento in a public place that celebrates the past and 'says goodbye' to an old brand or culture.

The aim is to create a Vision, Mission and Values that everyone can share and which matches their own personal aspirations. Only then will people start to let go of the past and embrace your company's future.

9

Management Theories X, Y and Z

by Fiona Robertson

In the many studies of management that have been conducted over the past 50 years, it has been shown that management style is dictated by the assumptions managers have about people generally – and specifically about the people under their authority.

In 1960, social psychologist Douglas McGregor attempted to explain the link between management and motivation. In *The Human Side of Enterprise*, McGregor explored a model that illustrated two very different styles of management, underpinned by two opposing mindsets, and looked at their subsequent behaviours and the impact these approaches could have on business. He called his findings Theory X and Theory Y[1] and stated that businesses (or their managers) were either of one type or the other. While his X/Y scale may seem a little stark, his theory goes a long way towards explaining the attitudes of managers and organisations, and the effects that their resulting behaviours can have on communicating with a workforce.

Theory X

Based on his observations, McGregor noticed that X-style managers hold the following beliefs:

- the average person has an inherent dislike of work so will avoid it, if possible;

---

1 *The Human Side of Enterprise: Annotated Edition* by Douglas McGregor, McGraw-Hill Professional, 2006.

- consequently, people must be coerced, controlled and directed to work towards the achievement of organisational objectives, or threatened with punishment if their efforts aren't adequate;
- the average person prefers to be directed, wants to avoid responsibility, has relatively little ambition and wants security above all else;
- people are inherently self-centred so are indifferent to organisational needs;
- by nature, people are resistant to change;
- most people are fairly gullible and not that bright.

THEORY X CHARACTERISTICS

Given their management style, Theory X bosses are often referred to as *autocratic* or *authoritative*. They make decisions alone to retain their authority and expect staff to carry out their directives; meanwhile their goals are task-orientated and driven by deadlines, with emphasis placed on getting a job done to the exclusion of all else.

Staff who are managed by a Theory X boss will tend to feel undervalued and disengaged so, even though particular tasks are being driven through from above, their productivity levels will reflect their dissatisfaction.

A typical Theory X manager will demonstrate some or all of the following traits:

- intolerance and short-temper;
- distance, detachedness, arrogance and elitism;
- unhappiness and anti-social behaviour;
- not participating or team-building;
- shouting;

- making demands, never asking;
- never thanking or praising;
- issuing deadlines and ultimatums;
- issuing instructions, directions, edicts;
- issuing threats to make people follow instructions;
- a lack of concern for staff welfare or morale;
- communicating one-way and being a poor listener;
- pride, sometimes to the point of self-destruction;
- fundamental insecurity and possible neurosis;
- vengefulness and recrimination;
- withholding rewards, and suppressing pay and remunerations levels;
- scrutinising expenditure to the point of false economy;
- seeking culprits for failures or shortfalls;
- seeking to apportion blame instead of focusing on learning from the experience and preventing recurrence;
- neither inviting nor welcoming suggestions;
- taking criticism badly – and retaliating if this comes from either below or their peer group;
- being poor at proper delegation – while believing they delegate well;
- thinking that giving orders is delegating;

- holding on to responsibility but shifting accountability to subordinates;
- relative lack of concern about investing in anything to gain future improvements.

Theory Y

In contrast, Y Theory managers hold very different assumptions about their workforce and tend to believe that:

- physical and mental effort at work is as natural for people as play or rest;
- external control and the threat of punishment are not the only means of inducing effort towards organisational objectives; a person will exercise self-control in the service of objectives to which they are committed;
- a person's commitment to objectives is a function of the rewards associated with their achievement. Rewards that satisfy ego needs and aid in self-actualisation are most significant (see Chapter 7 on Maslow's Hierarchy of Needs), and these can come from efforts directed towards organisational objectives;
- under proper conditions, the average person learns not only to accept responsibility but to seek it out;
- the capacity to exercise a relatively high degree of imagination, ingenuity and creativity in solving organisational problems is widely distributed in the population;
- within modern industrial conditions, only a small part of the intellectual potential of the average person is used.

THEORY Y CHARACTERISTICS

Theory Y managers exhibit a participative management style, in which they canvass their teams for ideas, delegate projects and give employees greater scope in the performance of their duties to enable them to give of their best. They presume that most people are ambitious, creative and self-motivated and therefore try to help staff to achieve their potential.

Being people-centric, Y managers focus on the relationships that exist between themselves and their staff, as well as between team members, to develop the unit as a whole. They also foster a sense of value and belonging amongst employees, resulting in good morale, high engagement scores and increased productivity. So although they don't focus on tasks as such, tasks get done more efficiently by Theory Y managers because they have instilled a healthier and more cohesive working infrastructure in their departments.

Linking Management Style and Motivational Approaches

McGregor stated that companies and their management approaches fall broadly into either the X or Y categories and that both styles can achieve powerful results, if the appropriate motivational levers are applied. McGregor's work was heavily influenced by that of Abraham Maslow, who's Hierarchy of Needs he took as the basis of his motivation model, and he meshed the two ideas together in the following way.

THEORY X MOTIVATORS

Maslow's Hierarchy states that there are certain deficiency needs which all people must address. If any of these needs are not being met and neutralised, they will become powerful motivators of behaviour: people will be compelled to attend to them and, if there is more than one type of need, they will always need to be addressed in the following order:

1. Physiological needs (biological necessities such as food, sleep, shelter, and so on).

2. Safety needs (security from harm or threat, laws, boundaries, and so on).

3. Belonging needs (relationships with others, belonging to teams, groups, society, and so on).

4. Esteem needs (respect, acknowledgement, praise, success, and so on).

McGregor linked Maslow's 'lower order' deficiency needs with Theory X management techniques. In the same way that hunger must be attended to, so must an authoritarian boss who is threatening to withhold your benefits. In both instances, the urgency is pressing so this will preclude you from doing anything unnecessary until the fundamental problem has been dealt with – thus prompting deficiency-eliminating behaviour.

THEORY Y MOTIVATORS

Maslow's Hierarchy also cites a number of 'higher order' growth needs, which inspire us to achieve more as individuals. Unlike the deficiency needs listed above, these can never be sated or neutralised so they act as continuous motivational spurs of behaviour. Again, these follow a sequence of importance (the first need will always take precedence over the second and so on), which is as follows:

1. Cognition needs (learning, training, knowledge, research, and so on).

2. Aesthetics needs (beauty, form, ambience, pleasure, and so on).

3. Self-actualisation needs (achieving one's own goals, realising one's potential).

4. Transcendence needs (helping others to develop and achieve their best).

McGregor linked these growth needs with Theory Y management processes. If you accept that everyone wants to grow in terms of their personal development, then an organisation or manager that allows staff to do this – and positively encourages their learning and progression – will result in a happier, brighter and more accomplished workforce.

Application and Results

This means that, before you can motivate your organisation, its managers and the workforce, first you have to identify which style of management prevails at your company. Having established whether Theory X or Theory Y is dominant, you can then apply the appropriate lower or higher drivers to greatest effect.

Although both styles of management can be effectively enhanced by using the appropriate motivations, McGregor observed that the results obtained by Theory Y always outperformed those of Theory X.

THEORY Z

Following the naming convention initiated by McGregor, in 1981 Dr William Ouchi published *Theory Z: How American Management Can Meet the Japanese Challenge.*[2] Also known as Japanese management style, Theory Z turns McGregor's idea around and looks at the relationship employees have with organisations rather than the way managers view their employees. Ouchi's ideas focus on the ways in which an employee's loyalty can be increased – a means of achieving exceptional employee engagement – so that staff can be entirely connected to the company for which they work.

In Japan in the 1970s and 1980s, the working culture was such that employees tended to work for the same organisation for life, becoming part of the culture of the business which, in turn, looked after their needs and well-being, both on and off the job. By vesting all their efforts, time and way of life with a single corporation, employees became inherently connected with their business; in turn, this business addressed all their deficiency needs in the short term, plus their growth needs as they developed with the company over time. Such extended careers led to stable employment, good morale and high rates of job satisfaction and therefore generated high levels of productivity.

Dr Ouchi's work is based on the 14 Points created by Dr Edwards Deming, an American theorist whose management and motivational theories were used to restructure Japan's organisational development and industrial revival after the Second World War. Some American firms have tried to apply the principles of Theory Z but their attempts have mostly proved unsuccessful. No doubt this is because the ideas contained in Theory Z are embedded in a different cultural approach to work, one which supposes a less fluid employment market and a focus on quality in all aspects of the work a business produces. The American/British approach to business is more task-driven, using management by objectives and shorter-term goals (for example, contracts rather than a lifetime's employment). These cultural differences have made it difficult to instill the approach of such a contrasting culture at work. Notable exceptions have been in the motor industry, where the principles of Kaizan – or continuous

2 *Theory Z: How American Management Can Meet the Japanese Challenge* by Dr William Ouchi, London: Addison-Wesley (Pearson), 1981.

improvement – have spread with the global growth of Toyota, a company that lives Theory Z.

Applying X, Y and Z to Internal Communications

What is important for anyone working in a communication role is that Theory Z's focus on employee satisfaction and engagement is now the key driver in internal communication. A Western reinterpretation of these principles is now at the heart of every major business worldwide, as organisations and their managements strive to connect with their staff in meaningful and dynamic ways. Moreover, legislation, such as the EC's Information and Consultation Directive, is backing these initiatives by setting such practices in law. However, some argue that legislation will merely fix best practice in concrete, rather than encouraging it to grow organically within organisations .

As yet, it seems that no one theory has managed to address all human motivation in business; but a fusion of Theory Y's participative management style and Theory Z's focus on employees looks like a constructive route to follow. And with the demographic changes taking place in Western Europe, where young talent is becoming more educated and more aspirational, it appears that businesses are being driven to offer Y and Z type workplaces, just to attract and retain quality staff.

10

The Johari Window

by Fiona Robertson

Designed by Joseph (Jo) Luft and Harrington (Hari) Ingham in 1955[1] as a graphic model of interpersonal awareness, the Johari Window is a powerful tool which can be adapted to assess the effectiveness of internal communication by individuals, working teams or whole companies and their strategies.

Personality Assessment

In essence, the Johari Window (Figure 10.1) asks a group to rate their perceptions of a subject; it then compares their notes with that of the subject itself. The information given by all the respondents is then mapped according to the Window to show whether the stated perceptions are shared, unknown or known only by the subject or the rest of the group. Taken together, this feedback represents a 360-degree view of the subject, detailing which perceptions are held and by whom.

In any assessment of feedback, there will always be information known by everyone concerned and some unknown to them all; but what is of particular interest are the perceptions held only by the subject, or shared by everyone except the subject. Luft and Ingham gave names to these four information scenarios:

1. Open Arena;
2. Hidden Area or Façade;
3. Blind Spot;
4. The Unknown.

---

1 *Of Human Interaction* by Joseph Luft, Palo Alto, CA: National Press, 1969.

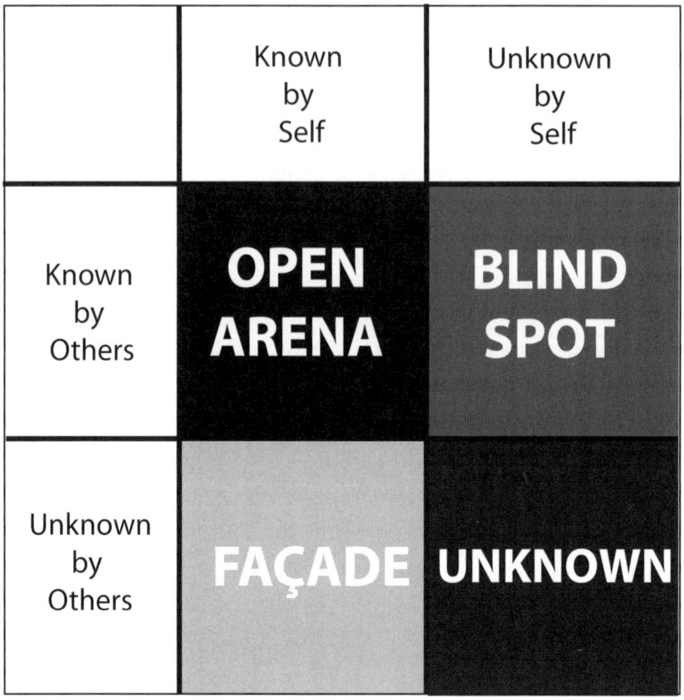

Figure 10.1 A Johari Window

The **Open Arena** refers to information that the subject has given about itself; it is therefore common knowledge among the group, known and shared by all.

The **Façade** covers any information held by the subject alone. Here, the subject has chosen not to disclose information to other people, making themself the sole keeper of these details.

The **Blind Spot** refers to the reverse situation, where everyone in the group shares information that the subject is either unaware of or blind to.

The **Unknown** area covers any information that is unknown to everyone in the group.

Effective communication is said to occur when there is a good balance between disclosure (the information we give to others) and feedback (what we learn from colleagues). Clearly, communication lies at the heart of this model because it evaluates:

- the disclosure of information by the subject (exposure);
- the absorbing of this information by another person (listening); and
- that person's response to the subject (feedback).

Given that the Johari Window demonstrates the balance of information exchanged in any given situation, it can be used to develop more effective communication by prompting a modification of either disclosure or feedback until the right balance is achieved – 'the right balance' – depending upon the circumstances you are assessing.

Employee Assessments

The Johari Window was originally designed to give people a greater awareness of their personalities by seeing themselves as others see them.

Interpersonal assessments are made by giving a set list of 55 positive attributes to both the subject of the assessment and their co-workers, who are all asked to pick the five or six qualities that best apply to that person. (Examples of the attributes are: mature, happy, capable, organised, modest, powerful and so on.) By mapping the overlap or difference between the responses, a grid of personality awareness can be developed.

However, such a profile only focuses on the positive attributes; it doesn't cover the flaws that also make up our characters. Therefore, the Nohari Window does just that: it is a challenging inversion of the original model, in which a set of 55 failings are listed. Using antonyms of the positive attributes employed in the Johari Window (for example, incompetent, weak, chaotic, smug, blasé, insensitive, and so on), the resulting grid highlights perceived weaknesses for the subject to address.

Applying the Johari Window to Managers

To give an example of how the Johari Window might be used to assess management style, let's assume a manager has withheld information from their staff unnecessarily, (they have assigned it to the façade pane); and that everyone in the department knows this manager isn't a good communicator – except the manager themself; (this information resides in the manager's blind spot).

If the manager can be made aware of their blind spot (that they are perceived as a poor communicator) by getting feedback from their team, then they can learn to share some of the information they keep back. If this happens, the façade and blind areas will shrink while the open arena expands, leading to a better, more direct flow of communication throughout the team.

With newly promoted managers, however, the opposite case can apply. If a team member has been promoted to become a team leader, they will need to learn to keep some information private, for instance, if one of their reports tells them something in confidence, or if the new manager is working on commercially-sensitive information, such as an acquisition. In such cases, the manager may need to censor themselves more than if they had stayed in their original job.

Applying the Johari Window Abstractly

The value of using the Johari Window in employee assessments is pretty clear. Interestingly, though, this tool can be modified and applied to teams, business streams or even communication strategies. It's simply a question of modifying the parameters that you set.

For example, if you wish to test the effectiveness of an internal message or campaign, you might create a series of statements that describe your message or, indeed, the company's strategy. These comments could then be hidden within a longer list of inaccurate remarks to see whether colleagues were able to select the correct statements. The feedback received from such an exercise will then tell you:

- firstly, how effective your message or strategy has been; and
- secondly, what employees think their company is actually trying to achieve.

By manipulating both the subject of the exercise (for example, corporate strategy, customer policy, team effectiveness, management style and so on) and the sample list of adjectives or statements from which employees are asked to choose, it is possible to apply the Johari/Nohari Windows to many aspects of business, to powerful and revealing effect.

Conclusion

They say knowledge is power; the beauty of this model is that it enables us to see those areas that are often hidden, blind or unknown. Armed with these insights, we can then take whatever steps are appropriate to become better, faster, stronger or more transparent and, ultimately, to communicate more effectively. However, the true power of the Johari model is that the more a manager operates in the open arena, the more their colleagues will respond to their honesty and openness. As a result, this virtuous circle leads to an ever larger open arena – and increasingly better results – over time.

But how do you apply the Johari Window to the arena of internal communication? One practical example is for live events: with most management conferences costing many thousands of pounds, it makes sense to get as much from your event as you can, in financial, topical and psychological terms.

To illustrate, when deciding the agenda of the annual management meeting, a common failing amongst senior management is to list the issues they want to talk about, then to carve up the agenda between them so that, on the day, they form an orderly queue at the lectern – regaling the audience with messages that are either irrelevant to the local business agenda or which have been said many times before.

A better approach is to ask your audience what they think of an agenda beforehand, using an online questionnaire. Be sure to ask whether there are any issues your delegates want aired – to help reveal any blind spots as well as to build an engaging agenda that will lead to better debate and more effective outcomes. And to ensure you get their feedback, engineer your registration process such that delegates have to give their input before they can book their seat at the conference.

11

McLelland's Needs-Based Model of Motivation

by Fiona Robertson

American psychology professor, David McClelland, devoted 20 years to studying motivation and the human need for achievement before finally publishing his theory within *Human Motivation* in 1987.[1] The conclusions he presented suggest that people aren't motivated by the concept of reward. Rather, each person has three types of need that exist in differing degrees and it is the combination of these three factors that explains our individual levels of drive as well as our preferred sources of motivation.

The three needs are:

1. Achievement Motivation (n-ach)
2. Authority or Power Motivation (n-pow)
3. Affiliation Motivation (n-affil).

Achievement Motivation

The need for achievement, written as n-ach, exists within us all but for some people, this need is dominant. We therefore describe n-ach people as 'achievement-motivated' since their primary focus is usually winning or succeeding in some way, either through the attainment of challenging but achievable goals or by job advancement. As well as achievement and progress,

---

1 *Human Motivation* by David McClelland, Cambridge: Cambridge University Press, 1987.

n-ach people have a strong need for feedback since it completes their sense of accomplishment.

McClelland argued that, with their strong motivation to achieve, n-ach people make the best leaders, both in terms of goal-setting and inspiring others with their own vision and determination. However, these same qualities can bear an inherent weakness in that n-ach managers tend to demand too much of their staff, assuming their teams to be as highly goal-focused and results-orientated as they are.

Given that most people aren't n-ach, such managers can appear out-of-step with their direct reports, who usually respond to very different motivational needs.

Authority or Power Motivation

With n-pow people, their overwhelming need is for control so these 'authority-motivated' types are spurred on to direct or sway those around them. As such, they are driven to become leaders, requiring high personal status, prestige and influence over others.

While managers with this need will generate a determined work ethic and foster commitment to the company – in themselves as well as in those around them – leaders with an n-pow driver may lack the flexibility and people-skills to motivate their teams effectively.

Affiliation Motivation

In contrast, the n-affil person is 'affiliation-motivated' so their primary impetus is interaction with others in order to establish friendly relationships. They need to be liked, to be popular and to be held in high regard so they're driven to belong to teams or social groups for emotional sustenance and energy.

As a result, managers whose need is n-affil may find their objectivity compromised by their desire to be liked since it affects both their judgment and decision-making ability.

As mentioned above, everyone has elements of all three needs, though one or two are likely to be more pronounced, determining both our characters and the way we behave at work. Our particular mix of needs will establish not only what motivates us but also how we inspire and manage others – hence management's fascination with McClelland's theory for the past 20 years.

N-ach Characteristics

Of the three types of need, McClelland was particularly interested in the concept of achievement motivation and the consistent ways in which n-ach people behave. Relatively few people possess strong achievement motivation although many will have minor n-ach tendencies. Of those who can be classified as n-ach, McClelland found they consistently approach projects with a need for 'balanced challenge', regardless of the importance of the task itself. They shy away from anything too easy or the flatly unattainable; instead, they create achievable tests for themselves that might exercise their abilities initially but which, eventually, they will master.

This approach mimics the 'overload principle' in biology where, to develop strength or fitness, an exercise needs to be taxing enough to stretch someone's current ability but not so demanding that it will result in injury. N-ach people appear to have internalised the overload principle, as seen in their cognitive approach to life: by seeking or setting tasks that test their abilities, they derive achievement, pleasure and motivation once these have been successfully accomplished.

Typically, they prefer challenges with an outcome they can influence and where the extent of their input is evident, approaching tasks in a determined, results-driven manner. There is no wishful thinking or risk-taking involved; their actions are focused on achieving a specific conclusion and they pursue this doggedly – a characteristic shared by most successful entrepreneurs and businessmen the world over.

Consequently, n-ach types are great at galvanising their staff into action: they make things happen and get results, skilfully extending their drive and influence to other areas of a business or to external resources, as required.

However, often this is managed at the expense of their team, who can be seen as a means to an end. Individual requirements are subsumed to the task at hand because the needs of an n-ach's co-workers are rarely considered; for those who are achievement-motivated, the important thing is that a project succeeds.

McClelland observed several other characteristics that were particular to people of an n-ach disposition. Namely, that:

- Achievement is more important to them than material or financial rewards. Security, status and money aren't motivators in themselves although financial reward is seen as a benchmark of success.
- Accomplishing a task gives the n-ach person more personal satisfaction than receiving praise or recognition. However, feedback on each task is critical because it enables them to assess how well they've done – so they prefer factual data to support their achievement rather than praise or congratulations.
- Having completed something well, an achievement-motivated person will continually look for ways to improve the task so that each time a process is repeated, the job is being done better every time.
- N-ach individuals naturally select roles and responsibilities that satisfy their needs, namely flexibility and the chance to choose their goals – as well as the terms by which they will achieve them. This way, they can create their own 'balanced challenges' at all times.

All three character types are important players in the internal communication mix. For instance, in many organisations the internal communications unit sits within HR, which tends to be run by n-affil types. Yet the CEO is more likely to be n-ach while department heads might be n-pow. You yourself should be aware of your own dominant characteristic as this will colour your interactions with others. The important learning from McClelland is to adjust your own language style to meet the characteristics of your audience. And when you are talking to a general audience, either through a speech, a video or a printed article, try to include a variety of language and metaphors that will appeal to all character types.

12

Herzberg's Two-Factor Theory

by Fiona Robertson

In 1959, Frederick Herzberg published *The Motivation to Work,*[1] a book which built on the observations made by Maslow but distilled its findings into a more straightforward 'Two-Factor Theory' of human motivation in the workplace.

Herzberg studied 200 engineers and accountants in Pittsburgh and found that the factors which make workers dissatisfied are entirely different from those that bring about satisfaction. Consequently, by addressing a dissatisfaction issue, Herzberg discovered that you wouldn't achieve satisfaction; you would simply neutralise the grievance. In order to actually create satisfaction, you had to introduce something entirely different: a motivational factor. Realising that there were two separate forces at work – one to diminish discomfort and another to maximise potential – Herzberg divided the issues that affect employees into groups of either Hygiene Factors or Motivators.

Hygiene Factors

Hygiene factors cover our essential needs as people within the context of a working environment. Namely, that we require reasonable conditions and good relationships with our fellow workers as well as pay and benefits for the services we provide. To give a more comprehensive list of Herzberg's hygiene factors, they include:

- company policies;
- relationships (with our bosses, peers, direct reports and subordinates);

1 *The Motivation to Work* by Frederick Herzberg, Bernard Mausner, Barbara Bloch Snyderman, New Jersey: Transaction Publishers, 1993.

- working conditions (heat, light, space, refreshments, and so on);
- salary;
- perks and bonuses (for example, company car, incentive meetings);
- status or job title;
- security (job, financial and physical);
- personal life.

In themselves, none of these items spur us on but, without them, we find it difficult to function and become miserable. In broad terms, hygiene factors equate to Maslow's Deficiency Requirements since they address our fundamental needs. As regards motivation though, they simply keep us on an even keel; a dearth of hygiene factors will make us unhappy whereas adequate hygiene maintenance will render us emotionally neutral. Moreover, the satisfaction we derive from meeting these needs is momentary so the positive effect soon wears off. Hence it is that money isn't enough to make staff stay in jobs that leave them bored or unfulfilled; a pay rise might cheer someone up in the short term but they'll still lack a sense of personal growth.

Motivators

Motivators, on the other hand, take us out of our neutral state and propel us forward so they exert a positive influence on us all. Challenge, autonomy, interest and creative opportunity are the personal drivers that promote growth, expansion, passion and creativity in business – the sparks that ignite an organisation, generate momentum and force progress. Not surprisingly, it is these factors that lead to employee engagement, job satisfaction and high levels of productivity. Herzberg identified the following as key work motivators:

- achievement;
- recognition;
- work of an interesting nature;

- responsibility;
- advancement;
- personal growth.

Herzberg's research has been replicated time and time again and his original results still hold true today. His distinction between motivators and hygiene factors has given profound insight into what motivates a workforce and how employee engagement can be achieved. Herzberg's Two-Factor Theory is therefore seen to be one of the most influential models for explaining the psychology of human motivation at work.

The implications for communication are abundantly clear. Where communication is needed to reinforce hygiene factors – such as a health and safety video or an induction programme for new employees – you have to make sure that the piece of media or collateral does its job so test it with audiences to ensure that it removes a grievance or satisfies a need. You will have scant credibility as a communicator if these basic functions are not addressed correctly and kept up-to-date. I have heard eminent communications professionals argue that hygiene factors are not the task of their departments. Yet it is only when these factors have been dealt with that a communicator can proceed to concentrate on the Motivators that will drive engagement and encourage further discretionary effort.

13

Mayo's Hawthorne Study

by Fiona Robertson

In 1924, Elton Mayo of Harvard undertook a study of Chicago's Western Electric Hawthorne Plant[1] in an attempt to find out how lighting affected the company's workers and their performance. The focus of his study was whether electric light would keep workers awake, thereby boosting their output, or whether the artificial lighting actually made them more tired.

One of the earliest studies of human behaviour in the workplace, Mayo's findings had a profound impact upon people management when they were first published in 1927 – and the ideas underpinning his results are just as relevant today.

What Mayo discovered was that the physical conditions in which employees work have little or no impact on their performance in terms of motivation. The factors that matter involve the social aspects of working for an organisation – and these alone can actually boost motivation and productivity, regardless of location, industry, class, education or other socio-economic elements.

The interest that Mayo took in all the individuals of the Hawthorne plant was unusual for its time and it made each of them feel important, respected and valuable – so much so that this attention alone was enough to significantly increase their efficiency and output.

Surprised by his findings, Mayo went back and expanded his study into what are now known as the Hawthorne Experiments; meanwhile, his original studies have been replicated many times over in the intervening years. Time and again, the results continue to show that, when companies value their staff by listening to their ideas and opinions, this respect motivates employees to give of their best, resulting in higher standards of performance and achievement.

1 *Elton Mayo papers*, Baker Library, Harvard Business School, 1909–1960.

So, when companies treat their employees as a group of individuals rather than a standardised unit of production, workers are able to act as the sentient people that they are, increasing self-esteem and their sense of unique value.

Key learnings from Mayo's Hawthorne study are as follows:

- work is a group activity;
- an adult's social life is primarily arranged around work;
- the need for recognition, security and a sense of belonging are more important in determining an employee's morale and productivity than are the conditions in which they work;
- complaints at work aren't necessarily about the stated facts; often they are simply manifestations of someone's underlying concern about their status;
- an employee is a person whose attitudes and effectiveness are conditioned by social factors – from their home life as much as by their place of work;
- informal groups at work exercise strong social controls over the work habits and attitudes of individual members of staff;
- organisations can be described as adaptive societies – where employees have to keep up with new technologies and ever-changing work practices. The constant shift that is inherent in all business disrupts the social structure within companies and has a negative effect on industry in general;
- for group collaboration to occur it must be planned and developed – but when it is achieved, the resulting cohesion can negate the disruptive effects of an adaptive society.

Put simply, people respond to the human dimension of being among a group of individuals in the same way as they would in society – the fact that this occurs in a work context is neither here nor there. We are a social species, programmed to inter-relate with one another, and the need to fit into whichever subset of society we are faced with is hard-wired into each of us. First and foremost, we have a primitive need to belong; next, to find our place within a group; then, to try and distinguish ourselves from our colleagues in some way. This behaviour takes place in societies all across the world so it is inevitable that it happens at work as well.

Historically, companies viewed their staff simply as a resource and the dehumanising effect this had on their employees caused great dissatisfaction – with the knock-on effect that morale and motivation were low.

Mayo's studies stumbled across this phenomenon when they began singling out each member of staff to ask for their opinions. By treating each worker as a valued individual whose voice would be heard and respected, the Hawthorne plant was transforming its collective workforce into a team of people, giving all of them the attention and differentiation that they naturally craved. And, by fostering a sense of community in which staff were encouraged to interact on a social level, this positive effect was compounded. So of course the lighting conditions became irrelevant compared with the spark of human feeling that had been ignited. Society, belonging, individualism, respect and value had inadvertently been introduced – producing a groundswell of motivation and productivity.

These concepts are what form the basis of employee engagement today: two-way communication, involving staff, listening to their ideas and opinions, and trying to create a positive culture at work. In their book, *Follow This Path: How the World's Greatest Organisations Drive Growth by Unleashing Human Potential,*[2] Curt Coffman and Gabriela Gonzalez-Molina echo the essence of Mayo's research thus,

> *The success of your organisation doesn't depend on your understanding of economics, or organisational development, or marketing. It depends, quite simply, on your understanding of human psychology: how each individual employee connects with your company and how each individual employee connects with your customers.*

For the communicator, the lesson is simple; listening – and encouraging a listening culture – is as important a part of the job as communicating 'at' people.

---

2 *Follow This Path: How the World's Greatest Organisations Drive Growth by Unleashing Human Potential* by Curt Coffman and Gabriela Gonzalez-Molina, The Gallup Organisation, Warner Books, 2002.

PART III

Skills and Media

14

Writing Skills

by Marc Wright

George Orwell was a master of writing style and how it could be used to evoke certain emotions in audiences. In his famous essay, 'Politics And The English Language,' written in 1946,[1] he laid out six key rules that will guide you to better writing straight away.

1. Never use a metaphor, simile or other figure of speech which you are used to seeing in print.

2. Never use a long word where a short one will do.

3. If it is possible to cut a word out, always cut it out.

4. Never use the passive where you can use the active.

5. Never use a foreign phrase, a scientific word or a jargon word if you can think of an everyday English equivalent.

6. Break any of these rules sooner than say anything outright barbarous.

Never Use a Metaphor, Simile or Other Figure of Speech Which You are Used to Seeing in Print

Newly created metaphors and similes are very powerful; they sum up in an image what could take a paragraph to describe.

1 *Horizon Magazine*, London, April 1946.

For instance: 'Our client retention strategy is about as useful as serving soup in a basket' is considerably more powerful than, 'On the whole, looking back at the previous quarter's sales compared with lost revenue from defaulting clients, shows that our retention ratios leave cause for concern.' The trouble is that, in business, we tend to fall between these two verbal stools and end up using metaphors that have lost their power, for example: 'Client retention has fallen off a cliff,' and 'Our Strategy has gone pear-shaped.'

The first few thousand times these metaphors were used, they evoked a mental picture; but now they pass through our brains without leaving a trace. So, when you are writing, ask yourself whether the language you are using is as fresh as a Spring croissant in a Parisian cafe or as stale as last-night's takeaway.

Never Use a Long Word Where a Short One Will Do

The longer the word, the more likely it has a Latin root. In mediaeval Britain, Latin was the language of politics, jurisdiction and management, whereas Anglo Saxon was the language of work and things. As a result, English tends to have two words or phrases to describe the same thing or activity. Where you have a choice, go for the Anglo Saxon since these words are grounded in everyday life and tend to be more meaningful to the listener.

Latinate	**Anglo Saxon**
Objective	Goal
Consult with	Ask
Develop	Build
Increase	Grow
Communicate	Talk
Strategy	Plan
Perceive	See

Still not convinced? Try using short Anglo Saxon phrases to emphasise the positive and lengthy Latinate words to decry the negative. To make the point, take a look at the following speech by Winston Churchill:

> *I say to the House as I said to ministers who have joined this government, I have nothing to offer but blood, toil, tears and sweat. We have before us an ordeal of the most grievous kind. We have before us many, many months of struggle and suffering. You ask, what is our policy? I say it is to wage war by land, sea and air. War, with all our might and with all the strength God has given us, and to wage war against a monstrous tyranny never surpassed in the dark and lamentable catalogue of human crime. That is our policy. You ask, what is our aim? I can answer in one word. It is victory. Victory at all costs; Victory in spite of all terrors; Victory, however long and hard the road may be; for without victory there is no survival.*

Notice how all the exhorting words are Anglo-Saxon: 'blood, toil, tears and sweat' whereas the enemy is described in long latinate phrases: 'monstrous tyranny... lamentable catalogue'.

Churchill was a professional writer as well as a politician and his use of language is always worth studying. So too are the speeches of Martin Luther King:

> *I say to you today, my friends, so even though we face the difficulties of today and tomorrow, I still have a dream. It is a dream deeply rooted in the American dream… I have a dream that one day, on the red hills of Georgia, the sons of former slaves and the sons of former slave owners will be able to sit down together at the table of brotherhood. I have a dream that, one day, even the state of Mississippi, a state sweltering with the heat of injustice, sweltering with the heat of oppression, will be transformed into an oasis of freedom and justice… I have a dream today.*

'Table of brotherhood' with earthy, Anglo-Saxon roots contrasts with the Latinate 'injustice' and 'oppression'.

If it is Possible to Cut a Word Out, Always Cut it Out

Look at these phrases:

- render inoperative = break;

- make contact with = contact;
- be subjected to = suffer;
- give grounds for = make;
- have the effect of = effect;
- play a leading part/role = lead;
- exhibit a tendency to = tends;
- serve the purpose of = serves.

Verbal padding will make your sentences meaningless. This is because the eye skims over words that don't need to be there so the reader assumes that the writer does not have much to say. Each wasted word you use devalues the currency of the pithy ones. Consequently, the more words you use, the more you dilute your message.

We use verbal padding to buy us time to think. Fine if you're in conversation with a friend, but otherwise it's far better to spend time honing your writing down to the essentials. 'I didn't have time to write a short letter, so I wrote a long one instead.' This quote is so true that it has been attributed to numerous writers – Mark Twain, George Bernard Shaw, Pascal and others, as far back as Cicero.

Never Use the Passive Where You Can Use the Active

Active language makes your emails, websites, scripts and copy more vibrant, accessible and memorable. Any sentence can be written in either a passive, or an active, form.

To illustrate:

- Passive sentences:
  - 'Service targets were broken this month by the Liverpool call centre.'

- 'The practice of smoking in public places, such as pubs and restaurants, has been banned by the Irish courts.'

- 'The new company identity is being implemented throughout the organisation's many locations, in a programme led by the marketing and xommunications department.'

versus

- Active sentences:

  - 'The Liverpool call centre broke service targets this month.'

  - 'Irish courts have banned smoking in pubs and restaurants.'

  - 'Jane Smith and her team are rolling out the new identity throughout the company's 17 sites.'

Active language is shorter, more to the point, and the person doing the action comes before the verb. School and college encourage us to use passive language – to appear more detached, objective and, well, academic. The trouble is that, when we take these writing styles to work, they muffle our prose and stifle the impact of our messages. Passive language puts people off your message – and perhaps to sleep.

Americans tend to use active vocabulary more than the British. You can see it in traffic signals: 'Walk', 'Don't Walk'; in advertising: 'Just do it'; in film titles: 'Jaws'; and in political rhetoric: 'I love America!'. It is a gutsier, more vibrant language style that grabs your attention.

English language, perfected and honed over the years, has developed Byzantine constructs and lengthy sentence structures that reflect the British uneasiness with direct confrontation and instructions. Although extremely elegant, corporate English degraded into the bureaucratic and opaque by the eighteenth and nineteenth centuries. Dickens satirised this national characteristic in Little Doritt in his hilarious description of the Circumlocution Office – a mirror of many British government departments. For an example of active vocabulary, here is a well-known verse from Ecclesiastes:

I returned and saw, under the sun, that the race is not to the swift, nor the battle to the strong, neither yet bread to the wise, nor yet riches to men of understanding, nor yet favour to men of skill; but time and chance happeneth to them all.

Here it is, translated by Orwell into what he calls the worst kind of modern English:

Objective considerations of contemporary phenomena compel the conclusion that success or failure in competitive activities exhibits no tendency to be commensurate with innate capacity, but that a considerable element of the unpredictable must invariably be taken into account.

Before we laugh, we have to admit that most corporate English is closer to Orwell's nightmare example than to the poetry of Ecclesiastes.

Never Use a Foreign Phrase, a Scientific Word or a Jargon Word if You Can Think of an Everyday English Equivalent

Communicating at work is a constant obstacle course of jargon and acronyms. Communication professionals are as bad as any group in using obscure language where everyday English will do. Here is my favourite list of management jargon that you can use to play jargon bingo at your next meeting.

Break Any of These Rules Sooner Than Say Anything Outright

Off Line	Push the Envelope	Culture Change	Outside the Box	Empowerment
Sign Off On	Drop Dead Date	Deliverables	Proactive	Matrix Management
Leverage	Focus	Drill down	Touch Base	Transition
Take Ownership	Bite the Bullet	Red Flag	Solutions	Dialog With (v.)
Guesstimate	Close the Loop	Impact (v.)	Scenarios	Synergy

Barbarous

Orwell's sixth rule is to use common sense. Trust your own ear. If something you have written or said sounds heavy because you have followed his previous five rules, strike it out and start again.

15

How to Commission a Video

by Kelly Kass

You've just been asked to jazz up the welcome session of a large pharmaceutical conference. Your boss is looking for a mood setter; something to excite a roomful of 700 delegates who must then sit through 90 minutes of speaker presentations. The solution? A 2-minute opening video.

This is just one of several ways by which you might come to commission a video – but before you launch yourself head-first into the world of production, stop and ask yourself a few key questions concerning its function and usage:

- Why is a video needed: what purpose will it serve?
- What is the message, theme or point to be made?
- Who will see the video?
- When, where and how will it be viewed?
- Will the material have a secondary use?
- If so, will copies need to be made? And on which format?
- Exactly how big is the budget?

Answering these simple questions at the outset will help you to focus on what you want a video to achieve – its content, its impact, its message.

However, it is how your video will be used that will determine how it should be made – the script, the production process, the aspect ratio, the stock and the equipment used during filming will all result from looking at the project from the following perspectives. The answers you give will help to establish a number of factors critical to the production of your *opus magnum*; they will also highlight the elements to be included in your production schedule, giving shape and momentum to your commission.

Stage 1: Should it be a Video in the First Place?

Video is most effective at communicating the following:

- general messages, not fine detail;
- emotional stories and testimonials;
- capturing your people and personalities;
- presenting visuals to support your new product, process or initiative, adding clarity and credibility.

Stage 2: What is the Message, Theme or Point to be Made?

- Are there elements of the production process (for example) that can be shown more easily than they can be described?
- Will a video help the audience to understand what the new product or process will involve?
- Will it educate them in an informative and entertaining way?
- Could it also help expose them to remote locations, affiliated suppliers, end users or practical applications of their product that otherwise they might not see?

Stage 3: Who Will See Your Video?

- Exactly who will see your video? Will it be one small group at the conference or can the video then be rolled out to the rest of the company (for example, via the intranet or DVD duplication)?

- Will it be seen internationally? If so, will subtitling be necessary?
- Examine the languages and culture in your organisation – will your video cross frontiers in a global company?
- Is the theme of your video a universal one that all company members can relate to?
- Which voice should you employ? (Formal, informal, authoritative, knowledgeable, and so on.)
- What sort of language do you want to use? (Engaging, humorous, informative, and so on.)
- Will the use of jargon or industry shorthand be appropriate?
- Does the video fit with the company's image? (For example, would a *Pop Idol* spoof work at a top accounting firm? Probably yes.)
- Try to match the style of your video to your audience and nudge them with its content; don't shove them.

Stage 4: Examine Your Viewers' Understanding of the Issues Concerned

- How informed is the audience? Will viewers be vaguely aware of the issues involved or do they need a thorough explanation of the situation with background details?
- What are the key messages that you want to put across?
- How are these messages likely to be received?
- Do they need additional clarification to prevent alarm or miscommunication?
- What do you want viewers to take away, as a result of viewing the video?

Stage 5: Creative Elements to Consider

- Video treatment: if you are doing anything more ambitious than a talking head then consider hiring a production company to prepare a treatment. If you like what they pitch then hire them.
- Video style: use the most appropriate style for your content:
  - drama;
  - comedy;
  - talking heads;
  - documentary;
  - presenter led;
  - voice-over led.
- Stills: if you'd like to incorporate digital pictures such as product shots or company photos, make sure you resize them for video.
- Graphics: are there specific points that would be better made using graphics on-screen? (Perhaps your product has reduced the risk of cancer by 25 per cent or maybe you want to list the two dozen countries in which it has made a difference?)
- Animation: this is used to add motion and fluidity to a piece; it's also a great way to bring your theme and logo to life.
- Music: a soundtrack brings energy and emotion to a video.
- Basic rules
  - keep your video short;
  - remember: less is more;
  - present a beginning, a middle and an end;

– show, don't tell.

Stage 6: When, Where and How Will Your Video be Viewed?

- In the office, on a laptop or in a conference room?
- At home (say, via a DVD player)?
- If so, will copies need to be made? And on which format?
- Will it be projected on a screen at the conference venue? If so, you will need to look at the size of the audience and the dimensions of your venue to work out what sized screen (or screens) will be best.
- The screen size will determine the aspect ratio in which images are shot (most modern plasma screens are 16:9 compared to the old 4:3) as well as the quality of imagery required.
- Will the video be physically distributed to attendees on DVD? In which case, you'll also need to factor in duplication and packaging costs, as well as a design for the label, sleeve or case.
- Do you want employees to be able to access the video online?
- Perhaps you want to opt for video streaming? While it's cheap, accessible and easily updated, beware of bandwidth issues; also keep your image size in mind.

Stage 7: Will the Material Have a Secondary Use?

- Will the video you make be of use to other employees not attending the meeting? If so, either the video's content will need to be suitably generic for all audiences or you'll need to shoot additional material that can be used to create a second version for your other audiences.
- Might the video be helpful for training staff or in the induction of new joiners?

- A third version of your material might be required for these purposes. By filming additional links and spending an extra couple of hours in the editing suite, your video might acquire considerably more mileage and added value.
- Can it be used externally? (for example, in advertising, for the press or at shareholders' meetings?) If so, you will need to produce material that is of broadcast quality.

Stage 8: Budget

When you commission a video, remember that video production is a team effort requiring many skills – so you'll have to pay for all of the following:

- scriptwriter;
- producer;
- director;
- production coordinator/assistant;
- camera person;
- tape stock;
- make-up artist;
- actors;
- editor;
- edit suite;
- graphics operator;
- the rights to any music or stock footage used;
- miscellaneous production expenses (meals, transport, and so on).

Depending on the size of your budget, you may decide to use just some of the above and, these days, ever more clients are cutting costs, opting for more simplicity and less glitz. Where once they might have chosen a top notch graphics designer, companies are now realising that it's easier and cheaper to create simple text graphics directly in the Avid or on Final Cut. In addition, many coordinators now work without the help of a production assistant; at shoots, some PAs now take on the role of make-up artist; and more than a few producers (like myself) even do their own shooting!

Remember that as the costs of shooting and editing are going down, what makes a prize-winning effective video programme over a prize turkey is the quality of the talent you employ – and good writers, directors and actors will always command a premium. And a good producer will keep your project on budget and on schedule.

16

Better Presentations

by Fiona Robertson

Giving a presentation is one of the most stressful experiences you can put yourself through, this side of divorce, moving house or bereavement.

When it comes to excellent presentations, there are just three secrets for success: preparation, preparation and preparation… so give yourself a break and learn how to prepare for the next – or first – time you have to get up in front of an audience. Don't be fooled by those very fluent and confident presenters who appear to be making it up as they go along. In fact, they are delivering a performance they've refined and honed through practice.

And don't believe that you can wing it on the day either; allow at least 2 weeks in which to get yourself ready. That's the minimum of a week in which to create the script and prepare your slides; and at least 1 more week to craft your performance.

Creating the Script

Double-check the brief to establish what needs to be covered and in what depth, then talk to the organisers and other speakers to find out how your presentation fits the objectives of the meeting.

Think about your audience. Reduce them down to two or three people who you know and consider:

- What level of information do they want from the presentation?
- What do you want them to leave your presentation thinking?
- What tone should you take?

Go and talk to that representative sample. You might be surprised at what they already know, and at what they want to find out. Remember, it's not about conveying lots of information; it's about editing down all that information to help people understand what's important to them. Your audience wants to listen to your advice so they know what to learn and what's safe to ignore. If they just wanted an overview of the subject, they could read an article.

Check the running order to see how much time has been allotted to you and that this fits your brief. Don't pad out a simple presentation to fill the time and don't skim over important details because your slot's too short. Rather, let the subject matter determine how long your presentation should be. If your slot is too long or too short, speak to the meeting's organisers and revise the running order (or the brief) as early as you can.

Make sure your presentation has a beginning, a middle and an end, that there is a logical sequence to your material and that the flow of it has 'pace'. This doesn't mean writing your presentation from start to finish – you'll only write yourself into corners and waste time. Instead, map out all the parts of your presentation on a large sheet of paper, connecting different themes and grouping different points. Then decide which areas make up the beginning, which middle bits develop your argument and where you want to take your audience for the end point. If your script isn't right, keep working; it's all you've got so make it good.

As a general rule, each paragraph should contain a single thought, and each sentence should be a separate beat in the argument to get that thought across. Always build in a logical direction; darting backwards and forwards will confuse your audience. And if you can't get it right, get someone who can – employ a professional scriptwriter with a track record in your field or area of business; We are all trained to write for the written word; writing for the spoken word is a different art altogether. And remember, do your script first and your slides second. Yes, it is harder that way – but the result will be better. Otherwise, you risk bending your arguments to fit the pieces of clip art you've found!

Preparing Your Slides

Slides are almost universally prepared using PowerPoint software. The ubiquity and popularity of this package means that just about anyone can achieve a professional result themselves. If you haven't the time to learn how to use the software, or your presentation is part of a high-end production, use a company that specialises in graphics production; their expertise means they will be able to create outstanding presentations in a relatively short space of time.

Every presenter should receive the same few templates (name slide, holding slide, subject headings, bulleted lists, and so on) with guidelines on colours, fonts and font sizes, punctuation styles, layouts, charts and graphs, and so on. Go through the final version of your script and pick out the key pieces of data that you want to highlight. Next, look at any elements that are easier to demonstrate than to explain (including logos, employee photos, advertising stills, flowcharts, schematics, maps, charts or illustrations, and so on). The golden rule with slides is 'show what you can't say' and 'say what you can't show'.

For example, the picture of a group of your smiling colleagues will convey a thousand times more meaning than a bullet saying 'Teamwork'. Equally, there are times when words will create a mind picture that outstrips anything you can get from a picture library, for example, 'No man is an island'; 'Treat others as you would have them treat you.' Never use clip art: it's lazy, clichéd and everyone has seen those rather poor cartoons before. List all of the slides that need to be created, in sequence, and make notes about where particular data can be obtained. Follow your style guidelines about slide builds as well as for transitions from slide to slide.

DO NOT put lots of information on any one slide – your audience will struggle to read it and will probably fail. They'll then waste time wondering what they missed and might not hear the next vital point of your presentation as a result. If you need to give a large amount of data then why not:

- send it to your audience beforehand by email;
- give handouts at the end of your presentation;
- send it to your audience afterwards by email;
- post it on the web or intranet and tell them where to find it.

Your slides should reinforce what you say; they should never lead your presentation. Remember, they are not a form of autocue. If you can't remember the script, use a prompting system. Try to use a holding slide between those that give specific information, to act as a sort of graphic wallpaper. This will encourage your audience to look at you rather than at the screen. Consequently, during your presentation, the shift from wallpaper to information will be more pronounced, making your use of material more effective. Whatever you do, don't read your slides aloud; the audience will do that for themselves.

Creating Your Performance

Learn how to read your script *and* have eye contact with your audience. It's easier than you think. Because your eyes and brain can read much faster than your mouth can talk, you can read to the end of a sentence well before you reach it with the spoken word. So, halfway through the sentence, look up and deliver the second half while looking at your audience. Practise this technique in front of a mirror: you will see yourself put more visual meaning into your words as you convey the information.

Pace yourself; this means varying the speed you use to give information. Speed up over the obvious parts of a sentence – the bits that your audience can assimilate easily and slow down over the part you want them to register. Practise your speech at least seven times from beginning to end; even seasoned politicians will do this. If you want help with your performance, have some presentation training; a sense of stagecraft will give your delivery more polish and confidence.

USING THE SCRIPT

If you want to work from a written script then learn how to read your script *and* have eye contact with your audience by using this simple technique – it's easier than you think! Because your eyes and brain can read much faster than your mouth can talk, you can read to the end of a sentence well before you reach it with the spoken word. So, halfway through a sentence, look up and deliver the second half while looking at your audience. Keep your thumb on the line you are reading so that when you return to the script, you can pick up the next sentence without hesitation. Practise this technique in front of a mirror: you'll soon see yourself putting more expression into your words as you convey information.

Start to free yourself from your written script. This will allow you to move away from the lectern, engage more directly with your audience, and impress them with your ability to speak fluently. How? First, write your script out in full; then look at each paragraph and break it down into bullets that remind you of the key points to be made. Write these bullets down on postcards so you can see them clearly at arm's length. Collect these 'cue cards' together in sequence, hole-punch them in one corner and secure them with a small piece of string so that, if you drop them, they will remain in order. Have them in your hand and refer to them when you get lost. But remember to pause as you look at your cards; this adds dramatic effect as well as improving your concentration.

Alternatively, use a prompting system. Performing a similar function to cue cards, monitors are placed in front of the stage and these screens show slides containing your bullet points. You could also use an autocue system, where your entire speech rolls across a glass screen, keeping time with you as you speak aloud. The screen is usually placed next to the lectern and, being small and transparent, is virtually invisible to the audience. Otherwise, a larger screen is used, situated in or behind your audience, in front of the stage. It takes some practise to get used to an autocue system and to realise that the operator is following your speed of delivery rather than the other way round.

Always use two autocue glasses: this will help you to address both sides of your audience and they will ensure an unobstructed view of you to the front. Generally speaking, autocue is used only by those who do not have time to familiarise themselves with a script (such as senior politicians, who may give two or three speeches a day). But no matter how polished your delivery, autocues are not a good thing as your audience will suspect you are reading someone else's words. Eventually, you will know your material so well that you can cue yourself from your PowerPoint slides, if needs be. (Though, ideally, your verbal delivery should lead your slides and not the other way around.)

DELIVERY

Position yourself on the left hand side of the screen, from your audience's point of view. It is natural for people to scan from left to right when they are reading so, by standing here, they'll look at you and then the screen. (And by extension, the opposite applies in those countries that read from right to left.) When you are introduced, take possession of the lectern, check that the right slide is up on the screen, look round at all parts of your audience and, only then, start talking. During that period of silence, you will get everyone's attention.

Understand and use the presentation triangle, shown in Figure 16.1.

Position A is behind a lectern. Stand here when you want to make minimum impact; for instance, when you are showing a video on-screen.

Position B should be adopted when you want to make a point about a picture, bullet or quote on the screen. Stand here, next to the screen, and point with your left hand, looking out at the audience as you do this and keeping your hand there while you make the point. (You can also use this moment to check how long you've been presenting – so wear a watch on your left wrist.)

The greater the connection you want to make with your audience, the closer to position C you should move. Try to present your key arguments from this point. In theatrical terms, this is known as downstage; it is where an actor will go for maximum rapport with their audience.

Don't wander aimlessly about the stage – this just makes you look nervous; instead, move with purpose. As a rule, you shouldn't give important information while your feet are moving. Use your body language – and

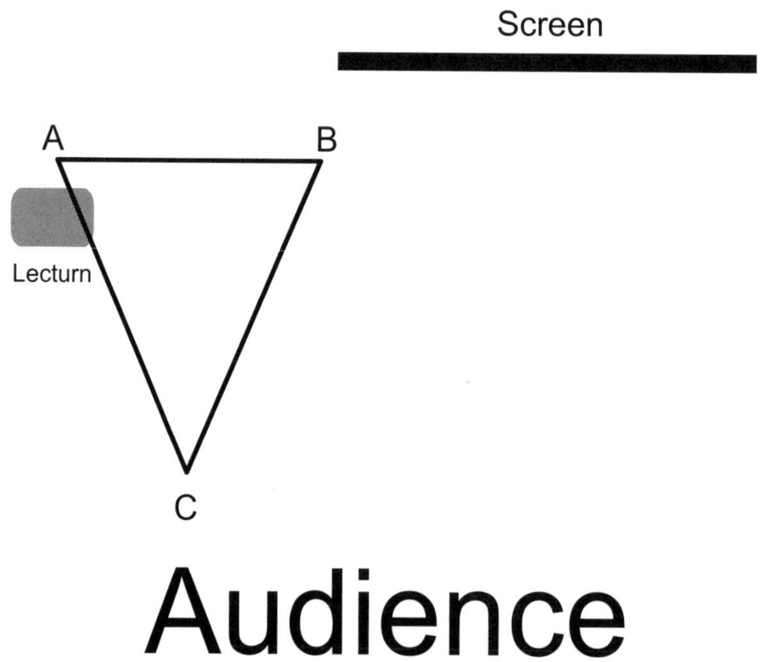

Figure 16.1 The Presentation Triangle

exaggerate it correspondingly so that those at the back will still see what you're doing. Remember that tiny gestures will be lost in a large auditorium.

PERFORMANCE

Understand the sound dynamics of the PA system by studying the presenter before you. Notice where a speaker's voice goes off-microphone (for example, when they turn towards the screen). Watch out for areas where feedback occurs (the awful screech that comes through the speakers) – usually it happens when a mic gets to close to the speaker unit so make a point of noticing where speakers have been positioned and give these a wide berth. Before you start, make friends with the sound engineer and insist on using a lapel mic, which will be clipped centrally to whatever clothing is covering your sternum (usually a tie or shirt plaquette). Should your radio mic fail, return to the lectern and direct your voice towards the lectern mics as you speak.

Arrange to use a cue light system or remote mouse to move your slides along. Keep this in your right hand and make definite clicks when you want the AV engineer to proceed to the next slide. Your left hand will then be free to gesture towards the screen, if necessary. If the operator makes a mistake with the slide cueing, speak to them by name and talk them through to the right slide. Be clear and take your time with them as they could be having technical problems that you are unaware of. Never blame someone else, even if it is not your fault. By taking responsibility, you will appear both magnanimous and in control.

These days it's more common to operate the graphics yourself via a PC. Make sure you know how to use the clicker and familiarise yourself with the PC's keyboard if not using your own machine. Before the event begins, ensure any other programs on the 'show PC' are closed to prevent pop-ups, email alerts and the like.

And never drink alcohol before a presentation: instead of settling your nerves, it will make you forgetful; and it will take the edge off your performance.

INTRODUCTIONS

Write out the words you want your introducer to use about you, keeping your introduction brief. Give them a short script and help them with any words or pronunciations. Remember, it's your responsibility to get the introduction you want. Your introducer will build you up – after all they invited you and want to justify their choice – so your first task is to start with some self-deprecation to win your audience round. And because you wrote the introduction, you have the perfect set up to make a self-deprecating joke, for example:

> *The popularity of a speaker is directly proportional to how far in advance you have to book them. I understand that if you want Bill Clinton to give a presentation he's booked 12 months ahead, and to get Nelson Mandela you need to book him 2 years in advance. So last week when John asked me to talk to you...*

STORYTELLING

Use storytelling techniques to capture your audience and make your presentation memorable. Start your presentation with an amusing, informal story about yourself. This will warm up your audience, make them laugh and help them to understand who you are; it will also make you appear more human and accessible.

AUDIENCE INTERACTION

Interact with your audience by asking them questions. Do this to make them look clever, not you, so don't ask questions that your audience cannot answer. They'll get frustrated and you'll come across as a know-it-all. Try to find areas of common ground on which to build your arguments, (such as marriage, – a fairly safe and universal theme).

If someone shouts out or asks a question, react to it and build it into your argument. If you don't understand the question, ask them to repeat it, and if you still don't understand, admit this and ask someone else in the audience to explain. They are probably just as baffled as you.

THEATRICAL DEVICES

Use pauses – both for effect and to give your audience thinking time to digest what you've just said. You can also use jokes – but only ones that work. Try your jokes out on friends, relatives and colleagues. If they don't laugh, drop them. Good jokes are like gold dust; and the more you use one, the better you will be at fine-tuning it for effect. Just don't use it twice for the same audience!

Appear spontaneous. Pretend that a thought has just struck you, bend one of your stories to something that happened on the way to the conference or adapt a point to something you read in that morning's newspaper. You could also refer to comments made by a previous speaker.

Lists are highly effective rhetorical devices for getting key points across. Two items do not make a list, while four are harder to remember so use three-part lists. For example, 'Our mission as a business is to make some money, have some fun and do some good.' If you want your audience to applaud (say, to thank someone or acknowledge their achievements), then give them some key clues. Build to a crescendo, throw your voice out to the audience, and start applauding yourself. For example, 'Some would have thought it too hard to try in the first place; others would have given up when things got tough; but Maxine Yates overcame all obstacles to bring the project in, 6 months before schedule'… (pause)... 'Let's hear it for Maxine!' (then start applauding…).

Presentation Structure

Tell your audience what you are going to say; tell them your presentation; then tell them what you said. It's an old system but it works. You can ring the changes by witholding the punchline of a story to the end of your talk, then using it to reinforce your key message. For example, 'Why did I call this presentation *The Ears of the Hippopotamus*? Because there's often a great deal more to a subject than appears on the surface. So when you are working with colleagues across continents, keep your eyes peeled for those hippo ears.'

Be aware that an audience's attention drops off after 20 minutes of listening so, if you speak for longer, make sure you have something very interesting to say. End your presentation with reference to a comment you made at the beginning. This will complete the circle, giving your speech 'roundness' and a thematic elegance.

After the event, listen to feedback about your presentation and study any audience evaluation sheets. You probably won't agree with much of it but the truth of your performance is in the *receiving* of it rather than in the giving. Also use evaluation techniques (such as exit questionnaires) to establish just how many of your messages are getting through.

Joint presentations can be effective where two of you can give a bigger picture or increased credibility, or you can just be more entertaining. However, rehearsals will take twice as long.

Using video within your presentation is a great way of bringing your story to life. Just ensure clips are short and to the point or you'll risk losing the narrative thread of your argument. Props and costumes can also heighten a performance as long as they work with your theme. Coming onstage in a clown's outfit may make an amusing entrance but, 15 minutes into your speech, the joke can wear pretty thin.

In general, you will have the greatest impact at the beginning of your speech (when you are fresh to the audience's eyes and minds) so get your key argument in early – then develop it as you go along.

If you are presenting to a foreign language audience make sure you meet your interpreter before the event. Go through the presentation with them, explaining names or references that may be unfamiliar. Remember to allow twice as much time to deliver your speech (or cut the content down by half). 'Consecutive translation' is where a speaker makes an utterance and the interpreter then repeats this in the audience's language. This means you need to keep your thoughts succinct. A rambling series of subordinate clauses will not only confuse the translator but they may have to interrupt you mid-flow.

Simultaneous interpreting with headsets can be more effective but beware of the time lag effect. If you make a joke, people might not laugh until you are well into your next point. Finally, be careful how you use idiomatic English and metaphors. In the European Parliament the phrase 'the spirit is willing but the flesh is weak' was once interpreted as 'the vodka is OK but avoid the steak'.

17

The Concern Scale

by Marc Wright

The Concern Scale (see Figure 17.1) – sometimes called the Significance Scale – is a useful tool for developing your communication channels. The basic idea is that the more your messages concern your audience, the more effective face-to-face media will be as opposed to any other channel. This has led to the creation of a scale, which you can use with your managers to agree how certain messages are communicated to colleagues.

The Post-it Note

Consider this scenario: You get up early one morning and make yourself a cup of coffee. Flicking through your emails, you come across some astounding news; you have been accepted for a great job – a job you have long been chasing. But it means relocating to another country.

Your young family is fast asleep and you don't want to wake them this early, yet you have to go into the office immediately for a meeting with HR. You stick a Post-it note on the fridge announcing that you are all moving to another country and sneak out the door.

Sacked by Email

This may sound ridiculous, yet just this use of inappropriate communication channels persists in the workplace. UK insurance company, The Accident Group, famously laid off its workers by sending them all a text message, and Liverpool City Council once fired staff by sending written letters to their homes by taxi.

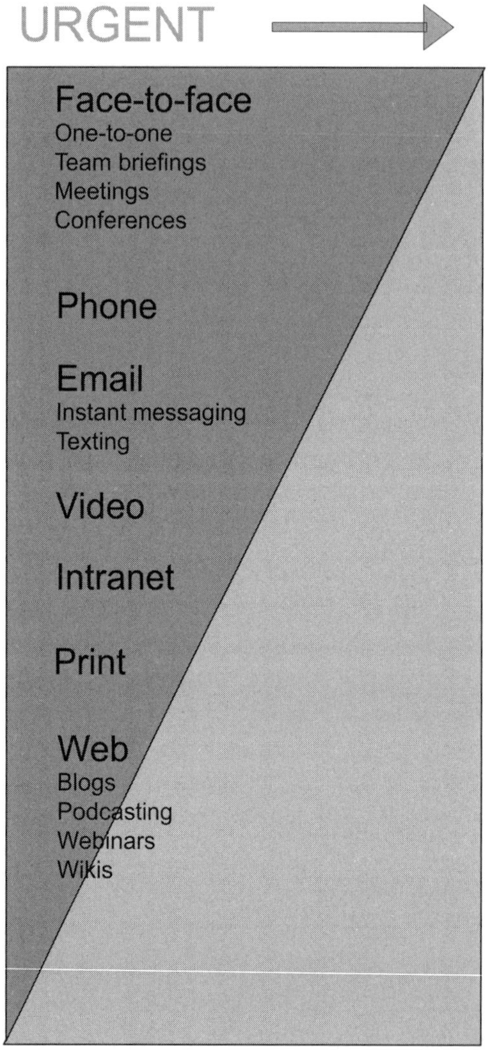

Figure 17.1 The Concern Scale

The problem is that we sometimes allow the speed of communicating override the significance of the message. The result is that your audience may get the message quickly – but they will be far more hostile to the news you are conveying because of the insensitive way in which it was delivered. And if that news requires their goodwill to turn it into action, then you have truly shot yourself in the foot.

So what are the rules of the Concern Scale?

HIGH CONCERN MESSAGES

For *high concern messages*, use face-to-face communication. If the issue involves someone's job, livelihood, self-esteem or material circumstances, you really need to communicate on a one-to-one level; and that job is best done by an HR professional or a line manager who has been briefed and trained in communicating the changes.

They must be able to tailor the message to the particular needs of that audience of one; they need to be sympathetic, knowledgeable and capable of giving appropriate news, advice and counsel. They also need time as they will have to coach their colleague through the Change Curve over a number of meetings.

If the changes affect everyone in a team equally, then you can brief them together in a small group (which means no more than the number you can fit around one table). It's critical to allow everyone the chance to ask questions and internalise the message. Facilitation of these meetings requires training and skill; people are most likely to change when they see someone they respect within their own work team start to adopt new language and behaviour that implies acceptance of the change. If I see someone who does the same job as me and works in similar circumstances, and they are further through the Change Curve than I am, then I will be more disposed to follow the same journey.

CEO versus Line Manager

Should you use CEOs and senior executives to deliver high concern messages?

On the one hand, consultants such as TJ Larkin[1] are adamant that the only effective communication channel in these circumstances is through the line manager. Others, such as the measurement expert, Angela Sinickas, and the social media guru, Shel Holtz, argue strongly for a combination of line manager and senior executive communication. Larkin points to research by the Hay Group, which found that communication from one's own manager creates four times more employee support than from a senior manager/town hall type meeting, and nine times more employee support than an article in the

1 *Communicating Change* by TJ Larkin, New York: McGraw-Hill, 1994.

company newsletter.[2] Larkin argues that, if time and resources are limited and you can only do one thing, then communicate through line managers. Sinickas and Holtz, on the other hand, believe that it is equally important for the CEO to provide the context of the change; to give the Big Picture.

The best advice we can give you on the current evidence is that if you can do both, then do both. Get out the communication to staff from the top and then immediately go into smaller group meetings with line managers, who have been fully briefed and trained up for delivering high concern messages.

Conclusion: Using the Concern Scale

First, establish your own personal concern scale in your working and private life. Think about the significance of what you say to your audience and then use the scale to decide what is the best medium or channel. Clearly, if you are announcing to your loved ones that they are all going to move to another country, you probably want to have a round table discussion about it rather than leave a Post-it note on the fridge.

Then look at using the scale at work. Introduce it into your training with managers and start to encourage a consistency about which channels are used for which subjects. Reach agreement around which programmes need face-to-face communication and which can be handled by print, email or the intranet. Remember that men will always prefer the Post-it note while women are more inclined to pick up the phone.

So use the Concern Scale to get some kind of consistency based on audience needs rather than the preferences of the message-giver.

2 Hay Group, *Communication Measurement – An Oxymoron Bites the Dust Strategic Communication Management*, February–March 1997.

18

How Intranets and Related Technologies are Redefining Internal Communications

by Paul Miller

By 1998, when the last edition of this handbook was published, it was clear that technology would redefine the internal communications profession. What is surprising is that the impact of technology has been so slow and yet so far reaching. That said, organisations are complex beasts that generally change gradually. The most sustained shifts in the way work is performed happen progressively and that is certainly the case here. The question is, where will we be in 2018? Will the internal communications field still exist at all and does it still exist now in any meaningful form?

This chapter explores:

- How intranets and related technologies have grown within organizations.
- The impact such technologies have had on how organisations communicate.
- Two case studies that describe the emerging future environment for internal communications.
- Extinction or adaptation – the internal communications challenge.
- How to survive and thrive in internal communications.

How Intranets and Related Technologies Have Grown Within Organisations

Intranets, portals and the entire digital landscape within organisations represent the most radical shift to date within what we call internal communications. Just as on the external web, online tools and network technologies are empowering amateurs to gain a voice and exposure never seen before, so behind the firewall, a sea change is happening that is redefining internal communication. For the record, the footprint such online services have within enterprises reaches far beyond internal communications, affecting virtually every aspect of work, so those in internal communications can feel reassured to know they have not been singled out for unique levels of disruption.

The impact of intranet services or online services behind the firewall started slowly: a few servers under geek desks profiling all the people in the supply chain team so you could find out all you needed to know about these fascinating individuals. It was not pretty and as a result, the user experience community became involved and started involving user groups across the business; asking, 'What do you do, want, need and so on?' New interfaces, some governance and improved applications started to emerge and the intranet landscape evolved to become more useful to certain groups.

Internal communication, along with HR, saw these technologies as just another channel for communication. Put another way, the internal communication profession (with notable exceptions such as the communications teams within the likes of IBM and Hewlett Packard) were threatened by technology and chose to present their fears through a kind of strategic arrogance: Yes intranets were a good thing, but they were really just another communication channel such as print, face-to-face and electronic – all able to carry the directional (generally top-down) messages that the organisation wanted to issue. Interestingly, some non-technical tools at the time (during the late 1990s) were being used more interactively than was the case with technology. Managers led sessions with paper-based materials that opened dialogue and discussion in ways that the technology did not yet provide.

This was a period of intense resistance from internal communicators to a new set of tools and services that had the power to eat their lunch. Perhaps this was inevitable. Certainly, some internal communication mavericks in technology-based organisations like Microsoft and Oracle saw the possibilities that online services offered. It took people's breath away when in the early

2000s IBM used its technology to host a 48-hour 'IBM Jam' involving all staff across the globe in a shared conversation around an issue of importance to IBM. For 2 days they talked about corporate social responsibility and then took action based on the ideas generated.

This event was a sea change in the relationship between internal communication and technology. In 2007, Philips had a 7-day period focused on its core company value of simplicity, using its intranet and related tools. Deloitte in the US hosted the Deloitte Film Festival on its intranet where staff generated their own films about 'My Deloitte' and these were then archived, with the best four films used in the recruitment process for new hires.

The lasting effect of the slow take-up amongst internal communicators of intranets may prove to have lasting damage to the profession. When you do not take a lead in an area that is reshaping your work, you are left vulnerable to its journey. HR has been hit hard by self-service online tools which allowed multiple outsourcing of HR services and radical reductions in HR staff. One major global corporate firm has identified 5,000 people in their company with a job title that includes the word 'communication'. This growth in the head count has been the result of duplication and fragmentation of communication roles and the company now believes they need 250 employees to manage this function at most, with the rest of the work performed through the intranet and related tools.

The Impact Technologies Have Had on How Organisations Communicate

At one level, the impact of these technological tools on how we communicate is quite straightforward. Historically, internal communications has meant (going back a few years) top-down communication and then (more recently) bottom-up communication. Now through new tools such as advanced intranets, portals and social software we have peer-to-peer communication as employees and contractors take over the means of communication. Collaboration tools can be deployed within minutes and at little cost across virtual teams. They proliferate and people love them. In many cases internal communication professionals are barely involved in this change.

We have three types of communication; top-down, bottom-up and the third moving laterally across the organisation. This third element enables people to communicate in unique and previously impossible ways and produces, in its wake, new connections, conversations and relationships. It has consequential impacts on the power relationships in the organisation and gradually dilutes the other channels of top-down and bottom-up communication.

By way of example, let's take a change in group pension policy in a large, global energy company. Previously an email/intranet news article would have been posted across the company to announce the change which would provoke calls/emails to HR which were then handled on a case-by-case basis. Some people were likely to have been confused or unhappy with the change and would grumble to colleagues over coffee or lunch, but the new policy would stick and the communication process was reasonably well controlled by internal communications and HR.

Introduce into this scenario, peer-to-peer communication generated via personal/group blogs, collaboration sites used by hundreds of teams, instant messenger chats, social software sites within the organisation and externally on the Internet. Collectively, these play host to a volume of conversation and discussion that is impossible to control. Some individuals in the organisation have a new influential role as gate keepers of knowledge and communication. This scenario is based on a real-life example. The organisation in question asked senior HR staff to enter the conversations and present the rationale for the change in various ways, responding to questions, correcting inaccuracies and so on. The final outcome was that the pension shift happened; some tweaks were made to its implementation; its impact was well understood; staff felt heard and engaged; and local regional issues were aired and addressed.

Where were the internal communications staff in this process? Virtually absent, as the process was self-managing with HR leaders choosing to engage directly.

Examples of the Emerging Future Environment for Internal Communications

MICROSOFT

> *'It just happens that our corporate culture is one of trust and empowerment.'*
>
> Rob Gray, former Product Marketing Manager
> (SharePoint Technologies), Microsoft

The atrium of Microsoft's UK HQ is a space that is dedicated to allowing people to sit, talk and share ideas and knowledge. On each of the several small tables spaced out across the floor, advertising for the next big Microsoft product, 'Office Communication Server 2007', a presence, VOIP and Instant Messaging Platform communicates to all staff and visitors that Microsoft is gearing up for another big product launch.

For Rob Gray the biggest recent change in the industry is the new people joining. In the current technological climate, email itself is becoming out-dated and new graduates, entering the workplace at just 21 or 22, have been using the Internet for most, if not all, of their lives. When they arrive in their new place of work, they have a high expectation of the communications technology that will be available to them, having become accustomed to using Facebook, MySpace and other networking sites. If they arrive and find only email and a shared drive they will be severely disappointed. Part of the pressure to provide new technology in the workplace is the perceived need to satisfy and appease the new recruits.

Email is now, more than ever, viewed as an irritant; something which drags us away from our work, although it is still being used as the dominant form of communication, even within Microsoft. However, Microsoft is changing, driven by the demand for change amongst a more demanding new intake of employees. Such is the current high level of disregard for email, that only one man within Microsoft could genuinely command people's attention through the medium: Bill Gates. Gates, however, did not expect his employees to read pages and pages and encourages the use of the company intranet by sending a short email with a link to the full story which can be found on the company intranet.

Microsoft has two approaches to internal communications: the first involves top-down information fed through the company intranet. The second is much more innovative and built around Microsoft's SharePoint and MySite, which allow all employees to shape and decide what information to share around the organisation. The intranet, Microsoft Web, is probably the biggest source of communications within the organisation and supplies the usual knowledge that an intranet would be expected to provide – news, information, employee services and more.

All of the news alerts on the intranet can be subscribed to through RSS feeds, this allows people to pick and choose information that they are either interested in, or that is relevant to their particular work. The emphasis is on the user to filter out news that they do not want to read. For key messages, however, Microsoft will send information direct to employees' inboxes and reinforce these messages through the intranet and blogs.

As you might expect, Microsoft makes considerable use of other technologies to help them communicate more effectively. Live meeting technology saves the organisation a good deal of time and money. Each employee has a live meeting account and may invite any other employee to that meeting.

Through the live meeting technology, virtual teams within the company are able to meet on a regular basis without losing any time travelling; regardless of whether they operate from Reading or Richmond in the US. To help ease the pressure on emails, Microsoft uses an instant messaging system, called Microsoft Office Communicator, which is very similar to the MSN instant messenger that we have become so used to in our private lives.

Microsoft Web is awash with information. An employee might easily be able to spend 8 hours a day just watching webcasts or reading news updates that only relate to Microsoft. This is why Microsoft takes a mixed approach to internal communications. Structured communications are necessary to communicate what Microsoft is doing, but to communicate how to achieve its goals, an unstructured approach to communications can help to bring untapped potential within employees to the fore.

The second aspect of Microsoft's internal communications is the more vibrant and exciting arm – within the intranet, employees can create their own pages, akin to creating your own MySpace page, in which they can put information about their work. This page, known as MySite and part of Microsoft's SharePoint software, is not managed by a content manager: the onus is absolutely on the individual to be responsible in choosing the content with which to populate their MySite. MySite is also integrated into the telephone system, so employees can telephone each other directly without needing to pick up the phone.

One of the most useful components of MySite is that it allows employees to post documents on their site which others can then pick up. Just as with Facebook, you can choose who is allowed access to your MySite – those who can access your site can also pick up your documents. The end result of this is a big reduction in the number of internal emails involving colleagues asking one another to send them a recent presentation or key slides. The underlying philosophy is that if SharePoint is used well, it should empower its users to find the answers for themselves.

A further useful innovation within Microsoft in recent months has been the embedding of SharePoint Server 2007 search technology within the intranet. The search technology allows employees to search under three areas; Intranet, People and Customers. The new method of searching for individuals within the system, by allowing you to find the account manager, product manager or whomever you may need, saves numerous telephone calls and emails to colleagues and can bring information on any individual within Microsoft's immense database within a few seconds.

Even within Microsoft, there is still a role for face-to-face communications. When a new team forms, face-to-face meetings are still the order of the day, to allow the team to gel and get to know one another. Once the team is established, it may switch to virtual meetings, emails and telephones. Microsoft continues to make use of face-to-face communication at its annual conference: around 15,000 Microsoft employees would meet up to listen to Bill Gates and other senior executives – this event gives new staff in particular, the chance to put names to faces. For those who cannot attend, this event is opened up online to all employees, allowing a greater reach and a massive reduction in costs.

Even though the new technology could be viewed as a threat by the internal communications team, as it becomes easier and easier to circumnavigate traditional communications, there is still a role for the traditional internal communications manager. If anything, the role has become more challenging as the sheer bulk of communications continues to grow.

While at Microsoft there is no policing system, it is important to make sure that at least the key messages are getting through and are delivered loudly and effectively enough to resonate with employees. To that extent, Microsoft Web is quite closely managed in terms of the top, high level messages.

Extinction or Adaptation: The Internal Communications Challenge

The options for communicators have expanded hugely. Also 'people tend to trust their peers more than authority figures.' says the 2006 Edelman Trust Barometer,[1] putting the employee ahead of the organisation's leadership.

1 The Edelman Trust Barometer is published annually on www.edelman.com

According to Edelman, around 33 per cent of leading organisations use blogs and one-third of them are aimed at internal audiences. The advantages of new media for internal communications are evident. From internal expertise and information sharing, to openness and collaboration, from accountability and speed to engagement, communication matters.

So what are the points to watch for?

- Many heads are better than one: can a wiki handle your internal documentation? With this new collaboration tool, you can witness a new found passion for sharing and integration among staff.
- Leveraging internal skills: you can harness staff expertise for the organisation. By connecting, time is reduced dramatically.
- Beta test: get feedback to improve. Test with employees. Fine-tune applications.
- Build policies: shape policies for new media usage before the media overruns your organisation. IBM arrived at their policies with the help of employees.
- Start a conversation: replace email with a blog and start the conversation. Engage communities of practice on the intranet.

The most dangerous thing that we can do is ignore the social networking phenomenon. Social networks have fundamentally shifted the way that we communicate from verbally to horizontally on the web. But there are threats:

- Social networking sites are a threat through draining business resources, both in terms of time and network bandwidth.
- Intellectual property, network security and commercial reputation.

On Facebook, the social networking site, an employee of a large retailer hit back at comments from appreciative customers: 'Well I'm glad u all think its so great, u should try working there, does my head in.' The employee provides his name, a photo, and more details about his personal life than most people would want to know.

This may be harmless enough, but it is an example of the lack of caution that is causing companies to worry about Facebook and its like. Sometimes the incaution hits the headlines. UK retailer Argos fired an employee who was reported as telling the world on Facebook what he thought of his employer. Similarly, the company that runs the directory service 118 118 spent months trying to get Facebook to remove a page dedicated to insulting its customers.

Telling staff you do not trust them is, of course, an option. But, better surely to point out that personal rants could damage them more than you and that posting personal details puts them at serious risk from hackers. Explain to them how to increase the security settings on Facebook, and use traditional management techniques to keep them productive in the office.

How to Survive and Thrive in Internal Communications

Will there be an internal communications role in the future? Given the scale of change, the answer is not yet clear, but certain rules are worth following to ensure your future value:

1. Stay informed about how new technologies are shaping the Internet and keep up to date with the ways in which the leading edge players such as HP and IBM are experimenting.

2. Don't try and obstruct communication. Understand what people want to achieve and provide guidance and policy with standardised tool sets. You have a role as an expert and monitor.

3. Remain flexible in your current role and add value in innovative ways.

4. Introduce clear measurement and tracking systems so you can report on what is happening across the technology enabled channels.

5. Be an advocate of technology not a resistor and gain a reputation as an informed voice of sense.

19

Appreciative Inquiry

by Jonathan Priest

Appreciative Inquiry (AI) is a radically alternative approach to organisational change.

If the thinking behind traditional change management strategies can be summarised as, 'Let's look for the problems around here and fix them,' an AI approach would be, 'Let's find out what's already working around here and allow these positive experiences to influence the rest of the organisation.'

What is Appreciative Inquiry?

The assumption of AI is that there are already lots of good things going on within most organisations but, because they are ad hoc and unrecognised, they have little influence. AI brings these positive influences out into the open in the form of stories that can be shared, and whose positive influence can spread in a viral way.

The term AI is based on the interviews with members of organisations which generate these positive stories, the first step in any AI engagement. Of course it's far more subtle than simply accentuating the positive because the whole mindset changes when you turn away from a re-engineering mentality and focus on people's achievements instead.

The concept of AI was developed by two American organisation behaviour professors, David L. Cooperrider and Suresh Srivastva, his doctoral supervisor. Their paper, *Appreciative Inquiry: A Theory of Organizing and Method for Changing Social Systems,*[1] is regarded as one of the more significant innovations in action research.

---

1 *Appreciative Inquiry: A Theory of Organizing and Method for Changing Social Systems* by David L. Cooperrider and Suresh Srivastva, 1987; *Appreciative Inquiry Handbook* by David L. Cooperrider,

Action research is distinguished by the fact that researchers involve their 'subjects' as co-researchers as opposed to the more detached approach embodied in time and motion studies.

Channelling Positive Energy

The thing that caught my imagination when I first went to a presentation about AI by Organisational Consultant, Ann Radford,[2] is the simple notion she described of how one's 'energy' can be directed by negative assumptions:

If you talk about negative stuff, that's where people's energy will go.

Energy, in this sense, refers to the process of engaging and focusing your attention towards a particular subject. For example, if I describe a system, organisation or team in terms of its dysfunctional qualities, then you will immediately have a generally pessimistic and guarded approach towards that system.

On the other hand, if I describe that system in terms of its successes but suggest that there might be ways to make it work even better, you will see it in a more positive light. The way you frame your communication completely changes the context – and hence people's attitudes and expectations.

This principle also applies to corporate communication, which is why it tweaked my cord. There's more than a subtle difference between a communication that has been sanitised and one that sets out to accentuate the positive. The assumptions we make about how we work in an organisation reinforced in the way we describe them and the type of questions we ask about them help create a negative or oppressive company culture.

So before you open your mouth on any issue, consider where you want people's energy to go and think about the assumptions implied in your approach.

Diana Kaplin Whitney and Jacqueline M. Stavros, San Francisco: Berrett-Koehler Publishers, 2003.

2 Ann Radford, AI Resource Centre, www.aradford.co.uk.

THE EIGHT ASSUMPTIONS OF AI

In Sue Annis Hammond's *The Thin Book of Appreciative Inquiry*,[3] she talks of the Eight Assumptions of AI:

1. In every society or organisation, something works.
2. What we focus on becomes our reality.
3. Reality is created in the moment, and there are multiple realities.
4. The act of asking questions of an organisation or group influences the group in the same way.
5. People have more confidence and comfort to journey to the future (the unknown) when they carry forward parts of the past (the known).
6. If we carry parts of the past forward, they should be what are best about the past.
7. It is important to value differences.
8. The language we use creates our reality.

Margaret Philips specialises in organisational development and change and has used the AI approach for several years, though now she tends not to label it as such:

> *The way AI differs from change processes that are more interventionist is that the research is conducted by the participants themselves and the discoveries that emerge are their own.*
>
> *We start by putting people into pairs, with a list of questions. They interview each other for about twenty minutes and then summarise their partner's responses to the rest of the group. Great care goes into formulating the questions, which are designed to help people build up*

3 *The Thin Book of Appreciative Inquiry* by Sue Annis Hammond, (2nd edition), Oregon: Thin Book Publishing Co., 1998.

a comprehensive picture of their role within the organisation and how they have contributed to its success.

From these revelations about positive behaviours, the group chooses those they would like to prioritise for wider implementation.

The Appreciative Inquiry 4-D Cycle

The overall process used is called the AI 4-D Cycle:

Discovery: the AI approach to personal or organisational change begins with the process of looking for what is working. You *APPRECIATE* the best of your experience. This discovery is based on interviews and stories designed to discover strengths.

Dream: this is where you *ENVISION* what might be by creating bold statements that describe ideal possibilities, no holds barred.

Design: you start to turn the dream into an agreed and shared reality; you *CO-DETERMINE* what should be the ideal, establishing principles and priorities.

Destiny: you take sustained action to *INNOVATE* in order to create what will be. But of course you don't stop here; AI is an ongoing process and you will always be on the look-out for new discoveries to feed into the mill.

If all this sounds a bit happy-clappy, especially to the hard boiled cynical Brit (to which tendency I belong), I suggest you suspend your disbelief. If you are in the business of leadership and organisational change, and haven't already come into contact with AI, then you may well find it to your advantage.

As Margaret Philips and many other AI practitioners have discovered, the effects of AI are sustained because ownership starts and ends with the individuals in the group. There is never a stage at which a big idea, formulated in part by an outside consultant, is then tossed back to the team for implementation.

The ideas for change are all theirs, as are the processes for delivering them. It all happens there in the room; they own the whole process.

Appreciative Inquiry in Practice

Here are some examples of the types of change initiative for which AI is appropriate:

- team development;
- organisational culture change;
- leadership development;
- work process redesign;
- diversity initiatives;
- strategic planning initiatives;
- developing partnerships and alliances;
- career planning.

AI is essentially a facilitated change process that relies on a skilled practitioner to take the organisation/team though the process, step-by-step. There will be many cynics and disbelievers to be brought on board. Some will find it hard to recognise the good and positive behaviours that surround them. It takes a good facilitator to sustain the momentum, not to mention a certain amount of courage for a manager to expose their people to such ideas. AI is an idea from which there is no going back and it has to involve the whole workforce otherwise, what's the point? AI was born during the era when the corporate grip was being loosened and rigid hierarchies swept away. Perhaps in times or places where the future is less secure, managers will be less inclined towards more liberal strategies. But the underlying principle of directing people's energy towards the good and the positive cannot be regarded as a passing fashion.

20

How to Run a Focus Group

by Patrick Williams

If you feel you can make the case for face-to-face communication to decision makers and secure senior leadership's commitment to modelling best practices, then you're ready for your toughest and most important audience: front-line managers and supervisors.

Supervisors are busy, paid to hit their numbers and often more comfortable exercising their technical skills than managing people. They think communication is a soft skill. They don't get the business case.

Yet supervisory face-to-face communication is the first, last and most important step in the process of employee engagement, leading to customer retention and profitable growth.

So, it's not a question of *whether* or *why* front-line supervisors should be enlisted as the most important link in the employee communication process, but *how*.

Using Research to Gain Attention

All successful communication begins with one and the same act: listening. Building your face-to-face process and garnering the support of employees and front-line supervisors is no exception. In this case listening must be structured carefully, through focus groups with employees and focus groups with supervisors.

Most professional communicators will be experienced in conducting focus groups using established best practices. The reasons you want to use focus group research – rather than quantitative research – for this effort, should be obvious:

- The face-to-face, qualitative (or verbal) medium of the focus group gives a more accurate picture of the state of face-to-face communication in the organisation than a written, quantitative (or statistical) survey. The medium is the message.

- The focus group itself is a forum for speaking and listening, central skills in the face-to-face initiative; and focus groups place the communication process within the culture.

- Participating in the focus group research will inform the basis for structuring your face-to-face process, heightening support through ownership. That is, people's support for a decision or plan is directly proportional to their perceived role in helping to inform the decision or plan.

- Above all, of course, well-conducted focus group research, like all research, provides accurate information on which to base your plan for a face-to-face programme.

Facilitation and Participation

The standard approach to well-conducted focus groups is as follows:

- create separate focus groups for supervisors and employees;

- make no focus group larger than 8–12 participants;

- select participants at random, from a pool stratified by function and job level;

- hold enough focus groups until you have results that are representative of significant audience groups, and that are useful enough for planning purposes (four, 1-hour focus groups with supervisors and eight with employees over 2 days should do it, especially if everyone will participate in the subsequent training, see the results of the research and participate in the actual face-to-face communications that come out of the focus groups; and

- ideally, focus groups should be conducted by an outside professional, for reasons of objectivity and expertise.

QUESTIONS TO ASK EMPLOYEES

Remember that the purpose of focus groups is not to satisfy an insatiable curiosity but to gather accurate information on a specific or focused topic. With this in mind, consider using these questions in focus groups with employees:

- For the most important information you want at work, where do you want to get that information?
- What information do you want (and why)?
- Are you getting it?
- Do you get the information you need to do your job the best you can?
- Do you know what your job is?
- Does anyone care about your performance?
- Do you know what others are doing, so that you can work with them (in your own area, or in other departments)?
- Do you know the goals of the company?
- Do you know what you can do to help the company meet its goals?
- What do you see as your role in the communication process?
- If you were to get the sorts of information you've been telling me about, and to have the voice you're seeking, how would that change your performance?

- What would you be willing to do differently to improve communications with your supervisor?
- How would that help the company?
- How would you evaluate your supervisor's communications skills?
- How would you evaluate your own?
- What one thing would most improve communications between you and your supervisor?

QUESTIONS TO ASK SUPERVISORS

Always conduct separate focus groups for employees and supervisors and managers to gather the most honest and insightful feedback. To ensure consistency, develop questions for supervisors to complement the employee focus groups:

- For the most important information you want to communicate to your direct reports at work, where do you want to get that information?
- And what is the information you want?
- Are you getting it?
- Do you get the information you need to help your reports do their job the best they can?
- Do they know what their job is?
- Do you care about your reports – not just their performance, but their needs as people?
- Do you know what other supervisors are doing so you can work with them?
- Do you know the goals of the company? Do your reports?

- Do your reports know what they can do to help the company meet its goals? In other words, do you tailor the goals of the company to the specific work of the people in your area?
- What do you see as your role in the communications process?
- If you were to get the sorts of information you've been telling me about, how would that change the performance of your group?
- What would you be willing to do differently to improve communications as a supervisor?
- How would that help the company?
- How would you evaluate your reports' communication skills?
- How would you evaluate your own?
- What one thing would most improve communications between you and your reports?

For both types of focus groups, the two most important follow-up questions to ask are always these:

1. Could you please give me a specific example?
2. Why?/Why do you think that?

REPORTING ON FOCUS GROUP FINDINGS

Just as no act of listening is complete without follow-up, no research effort is complete without reporting the results and action plan to the participants and those they represent. Focus groups should always end – and probably always begin – with a commitment to participants where and when they will see the results of the research, along with a plan for improvement.

Typically, full research reports are presented first to the sponsors of the research, followed by a summary of results and plans to participants and a summary of results with an outline plan to the entire affected population. This latter communication can be done via a mass media vehicle such as an electronic or print publication.

It's important to have a well-structured, accurately written research report on your focus groups for many reasons:

- different audiences will be interested in different parts of the report, and at different levels of detail;
- the report can be used as reference in related communications efforts;
- above all, the research report provides the context to participants in planning.

The external focus group facilitator should write the complete report, with the internal communication sponsor tailoring the report and its parts to various audiences for various purposes.

Research report structure		
Section 1	Title	For example, Key Findings from Employee and Supervisor Focus Groups on Improving Face-to-Face Communications at X Corporation, February 9–10, 2008.
Section 2	Date and author	When the research report was written and by whom.
Section 3	Table of contents	Including a one-sentence summary of the Executive Summary, Introduction, Key Findings and Recommendations (see below).
Section 4	Executive Summary	Summarising each of the next three sections in one paragraph each.
Section 5	Introduction	Sharing the purpose of the report; purpose of the focus groups; methodology in selecting participants, number of participants, number of groups, facilitator of focus groups and credentials.
Section 6	Key Findings	These are best organised by focus group question, with summary analysis, representative quotes and minority viewpoints.
Section 7	Recommendations	Including all recommendations from focus group participants (not from the facilitator, sponsor or any other outside interest). Group these recommendations by topic, noting their recurrence or frequency. Your recommendations should always include a plan to publish the results of the research and action plan, as well as a planning session to structure your process for improving face-to-face communication.
Section 8	Transcripts	These can be verbatim or in summary form, including the focus group date, location, number and job category of participants. Remember, never identify a focus group participant by name in a transcript!

Managers and Supervisors: Communication Sessions

You may be asking yourself, 'Why am I doing all this research and planning? I know what to do. Why not just do it?' Or, 'Programmes for improving supervisory communications skills already exist. Why not just buy one and adapt it? Why reinvent the wheel?'

The whole purpose of face-to-face communications between supervisors and their reports is two-fold:

- **Tailoring**: to engage employees in helping the organisation meets its goals, by tailoring those goals to the employees' self-interest.

- **Listening**: to listen to the best ideas for systems and process improvement from the people closest to the product or customer – the employee – for accuracy of decision making.

If you yourself violate those two principles – tailoring and listening – in purchasing an off-the-shelf programme, your chances of success are diminished. Off-the-shelf programmes are never tailored to meet your needs.

As a professional communicator, you could have designed an effective plan for face-to-face communication without focus groups or employee participation. However, the crucial process of involving employees would be missing, along with the necessary support to implement the programme.

Once you have conducted your research and developed your plan, it needs to be distributed to everyone affected by it. Since that's everyone in the organisation, you may want to publish several versions of your plan, depending on the target audience:

- one for the team that will help you implement it: the whole thing;

- one for senior management, who must support you and budget the initiative: Executive summary;

- one for other managers and all supervisors;

- one for all employees: feature story in employee publication or on the intranet.

The plan has two principal values: firstly it unites a disparate organisation in support of a common goal based on shared information; and secondly it coordinates the efforts of the professionals most immediately responsible for implementing the initiative.

Many useful templates exist to conduct useful planning sessions with managers and supervisors to follow up on focus groups about improving the quality of face-to-face communication. But, in a nutshell, you want to:

- Bring a group of representative members of the organisation together, maybe 8–10 people, for a one-day planning session. These will obviously include people from communication, HR, training or organisational development, operations and representatives from the focus groups (ideally two supervisors and four employees).

- Use the research report as the basis for the day's discussions. Be sure everyone has read it in advance of the planning session.

- Lead the group through a step-by-step planning session, with interactive discussion as outlined overleaf.

PLANNING COMMUNICATION SESSIONS: A FOOLPROOF PROCESS

1. Review the research findings using a SWOT (strengths, weaknesses, opportunities, threats) analysis. Strengths might include such things as leaderships' support and opportunities might include supervisor training.

2. Identify the key issues; those consistent topics most in need of action. These might include the need for supervisors to find time to communicate, measuring communication performance, the need to listen, and so on.

3. Identify three to four initiatives that will address these issues. They might include a HR restructuring of performance reviews to reward communications skills, or hiring and promoting better communicators as supervisors. One initiative will very likely be instituting a comprehensive session to improve supervisory communications.

4. Brainstorm and select various tactics to support the face-to-face initiative. These should come right out of your research and might include such tactics as these:

    - training in speaking and listening skills;

- launching information sources to help supervisors tailor corporate-wide messages;
- redefining the role of the supervisor to reflect the need for better communications.

7. Identify key allies in the organisation. These will be the leaders you go to for support and endorsement.

8. Identify any barriers you might face, and how to overcome them.

9. Set a goal for the initiative, such as 'To improve supervisory communications'.

10. Identify your means of measurement, for example, 'as indicated by improvements in quality and productivity related to improvements in communications'.

11. Set a schedule and budget for the initiative.

12. Assign clear responsibilities and accountabilities.

AN OVERVIEW OF COMMUNICATION SESSIONS

We call the meeting at which we introduce our initiative a *communication* session rather than a *training* session for practical reasons. Although skills training will typically be a part of the session, it will be only a small part.

An important decision is *who* will go through the first sessions? Only supervisors? Supervisors and their managers? Just managers? Executives? In their own group or as part of other groups? Employees? Yes – employees! After all, communication is a two-way – or every way – process. Will it work if only one half of the participants in the dialogue – the supervisors – attend?

All arguments have their virtues. Sure, if resources like time, money and trainers are unlimited, put everyone through the communication sessions. If not, identify a few facilitators to administer the programme and put only the front-line supervisors through the session. Make it part of the follow-up to have supervisors cascade key messages and what they have learned from the session out to their reports, and in to their own managers.

To win enormous credibility, it is best if the communication sessions are attended by the executive team first. The session typically takes 4 hours (given people's busy schedules and shortening attention spans). It includes most or all of these elements, often in this order, depending on your research findings and planning:

1. a brief introduction by an executive, endorsing the initiative;
2. the agenda;
3. a review of the focus group research, stressing the business case for face-to-face and the central role of the supervisor. Some form of the research – either the entire report or a summary – should be available as pre-reading to attendees before the session;
4. a review of information tools and communications coaching support at the supervisor's disposal;
5. a review of speaking and listening skills, including meeting skills;
6. a review of the cascade model;
7. tips in time management ad making time to communicate;
8. standards of performance expectations, systems of measurement, rewards;
9. next steps and follow-up;
10. commitment to cascading the session both ways (out and in).

EVALUATING SUPERVISOR AND MANAGER COMMUNICATION PERFORMANCE

But first, a note of caution! A successful face-to-face initiative for supervisors is more than training in speaking and listening skills. The simple fact is that everyone seeks out their own self-interest, their economic interest. And what gets measured and rewarded gets done.

As important as leadership modelling is to the success of your face-to-face programme, so is your partnership with HR in incorporating measurement of supervisor communication in performance reviews, which establishes performance expectations and corresponding rewards.

Often – too often – performance review modules for supervisors include two or three questions related to communication performance, as evaluated by their manager. These usually include questions such as 'holds regular meetings' or 'is open to ideas from reports'. This won't work.

Supervisors must be evaluated – not only by their managers, but also by their employees – on such key areas of performance as these:

- My supervisor helps me understand the company's goals.
- My supervisor helps me see what I can do better to help us meet those goals.
- My supervisor helps me understand how I can work more productively with others in my area and other departments.
- My supervisor helps me define my job responsibilities.
- My supervisor listens to my ideas for improvement and follows up with me.
- My supervisor genuinely cares about my work experience.

Like that, and with some teeth in it! In other words, supervisors must be directed to excellence in communications performance as described by and structured into their performance reviews. And their direct reports must have a voice in that process. Performance reviews, in other words, are simply one more expression of effective face-to-face communication.

These standards and processes, of course, vary from organisation to organisation. The sponsors of the programme must work closely with HR in establishing standards of performance expectation and accompanying rewards. But this is an essential part of any successful programme in improving supervisory face-to-face communication performance, and must be presented at the first meeting to introduce the initiative.

IMPLEMENTING COMMUNICATION SESSIONS

The next and arguably most important step is to implement the plan with front-line supervisors. First impressions are lasting, so the (typically) 4-hour informational, training session for supervisors must be put together with great care. Planning the session will also ensure that you've put the support processes in place to heighten your chances of success.

Reviewing the best-practice template for meeting planning from Step 1: Leaders – A review of meeting skills, you'll notice that a meeting's success is often determined by what goes on before the meeting. In this case, you'll want to prepare the supervisor participants in a number of ways:

- Send them an agenda for the meeting in advance, using the steps outline provided here
- In addition, send them a letter of invitation to the session from the CEO, and copy their immediate manager.
- As pre-reading, send a summary of the research.
- Clarify the purpose of the session to help supervisors in executing one of their most important responsibilities: communicating with their reports to heighten company performance.
- Clarify their role in the session: to participate fully, to review their own communications support needs to present at the meeting, to ask their direct reports for any useful input, for example. 'What would most improve communications between them and the session participants?'.
- You may also want to heighten awareness for the importance of the entire initiative before the session by running a series of stories in your print or electronic publication, reviewing the focus group research and explaining the plan for improving face-to-face communications.

FACILITATING COMMUNICATION SESSIONS

A professional communicator or a professional trainer could lead the session. The ideal trainers or facilitators would be front-line supervisors, since they would have high credibility as peers of the participants. Each of these has obvious strengths and weaknesses.

Decide what's best for your organisation, what resources are available, and so forth. Two facilitators work better than one, so perhaps some combination of supervisor, communicator and trainer would be ideal.

Of course, your own sense of what will make for a successful session will determine room arrangement, handouts, refreshments and so forth.

This is where all your preparation and planning pay off. If you've put all the pieces in place, the session should virtually teach itself.

Appendix: Communication Session – A Typical Template

Timing (mins)	Topic	Notes
0:00–0:30	**Introduction** The introduction should be made by the CEO, or a member of the executive team. This person's job is to endorse the session and the face-to-face processes that come out of it, and to represent executive leadership's full, unqualified support for the process. Sample contents of this address include: • A personal anecdote from the executive's own career, on the importance of face-to-face communication to business success. • Endorsement of the business case for face-to-face, stating that employee engagement is the key to customer retention, which spells profitable growth. In other words, the executive must make the business case for face-to-face as a necessity, not a 'soft' skill. • Explaining that communication is everyone's responsibility. • Commitment to support the front-line supervisors: tools, rewards, modelling. • To conclude the introduction, the executive should say, 'But all successful communication begins with listening. So tell me: What would most help you be better communicators? What barriers do you face? What can we do to support you?' Here, one of the facilitators will want to capture the suggestions and questions of the participants on flip charts or white boards, organising them by topic, as structured by the agenda. The executive can address whichever issues they are comfortable with, or simply capture them. • Commitment to follow-up: the executive should conclude the introduction with a personalised statement of what they intend to do after the session to improve face-to-face communications, and get back to participants with action on their suggestions.	Although you want to be flexible with time, this section of the session should take about 30 minutes.
0:30–0:32	**Agenda** The facilitator should take a few minutes to introduce themselves and present the agenda.	
0:33–1:00	**Exercise: traits of a great communicator** During this early stage of the session and to conclude the first hour of the entire session, it's important to keep listening and to keep everybody active. Excellent questions to ask participants include: • Who is the best communicator you've ever known personally at work? • What skills or traits did that person possess? • What benefits did the person get from being a good communicator? • What benefits did this person's direct reports get? The point of this exercise, obviously, is to have the participants themselves endorse the class: To have them illustrate, in their own words and examples, that communication effectiveness directly correlates to business success. Some optional or additional questions (if you have the time), are: • What is the biggest success you were ever involved with in your business career? • What role did communication play?	The point of this exercise is to have participants make the case for the session, which includes: • That face-to-face communication is an essential strategic business practice and everyone's responsibility. • That any supervisor can improve their communication skills.

	• Was communication necessary to the success of the project? • What did the communications look like? • Would the project have succeeded without effective communication? • How can you apply those lessons to your own career?	• That you are here to help. The vital point to reinforce at this most sensitive stage in the session is that you are there to do everything in your power to heighten their chances of success as supervisors. They've demonstrated in their own words and examples that communication is necessary to success.
1:00–1:15	**Research findings** Now you must demonstrate that, in their own words and the words of their reports, there is a considerable opportunity for improvement. In other words, here you review the focus group research described in Step 2. That should gain you credibility for the session, and the initiative that comes out of it, in three ways: • The session is based on the input of the participants and their reports. • The session is tailored or customised to address the specific opportunities uncovered by the research. • The session content is also determined by the needs of participants. In other words, presenting a summary of the focus group research is in no sense an opportunity to beat up supervisors for having done a bad job. That's the approach to avoid at all costs. The purpose of presenting the research – and engaging the participants in discussion – is to gain credibility for the business case for face-to-face communication, and to assure participants that you are there to support their real interests in success.	The focus group research can be negative, and participants can be defensive. This would be a good time to ensure front-line supervisors of your awareness that they are the most important audience in the organisation: that everything depends on their ability to engage front-line employees, who touch the product or the customer. Presenting and discussing the research should take no more than 15 minutes, since they will have already read it.

1:15–1:45	**Measurement** How participants will be measured. We stressed the vital role of measurement in the previous step. A HR professional now presents the new way communication competence will be weighted and evaluated in supervisors' performance reviews. To repeat for emphasis, the purpose of measuring supervisory communication performance is to clarify their role, establish objective standards of performance, and to support them in that role through rewards. Those measurement programmes that seem to work best have several characteristics in common. They are: • Based on observable behaviour: 'My supervisor holds regular meetings'; 'My supervisor explains how my work contributes to the organisation's goals'. • Include the input of the supervisor's manager, peers and reports, to drive the supervisor's communications efforts in every direction: 360 degrees. • Link the supervisor's communications skills to business metrics: improvements in safety, or defect-free products, for example. • Are part of an ongoing process of review, rather than a yearly event with sometimes surprising results. • Exercise and questions for discussion: Here, the HR representative will want to share a sample performance evaluation with participants and ask them to evaluate where they are today.	The specifics of measurement must, of course, be determined by HR professionals, in partnership with Operations and Communication and others, within existing management guidelines and in alignment with the culture and goals of the organisation. This should bring the session to 1 hour and 45 minutes, leaving 15 minutes before the break, and inviting a brief discussion of time.
1:45–2:00	**Make time for time** The primary barrier to communications, a barrier that supervisors will identify in the focus group research and in this introductory session, will be lack of time. We've noted the reasons. The discussion will go on too long unless you control it. Just give it 15 minutes for two activities: • Gather their best practices in time management, to demonstrate to participants that their peers can do it. • Underscore the importance of (a) scheduling frequent, brief meetings; (b) incorporating communication into other activities (c) focusing on only a few key messages.	This should conclude the first half of the session.
COFFEE and TEA BREAK – Allocate a time when participants should return for the final 2 hours!		
2:00–2:45	**A list of possibilities** Of course, you'll want to have samples of these to show and pass out to participants during the session. Review the cascade process described in the Step 1, and offer brief practise in using it: • First, provide participants with a sample issue of importance facing your organisation. Show them how it would be communicated at the executive level, cascaded through your structure to their level, and how they might tailor the message to their direct reports. Do two to three of these as practise. • Also, give supervisors practise at gathering ideas and questions from their direct reports and cascading them 'in' to the right level of decision making, based on your organisation's structure. • Review the meeting planning template from the previous step. Again, give participants a relevant topic, and ask them to present the topic using the stages in the template. Try two or three of these as exercises. • Review your daily electronic newsletter, and ask representative participants to practise presenting its contents in a regularly scheduled daily 5-minute meeting. If you don't have a daily electronic news vehicle, this would be a good time to launch and introduce it.	Exercise: On the day of the workshop, choose either the most typical or the most pressing issue facing your organisation. As an exercise, present the issue and ask participants: 'Using all the tools at your disposal, which we've just reviewed, what would you say about this to your direct reports when you return to your teams after this session?'

	• Review your website and intranet page, the information available on it and how supervisors can use it. And do the same with some of the following: – employee print publication; – quarterly meetings; – annual meetings; – CEO and employee blog (if you've launched either or both, review their use here); – other feedback mechanisms – an annual Employee Opinion or Satisfaction Survey, for example; – other vehicles that support supervisors in their efforts to pass information along to employees, and take information in.	This exercise should bring you to about 2 hours and 45 minutes into your session.
02:45–03:45	**Speaking and listening skills** Many programmes in improving supervisory or managerial communications skills focus only on these two skills. My own sense is that that training should be only a small part of the session, for one simple reason: people have been speaking and listening their entire lives, and their styles can be improved only incrementally. For speaking skills, simply stress four techniques: • Eye contact – especially looking at several sets of eyes in a meeting. • Pace – speak at the rate people hear, either slower or faster than you currently speak. • Volume – speak loud enough for the person seated farthest from you to hear. • Language choice – be sure to use words that your listeners understand, especially if it's technical language. You may want to give the participants some practise here, but, in the interest of time, you may simply want to ask them to review those four points periodically when they return to work. Listening is much more difficult, and the session should spend more time on it. The reason is that supervisors in particular and everyone else in general spend more time speaking than listening, which is always a mistake. If our job as supervisors is to bring out the best in the people who report to us, the first and most important step is to listen to them. A proven way of conducting this part of the session is to ask participants to name the best listener they've ever known – inside or outside the workplace. Ask them to write down the name of that person. Then, ask them to identify the traits that made that person an effective listener. Next, ask them what *the listener* got out of the experience and what *the person listened to* got out of the experience. What you'll discover is that the traits of a good listener are these: • eye contact; • echoing for clarity; • asking probing questions; • listening without thinking ahead; • listening without judgment; • listening without distraction; • undivided attention; • letting the speaker narrate; • not offering advice unless it's specifically asked for; • follow-up. The last point is key: Please stress that the act of listening is incomplete without follow-up.	**Exercise:** A good listening exercise is to ask participants to engage someone they seldom listen to in conversation and, practising the listening skills outlined above, try to discover some information the supervisor can use for better decision making, whether it's a direct report, a peer in another department, or their own manager. Please assign and discuss. This last exercise should bring you near the end of the session. Remember best meeting practices: try to end early!

	You'll also discover that listening is a form of recognition, and a key to building trust. Simply listening to the thoughts and ideas of others validates their identity and worth, and bonds them to the listener. But the most valuable product of listening, for a supervisor, is that a supervisor is a decision maker, the best decisions are based on accurate data or input, and the employees have that information. In other words, listening helps the supervisor – more than any other skill – do what supervisors are paid to do: make decisions. No doubt many organisations have existing training programmes in listening skills. If so, you may want to adapt that training to this approach, while maintaining your strategic focus.	
03:45–04:00	**Conclusion** Please end the session by making these points: • This is what we've heard today. A skilled facilitator can briefly highlight the key learnings, and showcase once again the importance of listening in building trust. • This is not the end of anything; this is only the beginning of an important process – for the organisation, and for your career. • We are here to help you succeed in any way we can. Here are our contact numbers... • Do you have any concerns, ideas or questions that have not yet been voiced? (Capture these and assure participants of follow-up.) • We'll be contacting you to see how it's going and listen to you, and offer our support. • End with a compelling anecdote about the power of face-to-face communication from one of the session's participants. • End as you began, with listening: Ask participants to fill out the evaluation forms of this day's session. Because you'll be measured on your communication performance, and we're here to support you in your success, please do the same for us.	Just before you request participants to complete evaluation forms, ask them to take out a piece of paper, and write two things (and ask participants to please keep this paper with them every day): • What I will share with my reports and manager about this session when I return to my job. • The one thing I will do differently to improve my face-to-face communications with my reports beginning now.

21

Facilitation Skills for Line Managers

by Marc Wright

The Characteristics of Good Facilitation

When facilitating a group you are under constant scrutiny and you need to stay alert at all times. Remember that members of the group will see you as an equal, not a leader and therefore your power as a facilitator depends on your keeping the general goodwill of everyone. Here are the key characteristics of a successful facilitator:

Openness: if you do not know something – admit it and use the knowledge in the group to set you straight.

Honesty and fairness: do not appear to favour any individual, subgroup or particular point of view. Let the company line (if there is one) emerge through discussion.

Consistency in actions: if you give one person 5 minutes to waffle on, others will expect the same right.

Focus: remember the task set for the meeting: stick it on the wall and bring your people back to it whenever they wander.

Active listening: listen to what people are saying, rather than on your next question. Reflect it back to them if it is ambiguous so the whole group can be sure of the point being expressed.

Accessibility: make yourself available to everyone in the group, not just those closest to you.

Flexibility: if things take an unexpected turn think on your feet and follow the new line of inquiry if it adds to the debate.

Assertiveness: use your authority for the good of the group, for instance when a ground rule is being broken.

Enthusiasm: remain passionate about the subject and the discussion. If you stop contributing or pop out to take a call, everyone else will.

SETTING GROUND RULES

Every discussion is different but it is useful to establish a set of common ground rules such as:

- everyone arrives on time;
- all members participate;
- keep the discussion focused;
- no holding back information;
- no negative comments regarding other thoughts/opinions;
- be specific – use examples;
- value differences;
- be willing to accept the possibility that you may be wrong;
- do not take cheap shots;
- show respect for each other's opinions;
- be brief;
- no hobby horses;

- no clay pigeon shooting;
- 'Yes, and' instead of 'No, but'.

By publishing and adhering to these rules you will have a more productive and pleasurable session if people buy into the rules at the start. Then if anyone transgresses it is the power of the rules that you can enforce, rather than your own will.

KEEPING TO TIME

It is the role of the facilitator to manage the discussion on schedule. So keep an eye on the clock and remind the group where they are in the process of the task they have been set. If you are getting bogged down in an issue say something like, 'I think we have entered a swampy area here and we need to back out and walk round if we are going to get to our destination. Is everyone OK if we leave this subject and look at x?' Where an interesting issue is raised which is nothing to do with the objectives of the discussion use the 'parking' technique: 'That's fascinating, but not in the remit of this discussion. Can we park it and come back to it at another time?'

RECORDING OUTPUT

The key to recording output is to make it visible. The simple rule is: write it down, hang it up. Make notes on flip charts. When the chart is full hang it somewhere in the room where it is visible. Use lots of blu-tack and cover the walls if necessary. The human brain can remember no more than three key ideas at any one time, so give people visual props to show the development of the argument under discussion and refer back to earlier points as you go along.

Sometimes it is wise to appoint someone else in the group as the recorder, so that you can better demonstrate active listening. At the end of the session collect up the flip charts to show respect for the ideas that have been expressed.

HANDLING SIDE BAR CONVERSATIONS

If one or more members of the group start talking in side bar conversations allow a few words or remarks; they could be just explaining a point to a colleague. However, if they continue to talk in a breakaway group, address them directly and ask them to share their thoughts with the whole group. They will usually fall into line. Do not let side conversations to continue as these will undermine and corrode the group discussion.

MANAGING CONFLICT

If someone in your group starts getting aggressive or sarcastic towards another member of the group or to a particular idea, leader or section of an organisation then challenge them and immediately throw the subject open for others to comment on. 'That's an extreme view I haven't heard before. What do others think?' The important thing is to get the ball away from the destructive individual. If however there is much agreement in the room then you may want to rethink your first impressions and consider whether you have uncovered an important point that needs developing. Do not put up with personal attacks either on you or others. Use the agreed ground rules to rule the offender out of order.

HOBBY HORSES

A member of the group could use the syndicate session as a chance to air their favourite hobby horse even though it has little to do with the subject under discussion. Beware the well-tuned phrase or self-serving anecdote that has been polished many times in the repeating. Look out for other members of the group rolling their eyes or showing exasperation. When this happens, confront the speaker before they get too far into their stride: 'You have made your point very eloquently but how do you think this relates to the subject of x?'

CLAY PIGEON SHOOTING

You know when someone puts up an idea for discussion and half a dozen shoot it out of the sky with a bunch of reasons why it won't work? Well that's clay pigeon shooting and it is the biggest barrier to creating innovation in companies. The negatives that obstruct the new idea may be surmountable with a bit of thought and ingenuity. And sometimes the most implausible of ideas and blue sky thinking can lead you to unexpected breakthroughs. Make it a rule that 'no, but' interventions are banned. If you want to respond to an idea that has been launched you have to use 'yes, and' at the start of your statement. This encourages participants to build on the ideas of others until you get something that works.

PART IV
Leadership and Change Communication

22

Leadership and Engagement

by Bill Quirke

Introduction

In a world of turbulence and uncertainty, the job of leaders in setting direction and taking people with them is harder than ever. With tough markets, uncertain demand and increasing competition, leaders need to build stronger relationships with their people and establish firm foundations of trust. To perform well, organisations need their leaders to lead, and to do this, leaders require good communication.

In this day and age, change for organisations means being in a state of almost constant flux. The stakes are high, both for the business and for its leaders. In 2005, CEO departures doubled. Those organisations which are most fluid, anticipate change and adapt quickly will be the ultimate winners. In addition, organisations need their employees to engage their creativity, energy and commitment to succeed. A business can only achieve its best when everyone's energies are pointed in the same direction.

This chapter focuses on the research evidence for importance of engaging employees, the key role of leaders' communication in doing so, leadership styles, the Synopsis FAME diagnostic model, a host of communication techniques, two case studies and a summary.

Understanding is Not Enough

If companies want to engage their people, they must ensure everyone understands the key business issues – why they exist and what they are. They must also 'make the connection' to show how individual success contributes to company success. But understanding on its own is not enough. Commitment comes from a sense of engagement – the winning of hearts as well as minds.

So, When Do You Know an Employee is Engaged?

Engagement involves employees feeling a strong emotional bond to their employer, recommending it to others and committing time and effort to help the organisation succeed. Several experts have defined and demonstrated the tangible value of employee engagement.

The importance of employee engagement was the centerpiece of James Heskett's, and his colleagues' paper, 'Putting the Service-Profit Chain to Work'.[1] They demonstrated how engaged employees create loyal customers, who in turn create greater profit for the company. In 1998, the *Harvard Business Review* published a case study on the retail chain Sears, which had made employee engagement a fundamental plank of its strategy. Sears' leaders estimated that a five-point unit increase in employee attitude led to a 0.5 per cent increase in revenue growth.

In the same vein, Sirota Consulting studied 28 multinational companies during 2004 and found that the share prices of organisations with highly engaged employees rose by an average of 16 per cent, compared with an industry average of 6 per cent.

In 1999, The Gallup Organization published research that showed that engaged employees are more productive, more profitable, more customer-focused, safer and less likely to leave their employer. Similarly, Watson Wyatt found that high-commitment organisations outperformed those with low commitment by 47 per cent. They also found that organisations where employees understand organisational goals deliver 24 per cent higher shareholder returns.[2]

In a study of professional service firms, the Hay Group found that offices with engaged employees were up to 43 per cent more productive in terms of generating revenue.

'Driving Performance and Retention Through Employee Engagement', a 2004 Corporate Leadership Council survey of 50,000 employees in 59 global organisations, found that highly committed employees were 87 per cent less likely to leave their organisations and performed 20 per cent better than fellow disengaged employees.

1 *Putting the Service-Profit Chain to Work* by James Heskett, Harvard Business School, 1994.
2 Source: Watson Wyatt, 2003.

Leaders Play a Vital Role in Engaging Employees

The key to creating engagement lies with a company's leaders. It is their job to make the connection for their people and to communicate in ways that win commitment. This chapter describes how to do just that, and outlines critical lessons for success that every leader – at all levels of the business – needs to apply.

It is no longer enough simply to communicate and hope for compliance. Now the job has changed to one where leaders need to understand how to engage and motivate their people and lead their people through change, both good and bad.

A 3-year study of 40 major global companies[3] confirmed that a key driver of business profitability was the level of commitment shown by a firm's employees. The key factors behind this were the leadership skills of managers, the opportunities given to employees for personal development and the extent to which employees were empowered to discharge their responsibilities effectively.

Typically, organisations are keen to engage their people for a variety of reasons. They want to:

- unleash the talent and energy of their people;
- provide them with strong personal ownership for delivering their goals;
- give them the sense that we're all working for the same business; and
- harness their drive to achieve extraordinary things.

They also want to create a buzz around the workplace so that people enjoy coming to work, feel it's a great place to be and create a virtuous upward spiral of engagement and energy.

With all that to play for, it's no surprise that leaders are trying to raise the standard of leadership throughout their organisations. They know that

3 Source: ISR, People Management, 29 May 2003.

channelling their people's energy in the same direction will get the best from their people, both for themselves and for the organisation as a whole. The leaders' role in achieving this can at times seem fairly daunting. The list of qualities expected of leaders is seemingly endless. They have to be brave themselves and motivate and energise others, drive performance, support the organisation's vision and create positive working relationships across different parts of their organisation. Organisations with these kinds of aspirations for their leaders tend to benchmark themselves against high performing organisations, and therefore the standards they set for their leaders are continually rising. Whereas employee surveys in the past would typically ask an employee to rate their manager on giving them the information they need to do their job, now employees are more likely to be asked to rate their manager on their ability to inspire them to do their best.

Research shows that executives often suffer from an 'inspiration gap', the difference between how they rate themselves and how their employees rate them. A DTI report, 'Inspirational Leadership',[4] found that the chief executives they surveyed expected workers to show trust and respect for the people they work with and their customers. But, when 700 white collar employees were questioned, only 40 per cent thought their MD or chief executive had the same characteristics. 60 per cent said they were out of touch, and only 10 per cent said they inspired them. Employees felt that four in ten executives 'talk more than they listen', and just 50 per cent of employees felt there was a 'good buzz' at work.

So, at a time when leaders want more engagement from their employees, leaders are inadvertently disengaging their people through poor communication.

What Do People Want From a Job?

Employees have a range of needs from their jobs. They want:

- **A clear direction:** where the organisation is going and how it is doing.
- **Perspective:** an understanding of how they fit in, what they are supposed to do, how they contribute and how they will be judged.

4 Report prepared for the Department of Trade and Industry by Jill Garrett and Jonathan Frank, Caret Consulting, December 2005.

- **Relevant information:** once they have a clear idea of what their job is, where they need to go to get the information they need to do it.

- **Meaning:** excitement and a sense of purpose. What are we about, what are we interested in, are we playing a bigger game than making and selling widgets?

- **Feedback:** on their progress and performance, and the opportunity to develop.

- **Guidance on behaviour:** an idea of how they should behave, what is important to the organisation, and who they should emulate.

- **A sense of belonging:** to feel part of a community, to enjoy working with colleagues who they can talk to for information, trust and rely on.

The Corporate Leadership Council[5] emphasises the importance of gaining employees' commitment because it has an impact on two things:

1. **Their discretionary effort,** which is the extra work they put in which therefore has an impact on improved performance; and

2. **Their intention to stay or to leave**, which has an impact on retention.

The Council identified two aspects of commitment:

1. **Rational commitment**: the extent to which employees believe that following managers, teams or organisations are in their self interest – whether that's financially, professionally or in terms of their development; and

2. **Emotional commitment:** the extent to which employees value, enjoy and believe in their jobs, their managers, the teams they're part of and their organisations.

5 Source: 'Driving Employee Performance and Retention Through Engagement' Washington DC, Corporate Leadership Council.

These two sides of the coin of engagement – rational and emotional – are reflected in the global survey company, ISR's, useful description of the three components of employee engagement:

1. **How employees feel:** employees' sense of belonging to, and pride in the company.

2. **What employees understand:** the evaluation of the company's goals and values.

3. **How employees act:** the willingness to go the extra mile for the company and preparedness to commit to the future.

The vital component is action. However, poor internal communication often undermines employee engagement, by failing to help employees feel, think and do. Employees may not:

- **feel** that they truly belong to the organisation, are valued by it, or feel pride in the company they work for;

- **understand** what the company is trying to do, or why it is trying to do it. Kaplan and Norton (creators of the 'Balanced Scorecard') discovered from their research that on average, 95 per cent of employees are unaware of, or do not understand, the organisation's strategy;[6] and

- **know** how the overall strategy relates to their daily job, what precisely they're supposed to do to contribute, and how, concretely, they can help.

There is a clear link between poor leadership communication and low employee engagement. Engagement is damaged by a leader's shortcomings in communicating, when they:

- lack clarity about strategy, and a clear focus about direction;

- do not translate corporate rhetoric into concrete specifics, so their communication sounds like 'motherhood and apple pie';

6 Source: *Harvard Business Review*, October 2005.

- are inconsistent in their messages, signalling a lack of alignment with fellow leaders, and a lack of certainty which only encourages employees to wait a little longer for a clearer picture to emerge;
- tend to communicate in a way that is rational rather than emotional, and fail to paint the bigger picture. They use management speak and an impersonal style, and cannot bring a vision to life or generate enthusiasm in themselves or others;
- are reluctant to give employees the freedom to ask tough questions or to answer those questions without dodging the issues. This signals a lack of respect for employees and undermines the credibility of leaders. Employees take from this that they are not valued or listened to, which undermines their identification with, and pride in, the organisation; and
- Do not walk the talk. There is an obvious disconnect between the espoused values of the organisation and the behaviour of its leaders. Employees then listen less to what leaders say, and instead observe how they behave.

Why Leadership Communication is Important

Leadership guru Warren Bennis identifies the central role of communication for leaders as follows:

> *Communication creates meaning for people. Or should. It's the only way any group, small or large, can become aligned behind the overarching goals of an organization.*

Line managers and leaders have a clear influence on employee attitudes and behaviours.

Survey after survey reports that employees feel the most important – and preferred channel for communication – is their line manager. However, this shifts depending on the kind of information which is being communicated. For example, where significant structural changes that have an impact on people's jobs are concerned, employees often want to hear it from the most senior manager available, on the principle of getting it straight from the horse's mouth.

Ironically, many shortcomings of leaders' communication described above are inadvertent. The disengagement of employees can be the result of leaders playing to what they see as their own communication strengths, and using the winning ways which have helped them succeed so far. Unfortunately, many of these ways were developed in organisations that did not require high levels of employee engagement, and during less complex and demanding times. What has helped the leaders succeed so far may not be what will help them succeed in the future.

LEADERSHIP STYLES

Part of the problem is that there is no one ideal model of a leader. There are different types of leaders who are good in different situations. They each have different communication styles, communication strengths and, inevitably, communication weaknesses. Different people react differently to different leaders. For example, the charismatic chief executive, who passionately paints the company vision that inspires the sales and marketing teams, can seem a little short on substance and specifics to the engineers in the manufacturing division. A good first step for leaders is to understand what kind of leader they are, and what kind of leader they need to be in future.

In any leader's role there are two aspects: the task dimension of the role – setting a clear direction and helping employees understand their role and what their efforts mean to the organisation; and the relationship side of the role – communicating with people in the way that builds constructive relationships and makes them feel valued and respected.

Authors of *Primal Leadership*, Goleman, Boyatzis and McKee,[7] identify six styles of leadership based on research data from 3,871 executives. These six distinct styles are very helpful in identifying leaders' communication preferences and styles, as outlined in Table 22.1.

Each of these leadership styles lends itself to one element of the leadership communication job. Some lean more toward the task side, and the rational; others emphasise the relationship side, and the emotional. The problem is that leaders tend towards one dominant style, and either find it hard to adopt other communication styles, or do not realise that they are supposed to do so.

7 http://www.businesslistening.com/primal-leadership.php#leadership-styles.

Table 22.1 Overview of leadership styles

Leadership style	Description
Visionary	Leadership that inspires people by focusing on long-term goals. An effective visionary leader understands the values held by the individuals within the organisation, and can explain their overall goals for the organisation in a way that wins support.
Coaching	Leadership that delegates responsibility for elements of the organisation's strategy. An effective coaching leader listens one-on-one to employees, establishes rapport and trust, and helps employees identify how their performance contributes and where to find the resources they need.
Affiliative	Leadership that creates a warm, people-focused working atmosphere. An affiliative leader listens to discover employees' emotional needs, and how to accommodate those needs in the workplace.
Democratic	Leadership that involves everyone in the group, listening to everyone's opinions before proceeding.
Pacesetting	Leadership that leads from the front, sets ambitious goals and continually drives progress.
Commanding	Leadership that issues instructions without asking for input, and says 'do it because I say so'.

THE PROS AND CONS OF DIFFERENT LEADERSHIP STYLES: FINDING THE RIGHT BALANCE

Visionary, Pacesetting and Commanding leadership styles tend to be used by leaders who are task focused, high energy and 'make it happen'. Their tendency can be to 'shoot from the hip', and get messages out, rather than think them through. The temptation among such leaders can be to communicate *at,* rather than *with,* their people. Such leaders have usually succeeded in the past by being directive and task focused. The communication skills they have developed are usually more suited to telling than to asking and engaging.

The skills needed to engage and create conversation are different from those required to make a strong PowerPoint presentation. Leaders who believe they can simply apply their existing communication skills to a different communication job usually do not get the results they hope for. A typical pitfall is to focus only on what messages they want to tell employees, rather than on understanding how employees may interpret and decode their communication. Without a good understanding of their different audiences, and without a good feedback channel, such leaders are not genuinely communicating, just broadcasting.

As a leader, if you are trying to engage your people, adopting a campaigning approach will seem like a superficial 'flavour of the month', which will hurt rather than help your credibility. People need to feel that their views are understood, and they are reflected back in any communication. It is important for the leadership team to understand their people's concerns and likely reactions, before they start communicating.

More people-focused leadership styles such as Coaching and Affiliative, outlined in Table 22.1, create a warm, people-focused working atmosphere. An affiliative leader listens to employees closely, with the danger of focusing more on the emotional climate and ignoring the work itself. It is therefore all about finding the right balance.

Democratic leaders tend to listen to everyone's opinions and gather information. The danger for them is being seen as 'dithering', such as when meetings drag on for weeks without making tangible progress.

In summary, there is no one best style of leadership. The directive approach, for instance, is useful in crises or when a leader must manage a poor performer, but overuse stifles initiative and innovation. The affiliative approach is appropriate in certain high-stress situations or when employees are beset by personal crises. Pacesetting can get results in the short term, but it's demoralising to employees and exhausting for everyone over the long haul.

The most effective leaders are adept at all six leadership styles and use each when appropriate. Typically, however, leaders default to the styles they are most comfortable using. Leaders who are motivated mainly by achievement, for example, tend to favour pacesetting in low-pressure situations, but become directive when the pressure mounts.

WHAT DOES THIS MEAN FOR LEADERSHIP TEAMS?

In *Leadership Run Amok, The Destructive Potential of Achievers*,[8] authors Scott W Spreier, Mary H Fontaine and Ruth L Malby warn of the impact of overachievers, who, they say:

> *Tend to command and coerce, rather than coach and collaborate … take frequent shortcuts and forget to communicate crucial information,*

8 *Leadership Run Amok, The Destructive Potential of Achievers* by Scott W Spreier, Mary H Fontaine and Ruth L Malby, *Harvard Business Review*, Reprint No R0606D.

and may be oblivious to the concerns of others. Too intense a focus on achievement can demolish trust and undermine morale, measurably reducing workplace productivity and eroding confidence in management both inside and outside the corporation.

Leadership teams usually comprise different functional specialists who have developed different leadership styles. So it is no surprise that they focus on different elements of communication with different priorities. These differences in style can reinforce the danger of leaders not being seen to 'sing from the same song sheet'.

Pacesetting leaders, for example, may not spend enough time agreeing precisely what they are saying and how they are going to say it, or thinking through the possible negative perceptions of what's proposed, and agreeing their responses. Lack of preparation and discussion drives inconsistency, and inconsistency drives conspiracy theorists who look for differences in tone, interpretation and emphasis between the leaders that they then take to be signals of discord. A communication about change, for example, is then undermined when the top team is not seen to be united behind the proposals.

BUILDING TRUST IN LEADERSHIP

At a time when trust is declining in leadership, leaders are casting around to find out why. Trust is declining in a number of institutions – religion, government, the media – and employees are equally sceptical about their leadership.

Only 51 per cent of employees have trust and confidence in the senior management of their companies[9] and only 44 per cent of employees believe senior leaders are trying to 'do their best' for their employees.

There may be a number of different reasons why employees do not trust their leadership, such as:

- **Invisibility:** they don't see them, and so don't have a sense of what they're like.

- **Lack of respect:** they suspect their competence – they seem like good people but not capable people.

9 Source: Watson Wyatt, 2003.

- **Body language:** they're not approachable or human.

- **Lack of credence:** they're not credible – they've got a strategy which doesn't seem to hold water, and no clear rationale for having arrived at it.

Employees seem to look for five things if they are to trust their leaders. To be trusted, leaders must be seen to be:

- **Competent:** judged to know what needs to be done for the company to succeed, and felt to be capable of leading the organisation effectively in the right direction.

- **Open and honest:** telling the truth and feeding back the 'whole story', not just good news.

- **Concerned for employees:** showing they understand why employees feel as they do, and demonstrating empathy.

- **Reliable:** making sure that commitments they make are followed through and that 'words and figures' match.

- **'In the same boat':** perceived to share a common identity, experience and commitment with employees.

However, there are a number of things leaders do unwittingly which do not help them build trust, such as:

- **Leaders leak:** what they are like inside leaks out of them, usually at unguarded moments. Any difference between what they espouse and what they actually believe quickly becomes apparent.

- **Leaders are inconsistent:** they emerge from meetings at which they've agreed a collective line and then communicate a different version, often more favourable to themselves.

- **Leaders react under stress:** and say something which is completely uncharacteristic – which is then taken to reveal their personality. Employees have an 'aha' moment – they see the mask of their leaders slip, and feel they have detected the true person beneath.

THE IMPACT LACK OF TRUST IN LEADERSHIP HAS ON EMPLOYEES

There are other brakes which leaders unwittingly put on their own efforts. While one foot is pumping the accelerator of engagement, the other is firmly planted on the brake of poor communication.

As outlined earlier, where employees perceive there is a lack of urgency, and where they cannot quickly perceive how they can help, they tend to disregard increasingly strident urgings from the boardroom to change and change quickly. Where they do not understand how the strategy was arrived at, where the strategy would take them and how they can contribute to it, employees are slow to put their hand to the plough. Where the strategy is simply not credible, where it is an apparent repeat of something already tried some years ago and where the leaders themselves are not seen as credible enough to achieve it, employees slow down again. Finally, where the destination is unclear, it is unlikely to be motivating, and so employees feel neither willing nor able to head in the recommended direction.

WHAT MAKES A LEADER A GOOD COMMUNICATOR?

It is useful to be able to give leaders an understanding of the different components of the job they have to do as communicators. Usually, each leader has a leadership role model in their head – a leader they admire, who is effective and is a great communicator. However, each of these leadership role models can be quite different.

While leaders talk to each other around the boardroom table about the need to communicate, they usually mean quite different things depending on their personality, their character and their values.

A useful exercise is to ask leaders to identify another leader who they feel is an effective communicator. The leader they choose can be from any walk of life – political, sports, military, religious – living or dead, known by all or simply someone they've worked with during their career.

We often find that people will pick leaders such as Winston Churchill, Bill Clinton, Jesus Christ, Nelson Mandela, Colin Powell, Akio Morita, Lee Kwan Yew or even Mother Teresa.

When asked why their chosen leader is effective as a communicator, they come up with another wide range of answers:

- **Winston Churchill:** because of his ability to articulate the feelings and determination of a nation and express them compellingly.
- **Nelson Mandela:** because of his strong sense of values, being a model of compassion and understanding, and embodying reconciliation within South Africa.
- **Bill Clinton:** because of his charm and his ability to make people feel like they're the only one in the room he's talking to.

What's useful about this exercise is that it shows that leaders incline towards a favourite way of communicating, and tend to neglect or downplay other styles. Each of the leaders they choose tends to reflect the chooser's own priorities and values. For example:

- **Margaret Thatcher:** someone with a strong task focus and a desire to set strong direction may choose this memorable Tory leader.
- **Martin Luther King:** someone believing in the importance of articulating the mission of the organisation in an emotional and compelling way may pick this African-American visionary.
- **Nelson Mandela:** a person who believes in the importance of 'walking the talk' and the importance of demonstrating their values may pick Mr Mandela.
- **Bill Clinton:** someone who believes it is important to get on the same wavelength as people, to relate to them empathetically, and to 'feel their pain' may choose this past US President.

These are four *very* different types of leaders, with different characteristic strengths.

TASK VERSUS RELATIONSHIP FOCUS

A senior manager's selection of a leader who they believe is an effective communicator is usually a clue to whether their own leadership style leans towards the task side or the relationship side. Task and relationship in leadership are like the two pedals of a bicycle, you need to be able to push on both. However, senior managers tend to lean more heavily on one or the other.

Task-focused leaders tend to be good at providing focus, setting direction, giving a clear sense of mission and direction and setting a challenge for the organisation to fulfil. They may be less good at articulating their vision in emotional and compelling ways that bring their people with them. They may not be able to see things from their employees' point of view, nor be able to engage with them.

Conversely, some senior managers have a strong sense of values and are deeply empathetic with their employees – but they don't put enough time and effort into clarifying what the direction is, what the specific and concrete examples of what employees could do are, and they do not feedback on progress and how well targets are being achieved.

Effective leadership means balancing the 'hard task' and 'soft relationship' aspects of communication. The task side includes helping employees understand their role and what their efforts mean to the organisation and its stakeholders. The relationship side involves communicating with people in ways that build constructive relationships and make them feel valued and respected.

Making leaders more effective communicators means acknowledging that they have been successful by using the skills they have developed to date – it requires building on those skills, and understanding those areas where they are not yet as strong as they need to be. Senior managers in organisations have often been promoted for their 'task' side – they have high drive, clear vision of where they want to go and can deliver results. However, in the past they may not have had to exercise their 'relationship' side – the ability to empathise, engage and articulate.

This is reflected in the drive with which organisations pursue employee engagement. Task-focused organisations often find themselves aspiring to relationship-based engagement – but pursuing it in a task-focused way, adopting detailed step-by-step processes optimistically intended to create engagement with their people. A clear case of stamping on the brake and wondering why we're not going any faster.

Part of the problem may be taking a purely rational approach to developing strategy. Research by strategy consultants Cognosis suggests that managers are crying out for strategies that engage both heart and head. Only a quarter of the 1,600 managers surveyed said that they found their organisation's strategy exciting. Half didn't feel sufficiently involved, and did not believe that their opinions were listened to. According to the research, there is a strong correlation between emotional and rational 'buy-in' – and both are needed to succeed. Stronger engagement and commitment can only be achieved where employees are persuaded emotionally as well as rationally, that a planned strategy makes sense, is credible and doable. The Cognosis survey also revealed that 10 per cent of managers were 'super-engaged'. Intellectually they liked the rational rigour of their company's thinking, and were committed to achieving clearly understandable goals, but emotionally, they also felt their organisation had a common purpose and that leaders were united round it.

The Corporate Leadership Council survey mentioned above found that emotional engagement was four times more valuable than rational factors in driving employees' effort. The vital combination of rational and emotional is reflected in the words of Professor Henry Mintzberg of McGill University in his co-authored work *Strategy Bites Back*:[10]

> *Strategy doesn't only have to position, it has to inspire. So an uninspiring strategy is really no strategy at all.*

Thus, many high performing organisations are impatient to drive up engagement by having leaders who are inspiring. However, few are helping their leaders connect with their people in any way which is inspirational.

THE FAME MODEL

Research done by Synopsis showed that effective leaders – in business or otherwise – excel in four key areas of communication. This enables them to engage their people in both good times and bad, throughout stable times and turbulent times.

These four areas are summarised in Table 22.2.

For successful communication, leaders need to understand that all four aspects of communication are important, at different stages and times. They

10 *Strategy Bites Back* by Professor Henry Mintzberg, New Jersey: Prentice Hall, 2004.

Table 22.2 The Synopsis FAME model

Acronym	Summary
Focus	Leaders must ensure that everyone understands both the external and internal issues facing the organisation and what employees must do to contribute to company success.
Articulate	Leaders must be able to paint a picture of where the company is headed.
Model	Effective leaders are champions of the values they stand for. They also understand the power of informal communication.
Engage	Engaging leaders are good at listening, facilitation, asking effective questions and handling difficulty. They are described as being approachable, enthusiastic and interested.

also need to be able to build on their existing strengths and to adopt new styles so they can adapt their communication to different audiences at different times. This section expands on each of the four FAME areas of leadership communication:

Focus

The chief aim of the leaders' communications is to ensure that everyone understands both the external and internal issues facing the organisation and what each must do to contribute to the organisation's success. Mercer Human Resource Consulting discovered in a study in 2000 that when senior managers do not communicate a clear vision for the future, employees are more likely to consider leaving the organisation. Employees often complain about the lack of connection between initiatives and the inconsistency of leaders' messages. Leaders therefore have to communicate a clear focus on business issues, set a few clear priorities, which they repeat and reinforce consistently, and identify clearly what they want employees to do.

The 2004 Corporate Leadership Council survey identified the top levers for driving employee effort as the employee's understanding of the connection between their work and the organisation's strategy and the importance of the employee's job to the organisation's success. Employee research consistently shows that less than 50 per cent of employees know where their companies are going or what they are trying to achieve. This indicates that organisations are not telling their people the thing that would most increase employees' efforts. The same research also shows that employees are convinced that they themselves are doing a great job. They do not know where the business is going but they are all too confident that they are helping it get there.

This break in the 'line of sight' between a company's strategy and what individuals at the sharp end are expected to do is a common failure of leadership focus. Giving people clarity about what is expected of them, and how their efforts relate to organisational goals, has been shown[11] to have the strongest link to productivity.

Articulate

Great leaders can turn a vision into words succinctly. They paint a picture of what they want to achieve, turning 'management-speak' into plain language. They make messages memorable and ensure that everything they say fits together into an overall picture. Leaders may want to engage employees' emotional commitment but they tend to appeal for it in dry, intellectual language. Leaders have to be able to turn the vision into an elevator speech, and paint a picture in a more emotional language.

Effective leaders invest time in planning how they will convey their message. Leaders such as Martin Luther King and Winston Churchill painted their 'bigger picture' messages in emotional, engaging language, which they took the time to prepare and craft.

Model

Effective leaders are champions of the values they stand for. They lead by example, and model the right behaviour for others. If leaders want to inspire and motivate their people then how they behave and what they signal are often the most powerful parts of their communication. Commitment goes beyond simply agreeing and repeating messages, or going out on the road to meet people. Senior management need to walk the talk, and be committed, because lack of commitment is transparent and readily detected.

Nelson Mandela is not famous for his words, but for his actions. When South Africa hosted the Rugby World Cup in 1995, he walked out on the field wearing the South African rugby shirt. This was a symbolic action, signalling reconciliation across racial divides, in what Mandela saw as the creation of

---

11 *Leadership Run Amok, The Destructive Potential of Achievers* by Scott W Spreier, Mary H Fontaine and Ruth L Malby, *Harvard Business Review*, Reprint No R0606D.

'the rainbow nation'. Since 70 per cent of communication in organisations is informal, and employees consistently report that they get 70 per cent of their information via the grapevine, it's important to understand the impact of leaders' *informal* communication.

Leaders are influential, and have greater impact on their people when they are communicating informally – whether around the water cooler, in the bar or in a car on the way to a meeting. Employees pay far more attention to leaders when they are apparently 'off duty' than when they are standing on stage in a formal setting.

As mentioned earlier, it is important for leaders to understand that 'leaders leak'. What leaders truly believe, and how they really think 'leaks out' of them, unbeknownst to them, as they talk informally in off duty moments. So it is that employees become experienced 'Kremlin watchers', looking at the behaviour of their leaders rather than just what they say. Informal communication is the most powerful, but it is also the most likely to lead to misunderstanding.

Even where leaders believe that it is formal communication events that have the greatest impact, they typically do not prepare for them. Leaders fly to vital management conferences only finalising their slides on the plane. They do not allow rehearsal time with each other, and do not ensure that each individual leader is singing from the same song sheet, and harmonising with their colleagues. Such a lack of alignment and consistency may be survivable in a formal setting, but is deeply damaging when it comes to informal communication.

Inconsistencies in messages between leaders are almost inevitable. Leaders tend to agree on generalities, but disagree on specifics, since they do not take the time to dig further down into the issues on which they disagree. So their informal chats inevitably signal differing views. Employees perceive there is a gap between different leaders and then watch more carefully to see how these disagreements will be resolved. This costs an organisation time. Where strategy has to be translated into actions as quickly as possible, and there's urgent need for action, unprepared communication and lack of alignment between leaders act as brakes. Employees will slow down rather than speed up because they get mixed signals, and so await a clearer signal of direction before proceeding.

Engage

Bill Clinton described leadership as, 'The art of getting others to do something you want done because they want to do it.' Effective leaders engage people by providing context and making the connections between their agenda and the individual's agenda. They are good at listening, facilitation, asking effective questions and handling difficulty. Increasing employee engagement means understanding what engages people. Employees want to work for an organisation that is succeeding and is going somewhere. They feel it is fun to work with interesting people in an organisation fulfilling a bigger purpose. However, how leaders engage with them is a vital part of whether they feel valued, involved and heard.

Employees report that what engages them is the chance to talk and the feeling they are listened to. They want to feel safe to speak, to have their say and to be able to exchange ideas with their leaders. Leaders who are thought to be engaging are described as being approachable, enthusiastic and interested. They ask questions and listen carefully to the answers. They can get on the same wavelength as the people they're talking to, they can ask thoughtful questions to explore issues and they understand the concerns that their people express.

FOCUS AREAS FOR LEADERS

As a consultant, working with leaders to improve how they engage their people has provided some useful lessons. One key lesson is where leaders focus. Typically, task-focused leaders have a very clear idea of what they want to achieve but they tend to be less good at understanding what their various stakeholders want. In one organisation, for example, leaders had the clear aim of improving the margins of their business. Their intended message to their employees was clear – we have to compete more effectively, reduce our cost base and get our margins up to provide greater shareholder return.

Asked to identify what was the focus of their communication, leaders looked at a few simple questions:

- Q1. What's the outcome I want in this situation?
- Q2. Where are my people now and how do they regard the current situation?

These are deceptively simple questions, and it is surprising how often leaders find them difficult. Take the first one. Leaders tend to be very clear about what they want to say to their people, for example 'reduce cost, improve margins and increase shareholder value'. They tend to be less good at identifying what communication is supposed to achieve. What should be the change in attitudes and behaviour as a result of successful communication, and how would they recognise success if they saw it? What this often reveals is that leaders focus on the message they want to give, rather than the change they're trying to make.

Leaders should focus on the outcome by asking themselves the question, 'What do I want my people to do differently, how do I want them to behave and what is my picture of success?' Grappling with these questions, leaders often come up with abstract terms with few specifics, such as, 'I want people to buy-in to the change,' or, 'I want people to feel energised and empowered.' The point is not that these answers are wrong, but they're not specific. How would you know whether your people bought in? Would it be enough for them to nod and smile pleasantly in agreement or do you want them to behave differently with customers?

WHERE ARE YOUR PEOPLE NOW?

It is extraordinary how often the leaders of initiatives are convinced that employees are waiting with baited breath to hear more about their programme. Because something is so important to its owner, it's easy for them to overestimate the enthusiasm of employees elsewhere. Enthusiastic project owners tend to project their enthusiasm on to others. A typical response to the question, 'How do your employees regard this initiative?' is 'fantastic, very positive, very keen, very enthusiastic' and so on.

In one organisation, the global IT function was about to launch a major change programme across the organisation. Asked about how employees might regard this new initiative, they were initially positive and enthusiastic. Questioned a little further, they began to become less certain and less enthusiastic. Why were employees so positive? How did they regard the last IT initiative, what was their perception of the global IT function as a whole and how did they regard the level of service that the function provided? Rapidly, the assessment of employees' views shifted. The last IT programme was widely perceived as being a disaster. Why was that? – 'Because it was a disaster,' said the IT team.

Senior managers need to take a slightly more sceptical view of their own initiatives, and to identify employee attitudes as they are, rather than as they wish them to be. This is because if you're trying to get on the same wavelength as people, and trying to connect your agenda to theirs, it helps if you have a realistic picture of their views.

However, leaders can often view this as 'being negative' and can be unwilling to acknowledge and confront employee attitudes that they regard as negative, ill-informed and uncooperative.

This may explain why so much communication adopts a relentlessly cheerleading tone, and focuses on the positive – an approach that is reflected in employee attitude surveys which say that management too often tell employees the good news, but don't tell them the bad. This in turn undermines the credibility of the leadership, the trust of employees in them and the levels of engagement in the organisation.

ARTICULATING MEMORABLE MESSAGES

Senior managers or project owners can find it difficult to articulate their message. This is often because they:

- do not put themselves in the audiences' shoes and see things from their viewpoint;
- express things in 'management-speak', using jargon which is meaningful only to management;
- favour complexity over simplicity and make things complicated not simple; and/or
- create communication to be read not said.

Articulating is about the leader's ability to put things into clear pictures, memorable phrases and compelling words. Articulate means being able to drive home your point by using language expressively. Leaders who are seen as great communicators such as Winston Churchill and Martin Luther King are often praised for the masterly way in which they use language. People remember Churchill's rousing call to action, 'We shall fight on the beaches' and they remember Martin Luther King sharing, 'I have a dream.'

Both of these leaders were trained in oratory, and had studied how to write their speeches and how to use their powers of speech to create a powerful impact upon their audience. That they could connect so closely with their audience testifies to their ability to express so precisely the thoughts, feelings and aspirations of their people. Their expressiveness, their spontaneity and their impact was helped, not hindered, by the preparation and forethought they put into their words.

It is noticeable that the quotes of political and religious leaders can be recalled and repeated. It is much harder to recall the sayings of business leaders.

The power of good storytelling

Politicians understand the impact of the cadences of their words, the construction of their sentences and the style of their delivery. They take advantage of the fact that, for most of us, the rules of communication are based on an oral tradition – on words said rather than read. Literacy in the west is a relatively new phenomenon whereas the oral tradition of storytelling is thousands of years old. Formal communication depends on the rules of written language, whereas informal communication is based on conversations using the rules of an oral tradition – the rules of storytelling, joke telling and anecdote swapping.

This may explain why so few employees can remember and repeat their business's strategy, but they can repeat a joke they have heard. This may also explain why the grapevine is such as powerful means of communication; because it relies on rules of communication we're all so familiar and comfortable with – the rules for telling and repeating stories. Seventy per cent of the communication within organisations is informal, whether that is networking or gossiping. Formal management-speak communicated occasionally via formal communication channels cannot match the power and influence of day-to-day informal storytelling.

Three is a magical number

What is remembered gets repeated. For example, the story of Goldilocks and the three bears is familiar and repeatable for a number of reasons. There are three bears, which is easy to remember. Each time Goldilocks tries something – a chair, a bed, food – the first is too this, the second is too that and the third is always just right. Imagine the confusion had there been six bears, and not just three bowls of porridge, but a buffet of food, each kind of which had to be remembered and repeated.

In the stories I told our three daughters, there were 'Three Billy Goats Gruff'. In fairy stories, magic rings provided three wishes, there were three sons who competed for the hand of the fair princess, and three wise men. Three is a magic number. It features strongly in oral tradition, perhaps because people can remember three to five things before they start losing detail. This may be the reason why although Snow White met seven dwarfs it is so hard to remember all their names. Three is the magic number in speaking too. There are often three words – 'liberté, égalité and fraternité'. There's Tony Blair saying the most important issue is 'education, education, education'. The most important issue in buying property is 'location, location, location'.

There's the good, the bad and the ugly; lock, stock and barrel; hook, line and sinker. Politicians always seem to answer questions in three ways. Listen to any bulletin and you'll hear spokespeople giving their lists of three, 'We will protect American lives, restore law and order and prevent chaos.' There's an important lesson here for leaders. Use rules of communication which are already established, rather than trying to overlay less successful rules. Your employees will not remember your PowerPoint slides, but they will remember your jokes. They will remember your strategy if it is structured in a way that helps it to be more memorable.

Remember, 70 per cent of internal communication is informal conversation in the corridor or around the water cooler, using the rules of oral communication. If you can craft your communication to follow the same rules, your messages will be remembered. What gets remembered gets repeated, and what gets repeated gets reinforced. The more formal the communication, the less likely it is to be repeated. Managers often feel uncomfortable 'communicating' with their people because the language they're asked to use is so unnatural and artificial. Leadership communication that is written in 'management-speak', as bullet points on a PowerPoint slide, stands less chance of being translated into day-to-day action.

LEADERSHIP SECRETS

The secret to effective leadership communication is to make it simple, memorable and repeatable. As a first step this means avoiding complex words, and exploiting words that already work.

Alliteration

Before the advent of widespread literacy, techniques were used by people passing information to each other to ensure its memorability and repeatability. One of these techniques, for example, was the use of alliteration – using words that begin with the same letter, or the same sound. We have phrases in our language such as short and sweet, heaven and hell, chalk and cheese, cheap and cheerful, which owe their use to their alliteration.

News media are often very good at simplifying a story, and expressing it with alliteration so that it is remembered and repeated. Affluent ladies who were opting to pay for caesarean delivery of their babies, rather than waiting for natural labour, were labelled as 'too posh to push'. Alliteration is an aid to memory developed by oral tradition. Another is adopting phrases that already exist. For example, in one recent news story, controversy had arisen about four-wheel drive vehicles being used by affluent drivers who claim they are for off-road use, but only use it to go to the supermarket. The press started referring to these as 'toff roaders'.

Metaphors

Another aid is metaphor. People think in pictures, and a picture is worth a thousand words. If a chief executive exhorts his people to, 'Increase operational efficiency, raise the quality of product development, and focus on higher quality products and services,' his message is more likely to be remembered and repeated if he summarises it by saying we want to be a 'Ferrari, not a Ford'. We use metaphors in everyday conversation. We say things like 'we won't even get to first base', we will 'leave no stone unturned'. We complain 'the baby has been thrown out with the bathwater'. One director talking about the future of his industry said, 'The traditional business model is sinking like the *Titanic*, and it's the small boats that will survive in the future.' Such pictures have high impact and are memorable.

A manager of a risk management department was frustrated at trying to engage other departments in the vital but apparently boring process of risk identification and logging. Each time they contacted colleagues for meetings to discuss the 'Risk Evaluation Process' (REP) they couldn't get the time of day, as colleagues remembered they had to be elsewhere to do something much more important. In a burst of frustration, the risk manager said that the way they were currently operating was, 'Like a fleet sailing into troubled waters without a minesweeper – at some point they were going to hit the mine field.' Most of his colleagues didn't understand what the REP process was, but they did understand what a minefield was. Communicating in this more vivid way got them greater engagement and greater cooperation.

Unions' very effective communication is often due to their very good use of metaphors. Whereas management talk about 'optimising processes and rightsizing resources' in an apparently abstract and bloodless language that may conceal more suspect motives, unions fight back with vivid metaphors in protest. Plans are, they say 'the thin end of the wedge'; this is simply 'death by a thousand cuts'. One union recommended its members reject management's proposals by saying that 'this deal has more strings than the London Philharmonic'. Few of their members understood the details of the deal, but they repeated the sound bite knowingly. In the race for employees' hearts and minds, the metaphor beat the management-speak.

Metaphors are, of course, a two-edged sword. They can work for you or against you. One chief executive described to his senior managers the journey they had embarked upon. He was keen to get them engaged, and reluctant to be side-tracked by long debates about detailed issues of implementation, which could only become clearer once they got started, and at a later date. Unfortunately, he described the journey in terms of being on a boat sailing troubled waters. What he wanted to say was that some details would only become clear as we got closer to them. He could have said that we were sailing towards the horizon and details would emerge as we got closer. Instead he described the uncertainty as 'sailing in fog', which, his senior managers muttered was like him – thick and wet. When he declared, 'We're all in the same boat,' the rejoinder came, 'Yes, and it's the *Titanic*'.

The elevator speech

A number of these oral techniques come together in having leaders summarise their strategy in an 'elevator speech'. The elevator speech is a brief encapsulation of an idea, concept or argument. It is named after the challenge of stepping into the elevator, and being asked by a colleague about something you are working on and being able to give them the short version in the 30 seconds it takes for the elevator to travel between floors.

The more conversational you can make the summary, the more likely it is to be remembered and repeated. However, to encapsulate everything in 30 seconds, requires some clear structure.

Jokes

Stories and jokes have a clear structure. They have to, if the storyteller is to remember them, and the listener is to be able to repeat them. For example, many jokes begin, 'An Englishman, Irishman and a Scotsman walk into a bar.' The Englishman goes first and does something, the Scotsman follows with his version, and then the Irishman does something different and brilliantly clever. In telling the joke, the teller knows that there are three cycles he has to remember (remember, the magical number is three!). He knows there is a set up, three cycles and a punch-line. That gives the teller a clear structure and a roadmap of the story. It helps organise the ideas, not omit anything and put the emphasis on the punchline.

Similarly, for the listener there are clear signals about what to expect. There's a clear structure, there's a simple sequence and there's a clear takeaway – the punchline. Importantly, structure helps both the teller remember what to tell and the listener what to expect and what to repeat in turn.

THE 30-SECOND EXERCISE

So, when leaders are asked to write an elevator speech, and then follow a clear structure, it must be written to be said, not read. It must be short, clear and simple. It must use conversational language, not management – speak and jargon.

The structure for the elevator speech is taken from storytelling and joke telling, and follows the 'rule of three':

- **A one sentence summary of what the strategy is trying to do**: for example, 'We are changing the way we serve our customers, so that we focus on what's most important to them and more profitable for us.'

- **Three reasons why we're doing this**: for example, because customers are demanding higher levels of service, need greater levels of resources and are becoming more demanding about price.

- **Three things we're going to be doing**: for example, we're going to focus on those customers who spend most with us, we're going to retrain our sales people to act more as account managers and we're going to provide a smaller number of customers with higher level of service.

- **Three benefits of this approach**: for example, this way we will make customers happier, have more demanding but more interesting jobs, and more secure and interesting careers.

Typically, leaders are brought together in groups to translate their strategies into elevator speeches. They're then challenged to stand up and deliver these in 30 seconds against the clock. What's interesting about this exercise is that leaders often protest that their strategies are too sophisticated to be boiled down into such a short amount of time. In the BBC, for example, one broadcaster said he couldn't possible encapsulate his pet project in under 40 minutes if people were to understand the full richness of the subject. However, he acknowledged that BBC radio news programmes covered complex geopolitical issues in 30 seconds.

The challenge of condensing your story into 30 seconds is a useful discipline. It forces you to focus, prioritise and emphasise what is important. What becomes clear from the delivery is that the strategy is clearer, sharper and more memorable. This is not to say that all strategies must be restricted to 30 seconds – merely that the exercise helps crystallise what's important, valuable and necessary.

WHY ARE ELEVATOR SPEECHES USEFUL?

Employees frequently complain that the communication they receive lacks clarity, simplicity and impact. This is often because it is coming from senior managers who take great pride in messages they have developed. They may be so proud of their initiative, and so wrapped up in its complexities, that they can't see the wood for the trees. Explaining to these managers that they can make greater impact in a short amount of time by crystallising their message motivates them to think again.

Writing an elevator speech forces would-be communicators to get their message down to its bare bones. The rule for doing so is greater clarity, greater memorability, and greater repeatability.

Some organisations have also used elevator speeches to get greater consistency among their leaders. For example, at the end of a leadership conference at which the strategy has been discussed, a final session prepares leaders to communicate the strategy to their people. As part of this, leaders work together in small groups to develop elevator speeches. This has been useful in a number of ways. It:

- **Acts as a reminder,** and forces managers to remember what they've actually been told.
- **Encourages preparation,** and helps them begin preparing for onward communication – so they don't simply neglect to do so.
- **Develops consistency,** and checks for consistency of message across different managers before they go out and communicate.

Once leaders have had time to prepare, one individual from each group stands up and delivers the elevator speech within the time limit of 30 seconds. They initially feel that this is too short a time to get the message across. However, on hearing each other they tend to be impressed for a number of reasons:

- short communication conveys greater punch and energy;
- it sounds conversational;
- it sounds clear and complete.

Sounding conversational is important to managers. Forcing them to think about an informal conversational setting – like an elevator – shows how ludicrous some of their strategy communication is; filled with management speak and dependent on a long PowerPoint presentation to back it up. Managers are reassured when they hear their strategy encapsulated, sounding like normal conversation rather than some outburst of management speak.

Diageo Case Study: Developing Leaders' Communication Skills

Sixty-five per cent of CEOs are actively involved in developing leadership talent in their organizations[12] and Diageo is a good example of a company making precisely this investment.

12 Source: Hewitt Associates, US Top Companies for Leaders 2005 Study.

Diageo is the world's largest producer of alcohol beverages including Guinness, Smirnoff vodka, Captain Morgan and Crown Royal and was formed in 1997 as a result of the merger between Guinness and Grand Metropolitan. Two years later, the company acquired the Seagram's drinks business.

After 5 years of continuous change, the company decided it needed to rally its leadership in an effort to unite and engage employees. Because of the mergers and acquisitions, and the loyalty people felt towards the company they had come from, it was difficult to unite employees around the new company that had formed.

THE COMMUNICATION CHALLENGE

While Diageo was performing well, its leaders were confident they could boost performance to higher levels. The key was getting their senior leaders to connect with and inspire their employees.

They worked on the principle that, if you want to motivate and engage employees, you have to start by getting senior leaders to role-model positive communication behaviour. The communication team tackled this challenge head on through the development and implementation of a leadership communication workshop.

THE COMMUNICATION SOLUTION

Diageo began implementing leadership communication workshops for its senior leaders. Finding innovative ways to address leaders' communication styles, behaviours and skills is a difficult task. However, the communication team were able to get leaders to evaluate themselves critically by using real-life leadership examples, a number of hands-on exercises and a variety of practical application techniques.

During the company's leadership conference, the theme 'inspirational leadership' was unveiled and promoted as a key objective for Diageo's senior leaders. Diageo was serious about wanting leaders to develop the capacity to truly engage their teams. A fundamental part of that was helping them understand how their communication styles and behaviours impact the engagement of their people.

Diageo developed a programme of intensive, 1-day workshops designed to improve the communication skills and styles of Diageo's senior leaders.

The workshop curriculum was based around the FAME leadership model outlined earlier and designed to focus on Diageo's leadership and business objectives using specific, practical examples of the situations leaders faced. The workshop was designed to be very hands-on, focusing on the practical application of skills and techniques.

As preparation for the workshop, leaders completed a personal style assessment to get them thinking about their own communication style. They were also asked to think of a current project or particular issue to use as a practical example throughout the day (for example, the launch of a new programme, a change initiative or an issue they had to communicate to their teams).

LEADERSHIP WORKSHOP OVERVIEW

The overall objectives of the workshops were to help senior leaders to understand what Diageo expects from its leaders; identify personal communication strengths and weaknesses and use these to engage employees more effectively.

To kick-off the day, the facilitators helped workshop participants to brainstorm a variety of exemplary leaders from all walks of life – politics, business, sports, military and personal. The group then went through the list and pinpointed key attributes that have made these leaders successful and inspirational. Then, drawing from the list of leadership attributes, participants were asked to conduct a self-evaluation of their own leadership strengths and weaknesses. They then applied those attributes practically to a specific challenge they were facing, and had chosen to use during the workshop.

Participants were presented with the four essential leadership communication behaviours outlined in the FAME model to help guide them during the workshop's discussions and exercises.

Leaders took part in a variety of practical activities, including analysing case studies, role-playing and engaging in exercises around listening skills, using language with more impact and engaging people through the use of stories and metaphors.

According to Diageo, the workshops were less about training leaders on tactical communication skills, and more about increasing leaders' awareness of their communication styles and behaviours. Diageo does not claim that any one style is ideal. Instead, they highlight the positive and negative aspects to a variety of different styles and discuss which are most appropriate in different situations.

CONCLUSION

Diageo provides a good example of a world-class company that takes the impact of its leaders seriously. For Diageo, leadership is not limited to the top echelons of the organisation, but is a responsibility for those leading people, initiatives and brands at all levels of the company. While they would pride themselves on having strong leaders at the top, they want to build an organisation in which people are clearly led, leading in their own areas and strongly connected from top to bottom.

Disconnects Between Leadership Layers

In other organisations, the danger can be that a single charismatic leader does not provide a good role model for others in the organisation, but overshadows them. The danger with a charismatic leader is they can be tempted to go direct to employees, bypassing the line management and undermining their role. Such leaders often feel frustrated that their messages are being stifled by the middle manager 'permafrost'. However, the first disconnect in the line management chain is usually between the board level and the next level down. This is the area of greatest schizophrenia where people have strong views, but are political enough not to voice them.

The relationship between these two tiers is often a problem, and tends to have a knock-on impact on the rest of the organisation:

- **The role of the leadership group can be unclear:** are they there to discuss simply how to implement strategy, or to challenge, test and contribute to strategy? There is usually confusion about how directive the board should be, and how empowered and engaged the leadership group beneath should be.

- **The composition of the group can be unclear:** are people there because of the grade they inhabit, or because of their role as leaders of people? Grades may not spread consistently across different parts of the organisation, and those outside the chosen grades but who are influential may be included.

- **The role of their forums can be unclear:** is the purpose of their meetings to transfer information, or to discuss emerging strategic tends and encourage a broader view outside functional silos? Meetings are often stilted and unproductive because of the confusion of the leaders' roles, and their caution about speaking up.

The net result of this is that there is often a disconnect between the board and next tier down, and because of that confusion there is usually a further disconnect between the leadership group and their direct reports.

A study by HR research organisation, Hay Group, revealed deep division between senior and middle management caused by a widespread failure to communicate. The report showed that more than a third of senior managers – 38 per cent – believe their organisations are being 'paralysed' by middle managers who can't understand and don't feel committed to their strategic goals. Based on the report's findings, Hay Group estimates the middle management problem is costing the UK service sector alone £220 billion annually.[13]

However, this 'paralysis' is being caused by middle managers struggling to come to grips with the challenge of engaging their people. While leadership includes making the motivational speeches, it also requires managers to have challenging conversations with their people. They often have tough questions about communicating that they need to get answered:

- **How can I support the 'party line' of this message?** Managers are uncomfortable about having to sell a party line that they do not fully understand and do not agree with. They feel it undermines their relationship with their people, their personal credibility and their sense of integrity.

- **How should I lead the team through this change programme?** How do they explain the interrelationship between the multiple initiatives which seem to be running inside the organisation, explain

13 Source: Corporate, Hay Group, 2007.

the apparent contradictions between them and be able to shepherd their people through the various stages of the change cycle?

- **How do I bring our strategy to life for my team?** Confronted with a ream of management-speak and PowerPoint slides, which threaten to kill off any remaining spark of interest, how do I make sense of it all, speak plainly and paint a picture which is engaging, clear and motivating for my people?

- **How do I get the company's message across meaningfully?** How can I make a connection between the concerns, preoccupations and agendas of my people and those of the organisation?

- **How do I tell my people bad news?** How do I explain the apparent contradictions between our desire to make this a wonderful place to work and our continuous lay-off programmes which undermine any sense of security employees might have?

These, and more, are key communication issues for leaders. These are the kind of questions they ask when they are encouraged to act as leaders and engage their people.

Leaders and the Role of Communicators

Leaders should be helping their people to see a clear line of sight between company goals and their daily work, by providing direction, describing the larger business context, building understanding and commitment to the organisation's strategy, and establishing priorities. Organisations whose employees understand their goals deliver 24 per cent higher shareholder returns[14] and highly committed employees are 87 per cent less likely to leave their organisations, and perform 20 per cent better than disengaged employees.[15]

Leaders can have a huge impact simply by being visible and by being approachable. By walking around, running 'meet and eat' breakfast or lunch meetings, and town hall meetings, leaders can have a disproportionate impact by showing what kind of person they are and acknowledging their people.

14 Watson Wyatt, 2003.
15 Corporate Leadership Council, 2004.

'Leadership visibility' programmes run by some organisations are simply a structured way of making this happen.

Communicators have to step up to the challenge of engaging their leaders in being effective communicators. Communicators are vital in helping leaders understand their impact, clarify their goals, crystallise their messages and meet their responsibilities. Communicators should be providing communications counsel to leaders, identifying where they can most have impact, and challenging their thinking, their messages and their behaviour. Communicators can help their leaders provide clearer direction by helping them articulate their messages, increase consistency of messages and helping them remain 'on message'. They can also help leaders make the connection between the big picture and employees' contribution by helping leaders identify the 'so what?' of their messages for different audiences.

In terms of leaders' ability to model the right behaviour and 'walk the talk', communicators can help leaders identify where they should spend their time being visible and available. They can prepare leaders for these face-to-face sessions, and provide feedback about leaders' communication styles. They can coach them to align their style with their audiences', identify the impact leaders will have through formal and informal communication. They can provide feedback on how well leaders have performed, and how employees have interpreted their messages.

Communicators have to be the eyes and ears of the organisation, keeping their finger on the pulse of employee sentiment. They can help upward communication by raising issues which need to be resolved, and provide leaders with a barometer of employees' mood and level of engagement.

Case Study: AstraZeneca R&D Leadership

The whole pharmaceutical industry is facing change – cost pressures, new markets, outsourcing and changing regulations are just of few of the factors they face. Like its competitors, AstraZeneca is responding to these broader changes in the industry and R&D is a key area for its focus. Pharmaceutical R&D requires a huge amount of investment, and efforts there to bring about greater innovation, greater productivity and new discovery will result in real and worthwhile savings.

THE COMMUNICATION CHALLENGE

The AstraZeneca R&D internal communication team took up the challenge of engaging leaders in being effective communicators. Faced with major and sustained change, the R&D organisation of pharmaceutical giant, AstraZeneca, decided to coach, equip and support its leadership teams to engage people in what was happening. Communicators worked with leadership groups to align them, help them understand their roles and responsibilities and play to their combined strengths, and showed leaders how communication could help achieve real solutions to key business problems.

Engaging employees, particularly after earlier waves of productivity improvement, constant process improvement and change was a key task for R&D's Head of Global Internal Communication, Alex Kalombaris. He and his team adopted an approach which focused on coaching leadership teams and equipping communicators to support them. Each leadership team in R&D participated in a 1-day workshop. A total of 200 senior managers took part.

LEADERSHIP WORKSHOP OVERVIEW

The workshops were practical and focused each team on what they needed to do to bring about the necessary changes in their area. The entire day looked at how each group of leaders should articulate the direction for their teams, align behind the messages to their people, and prepare to engage their people in the changes ahead. Many participants were delighted that, not only did they acquire new skills and techniques, but they were also coming away with practical approaches to real communication situations that they were due to face.

A key aspect of the workshop was helping leaders understand their preferred communication style. A key distinction was whether the leaders were extroverts – lively, persuasive and entertaining, or introverts – accurate, logical and factual. We used a detailed analytical tool to help leaders understand their natural styles and what this meant for the way they communicated.

Looking at communication styles helped the leaders in three ways:

1. **Self awareness:** they could plan to make the most of the strengths of their preferred style and minimise the impact of its downsides.

2. **Awareness of peers:** they could spot other people's preferred styles and shift their approach to match, therefore increasing their chances of getting onto the other person's wavelength quicker.

3. **Flexibility:** looking at communication styles helped them understand that different people were likely to react differently to the messages they were putting across, and that more than one approach was needed to reach everyone.

Early in the programme, a workshop for the R&D network of communicators who would be working alongside the leadership teams was run. In this workshop, communicators learned the key leadership communication skills, and practised ways to support their leaders long after the workshops were over. AstraZeneca's investment in coaching their leaders highlighted the importance of the relationship between leaders and communicators. Their experience also provides useful lessons in how leaders should communicate in times of change.

10 LESSONS LEARNED

1. **Communicators and their clients often have different styles which can cause misunderstanding**. At AstraZeneca, communicators tend to have a different set of values and priorities from their internal clients. Whereas the communicators tended to be upbeat, spirited and considerate, their clients, most of who were trained scientists, were by nature more likely to be lower profile, systematic and considerate.

   Understanding more about communication styles helped the communicators change their approach to get onto their clients' wavelength and achieve common ground from which they could agree a way forward. Without this understanding, it was easy for the scientists to dismiss the communicators as 'all show' and for the communicators to see the scientists as too fact-focused, and both parties coming away from meetings frustrated.

2. **Members of leadership teams have different styles which can result in mixed messages**. In one team in particular, different styles were reflected in different strategies for communication. A spirited and direct, energetic and charismatic member of the team was

keen to talk to people in an unscripted and interactive way. More introverted members of the team were, however, uncomfortable with what they saw as an unstructured and undisciplined approach. The risk here was that different members of the team might take different approaches. The inconsistency that was likely to result could undermine alignment, and send mixed and confusing signals.

This was addressed by working with the team to agree the key messages and the 'story' and also reinforcing that the leaders needed to consider the preferred communication styles of their audiences and flex their approach to cater for them. They should be energetic and upbeat for those in their audiences who were extrovert, but also make sure they clearly link what's happening with business objectives and have detail and evidence for the more fact-hungry introverted types.

3. **Communicators have different styles which can result in mixed messages.** At AstraZeneca, communicators came from a variety of backgrounds and disciplines and had different styles themselves. Several communicators had been scientists themselves, and moved over to specialise in communication. Others came from journalism, and some through PR.

   Communicators were helped to understand their preferred style and think through how to get the most out of it. They also had chance to assess the preferred styles of the leaders they supported and how they could use this information to provide them with an even more effective service.

4. **R&D leadership teams focused on collaboration.** Many of the teams were successful because their leaders were skilled in building strong teams, bringing together functional and technical experts, and fostering cooperation. Their natural style was to be considerate and collaborative.

   In many ways, this style is useful during times of change – people expect greater empathy from their leaders, and to be reassured that they understand the pressures they're under and the pain they're feeling. On the other hand, the collaborative approach can also bring problems during change – leaders have to provide a strong sense of direction, and to be able to engage and motivate their people around the context for change, the compelling reasons for it, and the need to summon up another burst of energy for the new challenges ahead. Doing this means a shift to being more direct and upbeat.

5. **Scientists like fact and process.** Many appeared to be uncomfortable with emotion and story. The more introverted audiences such as many of the scientists do not like 'arguing from analogy' – they don't want images and metaphors of how one thing is like another. They believe that a thing should rest on its own merits and be tested for itself. Scientists may also want time to reflect on information, to process through its implications and to have a later opportunity for challenge and discussion. They are used to informed argument, to establishing hypotheses and then gathering data to test it.

6. **Leaders can be too close to the information and too far ahead in their thinking.** Many of the leaders were so close to the information that they forgot what their people did and did not know. This can cause difficulties when communicating change as an unwise word, or an inappropriate choice of phrase could trigger concerns that had not existed before. Leaders can also become impatient with teams that are grappling with facts and detail that they themselves digested some time ago and misinterpret their slow take up as resistance.

7. **Leaders can project their concerns and uncertainties onto their people.** For many leaders, the toughest objections to answer were those with which they privately agreed. Sometimes leaders would raise issues and concerns which their people may not have considered because the leaders did not want to be seen as corporate propagandists, or because they had their own concerns about how change has been rolled out, and the degree of detail which was available to them. Often, the end result can be extra confusion and concern.

8. **Leaders need to develop their own questions and answers.** Rather than having the communication team develop the list of FAQs, leaders responded better when they challenged each other with

tough questions, developed their answers, and tested out how real, credible and reliable these responses were.

It was also very helpful to challenge leaders to raise the questions they feared they'd be asked. In part this helped them prepare to deal with their fears, and it also helped them investigate what they were concerned about, get to the underlying issue and try and address and resolve it.

9. **Meeting format matters.** The leaders were especially interested in how best to put across their messages. The traditional way of communicating is to run large site events in which 200–300 people get the message at the same time. This minimises the use of the grapevine, as everyone hears the same message from the same person in the same way.

   However, these leaders also needed to ensure high degrees of engagement in order to maintain productivity and keep people focussed. Therefore they believed it was important to have discussions with their people, flush out their issues and increase their sense of confidence about the change.

   This meant they could not rely simply on the one-off large-scale events, since interaction at these would be low, and there would be little time or room for discussion. Indeed, it was more likely at any Q&A session the vocal minority would dominate, even if their views did not represent those of the majority.

   Many leaders therefore decided to follow up larger-scale events with smaller group discussions in which people could discover what the changes meant for their particular area of the business, raise their concerns and ask questions. They would also be able to challenge how well their leaders had created the vision for change, defended their interests and developed a feasible plan for successful implementation.

10. **Consistency is possible even when people see things differently.** One of the group heads was especially worried about consistency of message. They knew this would be difficult to achieve because

their department was spread across three sites, each of which had a distinctive identity and their own strong local leader.

Also, each of the sites was likely to be affected differently, and therefore would need not only different messages, but a different approach. For example, a site that was being severely affected by changes would not welcome an upbeat recounting of the benefits of the change to the organisation.

Each of the team clearly had different styles and different mixes of how much telling and discussing they were likely to follow. Therefore, even when the messages and slides handed out to the team were identical and consistent, they would inevitably be used and delivered in different ways, to audiences who were themselves different and distinctive – and who would start selecting different elements of messages that they might remember and pass on to other.

Faced with what looked like an almost inevitable guarantee of inconsistency, lack of control of what people might take out of the sessions, selective memory and decaying recall, the leader was naturally concerned. He was able to reduce his concerns by:

- **Preparation:** spending time together working through what the members of the leadership group actually thought, believed and felt confident saying.

- **Consistency:** agreeing as a group an elevator speech, key messages and answers to tough questions.

- **Rehearsal:** in which they could challenge each other, simulate tough situations they were likely to face and develop responses together, rather than coming up with something on their feet when delivering 'live'.

- **Summaries:** rather than leaving their answers in the Q&A sessions dangling, giving summaries of what they believed to be good about the changes and why they personally felt confident about it.

Summary

Leadership is a subject which is constantly debated in organisations looking for inspiration and engagement. There are some simple, practical ways communicators can focus the debate on how important good communication is to good leadership.

Leaders are the most effective way of influencing employees' attitudes and behaviour, and are at their most influential when they are communicating informally, in water cooler conversations and corridor exchanges.

Communicators need to move away from concentrating their time, effort and money on their formal channels, which are less effective, and need to get better at engaging their leaders in engaging their people. In all this, it's worth remembering that leadership is less about technique and more about attitude.

Everyone has their own favourite definitions of leadership, and one of mine is Peter F. Drucker's:

> *Leadership is not magnetic personality – that can just as well be a glib tongue. It is not 'making friends and influencing people' – that is flattery. Leadership is lifting a person's vision to higher sights, the raising of a person's performance to a higher standard, the building of a personality beyond its normal limitations.*

In helping their leaders show this level of leadership, internal communicators have the responsibility to show their own leadership, and the opportunity to be leaders of their leaders.

23

Communicating Through a Merger or Acquisition

by Marc Wright

Mergers and acquisitions are two of the most important drivers in increasing the need for internal communication in both the buying and the target companies.

In this chapter you can find out the eight key steps you can take to optimise internal communication when your company is acquiring another, or is being acquired or merged.

Mergers put a huge strain on communication managers as they find themselves truly between a rock and a hard place. On the one hand, senior management go into purdah as they jostle behind the scenes for the upper hand in negotiations while, on the other, staff panic about losing their jobs and related position, lifestyle and pension. Most communication professionals go through a merger or acquisition only once in a decade so you can afford to pull on a wide variety of external help and skills to get through a process that will stretch and develop you more than any other professional experience.

There is usually a management consultancy on board, who have come in to help with the rationalisation and restructuring of the merged business. They always put a high emphasis on the importance of communication. Studies by Booz-Allen & Hamilton indicate that over 70 per cent of merger objectives go unmet and just 23 per cent earns their cost of capital. However, change consultants are often involved flat out on their task of bolting two disparate companies together so they will have little time and expertise to help out the beleaguered communication manager stuck in the middle.

So what should you do when those first indications of a merger start blowing in the wind? Here we suggest an eight point strategy.

1. Build the Convincing Story

The first thing is to get together the big picture of why the merger is happening in the first place. This is none too easy since senior management will have different 'big pictures', depending on their views of how the pieces are going to fall post-merger. Remember that at least half of senior management are likely to leave following a merger, either with full pockets or hurt pride – sometimes both – so go back to basics.

You know with whom your company is merging and there will be speculation in the financial press on the reasons for the deal going ahead. Of course, the story given out to investors is not necessarily the story you want to promote internally; the fact that 40 per cent will be shaved from overheads or three vulnerable factories could be closed down will not play well in the canteens of your organisation. So be honest: resist attempts by senior management to proclaim a new age of prosperity and happiness and get the team behind a cast-iron story. Remember that the rules have changed. Morale and productivity are already in decline; (aren't you wondering how many people doing your role will be required in the new business?). Your job is to use communication to get staff through the Change Curve with the least amount of damage to productivity, morale and company reputation.

Do not wait for senior management to tell you what is going on. Make shrewd guesses, turn them into communication themes and test them against those who are in the know. For instance, 'If we are going to close the North West plant then we need to communicate the attached to the following audiences…' Taking a proactive line is a lot faster and you will get to the truth quicker.

When you have agreement on the main elements of your argument, test it on a few discreet peer colleagues around the office. Watch their eyes as you tell them the main points and you will know soon enough which bits of your story do not hold water. Tell the story without a prompt; your own memory will sort the wheat from the chaff.

Once you have a realistic story that will move staff through the Change Curve, force it on to the agenda at the most senior meeting you can find and get it signed off. Those responsible for the changes will be your biggest blockers as they will want to have all the answers off pat before they go public with any statement to staff. Point out what the staff are currently saying about the merger – it will always be worse than the truth. Then point them to the evidence about the vital role of communication in mergers. Don't worry about being bold during these periods. No senior manager will want to fire, demote or take on your job during this period and you can safely go to the next stage.

2. Capture the Radio Station

In times of crisis, it is no good rushing out an emergency version of the company newsletter (too slow) or using the editorial you write for the CEO on the intranet (too little credibility). Instead, create a new site on the intranet called 'Merger News' and get it up as soon as possible. You can email staff about its existence but, once they realise that this is the only channel for up-to-date, company-endorsed information, they will all be logging on six times a day – if only to see if you are refuting the rumour in that day's financial press.

Make contact with your opposite number at the acquiring or target company. Your bosses won't like this and will even say that you can't talk to them under the legal restrictions of The Financial Services & Markets Act 2000. This is actually untrue; their financial PR has told them to use it as an excuse to keep tight control of information among senior staff. If you are not inside that loop then threaten to resign again. Ensure that you are coordinating any internal announcements with your opposite number.

Once you have captured the radio station and broadcast your 'convincing story', you will then have the ticklish problem of having nothing more to say.

3. Talk About Talking

The worst message you can give out is that you have stopped talking. No talking means the worst is going to happen, in the minds of your staff, so start by *talking about talking:*

- Explain to people what facts are already available, signed off and in the public domain.
- Describe the process of consultation that is going to happen as the process moves forward.

- Establish a timetable for announcements of integration information and milestones – but be conservative. No one will mind if news comes quicker but do not break your own deadlines.

- Publish a list of FAQs and review them daily.

- Give out information about the target or acquiring companies and emphasise those values and characteristics you share. Give a history of the other company: the more your people learn, the less antagonistic they will become.

Quite legitimately, a company that is on the verge of acquiring a large competitor will want to talk as little as possible and – for instance in the UK – it is constrained by The Financial Services & Markets Act 2000. Companies often use legislation to avoid discussing issues internally, even though it is permitted within the guidelines of the city regulators.

The reason for this taciturn approach is that there is bad news on the way and it's just too hard to even think about communicating until the issues have been thrashed out. Senior management will argue there is nothing they can talk about to staff so they prefer to stay dumb.

However, this merely exacerbates the situation as the behaviour of management speaks volumes – and none of it is interpreted well by employees.

4. Use the Right Media

The Concern Scale (see Chapter 17) shows that the importance of information to an individual is in inverse proportion to their desire to have it broadcast from the rooftops. So:

- Use the intranet, mass emails and newsletters for the broad facts and major movements in the merger.

- Use team meetings to reveal changes in reporting lines and large-scale changes, such as shutting down offices or plants.

- Use individual, one-on-one meetings to discuss redundancies, moving locations or even promotions.
- Never, ever use mass text messaging or voicemail systems until the merger is a distant memory.

As a rule of thumb, around 80 per cent of your communication effort should be spent on going into face-to-face events with plenty of feedback. Hard work, but it's the only effective way to keep onboard the talent you want to retain. Make close friends with HR and ensure that you are working to the same timescales. Remember, they are the only people in all this who have a tougher job than you.

5. Remember the Survivors

Once the merger has been announced, meetings have taken place and the redeployment consultants and counsellors have moved in, you need to think about the survivors. Companies have got so good at softening the blow for the people they are letting go that it is the people who stay who can feel like the bigger victims of change.

Organise meetings for your workforce and allow them to get off their chests all the bad news about the changes. Accelerate them through the Change Curve as they cannot buy into the new company until they have gone through all the stages. If they aren't angry and depressed now, they will be later so try and get it over as soon as possible while you have the energy and resources to cope. Watch out for the signs of survivor syndrome: depression, lack of initiative, unwillingness to volunteer for projects, cynicism, lack of communication.

During the merger process, senior management will be further along the Change Curve than their staff so will be gung-ho for the new company. Make sure to temper their language about a bright new future while the rest of the company are still grieving for their lost colleagues and heritage.

6. Celebrate Your Heritage

Don't try to bury the past the minute you become the new merged company. Create a permanent memorial of the old company: a plaque of the old logo; a book of what you achieved together. You need to celebrate the passing of some very important emotional ties.

Give people the chance to mourn the old company before you expect them to embrace the new one. Texas Instruments has a 'corridor of honour', celebrating all the companies that they acquired on the road to growth.

7. Create a Network of Communication Champions

The change consultants will have set up a team of change champions already, to help with the integration of the new business. Recruit your own team of communication champions; they will form a crucial network for you in the months ahead. You will be overdosing on 'tell' mode as you impart news of the changes so use your champions as your eyes and ears around the organisation, alerting you to the major concerns of staff.

Establish a formal feedback loop so senior management have to take notice of your 'bottom-up' channels. Use peer pressure to encourage recalcitrant senior managers to keep their staff informed and motivated during these difficult times. Make sure you know what's on the rumour mill, what's old and unimportant and what's coming round the corner.

Also recruit some senior management champions (once you know who is staying) and use them as mouthpieces for the company. Select credible and, if possible, unreasonable people. If your messages convince them, then they will convince anyone.

8. Measure the Improvement

When you are fighting the alligators, it is sometimes hard to remember that you came here to drain the swamp. Whatever you do, do not try to get back to the levels of employee satisfaction that you enjoyed pre-merger in less than 24 months. You will only depress yourself and jeopardise your bonus.

Measure employee morale a month after the announcement and then test regularly for improvement. Remember that managing a merger is like going through crisis management – only it's much longer. You are going to need all the evidence you can find to prove to yourself, and the executive suite, that things are getting better.

Conclusion

So, as a communications professional, what can you do?

- Communicate often and regularly, even when you have nothing to say.
- Restate the position and emphasise that staff will know first, once there is news.
- Explain the process for consultation.
- Use the Concern Scale (see Chapter 17) to match the right media to the content of your messages.
- Create a dedicated channel for breaking news.
- Listen to the concerns of staff and feedback regularly to senior management.
- Deflate any rumours that are untrue.
- Agree your communication structures and systems throughout the merger process – don't wait until you have a major leak.
- Coordinate with communication managers in the target or merging company, as well as with any major partners or suppliers who are privy to sensitive information.

The last point is very important. One case in point is where the staff of a factory discovered they were due to be closed down when a supplier revealed that a piece of equipment, which was due for delivery, had been cancelled. The result was a collapse of trust in management and the wrecking of the entire consultation process.

And finally, remember that communication professionals have to operate on two fronts when their company or organisation goes through a restructure. On the one hand, you have to work hard to keep staff informed and on course while, on the other, you are fighting calls for cuts in your own department. So – whatever you do – ensure that you come out of the other side of the merger in the driving seat when it comes to internal communications. And try not to lose too many of your own team in the process.

24

Make Change Last

by Caisa Alpsten and Ulla Mogestad

Change has become part of the lifeblood for both management and communication teams in the great majority of organisations. But the successful implementation of new strategies that will change mindsets, create new ways of working and build commitment is still rare.

There are at least four reasons why it is so difficult to make change last:

1. Lack of insight. If people do not understand why change is necessary they are not motivated. If there are no visible threats, why change?

2. Top management giving up too fast. Top management often believe that change is a project implemented within a certain timeframe. But it is a continuous process requiring their full attention and commitment over years.

3. Managers are not mobilised as change advocates. As the direct line manager is the most trustworthy source of information when it comes to change of attitude and behaviour, all managers and supervisors need to be engaged from the start. If they do not understand the urgency for change, they send out the wrong signals and the message is blurred. In the worst case, they join the resistance: 'If my boss does not support it, it's no good for us nor the company.'

4. The organisation culture does not support the new strategy. If no efforts are made to align culture and reward systems with the new strategy, employees will continue to behave as before. 'Why change when it seems OK not to?' Culture will defeat strategy at every time.

Professional communicators can support change initiatives in many ways. Change communication is also a great opportunity to prove the value of communication. To succeed you will need a communication strategy that involves key stakeholders and a communication plan which is carefully monitored as you proceed. The following six-step process for successful change communication gives a structure for your planning (see Figure 24.1).

This chapter describes how communicators can support management in major business changes that involves most parts of the organisation. Smaller changes follow the same logic, but actions can be simplified and merged to fit the needs.

Step 1: Prepare the Organisation for Change

Set the scene for change at an early stage and generate a feeling of urgency. Many change projects are launched only when top management is ready to present the news. Very often this information is met by negative reactions and resistance, because front-line managers and employees are not prepared.

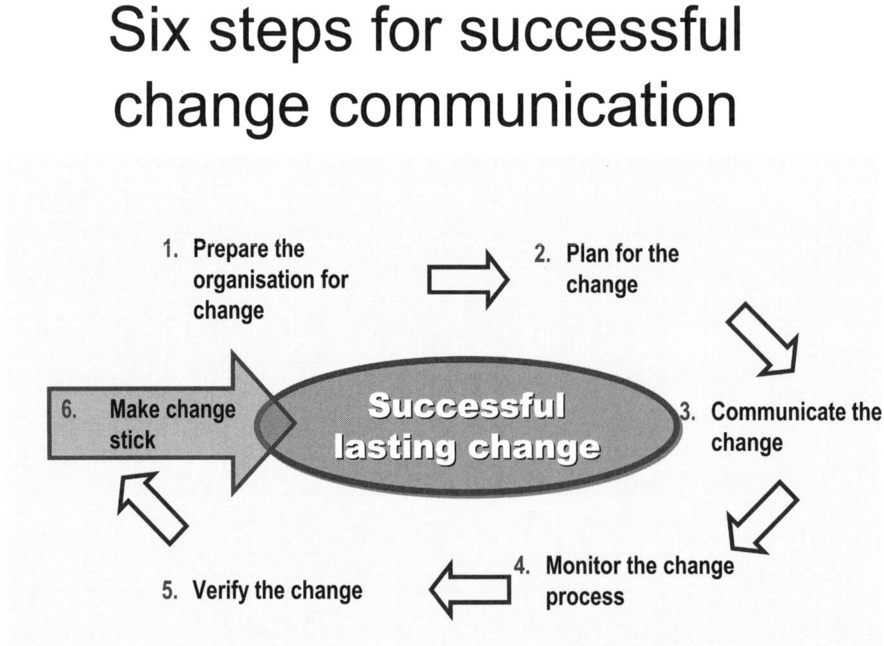

Figure 24.1 Six steps for successful change communication

Successful change projects begin much earlier, by creating a common knowledge of what must happen. By keeping people continuously informed of the company's competitive situation, market position, financial performance and customer requirements, a common awareness of the situation is raised.

RAISE AWARENESS USING DIFFERENT CHANNELS

Craft your messages carefully. Facts and figures are necessary but not enough. Make something that catches people's attention and use visible evidence. Help managers create a compelling background story and visualise the current situation in different ways, not only by numerical statistics and pie charts. Ask trustworthy people within the company or external specialists, clients or suppliers to give their opinion about the current situation. These kinds of actions will generate a feeling of urgency and people will understand the need for a change.

INVITE EMPLOYEES TO TAKE PART IN DISCUSSIONS

What actions support our business today and what will support it in future? What are the alternative future scenarios? Invite people to produce responses to important issues like these. Collect and use all good ideas and give people genuine feedback. Otherwise you risk a backlash – people will see the process as just another game or they will have a false sense of involvement.

ANALYSE THE STATE OF CHANGE READINESS

- Do people understand why change is necessary? If not, take actions as fast as possible.

- Do managers understand their important role in the communication process? If not, this will be the time for an extra reminder or training.

- Do you have the right channels in place? Will there be a need for new ones? Make necessary improvements.

- Do you have access to key stakeholders – top management, HR professionals, business unit heads and others? If not, start building these relationships.

- Does the culture support the change? If you do not know, make a culture analysis to find out what kind of resistance to expect.

TIPS AND TOOLS: THE CHANGE CURVE

We know that people always react on change, even when the most common reaction should be positive as is the case when implementing new strategies. Use the Change Curve to keep the communication right through different phases of reactions, as shown in Figure 24.2.

Initially, it is of vital importance that 'the uninformed optimists' are aware of the whole background to understand the new challenges.

FORMULA FOR CHANGE MOTIVATION

P x F x K > E

Present Pains x Future Happiness x Knowledge > Effort to Change

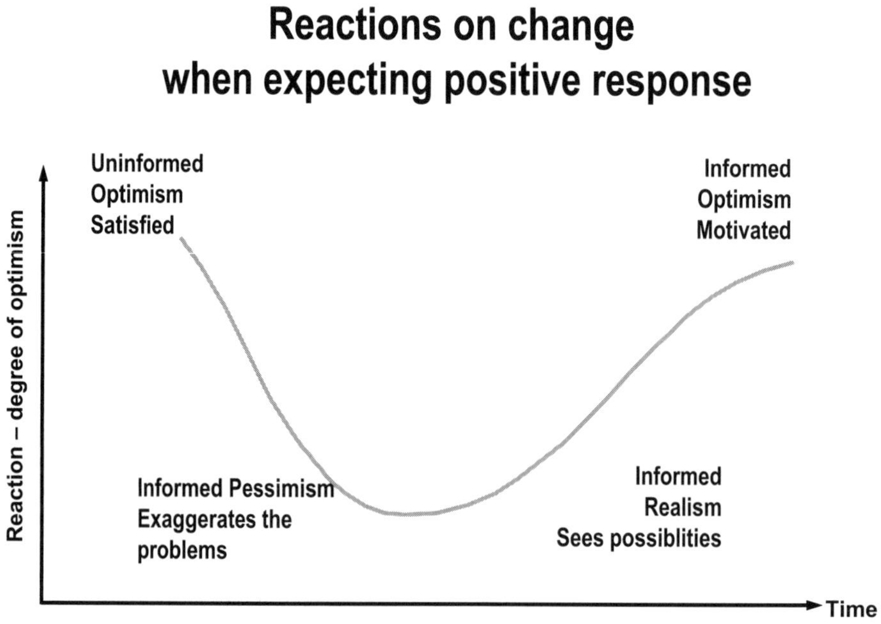

Figure 24.2 The Change Curve

This easy formula can help managers understand the challenge of change communication. Every change demands an extra effort. To be motivated for that effort, people need to understand:

- Why? – background facts, 'Present pains' made visible.
- What? – a compelling vision for the future.
- How? – knowledge and information to cope with the new situation.
- The formula tells you that people will buy-in, if the product of these three factors exceeds the necessary effort. Consequently, the result will be zero if any of these factors is zero.

SEMINARS: 'LET`S TALK ABOUT THE FUTURE'

As a communicator you can help management arrange workshops and seminars that will engage people at en early stage. Ideally, these workshops take place in many small groups at the same time, so that 50–100 or even more people can work together in the same room. That will raise engagement across functions and levels. You will need a number of facilitators depending of the number of groups.

Here is an easy process to get people involved in building scenarios:

- Open up the discussion with one single, open question: 'What are the most important things to do to make our business successful in future? Put yourself 5 years ahead, what will our business be like? What if…(and then introduce a short scenario)?'
- Facilitate the discussion in the small groups so that everyone is contributing. One person in each group is responsible for gathering outputs. Let people have a few minutes for reflection and jot down ideas on a piece of paper or on Post-its.
    - Go around the table and collect all ideas, one at a time, on a flip-chart.

- Discuss the ideas, analyse consequences and agree on the best ones.

- Write scenarios: what will happen if we take this idea and put it into action? As a communicator you can help by putting the outputs into clear words.

The outcome: one article from each group that will be published, in print or on the intranet. Publication should be very quick, ideally the day after.

COMMUNICATION WORKSHOPS FOR MANAGERS

Take an early initiative to train managers in change communication. The following three-step process has been successfully developed by AstraZeneca, Sweden Operations. The full programme involves three half-day seminars that imparts theory, methods and tools.

Basic communication theory

- Why planned communication?
- Communication basics and outcomes: Know – Feel – Do.
- Stakeholder mapping.

Change management and communication

- Road to dommitment: engagement and compliance.
- Rhetoric versus coaching; when to use what.
- Target setting.
- Risk analysis.

Communication tools

- Human brains and memory.
- Use all senses to influence.

- Messaging: main message and supporting messages.
- Communication strategy.

Step 2: Plan for the Change

In successful change projects the communicator is involved from the outset to advise on strategies at an early stage. The business strategies should provide the guidelines for content and direction of the change communication. It is crucial to identify the driving forces for the change project and present them simply and clearly; otherwise people will not understand why change is necessary for the future success of the business.

The change readiness analysis from Step 1 is the starting point for the communication planning. Keep the Change Curve in mind and be aware of how to communicate in different phases of reactions as is shown in Figure 24.3.

Go back to your change readiness analysis. How ready is the organisation? Also take into account what is going on externally – amongst customers, in markets and society – that can affect the change process? What risks are at stake?

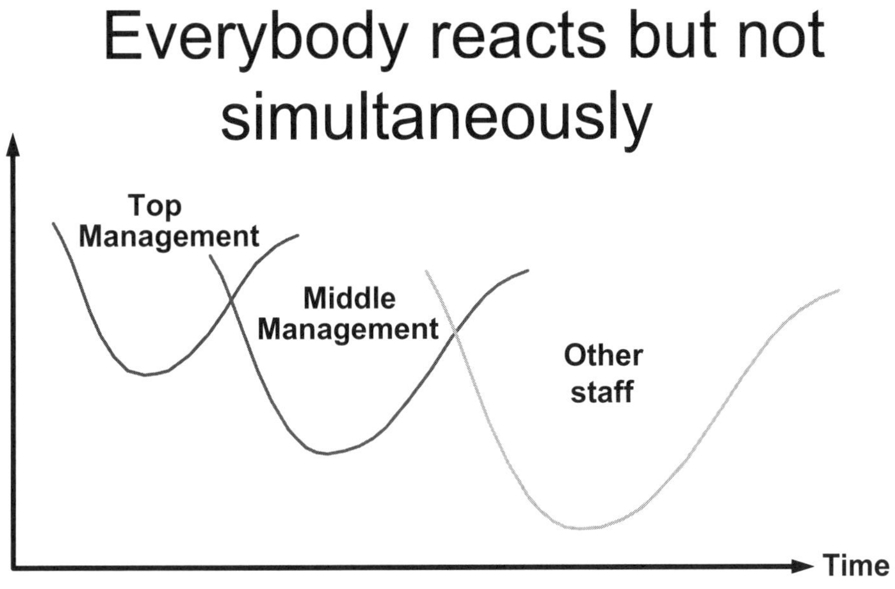

Figure 24.3 How to communicate in different phases of reactions

Management has the overall responsibility for communicating change. Communicators are there to support the process as professional advisors: crafting plans, messages and tools; creating channels for different messages; and facilitating face-to-face communication and regular feedback.

To secure successful communication the responsibility has to be organised. You could form a Change Communication Group with trustworthy people across functions and business areas, preferably headed by a communicator. This group should have access to all necessary information. Key stakeholders should be included such as business unit heads, frontline managers, HR professionals and, when applicable, the unions.

Create a clear and simple message that can engage people in the new vision and strategies. Ideally this should be done in a workshop with the management team. The power of a united team sharing an overall vision is the most critical success factor for a change project.

As a communicator you can help shape the key messages, addressing why change is necessary, what will be achieved and how to get there. Find supporting messages – arguments, facts and figures that give explanation and background for different stakeholders.

MAKE A COMMUNICATION PLAN

Decide on the right communication channels for the change project: Intranet and print for the regular information of facts while face-to-face communication from managers should be used for achieving motivation and engagement. It is important to coordinate internal and external activities.

Plan for the launch carefully and be sure to coach all managers and communicators involved well in advance. Prepare your presentation as well as your question and answer materials.

Do not forget that long-term planning will ensure successful and lasting change.

TIPS AND TOOLS: VISION WORKSHOP

The vision workshop is a half-day event that helps management translate vision and goals into key messages. Here is a step-by-step approach.

To make a vision easy to communicate, staff should find it:

- Meaningful: 'My contribution is important'.
- Positive: 'This feels right'.
- Clear: 'I understand, I can tell others'.
- Engaging: 'I believe in it'.
- Encourages action: 'I want to contribute'.

Agree on key arguments for the vision that meets most expectations, for example, things that both clients, employees and others find attractive. Thus you will have the basic elements for a consistent key message that can be communicated to all stakeholders. Agree on supporting arguments to use for different stakeholders.

COMMUNICATION PLAN FOR CHANGE

The plan is your and top management's main tool to ensure the right communication through different phases of the change project. We suggest you consider the following elements when making the strategic priorities:

- business drivers and desired outcomes;
- communication goals;
- communication responsibility;
- key messages (why? what? how?);
- communication strategy and channel strategy;
- risk analysis (and contingency plan);
- measuring and monitoring.

Apart from the long-term strategic planning you will need detailed 'action plans'. For example, a quarterly action plan to be changed according to measurement outcomes as well as weekly detailed action plans.

QUESTION AND ANSWER (Q&A) ROLE-PLAYING SESSIONS

Q&A is an effective communication tool to help people understand complex information. In times of change you can use it in all communication channels.

Q&A sessions, in which managers are forced to respond to real-life situations, are an effective way of preparing management. The idea is to encourage managers to handle tough questions with confidence.

Preparations

- Collect every potentially tough question and ask specialists to answer them correctly with accurate information. Create a draft Q&A document.
- Invite management and other key stakeholders who are responsible for answering questions about the change to a half-day seminar.
- Invite the management team to be themselves and the rest of the group to assume the role of the workforce. Give the management team the Q&A document and prepare the workforce to make their questions as challenging as possible.

Facilitation

- Facilitate the Q&A process by helping managers to formulate the best answers.
- Don't give up until every single question has a clear, simple and accurate answer, delivered convincingly.
- Make sure that everybody agrees on the final answers.

This process provides an effective Q&A document that all managers and other key stakeholders can use in their communication. You also have the option of publishing it on the intranet.

Step 3: Communicate the Change

If the two first steps of the process have been carried out successfully, the actual launch of the change will be easier. The most effective way to influence people's attitudes and behaviour is via managers at all levels. What managers say and do every day has a huge impact on the success of a change project.

As a professional communicator you can support the managers in many ways. You can coach them in change communication as they are taking on their communication responsibility. Remember there is a big time gap in reactions between management and staff. Most managers are not aware of this and tend to forget that employees need sufficient time to react on the information. Therefore, encourage managers to go on communicating in many different ways and repeat the key message until their staff knows why the change is necessary, what will be achieved and how they can contribute.

Check that all communication is simple, clear and honest; that it appeals both to minds and hearts. Facts and figures are not enough. People need to be emotionally involved in order to change their behaviours. Verify what managers say using other channels. Repeat key messages over and over again. Help people see the context and meaning of what is being said. Communicate regularly at agreed times and places – at least once a week, even if there seems to be nothing new to say. The consistency creates trust and minimises the risk of speculation and rumour. Stimulate feedback and use it to improve communication results. As much as possible cooperate with the unions and use the same facts and information material in all communication. Include mass media as an internal channel and provide everyone with as much information as possible. Comment internally every day on what is true and what is not in the external media.

Deeds are more important than words. Symbols speak loudly. What top management does sets the direction for everyone. Therefore, encourage openness and dialogue and keep as much as possible of the discussion within the company. Beware of too much chat and rumours, which take time away from constructive work with business and customers.

Provide managers with relevant information; facts and figures that are easy to use in their own communication. Give them hands-on support, face-to-face or via the intranet. Coach them in advance of big presentations and offer them feedback afterwards.

TIPS AND TOOLS

Create a change homepage on the intranet

In most organisations, the intranet is the prime channel for news and facts. Therefore, be sure to maximise the impact of your intranet. Here are some ideas:

- Brand the change project. Give it a name and a logo. Summarise the prime message into a short slogan.
- Make it visible on the front page, so that all news is easy to find.
- Gather all information on a special homepage/portal. Normally this is easily done and no special technique needs to be added.
- Publish facts and news regularly, at least every week. Let people know that they will find news, say, every Tuesday. The general rule is: even if there is no news to tell, tell it!
- Publish a calendar, so that people know what will happen in advance.
- Publish success stories and best practice regularly.
- Add some interactive functions, such as chats with senior management, whenever something vital is happening; Q&A as a living document adding new ones regularly; change project communities; wikis to let different groups of employees add content and ideas.

MANAGERS FORUM ON THE INTRANET

To help managers communicate let them have their own online forum where they can find the latest news and get tips and advice on change and leadership issues. Some examples of useful information:

- Regular news on the change project, if possible before it is published for all employees.

- Success stories on leading and communicating change.
- Presentations and support materials.
- Communication toolkits.
- Leadership community where managers can share best practice.
- Leadership issues in general.

COACHING AND DEBRIEFING SESSIONS FOR MANAGERS

Agree on purpose and goals with every person who is supposed to take an active part in the presentation. What do we want our target groups to know, feel and do afterwards?

Conduct individual discussions with each speaker to agree on what to say and do during the presentation. Go over the main messages, facts, figures and examples. Create preliminary slides for each presenter, but let them speak from the heart if possible.

Train all speakers beforehand and attune the presentation the day before. If possible this is a good opportunity for a practice with the Q&As.

The evening after the presentation, collect the speakers together with the communication and HR professionals. Discuss the performance by asking questions like: How do you feel about your presentation? What went well, what can be improved? What reactions have you met? What new questions need special answers and actions immediately? Discuss the next activities outlined in the communication plan. Is there anything that needs to be changed or done otherwise?

Step 4: Monitor the Change Process

You need to monitor the effects of communication activities regularly during a change implementation process. Otherwise managers will not know if the process is going in the right direction and communicators have no base for requisite improvements. As the saying goes, 'What gets measured gets done.'

- Have the various target groups properly understood the messages?
- To what degree are different groups engaged and committed to the new vision and strategy?
- What do we need to communicate right now to continue moving in the right direction?
- How effective are the different communication channels and the feedback system?

With proper analysis and quick feedback for everyone involved, monitoring becomes an excellent method for managing the change communication process and securing the desired outcomes.

TIPS AND TOOLS

There are several useful methods for keeping track of the process:

- You can appoint a group of employees representing different functions, levels, professions, ages and sexes and let them follow the process regularly in a variety of ways. Interview them initially to find out the state of change readiness. Test key messages, Q&As and channels with them. Interview them after important presentations and ask them to forward feedback from fellow workers. Invite them to participate as a test audience when managers' presentations are rehearsed. Consult them whenever changes or improvements are called for.
- Identify an informal group of leaders and key target groups who can keep track of the process from the leadership point of view. Meet with people from different parts of the company to discuss what is being carried on the grapevine. Compile a report describing rumours together with actual facts. Select key stakeholders for regular individual interviews and sample different target groups for focus group interviews.
- Draw a (different) sample of 10 per cent of the staff for a regular online survey, so that you can quickly check progress without

needing a response from the same group of people every time. If your company has a yearly employee survey, use it to measure what the effect is on staff morale, faith in the leadership and the perceived quality of communication.

Step 5: Verify the Change

Behavioural change takes time. However, you will want early evidence that you are on the right track. It is easy to kick-start a change and generate initial engagement. Once the initial euphoria has worn off people may start reflecting: 'Are the managers really doing what they said they would? Is this what I hoped? Do I really share the new values?' It is only once employees have a satisfactory answer to these questions that they will be ready to buy into the new strategy.

Top managers need to model desired behaviour continuously as is shown in Figure 24.4. They need to reinforce their personal belief in the change process by being visible and 'walking the talk'. Actions speak louder than words!

If there is a strategy of openness, managers should be open to discussion, invite people to talk and make sure they respect differing views. If there is a vision of innovation, managers need to encourage knowledge sharing

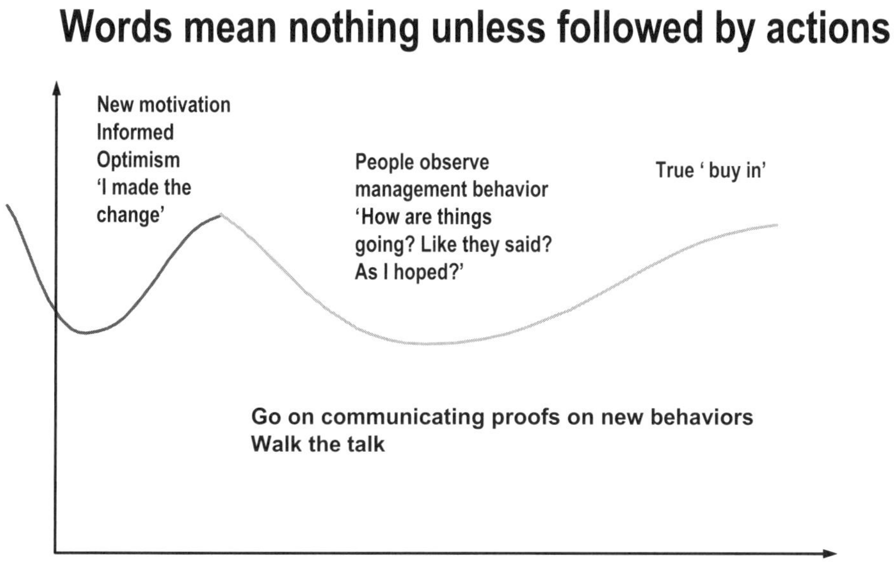

Figure 24.4 Words mean nothing unless followed by actions

and champion employees who come up with the best ideas. If globalisation is the core message, why not appoint one or more managers from overseas offices to the senior management team. If cost cutting is a key requirement, then managers should set an example by ensuring transparency in the use of expense accounts.

Many small steps stimulate further change. Establish systematic good news programmes so that people can see that their own contribution is working well. Produce and communicate short-term wins, which means that you have to show results quickly and make them visible continuously. If the new routine of up-to-date information about company performance has resulted in a new business contract, write a story about that and publish it. If leadership behaviour is a key issue, try to find best practice among the managers and publish them regularly. If cost effectiveness is a strategy for improvement show how one department has managed to cut costs immediately and still kept up good standards. These small success stories are critical, as they provide credibility and momentum. Reward people who do the right things – make them heroes and give them visibility in different communication channels. Celebrate successes, even the small ones.

TIPS AND TOOLS

Plan and monitor CEO communication

CEO behaviour is the single most important factor for successful change. A detailed plan of CEO activities that are continuously monitored is an important tool to help them to communicate effectively. Face-to-face communication with a personal touch is the most effective way. Here are some examples:

Help your CEO be visible in as many ways as possible. Prepare not just formal meetings but find different ways for informal conversations with front-line people. Have informal breakfasts or lunches. Give the choice to all people and draw a group of winners, say every month.

Walk the floor on a surprise basis. Whenever your CEO is visiting regions and divisions on formal purposes, schedule time for drop-ins and floor walks. If people in your organisation are on the move, let their CEO join them once in a while, whether it be a sales team, lorry drivers or a technical services team.

Facilitate formal meetings to let your CEO be as personal as possible. If they are not a great speaker at town hall meetings, try interviews. Most people come out better answering questions than presenting speeches. Dedicate a special website for CEO communication. Monthly notes, speeches, Q&As, discussion forums, chats or blogs. It should be in their own words.

Sometimes corporate stories and myths are well known and part of everyday conversations. Sometimes they are hidden and need to come up to the surface. In a period of change you need to capture new stories that reflect the new vision and strategy.

What are the stories and myths that are told in your organisation? Capture the actual stories by using structured workshop techniques or interviews. Make sure that people you talk to are representative of the whole organisation. Analyse the stories together with the management team. How would you like those stories to change? What is management's role in changing the stories? Are there any stories that reflect desired values and behaviours?

Choose the best stories and translate them into short, clear messages. Ask both the management team and a few teams of employees to assess the chosen stories. Are they really good? If not, make necessary changes. Tell the chosen stories over and over again. Let them be part of the prime message to describe the new strategy, values and behaviours.

Checklist to choose the best stories

- What is this story really about?
- Can you imagine the story into some pictures?
- What is the clue? Is it really good?
- Do you learn anything?
- Do you feel proud when you hear it?
- Does it make desired values/behaviours visible?

Step 6: Make Change Stick

A major business change normally involves sustained activities over several years. Successful change leaders need patience. Keep repeating the key messages in words and actions – using top managers as role models – until the new way of doing things is an integral part of the company culture.

Successful change leaders also make sure changes are embedded in the organisational culture. Likewise systems for reward, recruitment, leadership and communication are in line with the new strategy and culture. If they are not, you will need to develop both new systems and a new culture that can support the new vision and strategy. This is often the case, because management cannot foresee all changes needed at the outset.

There may still be some remaining gaps between objectives and outcomes, but it is important to come to completion, so that major successes can be highlighted. Identify and declare the objectives of the change project that have been achieved, acknowledge everyone's role in the achievement and underline the benefits that you have realised. Keep repeating the message of the vision and the new strategy and tell the story of the new successful organisation as often as you can.

Follow up lessons learned and build improvements into all your processes. Review the change communication process – what can we do better? Think about ways to develop the communication function and your skills to support the company's new strategy. Identify how to develop new competencies within the company for those processes where external resources were used during the change project. Develop a system for information and feedback that helps the company keep continuous change on the business agenda.

To change culture is difficult, but necessary if the existing culture does not support the new strategy. Such a project demands total support from management, including persistence, time, resources and patience. All leaders need to be bought in to such a dramatic plan before initiating such a project.

We suggest you follow these steps:

- Workshop with Management, where you anchor the need for culture development and define the issue: shall we talk about culture, a new way of working or what? Let management have their say about existing and desired culture and make sure they all understand their own responsibility to live the desired values. Finally, get their agreement for the development process.

- Set up a team with representatives from HR, communications and different business areas that will manage the project. Agree on realistic goals and timeframes for the project.

- Identify existing culture and desired new culture. What is supporting the new business goals and strategies today? What is not? Often you will need external experts but the most important point is to involve the whole organisation. The model in Figure 24.5 can be of help when making the initial analysis.

- Make a gap analysis. What is it necessary to stop doing and start doing? On the basis of this analysis, express the desired culture in words. Check it against business goals and strategies and consider the need of subcultures.

- Go back to management. Discuss the proposed new culture and what this will demand on management. In what way shall top managers show their belief in these new values? Get their understanding and agreement on a continuous process.

- Coordinate the new culture with the systems for leadership, rewards, communication, recruitment and external profile. What need to be changed and how?

- Develop a plan for implementation. Start with things that are visible: use new words and symbols, tell new stories, put new easy routines in place and so on.

- Let the new culture develop slowly. Stimulate a continuous dialogue about values and behaviour in the whole organisation. Give management and teams feedback and support. Follow up and reward correct behaviour. Communicate success and feature and promote new heroes.

TIPS AND TOOLS

If a real culture change is the issue an in-depth analysis is the starting point. The model outlined in Figure 24.5 can help you define the existing culture and find ideas for desired culture.

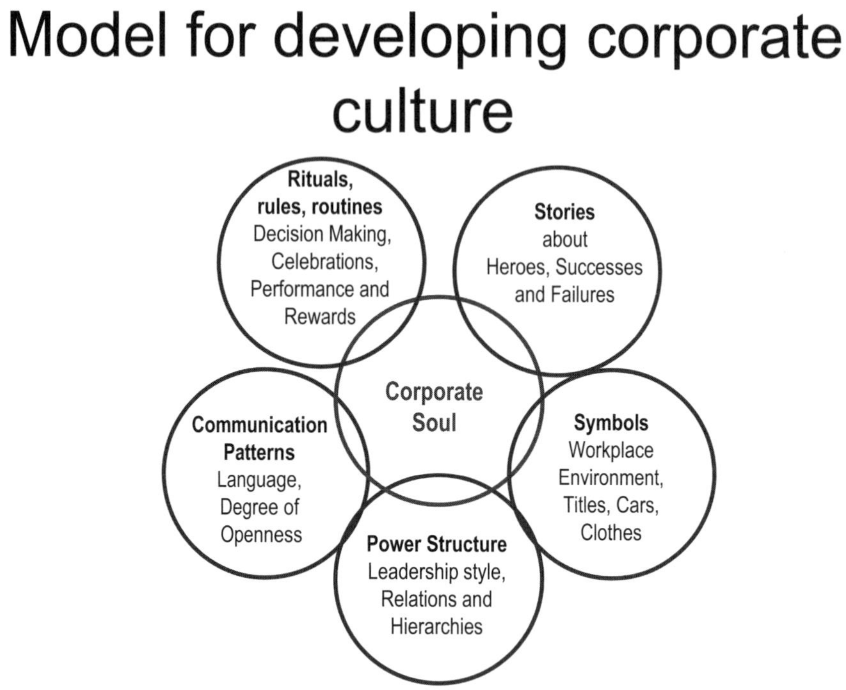

Figure 24.5 A model for analysing and developing corporate culture

Corporate culture has different aspects, as the five circles in the figure suggest. A lot of things are hidden whereas other things are quite obvious. The most effective strategy for a culture change project is to start changing things that are visible, for example words and symbols. Communication patterns, power structure and values are often hidden and more difficult to change.

Very often organisations explain their vision and values in words only. However, values have to be visible and lived by in our daily life. Otherwise they have no importance. The issue here is to make the values visible and to encourage people to live them.

25

New CEO: A Case Study in Communicating

by Lee Smith

The scenario is a familiar one. Your charismatic and much-loved CEO is moving on, only to be replaced with a little-known executive from another organisation. If you haven't faced this challenge yet, the chances are you will at some point in your career.

That was precisely the task the internal communications team for the Retail Division of HBOS, the UK's fifth largest bank, faced in 2006. To add to the challenge the new CEO had been lured away from their closest competitor and consequently the team was unable to talk to him until he arrived for his first day. By anyone's standards, quite a problem.

But that didn't stop them delivering a highly effective communication programme, one that put the new leader firmly on the map, built employee understanding of business objectives, and boosted advocacy on a number of levels. It also recently earned the team a coveted Communicators in Business (CiB) excellence award.

Context

HBOS Retail,[1] the UK's number one mortgage lender, savings provider and bank assurer, is a complex and diverse business. It includes major high street brands such as Halifax and Bank of Scotland, as well as strong UK mortgage brands such as Birmingham Midshires and Intelligent Finance.

---

1 Subsequent to the credit crunch of 2008 HBOS became part of the Lloyds Banking Group.

It's a large business – there are around 44,000 people working in 1,200 Halifax and Bank of Scotland branches, nine call centres and around 20 corporate sites across the country.

Early in 2006 it was announced that the then Retail CEO Andy Hornby was to become CEO of the HBOS plc, the parent organisation, and that he would be succeeded by Benny Higgins, who until then had held a similar position at the Royal Bank of Scotland.

It was at this point that the internal communications team was given the task of launching Benny to the business and, at the same time, driving up employee advocacy (that is, their propensity to recommend the banks products, service and employer to others).

The communication programme was developed and delivered by a team of four led by Retail IC manager Fiona Nelson. The majority of the work was done in-house, with a limited amount of external support on events and publications.

'This was a major communications exercise and the biggest of its kind for the business and the team,' says Fiona. 'As well as bedding-in the new CEO, we had to continue to deliver all business as usual communications, including our daily intranet news service, monthly online publications and a monthly TV programme. On top of that we wanted to raise advocacy levels in the business, one of our key strategic challenges for 2006.'

The Approach

Fiona and the team developed a simple communication programme based around two phases, 'Get to know the CEO' and 'Delivering for Retail'.

The first phase supported an initial 'listening' period; an opportunity for the CEO to tune into the business, hear the views and opinions of colleagues first hand and get under the skin of key issues and challenges. The second phase was about demonstrating tangible action.

Fiona explains, 'We knew that initially Benny's visibility and access would be key. Although he was already well known in industry circles, most of our people hadn't heard of him and so it was vital that they had the opportunity to see, hear and talk to their new leader. But we also knew that profile alone wasn't enough – colleagues needed to see that things were happening and know that Benny didn't just talk the talk.'

What followed was a high-impact multi-channel campaign that encompassed electronic publications, intranet content, business TV and, most importantly, face-to-face communications.

Phase 1: Get to Know the CEO

The first phase of the programme kicked off when Benny joined the business in May 2006. Branded simply 'Get to know the CEO' it was designed to create high awareness of the change at the top, to give colleagues a feel for Benny's style and approach and to capture employees' views and opinions on what needed to change.

A *Get to Know the CEO* intranet microsite was launched to provide colleagues with background information about the new CEO.

An electronic publication, HBOS Today, was issued to all Retail colleagues. It contained an interview with Benny and also highlighted the many ways in which colleagues could interact with him – via a special TV programme, an online Q&A system and a series of road shows.

Tell Benny was launched. This is an intranet site where colleagues can share their issues and concerns with the CEO or ask any questions they want answering. The feedback through this channel acts as a useful temperature check on the business.

Get to know the CEO TV was aired at the end of May. The BBC's Dermot Murnaghan put colleagues' questions (gathered in advance) to Benny during the programme, setting the scene for the face-to-face events that were to follow.

This context-setting activity was followed by the *Get to Know the CEO* roadshow. The team organised four colleague events during June and July. Around 1,500 colleagues at all levels attended. The objective was for Benny to listen to people's views first hand. These sessions comprised a short presentation followed by a Q&A session.

Finally, a number of electronic publications were issued immediately after each roadshow to all colleagues based in and around that location. This was done to ensure everyone had the opportunity to experience the discussion, whether they had attended the event or not. A wrap-up edition of HBOS Today, the group-wide electronic publication, was sent to all Retail colleagues following the fourth event.

According to Fiona, the first phase of the programme was a huge success: 'It quickly established Benny as an approachable, hands-on leader and engaged staff in a meaningful conversation about the business.'

Phase 2: Delivering for Retail

The second phase began late summer and involved letting colleagues know what the key priorities were for Retail going forward, to establish Benny as the owner of the major actions and increase advocacy of the divisions' products, service and people initiatives.

A series of promises – for customers and colleagues – were launched to give everyone a framework for the future. Importantly, each promise had a series of specific initiatives behind it to make sure it would be delivered. In line with Benny's direct communication style, the promises were kept simple, straightforward and relevant to all colleagues.

During September and October nine *Delivering for Retail* events took place across the UK. Around 7,000 management level colleagues attended. Each event included presentations on the key product, service and colleague initiatives that were planned for the coming months. Presentations were tailored to provide a local element to each event to make them attractive to all parts of the business. Importantly, a Q&A session was retained to continue the dialogue with colleagues and the top team. Colleagues at each event were also given a card to take away, detailing the promises.

Once again, an online publication, *Extra Online,* was published following each event for colleagues in each location. It covered the promises made, key content and a link to the presentation slides and transcript. A wrap-up publication was sent to all colleagues in Retail following the final event.

Another branded intranet site was created to give colleagues all the information about the events. Prior to events, it included information about logistics. Following events, it held transcripts, presentation slides and feedback. It was designed as a useful resource to help managers deliver key messages to their teams.

The key initiatives launched at the *Delivering for Retail* events were also communicated to all colleagues in Retail on a staggered basis. This was done using a variety of channels. For instance, when the Group's interim results were announced in August, a dedicated TV programme was produced for Retail. This included highlights from the first 6 months and an interview with Benny. TV was also used at the end of September to give colleagues across the business a flavour of the management events. Credit card-style handouts summarising the promises announced at the events were given to every attendee. After the final event, these were sent to every colleague along with a message from Benny Higgins.

The final strand of the communication campaign was *Benny Online*; an intranet-based conversation allowing colleagues to email questions to Benny and get an instant response. Around 300 questions were answered during the 3-hour session. All questions and responses from Benny were published online for all colleagues to see.

The Research

One of the hallmarks of a good internal communication programme is research and evaluation and the team identified early on a number of metrics that would help assess the contribution of communication during this period.

The results were impressive. Research by MORI showed that, between September 2005 and September 2006, employee advocacy increased significantly in a number of areas. Advocacy of HBOS as an employer increased from 56 per cent to 69 per cent, service advocacy from 45 per cent to 53 per cent and product advocacy from 62 per cent to 72 per cent. In addition, employee understanding of the business's objectives leapt from 69 per cent to 81 per cent.

Feedback from the *Delivering for Retail* events was also very positive – 90 per cent of delegates rated the events positively. Of these, 63 per cent rated them excellent or very good. HBOS colleagues also gave a big thumbs-up to the range of initiatives announced at the event. 91 per cent were positive about them, with 59 per cent rating them as excellent or very good. Furthermore, 89 per cent of colleagues said they felt more positive about Retail's prospects having attended.

Secrets of Success

So what were the keys to the success? Fiona believes that two factors underpinned the programme: 'Face-to-face was absolutely central and we worked hard to ensure as many employees as possible got to see, hear and meet Benny, regardless of their level or location. That worked incredibly well and got us off to a great start. Intranet, print and TV played a part too, but their role was to support the conversation, not to replace it.'

But Fiona also pinpoints the simplicity of the messages and the campaign's focus on delivering results: 'This was a straightforward, straight talking campaign focused on delivering tangible results. Colleagues really liked that simplicity.'

Following the success of the programme, it was decided that two further roadshow tours would be held in 2007. These kick off next month with a series of dedicated events that will report on progress and continue the good work.

PART V

Advanced Communication Skills

26

Corporate Social Responsibility and the Communication Professional

by Ingrid Selene

Corporate Social Responsibility (CSR) is the latest 'must have' strategy for large corporations. But is it a 'must do' item for employee communication managers?

The Background

There are many different definitions of CSR, and there are large variations between countries and companies as to what issues they focus on in their CSR strategies. Broadly speaking, CSR refers to how companies engage with all their stakeholders and make socially responsible decisions that conform to norms of ethical behaviour and comply with the law.

This chapter turns attention to CSR and the implications for the employee communication function.

Those companies that implement CSR may regard the programme as a way to:

- promote the company and its products;
- enhance the brand image and brand values;
- reduce regulatory constraints on the business or improve the regulatory environment in which they operate;

- facilitate a better, more cooperative working relationship with local communities;
- attract and retain employees;
- create a better work environment for employees that increases productivity and/or supports other strategic objectives;
- gain inclusion in ethical investment funds.

Other companies may only be reluctant supporters, introducing CSR programmes simply to meet compliance requirements in the country for which they have a stock exchange listing.

Most of for the benefits associated with taking up CSR cannot be achieved unless there is external promotion of the company's CSR activities. Governments, local communities, customers and potential employees need to be told about a company's CSR activities if they are to have the desired impact. It is therefore not surprising that from a communication's perspective companies have focused on their external PR, promoting their CSR credentials to their external stakeholders.

Less attention has generally been given to the internal promotion of their CSR activities.

Internal Communications and Corporate Social Responsibility

Employees are stakeholder too and it is important to understand the role that internal, employee communication should play in supporting a company's CSR objectives. At Aon Australia we are now looking at how we communicate our CSR programme internally and promote the associated activities to our employees.

While the internal communications team can (and should) be consulted when a company is developing its CSR strategy, and your views sought, you are unlikely to dictate the strategy yourselves. What you do have is an element of control and influence over the CSR-related communications to employees. These communications can enhance, ignore or potentially contradict the company's

CSR strategy. It's therefore important that both what is communicated and how it's done aligns with your CSR strategy.

Corporate Social Responsibility and What You Communicate

There are two categories of CSR communication in which you might be involved:

1. Special, one-off projects to promote a CSR initiative internally, for example, the introduction of an employee payroll deduction scheme for charitable donations.

2. Inclusion of CSR messages within existing internal communication vehicles on an ongoing basis. Articles in newsletters, features on the intranet (such as a CSR topic of the month) and feedback surveys that measure awareness of the CSR strategy are just some of the things to be considered.

In addition, you may consider:

- proactively adding a CSR perspective to stories, articles, presentations on other topics;

- avoiding communications that conflict with the CSR strategy.

The options you have to promote the company's CSR programme heighten awareness and provide regular information and updates will depend on your employee communication infrastructure. You have a particular responsibility when it comes to the communications you produce for the CEO and executive team. We know that employees won't see CSR as important to the company unless these messages come from the top, and are seen as being important to the senior management.

So when you are preparing communications to be issued by this leadership team you need to put them through a CSR filter. Is what you're saying consistent with the company's CSR strategy and values? Does it enhance or contradict these values? Should something else be included that further supports your CSR programme? Does the method of communication reflect the values espoused in the CSR strategy?

Obviously these considerations shouldn't be at the expense of other business objectives, or be given a higher priority, rather they should be in addition to them.

The internal communication teams will not be able to support the CSR programme unless they're well briefed on it. This suggests that you need to have a process in place for keeping up to date on the company's CSR strategy and activities. You also need to be aware of the external communication activities that are being undertaken relating to the strategy. This coordination should be relatively easy in those organisations where responsibility for CSR, internal and external communication are all in the same department. Formal structures, regular meetings and liaison protocols may, however, be helpful if these functions are spread across a number of different areas of the organisation.

Part of Corporate Social Responsibility is How We Communicate

There needs to be consistency between the values as espoused by the CSR programme, how the internal communication team works and how you implement the corporate communications for which you're responsible. There are a number of aspects to this, including:

- Timelines: for example, if your organisation's CSR strategy says that you will keep stakeholders informed about decisions that affect them then you need to make sure that your internal communications keep employees informed in a timely fashion.

- Inclusiveness: for example, if your organisation's CSR strategy says that you seek to be an inclusive organisation then you need to make sure that your employee communications don't exclude members of your workforce such as those that speak a different language or the deaf.

- Responsiveness: for example, if your organisation's CSR strategy says that you are responsive to the communities in which the organisation operates then you should have channels to obtain feedback from employees and communications that respond to the issues employees raise.

- Consideration of individual needs and differences: for example, if your organisation's CSR strategy says that you recognise and value individual differences then the internal communication team should demonstrate this (such as providing part-time work for those with caring responsibilities).

- Respect for others: for example, if your organisation's CSR strategy says that your organisation demonstrates respect for stakeholders, then the way the internal communication team is managed should demonstrates respect for the individuals in the team.

The individual CSR strategy of your company will determine the importance of each of these factors, their relevance and what specific issues you need to consider.

For example, if a company's CSR programme includes strong support for the local community then you need to support members of this community in your workforce, for example, by translating communications materials that come from head office into the local language.

As another example, if safety is a key element of the CSR programme you need to consider whether there are safety implications for a subject about which you are communicating (for example, a building refurbishment programme). You might not make the CSR issue a core element of the communication but it could be a good opportunity to reinforce the message and support this CSR goal.

In some organisations, the corporate communications department will also have the scope to devise and introduce its own projects that support the company's CSR programme. When I was the Director of Corporate Affairs at Pharmacia, Australia, I was able to develop and implement an employee volunteer award. A key objective of this programme was to demonstrate to employees that Pharmacia was a 'good company with good employees' at a time when there was considerable negative publicity about the industry and particularly one of our company's products.

It was a relatively simple programme designed to recognise and celebrate the volunteer activities of our employees. I launched the programme at a company meeting, made copies of the support materials and nomination forms available on the intranet, featured nominees in the monthly newsletter, and announced the winner at the end of the year with further company-wide communications.

Acknowledging the contribution that individual employees make to their local communities can be important for all companies, and critical for the success of their CSR strategy. The strategy may be met with cynicism or derision if employees feel that their own efforts are being ignored.

27

Storytelling and Business

by Ian Buckingham and Paul Miller

It's the 30th October 1938, and the roads are choked up as people across the USA head out of town in a panic. Across the country, folk are hiding in cellars, loading their firearms and preparing to defend themselves against Martians and their poison gas. Seventy years ago, the radio dramatisation of *War of the Worlds* by Orson Welles caused a stampede as listeners believed that the Earth was being attacked by aliens. Amazing what a well-told story can do! But surely people were more gullible back then?

It was the 1970's when a whole generation grew up with a fear (sometimes phobia) of 'what lies beneath' the calm surface of the ocean? Steven Spielberg managed to tap an archetypal fear and kept us perpetually on our guard from the dreaded shark. It was just a story, another piece of make-believe from the Hollywood story factory which exaggerated fact and was liberal with the fiction. But even if you are immune to both of these examples, then imagine how different is the feeling of lying in bed late at night listening to the creaks of your pipes and floorboards having watched a horror movie, than having sat through *The Sound of Music*. At one time or another, we have all been affected by the world of imaginary possibility we call 'Story'. If this is not so then perhaps you should visit your doctor; the sooner the better.

So how is it that a film, play or book can make us cry, laugh, experience joy and get angry and what's it got to do with business? People don't really die on stage – sorry to spoil the illusion for you – nor do they really get married, fight against justice, go to work in a bank or anything else. It's amazing though that our rational mind understands this illusion perfectly, yet still we connect with the story and shed real tears and have genuine palpitations of the heart. Have you ever paused for a minute and wondered what stories people working within your businesses are telling each other about the change process they're currently going through?

The Place for 'Storytelling in Business'

Generally, we take stories lightly, hence the dismissive expression, 'it's only a story'. If storytelling, in all its guises, is mere entertainment, a respite from reality during our leisure time, then in business it's a pejorative term. Storytelling belongs in the corner with all the other touchy feely stuff that doesn't get business done, and at best gives you a day out of the office (or if you're on linked into an online network, a day out *in* the office). But somewhere we are seriously missing the point, seriously misunderstanding our own needs as human beings. The fact that people in business ask 'what place has storytelling in business?' shows that they either don't understand that stories are the high denomination notes in the currency of communication, or that business has a serious fault-line and is suffocating a facet of our basic humanity. And suffocation surely has a detrimental impact on performance both of the individual and of the organisation. But before we examine the benefits of storytelling to business, let's examine storytelling per se: what purpose does it serve and what outcomes can we observe?

STORIES ARE EVERYWHERE!

Stories and storytelling are not the least bit alien to us. Stories are ubiquitous and for a good reason. Robert McKee, the Hollywood story doctor and guru, has this to say about story:

> *Imagine, in one global day, the pages of prose turned, plays performed, films screened, the unending stream of television comedy and drama, twenty-four hour print and broadcast news, bedtime tales told to children, barroom bragging, back-fence internet gossip, humankind's insatiable appetite for stories. Story is not only our most prolific art form but rivals all activities – work, play, eating, exercise – for our waking hours. We tell and take in stories as much as we sleep – and even then we dream. Why? Why is so much of our life spent inside stories? Because as critic Kenneth Burke tells us, stories are equipment for living.*[1]

Now perhaps Robert McKee and critic Kenneth Burke are siding with their own: art lovers taking a grandiose slant on the endeavour they have devoted their lives to? Then let's look elsewhere. Gregory Bateson in the book *Mind and*

1 *Story, Structure, Style and the Principles of Screenwriting* by Robert McKee, New York: Harper Collins, 1997.

Nature[2] tells the tale of a man who wanted to know if his computer could ever think like a human being, and put the question to it. The machine set about analysing itself. Eventually, the answer appeared – the words read, THAT REMINDS ME OF A STORY. Perhaps it's true as Milton Erickson proposed: 'humans are a 'story-telling species'.

WHY STORYTELLING IS POWERFUL

In the book, *The Art of Possibility* by Rosamund Stone Zander and Benjamin Zander,[3] the opening chapter is entitled 'It's All Invented', meaning that our individual perception of the world owes more to imagination than reality.

> *...All of life comes to us in narrative form; it's a story we tell. The roots of this phenomenon go much deeper than just attitude and personality. Experiments in neuroscience have demonstrated that we reach an understanding of the world in roughly this sequence: first, our senses bring us selective information about what is out there; second, the brain constructs its own simulation of the sensations; and only then, third, do we have our first conscious experience of our milieu. The world comes into our consciousness in the form of a map already drawn, a story already told, a hypothesis, a construction of our own making.*

If what we see is a representation of reality, then stories are one of the most effective ways in which we communicate our view of reality to others. And if we are all seeing the world differently, then how much more important is it to share our story and give others an indication of our view of the world, particularly if we happen to be in a leadership role or need to enlist others to help deliver for us (as everyone in an organisation needs to do at some point)? And how essential is this process of communication in the business world when we talk in our teams, groups and organisations about being on the same page? But let's not confine ourselves to the world of business just yet.

The science tells us that we are receiving information about the world around us through our senses, we are interpreting the world through sensory information. Where we put our attention (or is that 'where our attention is drawn'?) determines the input, that is, what we perceive. How we respond internally to the patterns inherent in what we perceive makes up our *experience*.

2 *Mind and Nature* by Gregory Bateson, re-issued by Hampton Press, Cresskill, New Jersey.

3 *The Art of Possibility* by Rosamund Stone Zander and Benjamin Zander, London: Penguin Books, 2002.

So, stories might be defined as the art of drawing attention to a very specific series of events that require the audience to see, hear, feel, taste, smell and think. Story is the art of taking another person on a tour of a different world or world view with the aim of elucidating a particular point or possibility. Good stories, stories that work, are *very* specific: a good movie doesn't have a wasted frame, a great play or novel rarely has a wasted word or line, because artists and writers are building a 'view', a flight of the imagination or the re-telling of past experience in which they want the audience to experience what they have experienced, ask the questions they have asked themselves, make a point for others to consider, and the effect is to mostly bypass the rational mind and appeal to the senses and emotions.

And if that is all a little abstract, then let's bring stories back to earth: stories are purveyors of beliefs and values. In the world of the story, in the specific *view* created, is an implicit set of values and beliefs. And if there is ever an example of how powerful a story is then look to Hitler and the Nazi dream of a new and glorious empire that honoured and favoured the superior (us), rid the world of it's imperfections (them), and conjured a world of pure art, fine architecture and all things 'decent'. To those that looked on from afar, from beyond the inner circle, it was an ugly and misguided fantasy – still it was compelling and pervasive enough to start a calamity that resulted in the deaths of 57 million people. Of course, it's a bit rich saying that stories started the Second World War, but much of Nazi ideology was spread through the story/myth of a super-race. It's sobering to reflect that much of what governs our lives is the sense we make from the stories we're told.

Storytelling and Business

To exaggerate the point, but to make it nonetheless, we are not advocating that ceremonial costume, dry ice, native drums and panpipes should be the new format for the Monday morning meeting or performance review (though the image is one to savour). Storytelling is never a replacement for effective procedures: coming into land at Heathrow airport in a Jumbo 747 you don't expect to communicate with air traffic control and hear a parable about a lion and a mouse which mirrors your current predicament…

Likewise, you need ropes, protective clothing and climbing gear to get up a mountain not a book of climbing tales… or do you? On television recently was a documentary concerning the ascent of Everest where a gung-ho member of the climbing team wanted to race for the summit. The team leader delivered a cautionary tale – with a pointed reference to the dead bodies that line the way. This soon brought about a change of heart and a bout of commonsense in the eager climber. A story, or *knowledge sharing,* may have contributed to saving their life, it certainly contributed to keeping the team together.

So, we all understand that stories are never a replacement for vital information or indeed action, but our contention is that today in business the tail is wagging the dog. That is, processes, procedures, facts and efficiency are valued above the *experience* of work. The world we created to make our lives better has to some degree and for some time asked us to sacrifice some of our personality, if not our humanity. Stories have been castigated as unprofessional in some way. People need purpose and they need to make sense of their lives, stories give them that. Even (or especially) stories about the business give them that. Do you think employees use flowcharts and procedure manuals when they relay the daily events to each other over a pint or a cup of coffee? So why do managers?

Information assists knowledge, but stories and metaphors create emotion and meaning. When working with a large IT firm we asked for analogies for the current state of play of the business. How revealing and how useful is it when someone describes the company as an enormous oil tanker with ten captains on board all arguing in which direction to steer the boat, whilst the crew are down below lobbing spanners into the engine? As this was accompanied by the laughter of recognition and the nodding of heads you can't help thinking that not only have you touched on something that would be missing if you studied the paperwork but you've effectively burst the emotional bubble, allowing a moment's catharsis and having gently coaxed the story from its cover, the underlying root causes could now be worked on together. Aesop's fables have long been used in a similar way – to enter our childhood consciousness like the metaphoric wolf in sheep's clothing and to warn, teach and to entertain.

Stories and metaphors at work are like icons on your desktop or zip files, they don't take up much room, but double click them and they open up to layers and layers of meaning and significance. They have a lasting effect because they make an emotional imprint on us; the sense is retained because stories create a felt-experience. And they work wonders in understanding situations and demands.

Leadership

If leadership is partly about inspiring a community of individuals to undertake a collective endeavour, then stories are essential to articulate that vision. Noel Tichy in his book *The Leadership Engine*[4] remarks that:

> *'The best way to get humans to venture into unknown terrain is to make that terrain familiar and desirable by taking them there first in their imagination.'*

And Antoine de Saint Exupéry remarked that:

> *'If you want to build a ship, don't drum up the men to gather wood, divide the work and give orders. Instead teach them to yearn for the vast and endless sea.'*

When a leader inspires, they breathe life and energy into their followers. When we reflect on the extraordinarily motivating speeches Churchill made, it's clear that no amount of PowerPoint (had it existed) and no amount of consultancy or accountancy models would ever have had the effect of his well-chosen words. And Martin Luther King had a dream, he didn't have a change imperative and wasn't at a critical point of inflection. Or was he?

The results of a study at the London Business School show how much of the message we retain depending on the vehicle of communication.

- Statistics = 5–10 per cent;
- Statistics and story = 25–30 per cent;
- Story = 65–70 per cent.

And the moral of this *story* is that if you are delivering the 'who we are' (brand identity), 'this is where we're going' (mission/vision) and 'this is how we're going to get there' (strategy) piece, don't rely too much on statistics alone to land the message.

4 *The Leadership Engine* by Noel Tichy, New York: Harper Business Essentials, 1997.

Business, Emotion and Non-sensory Language (or Why so Many Business Speakers are Boring)

Do you remember the strapline to the 1980's movie 'Alien'? 'In space no one can hear you scream.' These few words create an image (space), a sound (screaming) and a feeling (not a very nice feeling). Compare it with 'dedicated management capability' or 'randomised user-orientated response' These are non-sensory words and they abound in the corporate world. Now, if you put enough of these non-sensory words together you will trip something in the listener's brain and a film and a fog will appear before their eyes as they fall asleep or escape into daydream. These non-sensory words are the vocabulary of science, borrowed in business to give a veneer of credibility ('it must be true, it sounds scientific'). Somehow we are not reassured by too much feeling or emotion in business. After all, the language of love, romance, of the emotional life is the language of metaphor ('Shall I compare thee to a summer's day?'). This language excites the imagination; it creates *feelings, images, sounds, smells.* Remember your first kiss? The first record you bought? The smell of coffee roasting? The visual imagery of being surrounded by your loved ones? Often we believe that these feeling, these emotions, cloud and corrupt the experiment and enterprise we call business. Yet if you want to tell me about values, like trust and integrity, don't give me the science or the textbook definition, give me the metaphor, give me comparisons to help me understand, give me the story.

Getting the Story Straight: The Hero's Journey

The most effective and versatile storytelling tool must be 'The Hero's Journey'. There is no space to do justice to it here, but by way of a simple explanation, The Hero's Journey represents the central narrative that underlies any story of growth or change regardless of cultural origin. It is a framework which allows an organisation, team or individual to examine past and present change, both personal (largely emotional) and corporate (largely rational) and to anticipate and explore future change.

The Hero's Journey (Figure 27.1) formed the main plank of a leadership programme for a large petrochemical company. The requirement was for creative consultancy and support to ensure that the leadership models moved from theory to action. The metaphor of a journey in which their goal was perceived to be heroic and worthwhile was a powerful theme for the hard-nosed, analytical Top 200 worldwide. What might have been an adequate

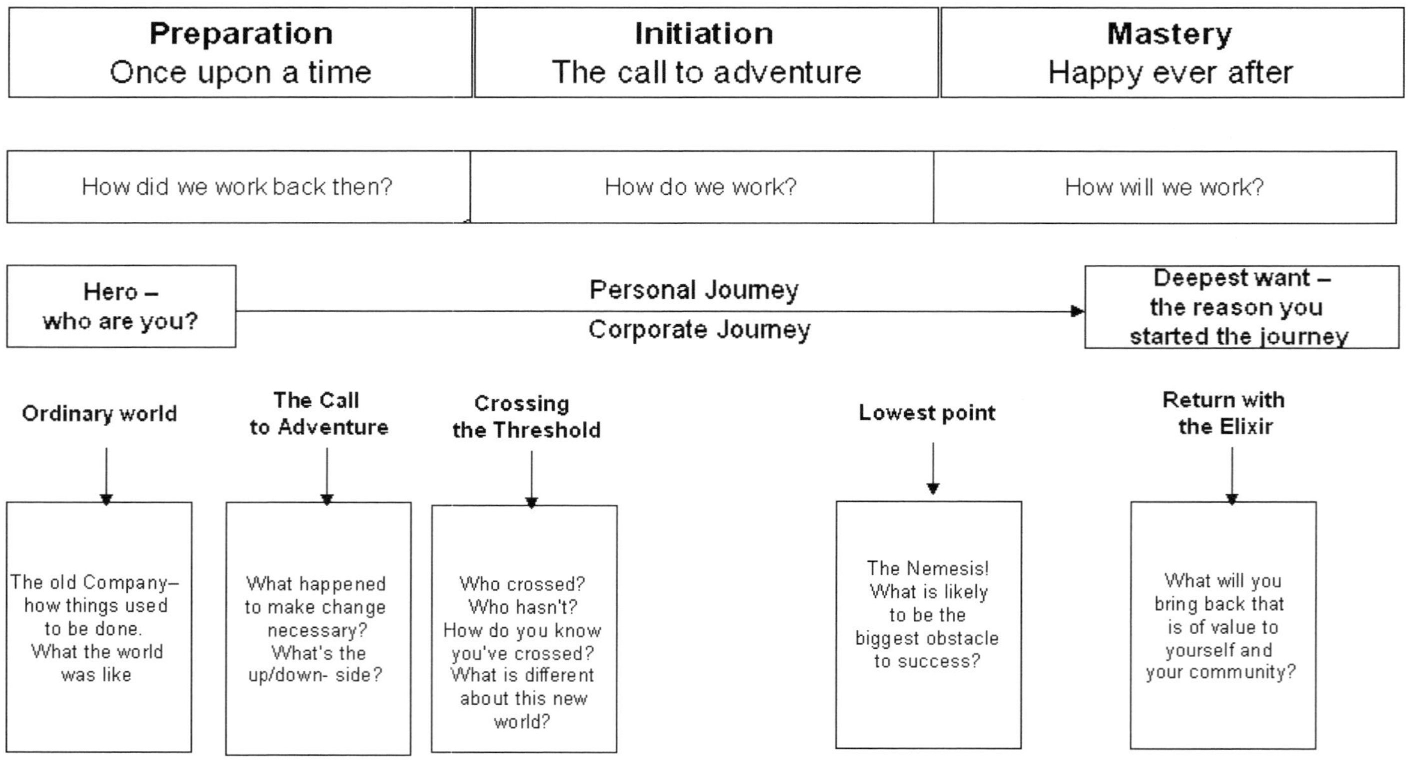

Figure 27.1 **The Hero's Change Journey**
©by2w.co.uk

leadership programme, turned into something of a movement once the goals, ambitions, leadership competencies, business targets and the roles of each individual were seen through the lens of The Hero's Journey.

The work of these leadership programmes was practical stuff with real-life outcomes, and the commercial objectives of the company were surpassed ahead of time. This success was correlated to the emerging inclusive culture instigated by the leadership programme and the tools and practices having been driven so deeply into the individual business units, in particular.

Storytelling has now become a widely accepted form of instilling advice and best practice in refineries. The global vice-president described the programme as being responsible for '... a phenomenon that's growing within our organisation'. When did you last hear that about a communication campaign?

Thus far, we've applied The Hero's Journey as a storytelling device:

- as a project planning tool;
- as a diagnostic tool for reviewing past projects;
- a means of aligning team goals and vision;
- a means of communicating an organisations mission;
- a tool for managing change;
- a 1:1 coaching tool, as a poetic device;
- a frame through which to view past, present or intended change.

Above all, The Hero's Journey is a means by which corporate objectives may become personal aims, and thereby create value, purpose and perspective.

Brand Values

The question 'What do you mean by integrity/teamwork/transparency?' is best answered with a story. There is a much quoted principle in dramatic writing that 'character is revealed under pressure'. Until a character is tested by circumstances then we know not of what they are made. Someone falls over in the street, or gets into difficulty in a meeting; do you rush over to help? Do you walk on by because you have an urgent appointment? Do you experience a little pleasure at someone else's misfortune? Stories reveal how people react in particular situations, they reveal what people believe ('It wasn't really stealing, everyone does it!').

While running an induction event for one of the big four accountancy firms, we used The Hero's Journey model as a way of eliciting powerful stories from participants and from speakers. We were privileged to hear a senior partner talk candidly and from the heart about his experience of being in the eye of the storm during the Enron scandal. It was a story of betrayal, of despair, of camaraderie, of fierce group loyalty, of stupidity, of duplicity, of pain and ruin and, ultimately, of success. What do you imagine this said to 200 new joiners? Young people sat in the audience with the burning questions, 'Have I done the right thing by joining this company?' and 'What sort of company have I joined?' The storytelling process developed its own momentum and recently won an industry award.

Positive Rumour: Celebrating Success Stories

Lessons learned are wrapped up in our past experiences. Often these are lost, but can be reclaimed through the telling of the story. These are more than cautionary tales (though cautionary they often are) they are a way of examining what worked and what didn't.

It's common practice in the petrochemical industry to begin meetings and conference events with safety stories, often about the personal lives of the workers as a means of putting their daunting industrial health and safety responsibilities into stark relief.

Below is an example:

> *I'd been told about putting knifes into the dishwasher with the sharp end facing down. Sometimes I'd remember, but sometimes I, or my wife, would do it the other way. Then a guy told a story about a young child falling onto the bottom tray and being badly hurt by the knives sticking out. It was such a strong story, I went home and established the habit of stacking the dishwasher correctly from that moment on.*

That's interesting, because it demonstrates that stories are a powerful tool in changing behaviour, but there's more:

> *... a few weeks later, my daughter, a toddler at the time, toddled into the kitchen whilst the dishwasher was being loaded, tripped and fell straight onto the cutlery basket. All the knives were face down, and she received no more than a large bump on her face. I'm so pleased I did what I did, and I share the story with you so you can do the same.*

Another organisation, an energy company, enlisted our help to harness the power of stories as part of their 'Have a Heart' (yes, that's what it was called), well-being in the workplace campaign. Thus far they had invested in stress-relieving balls and pedometers to sell the message. Short of an actual nanny handing the packs out to employees, they had managed, in their enthusiasm, to capture most communication clichés. Sensing an imminent engagement disaster, we encouraged them to undertake a series of face–to-face storytelling sessions, asking people to share stories exploring the importance of well-being at home, but in their own words. A gripping contribution was made by the 5-year-old son of one of the managers who drew a picture of his daddy lying down accompanied by a story about how he was scared that his daddy smoked and would soon go away and leave them on their own.

These are true stories and the reason we have included them here, is that we challenge you, especially if you have young children, to continue to stack the knives sharp end up, for example. We've never done it at home since hearing that story. Now think about how you can convey the same degree of emotion when communicating about well-being in the workplace. Still a dry subject?

Culture

Many years ago we were involved in a project for a high street retailer intent on creating a culture of openness and honesty. We agreed on a process called Forum Theatre, a process invented by the South American actor, director and activist, Augusto Boal, often now referred to as simulations, or when not fully understood or delivered correctly 'role play'. Boal developed a series of techniques and interventions that allow the audience to replay the past and road test the future. The difference between Forum Theatre and conventional theatre is the removal of barriers between actor and audience, the audience are encouraged to interact and make suggestions to the actors and may, at appropriated times, replace the actor(s) in the scenes.

Everyone was given the chance to feedback their stories of working in the business. The information was entirely anonymous and involved a diagonal slice of the organisation from cleaner to regional head. When all the feedback was collated and represented in 'scenarios' – short scenes based on reported experience – the reaction from the people at the coal face was, to quote a participant, 'Like seeing my life acted out in front of me – gave me a shiver down my spine.' Whilst the reaction from senior management, was roughly, 'I don't see the point of this, this just isn't anything like our day-to-day business.' Mmm. Interesting. When pressed on the question, 'Does anyone recognise these scenarios?' the room was ominously quiet. One shaky hand eventually went up, and a woman with a rather nervous voice said quietly, 'I do.' Someone had broken rank and for the first time there was some energy in the room. She continued, 'I think other people do as well, but are reluctant to say.' Reluctant or scared? This was an intensely revealing experience, as a snapshot of the culture it was perfectly apparent that honesty and openness were very rare commodities indeed. In fact, the aim of the project was too ambitious, but we had taken the first step – we had a barometer reading for the current state of play. Another way of looking at it is to say that we got a few actors to tell a few stories and almost caused a riot!

At the other extreme, in functional organisations, of which there are far more than the cynics allow, we find that stories, good and bad, are effortlessly and willingly trotted out. All that is required is to create the right circumstances (for example, trust, level playing field, non-judgemental approach) and ask astute questions. From a cold start we have learned some of the most surprising, fascinating and intimate details of people we are working with. This brings us neatly on to the next value of storytelling to business.

Collaboration and Connection

The myth goes that accountants, engineers and IT workers are tough to engage with. These people, we are told over and over again, are logical, rational, procedural individuals and we really will have our work cut out. Yes, it's true that some people are more adept or at home with left-brain activities, but they all have lives, a beating heart and a story to tell. Some of the so-called dull accountants we have worked with would rival Microsoft for their creativity, and would certainly give them a run for their money in staying up late in the bar! One such 'accountant' at Ernst & Young walked to the South Pole, solo. So badly frost-bitten was his toe that he cut half of it off with a penknife... Now there's a story!

Another example: in any room of 50 people you will nearly always find someone who has represented their county or their country at sport, and you will almost always find someone who has worked alongside them for years saying 'I didn't know that'. In terms of creating connections between work colleagues the story exercises that we run are like panning for gold and finding it every time. The question in all our work is how much of yourself are you leaving at the door when you enter work? Stories quickly turn accountants, lawyers, oil execs, burger flippers and so on, into mums, dads, enthusiasts, record breakers, lifesavers, romantics, extreme sportsman, musicians, explorers and more. And what is the purpose of this? Well, you break the work persona, you break the pattern of a person's thinking, you turn them in a direction they don't normally go and you create easy connections with others. For example, people who have overcome extreme hardship find admiration, respect and affection from others who have heard their story. And if you think we are talking therapy and counselling here, then let us point out one well thought out question, such as, 'What qualities did you possess in that experience that would be useful in your current work situation?' It sounds easy. It is.

Allowing people to import skills and competencies from other areas of their lives is a swift way of improving performance, whilst the exercise of revealing something of their life story is often the catalyst for deepening relationships with colleagues and with teams.

Stories are lying around waiting for a simple question to bring them to life. Think for a moment, what is the song that brings a tear to your eye/makes you feel joyful/drives you insane? There will be a story behind your answer. What is your most precious object? What memory does an aroma induce? Of what are you most proud? What's the best team you have ever been in? What's the worst?

Storytelling isn't a nice way to have distraction. Whether you like it or not, creative storytelling is at the heart of your culture and as leaders we have the choice of embracing, riding the current and using the energy or wasting time, energy and effort trying to build a dam of indifference. But for storytelling in business to have an impact and be useful, it presupposes acceptance, honesty, conscience, involvement and an ethical objective. Why not start by taking a long hard look at the sequence of planned events and significant internal engagement episodes (be they written or verbal) and consider what story the Top Team are going to tell about the next steps for the business and how you want your people to think and feel?

Charles Handy quoting Pierre Thuiller, French philosopher and historian:

> *A society is not a society unless it is able to invent ideal concepts and myths that mobilize individual energies and bind people's souls together.*

... and we wonder how those ideas and myths are best spread. Actually, that reminds me of a story...

28

Moving Minds

by Simon Wright

It is often said that moving home is one of the primary causes of stress in modern society. Whether we spend hours planning it or just go with the flow, it involves lots of emotional upheaval and significant change. Now consider that, according to the International Stress Management Association, over half of us experience stress at work and one in four take time off because of it, it doesn't require a giant leap to appreciate how office moves can be an extremely unsettling experience to a workforce.

So when the rumour mill begins and people start to hear the rumblings of an office move, a whole series of mixed emotions begin to appear. While there will be those who can't wait to leave their current location, there are often many more who will need to be prised away. After many years at the same desk creating a space which is comfortable and familiar, to be suddenly told that all of this is going to change, can lead to a lot of uncertainty.

It is no longer practical to impose office moves on to people, as little is gained but confusion, resentment and disengagement. However, if a move is handled well they can create quite the opposite effect. By investing time and a little resource into managing the communication of a move, significant benefits can be achieved. Indeed, there are many examples of high-profile office moves where internal communication has played a core role – from the various government department moves, through to the relocation of corporate HQs in to, and out of, London.

One such move was recently undertaken by the big four accountancy firm, Ernst & Young.

A couple of years ago, Ernst & Young completed the biggest move in its history, merging 13 offices in London into two state-of-the-art locations. The new head office, 1 More London Place, was opened in the autumn of that year and brought together over 3,000 people in a single location for the first time.

Jenny Moss, Senior Internal Communications Manager and a member of the project moves team said, 'The building was significantly larger than any of the previous offices in our estate and it required a step change in the way people used the facilities on offer and more importantly, it required real engagement before our people even set foot in the building.'

To achieve this, Ernst & Young put together a dedicated internal communications team which led the moves programme. The team developed communication channels ranging from a moves intranet, through to regular site visits and Q&A sessions. Most importantly, the team began engaging with the workforce over a year before the move, to give them time to ask questions, visit the site and to fully understand what the move meant and what changes would be required from them.

According to Moss, the move from closed-door offices to an open-plan layout was welcomed, 'By the time the people moved into the new location, they were aware of what to expect and were given lots of training and encouragement to use the new facilities and explore their new environment.'

Meeters and greeters ensured most people were fully operational within an hour of arriving at the new offices. Over the subsequent weeks, the communications team ran numerous orienteering sessions and various projects began to help the people utilise the new facilities as effectively as possible.

The moves programme has had some real commercial benefits and as Moss concludes, 'Our people say how much easier it is to work in the building. They can hold impromptu meetings and build relationships far more effectively which means an even better service to our clients.'

What Ernst & Young recognised early on, is that by maintaining a regular level of engagement with people, fear and uncertainty could be removed and replaced with an expectation of what was coming. Disruption in the outgoing offices was minimised and a smooth transition was achieved at the incoming offices. Not only was disruption reduced, but people soon began feeling a sense of pride in their new workplace.

Removing the negative elements associated with a move, for example, the worry of the unknown and the stress of change, can turn a potentially difficult time into a platform for positive change and a means to demonstrate real employee engagement.

Many organisations have also used a major move as a catalyst for general change. For the communicator, this can mean an opportunity to rethink existing communication channels and a time to implement latest thinking.

For example, at the new Ernst & Young offices, a network of over 50 plasma screens were installed to facilitate regular and timely electronic internal communication messages. This could never have been achieved in the existing offices due to the restrictions of the IT infrastructure required to support such a channel and the cost.

But employee engagement during a move is not the reserve of the large corporate. A simple desk move of four people can quickly generate similar levels of discomfort to those involved and those located around them as a major office move can. In fact, without adequate communication, the very real danger is that the rumour mill will take over and before you know it, speculation is rife about the impending restructure of a department or the wholesale move to some obscure location.

Office moves need not be damaging to the people involved and if handled carefully and considerately, can be a powerful tool to engage people, create a sense of pride and help improve productivity. Consideration of the impact the smallest move might make is just as relevant as the moving the corporate HQ. Perhaps the amount of time and resource allocated will be different, but the underlying reasons for ensuring effective employee engagement don't change.

Top 10 Tips During an Office Move

1. Start communicating early – at least a year before a big move.

2. Make sure you're part of the project team.

3. Treat it as a major change programme – don't underestimate the impact of a move.

4. Involve people in shaping their new environment – even the little things count.

5. Use the opportunity to review your internal communications technology and capitalise on the building as a channel.

6. Focus on the basics – like ensuring everyone is up and running within 2 hours.

7. Conduct orienteering sessions and tours around the building if appropriate.

8. Appoint meeters and greeters to welcome people to their new home and to help and advise during the first few weeks (and get them to wear a special t-shirt/uniform so they are instantly recognisable).

9. Use the move to drive through deeper changes (moving leaders from private offices to open plan can have an enormous impact on work climate).

10. Put in place a rounded communications plan including electronic channels and heavy use of face to face.

29

Perspective: The Hidden Dimension

by Mike Klein

It is not the most visible topic in the discussions about internal communication, generally taking a back seat to things like tactics, technology, technical skill and measurement. But perspective may actually be the issue that has more to do with the success of internal communication – and of an aware internal communicator – than any of its more technical or transactional aspects.

Perspective has an impact on internal communication from a number of dimensions. The three core dimensions include the communicator's perspective, the core client's perspective and the perspectives present in the audience. For the purpose of this discussion, perspective is defined as:

> *The values, biases, orientations and mindsets that govern an individual or group's participation in the process of communication.*

The Communicator: Common Perspectives

Given that this manual is geared towards the internal communicator, it makes sense to look first at the types of perspective communicators commonly hold – views that guide the way they communicate, the ways they position themselves relative to their clients and audiences and the ways they see their own role. Four main perspectives come to mind:

1. journalistic;

2. marketing;

3. facilitative;

4. advocacy.

The Journalistic Perspective

The journalistic approach is prevalent in large swathes of the industry, partly because clients perceive formal communication as a journalistic activity, and perhaps more significantly because many if not most internal communicators are hired on the basis of their journalistic experience and skills. Its influence is certainly felt in the continued reliance of publications and tools using journalistic formats and styles. But the most significant impact that the journalistic perspective – significantly, in the injection of the journalistic pretense of *objectivity* into organisational communication – is demonstrated in tone, impact and credibility.

The notion that organisational communication must represent – or look to represent – some kind of a neutral or normative position is one that some communicators adopt for a number of reasons:

- a belief that communications must be neutral to be credible;
- a desire to have one's internal communication look and sound like that provided by external media;
- a reluctance on the part of communicators to actively take part in the pursuit of the organisation's objectives.

While the journalistic approach may produce a product that sounds right, embracing a journalistic philosophy can hold numerous pitfalls for a professional communicator. The value of merely informing staff about what is happening around them is very difficult to substantiate and justify commercially. Adopting a position of journalistic objectivity creates serious strategic and emotional distance between the communicator and the work of the organisation. Maintaining the appearance of objectivity can often prompt a communicator to take a more detached or even negative view than facts justify, and much less than organisational success requires. Maintaining high production values while opting out of real support for organisational initiatives makes the communicator and their function a visible target for cost cuts.

The Marketing Perspective

For a number of years, the term *internal marketing* nearly became synonymous with the intentional practice of internal communication, with a clear focus on *selling* messages and outcomes to our own staff.

The marketing perspective approaches communication from the opposite end of the commitment spectrum to the journalistic approach. It has no pretense of objectivity – generally focusing on the positive impact of what is being discussed, and why the actions being discussed represent imperatives as opposed to options. It also treats staff as customers – parties to a transaction – rather than recognising the richness and complexity of their ongoing internal relationships.

Because of its emphasis on selling, the marketing perspective can often drive very visual or media-centred approaches: posters, brief videos, glossy brochures. The selling emphasis also brings up a number of major pitfalls.

Internal marketing often denies that staff have a choice about how they accept, reject, reinterpret or redirect organisational messages and such denial leads to the use of disempowering terminology – such as the use of the term 'we' to imply collective agreement on a topic or action where no such agreement exists. Internal marketing often adopts a tone that is cheerleading or unrealistically positive – where such statements contradict observable facts, the credibility of the organisation becomes undermined. A focus on using marketing to drive internal alignment can often be taken by managers as a signal that they can avoid taking their responsibility in communicating with and engaging their staff.

The marketing perspective remains popular because it offers the possibility of securing support/compliance for organisational initiatives without undue sacrifices or investment by senior and middle managers. And, for initiatives that require high awareness but relatively low commitment (protecting company property, following IT security procedures), this perspective still has something to offer.

The Facilitative Perspective

Facilitation collided with internal communication in the early 1990's, both from a conceptual standpoint (a belief that the right answer can be elicited from the *real* participants) and from a practical standpoint: that the communicator's role was about eliciting that answer and have the participants communicate it themselves.

Removing oneself from the development of solutions is at the philosophical core of facilitation as a perspective – with the facilitator giving far more emphasis to the process than to the product, and to emphasising the responsibility of the solution owners for the onward delivery rather than driving it themself.

The facilitative approach requires a similar level of expressed neutrality to the journalistic perspective – but it requires a far higher degree of strategic engagement with managers and leaders as they are the ones charged with formulating the solution and, in many cases, delivering the message. Still, the facilitative perspective has its pitfalls as well:

- Facilitation depends on the goodwill of the managers and leaders engaged in the process.
- It lends itself to top-down approaches, as many organisations consider multi-level facilitation unwieldy or politically unacceptable.
- It transfers responsibility for communication initiatives away from professional communicators, often to managers who have little commitment, interest or skills.

The Advocacy Perspective

A fourth perspective for an internal communicator which emerges is that of the advocate – that of the communicator who sees their role as creating a favourable environment for the outcomes of their clients. Essentially, the advocate role combines certain elements of the other perspectives: the partisanship of the marketer, the craft skill of the journalist and the engagement of the leaders/owners of the facilitator. But the advocate role moves beyond those elements with a clear focus and (often self-given) accountability for the achievement of specific, tangible outcomes.

The advocate makes no pretence of objectivity. Nor do they allow the communication effort to be a substitute for the required participation of leaders and managers in achieving the tasks at hand. But the communicator-advocate is also uniquely positioned to define success, particularly at certain milestones (the world will look like XXX when YYY is completed on x date), and of the end state as a whole (we will have succeeded when X has happened).

The advocacy perspective is not without its pitfalls; it is possible for the advocate's zeal and sense of ownership to alienate influential members of the client organisation – to the point where they resent or even sabotage the communication effort. The advocate's zeal may also lead them to press the organisation too hard to meet stated deadlines to maintain appearances. And of course, their efficacy may be limited by the perspective of the client they work for – which ultimately determines the tone, intensity and purpose of communication.

Client Types

While your own perspective certainly determines where you stand vis-a-vis the hiring organisation, the main overriding element of organisational communication is that it almost inevitably occurs with the participation and permission of at least one sponsor, or *client*. Because approval is critical, it is worthwhile also to look at some prevalent types of clients, and what may be required to align your own intent with that of the person signing the cheques.

THE DEFENDER

'The Defender' is a client whose first interest is that of the part of the business in which they operate – whether it is the organisation as a whole, the person's location, division or the project they direct. What is important to remember is that the defender will approach communication from the standpoint of whether it minimises risks or exposes the defender's agenda unnecessarily. Defenders tend to focus less on winning and much more on not losing, and communicators working with such clients can often benefit from acknowledging that element of the agenda without allowing it to subvert their own objectives.

THE BOSS

An entirely different type of client is someone called 'The Boss', more of an authoritarian figure who sees their role as being the person in the organisation who makes their subordinates do what needs to be done. Whatever your own view of power relationships within an organisation, the extent to which the boss believes they drive power and performance will be the operative perspective here. Leveraging communication with such a client may involve a look at the processes that work and the successes that have previously occurred in that organisation – balancing the client's perspective with the organisation's own sense of reality.

THE LEADER

Another type of client is focused most on the achievement of the task at hand, and less about dictating the process or protecting it (or their own) reputation – a client referred to here as 'The Leader'. An astute leader will often give a communications professional a relatively free hand – in terms of tone, vehicles, messages and strategic intent. At the same time, such a client may either have their own driving vision which may be less resonant to the other participants than to themself. Alternatively, a leader with a 'big picture' focus may not have secured sufficient commitment from other key players to allow communications efforts to do what's required. However, if both the communicator and the leader are aligned on intent and approach, the possibility of client resistance is highly diminished.

Audience Perspectives

Communication in organisations has little value if it makes no connection to the range of people involved in achieving organisational goals. While populations can be diverse, four basic kinds of audiences emerge with distinct perspectives of their own.

RECIPIENT

Recipients are seen by many as the masses – the large numbers of employees who are either apathetic, or whose interest in a topic of organisational importance is considered nice but not critical. Communication that treats audience members as recipients tends to be informative but not particularly engaging. And in some organisations, there are members who are indeed recipients – individuals, for whom the message has limited relevance and equally limited resonance – who don't necessarily want to be asked to pay more attention or make some accommodations for an initiative of peripheral interest. Assuming that audience members are mere recipients, however, entails substantial risks

– particularly if there are individuals or constituencies who can help achieve outcomes, or whose resistance can derail them.

PARTICIPANT

Conversely, another audience element is that of participants – people who do their jobs willingly, and want to understand as much as possible about what they can, cannot and must do at any point in time. Participants are aware of the extent that they have discretionary abilities to support or resist organisational initiatives, and effective participant communications generally show considerable respect to that ability to choose.

REBEL

A small, but potentially corrosive element in the audience population are members called rebels – staff members whose own views put them in active conflict with organisational objectives. While few rebels will reveal themselves openly, they are often wont to reinterpret organisational messages in cynical or hostile ways, and usually without direct traceability. Although there is little a communicator can do to remove the rebels from the mix, the resistance they put into the environment can be distinguished, openly discussed and erroneous arguments corrected.

CHAMPION

Another small group – and one with considerable utility to the internal communicator – are those called champions – committed supporters of the agenda who make tangible positive contributions. Communicators can not only use champions as examples of people who are making a positive difference and making the organisation's objectives achievable, they can also be identified and networked to communicate and share ideas with each other, and to engage participants, recipients and rebels in the relevance of the initiatives in their respective local areas.

Drivers

Among clients, communicators and audiences alike, there are a number of loyalties or drivers which lie at the core of their behaviour. These drivers tend to be of paramount concern to each player – despite protestations they may proffer to the contrary.

JOB

If a player in this world believes their job is vulnerable and wishes to protect it, that will be the framework that drives the person's proactive behaviour (to demonstrate their value) and reactive behaviour (not to cooperate with initiatives that could put the job at risk).

TURF

The issue of organisational jurisdiction or 'turf' is of paramount importance in terms of where a communicator sits in the organisation. A communicator sitting in HR will generally have to focus on the HR agenda, one working in corporate communications may have to defer to external messaging and one sitting in the programme office of the company's number two initiative may be asked to attempt to help reposition the initiative so that it is seen as 'numero uno'.

BUSINESS

Some communicators, particularly when seeing certain dysfunctionalities or discrepancies between what people do to protect their jobs and defend their turf and what the organisation claims to be about, may opt to embrace the business agenda and the values and principles espoused by the business. A communicator with strong senior sponsorship may be able to do so successfully – but without such sponsorship, seeking higher moral ground than one's client occupies may be a career limiting move.

Putting Perspective into Perspective

Organisations are different, situations are different and cultures are different. But organisational communication and organisational life have enough common dynamics – across industries, disciplines and borders – to merit looking at where one stands in relationship to what may be happening around oneself, and about where one stands on how to proceed in a way that is effective. In some cases, using the perspective frameworks offered here will allow for quick recognition of one's situation and help start the process of adapting to it. In others, this recognition will allow a communicator to challenge people coming from these perspectives and, in so doing, fundamentally change the situation in a way that helps achieve success.

30

Cultural Barriers

by Marc Wright

Understanding your organisation's culture is a key step in developing your internal communication strategy. Every company has its own culture and, if not understood and recognised, this culture will undermine your internal communication campaigns.

This chapter examines the four corporate culture types and how to adjust your internal communication strategy to be more effective within each.

Fons Trompenaars, in his seminal book *Riding the Waves of Cultural Diversity*[1] identifies four types of cultural diversity among corporate cultures:

1. Guided Missile;
2. Eiffel Tower;
3. Familial;
4. Incubator.

His work, written in association with Charles Hampden Turner, is based on understanding cultural differences within multi-nationals and across national frontiers, but these findings are also useful if you work within a single country.

Guided Missile Culture

A Guided Missile culture describes a company that is guided by objectives. These cultures are strongest in the US, the UK and The Netherlands. It is now

1 *Riding the Waves of Cultural Diversity* by Fons Trompenaars and Charles Hampden-Turner, New York: McGraw-Hill, 1998.

the dominant business culture in the UK – particularly in the service, technology, media and communication sectors – and has replaced the older command and control cultures, where staff were expected to do as they were told.

Command and control was prevalent in the 1950s, 1960s and 1970s, when the majority of senior managers had either fought in the Second World War or had done military service. They exported their behaviours and systems from the military straight into management practices and government departments. Command and control cultures tend to use communication to give instructions and lay down rules of behaviour. Such cultures can be extremely efficient (particularly in warfare) but the rise of an enquiring, well-educated workforce with a stronger sense of self has meant that such cultures have melted away in the UK. They are only really found in the armed forces and some financial services industries, where compliance is more important than initiative or customer service.

In guided missile cultures, the objectives of a particular project or mission are paramount. Staff are rewarded and focused on initiatives to move the business forward. When managers make decisions they will tend to be guided by targets set for their project rather than by the views of those working on different projects, no matter how senior.

What's good about guided missile cultures is that managers feel a high degree of ownership and are able to cut through and across departments to get the task done. Results are faster than in other cultures and there is greater flexibility as people work in smaller, sometimes virtual, teams to get the job completed.

What could be better is the complexity and conflict in a business that sometimes results from managers following separate agendas. These cultures, being target driven, can create high levels of stress and over-working in staff who strive to achieve the various objectives and key performance indicators they have been set.

So how do you thrive in a guided missile culture if it's foreign to you?

- align yourself to key projects;
- but hold onto the bigger picture;

- set yourself measurable and achievable targets.

Communication programmes in such cultures tend to become quite tactical, being designed to support whatever initiative is top of the agenda. Managers may have little time for communication projects that are company-wide as they will see them diluting the attention of teams that they would prefer to stay focused. If you want to get their support and a share of their resources, then align yourself to the key projects which need communicating. Concentrate, for example, on a new sales incentive plan, on health and safety issues or on a share-save scheme, which needs to attract the attention of large numbers of staff to be successful. If you spend your time communicating projects that are not seen to benefit the business on a day-to-day basis, then you and your department will lose credibility.

However, one of the challenges of the guided missile culture is that a company can easily lose sight of the bigger picture amidst the complex reporting lines of matrix management. There is a real opportunity for communication managers to work with the CEO to communicate the big picture, which shows where all the initiatives are heading. What binds the targets together? Where do all the initiatives fit? Consider creating or revitalising your own big picture; your boss will readily support that kind of initiative. And liaise with your HR department to see if you can bring alive your organisation's balanced scorecard by making all those targets available online so people can see how the success of their projects add to the company's overall mission and performance.

Eiffel Tower Cultures

Strict hierarchies are called Eiffel Tower cultures by Trompenaars because they are tall and inflexible and found mainly in France – although German companies can share many of these multi-layered characteristics. Instead of being target- or project-focused, here it's the relationship you have with your boss and your position in the hierarchy that drives management behaviours.

These cultures are very effective and strong; they are among the most successful organisations in Europe. However, they can be slower to react to change and this can be a problem when working in areas which require employees to be able to bend the rules to get the job done, or where there is a higher degree of ambiguity.

In rigid hierarchies, information is power. The communication professional, therefore, can be blocked by senior management's desire not to tell staff too much.

To counteract this tendency:

- cultivate side-to-side and bottom-up communication channels;
- develop both objective and measurable feedback channels;
- develop a senior champion for communications.

The Eiffel Tower model encourages communication in a top-down cascade model. By developing your feedback channels, you can beat the hierarchy at its own game. When feedback is objective and can be measured, it becomes a very effective tool for changing management behaviours. Imagine if your managers were giving messages directly to customers: the manager who alienated customers through poor or misleading communication would not stay long in the hierarchy as soon as sales began to suffer. What is measured dictates what gets done so, by measuring feedback rather than stifling it, you can use information to permanently improve the quality of internal communication.

Because hierarchical cultures are driven from the top, it is essential to get a senior champion for communication. Look for outside appointments who come from a different culture. These senior executives are more likely to already have been converted to the power of internal communication. Cultivate these champions and ask them for advice and mentoring. Then use examples from their part of the business to influence executives who are poor or unwilling communicators. The best champion is always the CEO so you need to develop their support.

It is no coincidence that more and more leaders of business consider strong communication skills to be an essential part of their personal toolkit. If your CEO is not a communication advocate, then perhaps they feel their own performance is not as good as they would like. Develop a programme of speaker training for your top executive and hire the best scriptwriter you can find to support them.

The Familial Culture

The Family or Familial culture is very widespread in Southern Europe, South America and much of the Far East. Here, the corporate culture takes its cues from the family, with its complex interweaving of influence and patronage.

Managers will make decisions in these cultures with reference not just to their line boss but also to the person who has sponsored their career or for whom they have worked in another part of the organisation. The culture relies heavily on mutual dependencies and trust.

Because the lines of loyalty are multi-layered, these types of company can be very flexible: if a key manager leaves, there is a network of 'relatives' who can take the strain. These cultures put a great deal of emphasis on honour, on keeping one's word and on reputation.

Family cultures have deep roots so although they can appear flexible; they are loathe to cut away from the past. As a professional communicator you can match this style by:

- communicating through example rather than by instruction;
- cultivating stories and legends to suit your cause;
- using celebrations and events.

Staff and colleagues are influenced not so much by what senior management say – as in an Eiffel Tower culture – but by what they do. When senior management promote and reward, it can often be in the face of statistical evidence. Where a 'Management by Objectives' culture will reward for attaining clear, concise goals, in a Family culture you can get promoted because you are liked; because the organisation feels that you fit and could do well in the future.

Loyalty from the bottom-up is often rewarded more than performance. Disloyalty to anyone is frowned upon. This gives rise to the archetypal 'saving of face' that is so remarkable in Far Eastern corporate cultures.

Internal communication in such cultures can become, therefore, anodyne and self-serving. Few managers are openly criticised, and information can degrade into mere propaganda. So rather than coming out with blunt and unwelcome messages, communicators turn to stories that can illustrate the message you want to get across without having to state the bald facts.

Stories have a strong potency in family cultures. Exploit the family culture's love of celebrations and special events to create significant moments that can accelerate change in your organisation.

Incubator Cultures

Incubator cultures are named after the incubator companies in Silicon Valley that developed with the rise of IT and the dot.com boom. It describes a culture where the idea is king and where people come to work to fulfil themselves. Just look at the original pizza-and-sleeping-bag cultures of Yahoo and Google, where staff are motivated by creating an ever-better search engine.

Management consultancies such as Accenture, IT providers such as Microsoft and Apple, and broadcasters such as the BBC, are full of individuals who get out of bed in the morning to follow an idea rather than a pay cheque. While these can be very exciting environments in which to work, for the communication manager, the job of internal communication can be like herding cats. This is because everyone feels themselves to be an expert in communication; in fact, they are only good at communicating what is of interest to them.

So how do you communicate successfully in an Incubator culture?

- develop a believable, authentic voice;
- encourage fanatics;
- use experiential techniques.

In Incubator cultures, hyperlinks undermine hierarchies, which means that anyone can find out the information they need without having to go up through the information chain to get it. As a result top-down communication ceases to have the hegemony it once enjoyed. Your own people leak like a sieve and external commentator and message boards have as much – or more – authority than your internal channels.

It is therefore essential to avoid spinning or obfuscation in any of your media channels. Tell it like it is or, if you can't, then say nothing. Incubator cultures are full of noise because they trade on ideas. Your task is not to add to the information but to attract attention to the information you want people to focus on. Blogging is a powerful tool – allowing staff and colleagues access to your genuine thoughts in your web diary.

Use Open Space Technology. This is a technique (sometimes known as an 'unconference') which allows delegates to drive the agenda at your next management meeting. If your people spend most of their lives on the Internet or intranet, then get them to come to a live event, where they have to leave their terminals behind. Use strong visual imagery, tastes, smells and sounds to reinforce your key messages. Don't depend on email. Use storytelling, interactivity, viral videos – anything that engages the senses that are not being used for most of your people's working hours. An open space event is determined by the participants. It starts with everyone putting up ideas for discussion and then a schedule is established. Delegates are free to come and go as they please to each session, grazing on information and learning or imparting ideas as they move around. It is a live event version of the 'wisdom of crowds' and can be a refreshing change from the usual orderly queue of senior executives at the lectern.

31

Using Pictures to Convey Strategy

by Hilary Scarlett

Today's communications professionals are constantly looking for methods which really engage employees in the business – a prerequisite for high performance, and for employee and customer retention. One highly effective approach that is being used more and more is a method that is thousands of years old – the use of narrative pictures. Pictures, metaphor and storytelling are being used by organisations as a way of encouraging dialogue and increasing understanding between managers and their teams. At first glance they can seem very simple – a piece of paper with images, depicting a story. However, they can be used to convey complex messages and to demonstrate, for example, the links between market context and business strategy, between organisation-wide initiatives, between activities of the organisation and its impact on the environment.

This chapter looks at how organisations, ranging from not-for-profit to manufacturing and to investment banks, have used the process of creating a picture to align leadership teams' thinking and to help those leadership teams create understanding of their strategies and change programmes.

What are They?

Strategy maps (see Figure 31.1), transformation maps, big pictures, rich pictures – there are lots of different names for them, but they are essentially large pictures (around A0 in size) used to convey information to audiences in an attractive and meaningful way. When used to their full potential, they do much more than convey facts about the organisation – they generate real discussion between the groups who are using them.

Figure 31.1 A typical strategy map created for a retail bank

Some use words, some rely solely on images to convey messages. Using words means that they have the advantage of being self-explanatory but creating a picture without words – relying on just the images – means that the picture is much more intriguing and demanding: the viewer has to look hard at the picture, think about what the images mean and interpret what they see.

Some organisations use them as part of team meetings, with the manager leading the discussion; others use them at conferences and workshops where they stimulate debates around the room.

Some pictures are complete in themselves; others need employees to add to them – either by 'graffiti-ing' on them or adding stickers. Some organisations use pictures for a one-off discussion, others choose to return to them again and again to identify what progress is being made since the initial discussion.

Why Use Them?

There are at least ten good reasons for using them.

1. THEY CONVEY A LOT OF INFORMATION QUICKLY

As the saying goes, 'a picture tells a thousand words' and these big pictures do have the benefit of being able to contain a lot of information. They can provide the context for change, what the future looks like and the steps that the organisation and every employee needs to go through to achieve the vision. They can home in on customer needs or environmental challenges, health and safety issues or personal development.

One bank was particularly attracted to using a big picture as they had lengthy documents and word-based presentations that tried to inform employees about its change programme, the consequences of not changing, the elements of its change programme and what would be required of employees. They knew that it would be hard, if not impossible, to expect employees to read these lengthy documents and take the messages to heart. All these messages, documents and slides could be summarised in one big picture and, in addition, the layout of the picture could demonstrate the links between the external world and the company's response to it, the company's change programme and the ultimate goals.

2. THEY ARE MORE VISUALLY ATTRACTIVE THAN WORD-BASED DOCUMENTS

From early cavemen to our own childhood, we are all drawn towards pictures. We like to explore them and try to make sense of them. Many big pictures use colour which makes them particularly vibrant and attractive. One member of a diversity team who had created a big picture to raise awareness of the importance of diversity, put their big picture up on the wall and said colleagues were constantly walking up to it to have a closer look – attracted by the look of the picture and intrigued to know what was in the picture and why.

3. THEY APPEAL TO A WIDER RANGE OF SENSES AND THEREFORE LEARNING STYLES

Because a picture appeals to people visually and aurally, it appeals to a wider range of learning styles: visual learners think in terms of pictures and learn best from visual displays. Auditory learners will benefit from listening to the story that accompanies the picture and from listening to the debate and dialogue amongst colleagues.

4. THEY ENCOURAGE DEBATE AND DIALOGUE

One of the greatest benefits of using a picture is that they encourage discussion. Whereas a slide-based presentation is often given in a darkened room with one person presenting while others listen, a picture needs to be put up on a wall in good light. Employees are encouraged to gather around the picture and explore it with their manager or facilitator. A manager using a picture can draw people in, ask questions of the group and get them to talk about what they see in the picture and how it is relevant to them. A major benefit that many managers experience is that employees feel much more comfortable challenging what they see in the picture, rather than directly confronting their manager. This means that rather than tacitly disagreeing, employees are more likely to question openly what they see, raise the issues that concern them and therefore engage fully in the conversation. A picture is therefore much more likely to bring out real discussion and debate.

5. THEY ENABLE CO-CREATION

Because of the very process that needs to be gone through to create a picture (which we'll look at later in this chapter), they encourage co-creation. The initial development might be done by the executive team with each contributing to what should be in the picture or by teams of employees who can look at early drafts, question what they see and suggest what the content should be and how it should be depicted. The important point is that employees at every level can be asked to contribute to the development of the picture. This means that not only is the picture more likely to resonate across the hierarchy and geographies, but also that there will be a feeling of ownership for the picture and its messages across the organisation.

6. THEY MAKE CLEAR LINKS BETWEEN MAJOR THEMES OR INITIATIVES

Because the picture is set up over a large 'canvas', employees can see how initiatives fit together or are sequenced. This is much more easily done on a large picture than in lots of pages of slides. Some pictures depict their change programmes as a journey and the picture can then show at what stage on the journey certain initiatives will be introduced. The black and white picture (see Figure 31.2) depicts the reasons for change on the bottom disk and the consequences if the organisation does not change, what the organisation hopes to achieve on the upper disk (customer focus, better global sharing of knowledge and so on) and is surrounded by four other disks which depict each of the four change streams. You can see a person being pulled through a hole in the floor from the current world to the future. The person doing the pulling represents a change agent as this was who the picture was initially designed for.

7. THEY ARE OPEN TO ALL EMPLOYEES AT EVERY LEVEL AND IN EVERY LANGUAGE TO INTERPRET AND DISCUSS

Pictures work particularly well in multi-lingual organisations, especially if no words are included. One manufacturing organisation chose a picture as its vehicle to communicate: it was a recently-merged organisation and the fact of having one picture, the same picture, being used by every team across their 120 sites was an important symbolic message in itself. With sites in many developing countries, having no words was also a great equaliser – the fact that some employees could not read was not an issue and they felt as able to discuss the picture as any other employee in any other country.

8. THEY HELP LEADERSHIP TEAMS IDENTIFY WHETHER THEY ARE ALIGNED IN THEIR THINKING

One extremely valuable outcome of using pictures is that they test alignment of leadership thinking. The development of pictures is usually based upon the

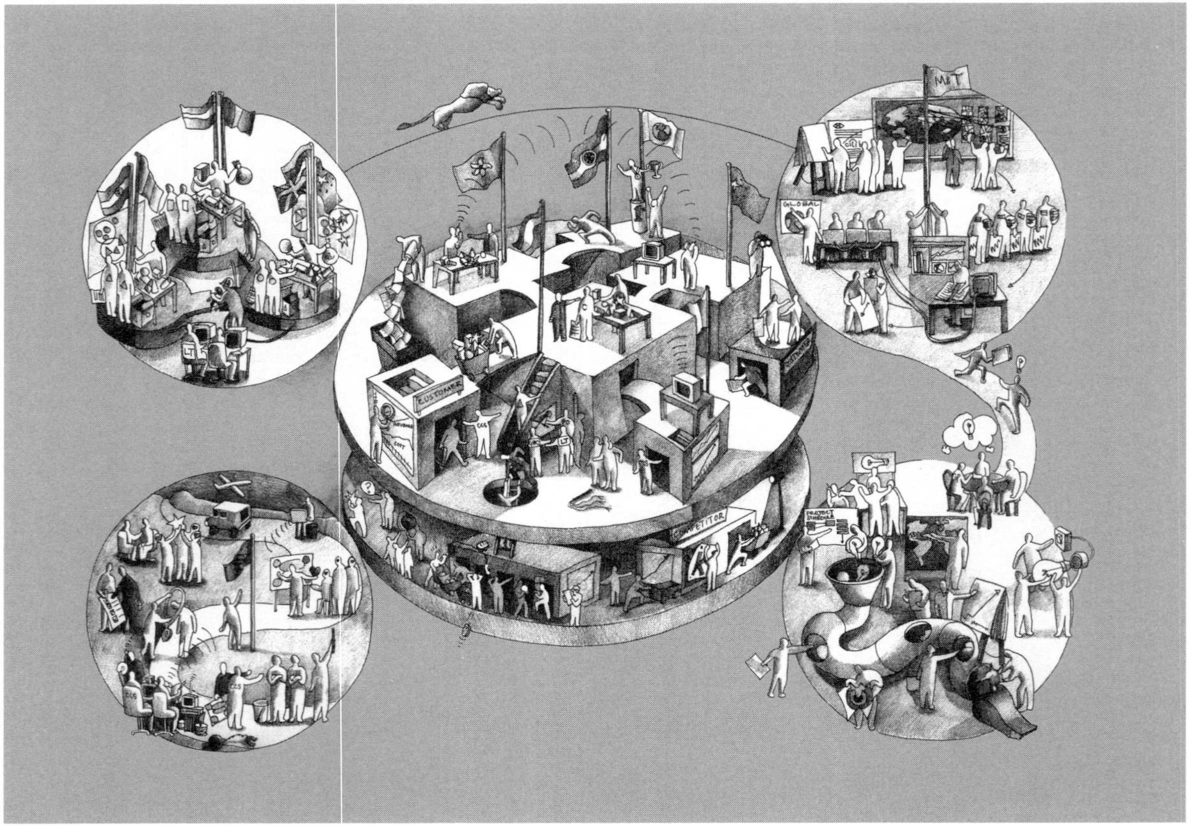

Figure 31.2 The change programme as a journey

input of leaders – each must input to the brief and this reveals whether they have the same understanding of the current situation and the same shared vision as each other. The leadership team also needs to see the first draft of the picture and this creates an interesting discussion. Before the next draft can be developed, the team needs to agree content (both what should be in the picture and what can or should be left out), emphasis, style and links between elements of the picture. This in itself is a useful exercise, enabling them to identify how unified or not they are in their opinions.

9. THEY HELP LEADERS AND MANAGERS THINK THROUGH THEIR STORY

Using a picture means that leaders and managers have to think through what they want to say and what messages they want to convey. They cannot fall back on reading words from a slide, they have to think how they will structure the session and how they will use the picture, how they will make the story relevant to their team and where they want to get their team to discuss and debate. Helping leaders and managers to think through their story increases their confidence and personal credibility.

10. THEY ARE MEMORABLE

There are probably not many slide-based presentations that employees will remember but the chances are that they will remember a picture or elements of it. In addition, to keep the picture and its messages front of mind, the picture can be used again: it can be left on the wall for a while to remind employees of its key messages. One retail bank used elements of the picture in the in-house newsletter and on the intranet to act as a regular reminder of the discussion employees had had.

Developing Narrative Pictures

1. ESTABLISH WHAT IS NEEDED AND CREATE A CLEAR BRIEF

The first stage is to be clear about what the purpose of the picture is – what it is trying to achieve, which groups of employees (or external stakeholders) will be using it, what the key messages are. Also part of this initial stage is identifying who should contribute to the brief and who should be involved in creating the picture. Creating a clear and detailed brief helps the process immensely: the brief forces those involved in commissioning the picture to agree what the picture should depict – getting the brief right means that there should be far fewer drafts of the picture, saving time and money.

2. CO-CREATION

The process of creating the picture is in many cases as important as the picture itself. This is what this second stage is all about. Those who have commissioned the picture must feel comfortable with the content of the picture before consulting more widely. This draft can then be taken to groups of employees for them to critique it – asking them to identify what works well and what needs to be changed. It is essential to think through which and how many people are invited to contribute to this process: involving many people can be very important in ensuring that the content is right and can also be an important, symbolic act of involving people. It also increases 'ownership' of the content and process. However, the wider the consultation, the more time-consuming the process will be. Consultation inevitably means lots of comments and many will be contradictory. It is important to be clear before embarking on consultation who will have the final say on what is amended in the picture.

3. COACH AND EQUIP LEADERS TO USE THEM

This is a crucial stage – few managers will have had the experience of running sessions using a big picture. Some will feel nervous about running such a session, others might assume that the picture should be used in much the same way as a slide-based presentation. Anyone using a picture needs to be coached in how to do this and in particular they need to be coached in how to use the picture as a means of generating discussion. Part of this preparation will also be about getting managers to reflect on how they will tailor the content of the picture to their employees – what stories they can tell to illustrate the points and where they need to get employees to participate in the discussion and agree actions. Using a picture does require preparation – there is no avoiding it – and managers need to recognise this.

4. USE THE PICTURE TO CREATE DIALOGUE; MEASURE

The fourth stage is to use the picture. Ideally every manager should be a participant in a session before they lead one so that they can experience what it feels like and what techniques work well in igniting the discussion. As ever in the world of communications, it is important to think about how the impact of the sessions will be measured. Conducting employee research before and after using the picture can help identify what shifts the discussions have created.

This is also the stage, if not earlier, at which to think about how the picture can be used in the long term: whether it is to be used as a reference point to which managers and their teams will constantly return and whether the images and messages can be conveyed via other internal media.

Pitfalls

Pictures and the process to create them can look disarmingly simple. Some of the mistakes organisations make include:

- Not getting the right people to input: if leaders are not involved early in the process, they can be reluctant to use the picture. If the right groups of employees are not consulted, the content might be wrong or might jar culturally.

- Not training managers: a manager who has not prepared properly for the session will not reap the benefits of using a picture and nor will the team.

- Choosing the wrong style of illustration for the audience: this is a very sensitive area. There are many different styles to choose from and it is important to get the right fit so that employees are drawn to the picture and want to work with it. Cartoon styles can be seen as very accessible or patronising; lots of words on the picture can mean that it is very simple to understand or that it lacks intrigue and might just as well be a slide-based presentation.

- Taking too long to create them: it can happen that if the process of design and consultation takes too long, then the moment has gone.

- Using them as a one-way monologue: as mentioned above, there is a danger if managers are not properly coached, that the manager uses it as a tool to talk at people – this undermines the very reason for using a picture.

How Some Organisations Have Used Big Pictures

An international bank created a picture to help their change team understand the overall objectives of the change programme and to look at how the team needed to work together. The picture was created based on the input of the leaders of the four strands of the change programme. This in itself was an interesting process as the leaders were interviewed individually and the interviews therefore would expose how aligned the thinking of the four leaders was. Fortunately, and unusually, the thinking was very consistent; when the four leaders each looked at the initial draft, there was just one small change to be made. This in itself was a positive message to the leaders – they didn't just need to think they were aligned in their thinking, they could be reassured that they really were aligned.

The picture was then used as the basis of a workshop with the change team which consisted of 25 people ranging in experience and nationality. The great advantage of this picture was that it did not use any words so that no matter what participants' first language might be, they would not feel disadvantaged by the picture.

The first half of the workshop consisted of the four leaders using the picture to lead a discussion about their strand of the change programme, encouraging team members to question and challenge what they saw in the picture – was this right? Were these really the challenges the company was facing? Have we depicted our solutions appropriately and given them the right balance? What's missing from the picture?

The second half was used to allow participants to get their pens out, study the picture hard and to amend the picture as they saw fit. This meant that they had actively contributed to creating the picture and had thoroughly debated and questioned the purpose of the change programme, its implementation and their role within it. As a result of the workshop, the picture was re-drafted to reflect the comments of the team. All members of the change team said that they would be confident to talk about the change programme and to use the picture as a means of getting a discussion going with their internal stakeholders.

Other Examples

- A government department created a picture to set out their 5-year change programme.

- A charity used a picture to get each of their offices to think about diversity and to get employees thinking about whether every aspect of their office and their interactions would encourage people in need from all backgrounds to come to them for guidance.

- A retail bank created a picture to equip thousands of managers to have conversations with their teams at every branch and in every call centre about the future direction of the bank and the role of every employee in achieving that future.

- A global manufacturing organisation created a picture to inform all its employees worldwide about health, safety and environmental issues.

- A communication team created a picture to depict the potential impact of well-managed communication and to illustrate how they wanted to work in partnership with their internal stakeholders.

> *I was attracted to using a picture because we needed to do something different to engage our people. We had had plenty of presentations and documents but we needed a method that was really going to get our people talking and discussing and thinking. The picture as a tool to prompt debate did exactly this for us.*
>
> Julie Everitt, ABN AMRO

With thanks to Lindsay Seers, Julie Everitt, Mike Pounsford, Domna Lazidou and Sheila Hirst.

32

Communication Champions

by Fiona Robertson

Resources for internal communication are usually limited, both in terms of manpower and budget and yet, all around your company, you have an untapped supply of the most powerful tool for moving the minds of your staff: Communication Champions.

By using a Champions Programme, you will be able to multiply the efforts of your communications team – ten, twenty, a hundred fold. And this resource is not only astoundingly effective, it's also completely free.

In this chapter, we explain why a Champions Network is such an effective and valuable communications resource and how to go about creating and managing your own team. Note that the techniques we feature here can also be applied to any form of champions programme, such as change programmes or 'living the brand' initiatives.

Communication Champions: How They Work and What They Do

- The reason why champions are able to magnify and accelerate your efforts is because they work on different levels, functions, sites and regions of your business, simultaneously and continually.

- Once a clear proposition or goal has been set for your champions network, they can then set about disseminating this message throughout the organisation, swaying co-workers at a grass roots level and effecting a seemingly-organic sea change within the company.

- Communication champions are most often used as communicators and agents for change.

- They are usually tasked with moving your company to the 'tipping point' of any given programme faster and more effectively.

- Champions can become your eyes and ears for internal research and measurement purposes.

- They can gather stories from around your company that, collectively, create your organisation's mythology, (for example, examples of great customer service).

THE ADVANTAGES

The advantages for the communications department, as well as for the company as a whole, are dramatic and swift results achieved with relative ease and all at little or no cost. The advantages for the champions themselves are equally positive: taking on this role gives them a sense of exclusivity; it makes their working week more varied; it builds their communication skills and advances their personal development and it gives them the opportunity to be noticed by senior management.

POTENTIAL STUMBLING BLOCKS

Note that resistance to a network of communication champions can come from senior management, who may be reluctant to give away man-days from their departments – especially if you want to recruit their most effective staffers – so it's vital that you obtain their endorsement.

HR may also object if you fail to include them in your plans. Otherwise, they may perceive you (and your network) as a rogue elephant, trampling over their detailed development and succession planning.

GETTING SENIOR MANAGEMENT'S ENDORSEMENT

Find a sponsor within the senior management team, (preferably the MD) and get their approval to have meetings with all the senior influencers in the organisation. At this stage downplay the amount of time for which you will need their staff. If you ask for more than 1 day per month, for 6 months you are likely to meet stiff opposition. Don't worry – just get as much as you can of their time – the champions themselves will commit more as they become more and more engaged.

Point out the personal development opportunities this network will present to their staff; they will be trained in presentation techniques and will be party to the organisation's bigger picture. Agree the role of the communication champions, clearly setting out the objectives of the programme to be implemented. It's a good idea to get the CEO and other senior management (including HR) to commit to a session with the champions, at which they will set out their proposals for change.

Set benchmarks before and after the champions programme, by which its progress can be measured (and its implementation justified). For example, the network's impact on the bottom line; internal feedback on particular information, attitudes and behaviours; and external feedback on something appropriate that the champions' work will have affected.

RECRUITING CHAMPIONS

Finding the right champions to spread your message is critical to the success of any champions programme so selection and recruitment is all important. Your champions' attributes and personalities are key so focus on the criteria below, rather than trying to recruit a representative cross-section of your organisation. Remember: if you recruit a representative spread across the existing company, you will simply prolong the status quo.

Effective champions tend to be:

- early adopters;
- good communicators;
- respected by their peers;
- already busy;
- representative of the major divisions, regions and functions of your business;
- from all levels of the company, down to supervisor (but no lower).

To find your champions, advertise the programme and ask for volunteers; people who nominate themselves tend to have the profile you want. Having obtained a number of potential candidates, ask for recommendations from other sources, for example, their line managers and HR. Unreasonable or difficult employees can make great champions; often, they're simply frustrated in their job so, with something to get their teeth into, they can turn their enthusiasm to your project. However, be wary of the candidate being foisted on you by a manager who is dissatisfied with their employee's performance so wants to offload the departmental dead weight. Sell the role to your candidates on the personal opportunities the position offers, the attention from senior management that they're likely to receive and the difference their contribution will make to the company.

When you have a keen group ready to be groomed, select most of them; it will make the role of communication champion more desired and aspirational. Tell those who weren't selected that the programme is full at the moment but that you'll be reviewing the team in 6 months' time and they are top of the list.

THE TIPPING POINT

For an idea, behaviour or programme to take root in your organisation, not only will you need to introduce it, you'll then have to let it spread and take hold, like a virus, until a sufficient proportion of your employees are behind this new approach. Once this tipping point has been reached, the speed with which your idea spreads will accelerate exponentially.

In any given community (or business), there will be a small number of Fanatics (maybe 2 per cent), a greater number of Early Adopters, a majority of Fence-Sitters, and approximately 20 per cent will be Reactionaries.

The fanatics are those people who continually come up with wild ideas though they tend not to see them through; their history is a series of aborted experiments so they get a reputation for not delivering.

Early adopters watch the fanatics in case they hit on an idea that might just work. When they do, they have the ability to present it in more practical terms and drive it forward. Early adopters are known for being open to and enthusiastic about new ideas; they have the respect of their peers and tend to be on the bandwagon before it starts to roll.

The fence-sitters watch what the early adopters do but they don't join in until a project has gathered momentum, credibility and approval from senior management; only then will they adopt the new approach.

The reactionaries are those who never change or embrace a new idea of their own volition. However, once an idea has gained significant momentum, it reaches its tipping point and then becomes adopted throughout an organisation, forcing the reactionaries to follow suit.

Given that this broad profiling exist in every business, its evident that early adopters are pivotal in influencing the climate of an organisation and in driving change. The reason why they are such a powerful group is because they are comprised of three different personality types – what Malcolm Gladwell in his seminal book *The Tipping Point*[1] classes as Connectors, Mavens and Salesmen.

Connectors are socialites – rare people with unusually extensive and elaborate social networks of friends and acquaintances. They spend time maintaining their social connections and are the central point of any organisation's network.

Mavens are the information gatherers of a social network; they evaluate the messages they receive and, when they pass on original communications, they also attach their views or personal interpretations. They give a critical appraisal of what's going on, thereby regulating the information being passed around a network, consequently, mavens have the power to control which ideas get transferred as well as how they are perceived.

Salesmen are persuaders – people who can propagate messages through force of character, and who can sell messages that are of importance to them. Their ability to persuade strangers to accept a message is why salesmen are important in tipping ideas to the point where they become adopted by the majority.

As regards your communications programme, if you can get the support of an early adopter within your senior management team, so much the better!

1 *The Tipping Point* by Malcolm Gladwell, New York: Little Brown & Co., 2001.

ENGAGING YOUR TEAM

The key here is not to frighten your champions off before they've started: the principle is to give them a piece of silken thread which they can pull on. Tied to the thread is a piece of string, and tied to that is a length of rope. By the time they are pulling on the rope, they are fully committed. So start with an invitation to test a pilot programme and then work with them to the point where they soon become the drivers of that programme.

Outline the features and benefits of the role that your new champions have taken on – namely, to be involved in something new, to be instrumental in making a difference, to learn new skills and to get noticed. Remember to make the project sound like fun, with little required in the way of time and effort. Organise a half-day meeting to bring all your champions together and explain the issues that you want the network to address. Pack this first session with fun team-building games and give them some quick wins through developing skills they can use day-to-day (for example, brainstorming techniques).

Encourage their opinions, get your new team to identify potential obstacles and then ask them to devise solutions to these issues. You'll find they gradually talk themselves into taking on the responsibility for implementing the actions they've outlined. Brainstorm all the ideas they've come up with until you have a plan that holds water; then arrange for the team to present this strategy to senior management. The more they give of themselves, the more committed they'll become… so soon you'll find you have a solid network permeating your organisation.

SUSTAINING THE NETWORK

Create an activity plan for your champions for the next 6 months, setting out their objectives; the benchmarks by which to gauge their progress; a few quick wins; opportunities for fun and any rewards. Measure your champions' progress using employee surveys which focus on the workforce's awareness of, or attitudes towards, elements of your communications programme, plotting shifts as they occur. Publicise the team's work and achievements company-wide through emails, newsletters, intranets, and so on.

Make a formal presentation to senior management towards the end of each 6-month period, including internal and external feedback on the subject of the communications plan, comparing results from before and after. Note the financial impact the network is having on the business, and include comments received from around the organisation on the work done, the stories compiled, and so on.

Celebrate successes and, each 6 months, give nominal awards for the champions' achievements. At the end of each 6-month term, replace at least one-third of the team to keep the champions feeling sharp and to allow new blood (and perhaps new avenues of communication) into the mix.

33

Better Emails: The W-H-Y Technique

by Marc Wright

Here's a simple technique you can learn to ensure more people read, and take action on, your emails. Emails you send are read by less than half their recipients and are acted on by even fewer. This page teaches you, in simple steps, how to write more effective emails and how to spread these techniques throughout your organisation.

The Challenge

The most used channel for communication in large organisations is email; however, it is also the most open to misinterpretation. Given that sending an email is a one-way system, senders cannot be sure that recipients have read, understood, or are acting on, an email's contents.

Solution: The W-H-Y technique

The W-H-Y technique has improved the efficiency of emails in large organisations such as British Airways. You can learn it in the time it will take to read this page, yet it is a technique that will stick with you for life. Just use the W-H-Y device when you sit down to write your next email. W-H-Y stands for the three paragraphs or elements of your email:

- 'W' stands for 'WHAT' – What is this email about? People are not interested in why you have composed an email or the pleasantries of opening chitchat. They have come to your email after reading about a totally different subject or doing some wholly unrelated task. So cut to the chase and tell them what the email is about; and do so using simple, jargon-free active language.

- 'H' stands for 'HOOK' – What benefit does the recipient get from reading your email? Think about the subject from their point of view and ask yourself, 'Why should the recipient give a damn?' Then get that benefit into your second paragraph.

- 'Y' is subject of the third paragraph – What do you want your recipient to say 'YES' to? It is the call to action.

Subject Title

The subject title of your email is crucial. As it is the only part of your email the recipient is guaranteed to read, as much care and attention should be given to it as a newspaper headline or an advertising copy line.

Write the subject title for your email *after* you have written your message. Look at your second paragraph then give your email a title that brings the 'hook' alive. Finally, check the sense of your message to make sure it is meaningful to anyone who might see it, even if they get to your email weeks or months in the future.

Benefits

- Using the W-H-Y technique consistently helps your reader to get straight to the point of your email, work out the benefits to them and see what you want them to do.

- People will read further down your email as you draw them into the subject and, by the end, will have a clear idea of what you would like from them.

- If you find your email does not fit the W-H-Y template, then perhaps email is not the best communication medium for your message.

- Communicating something for your recipients' general awareness should probably go on the intranet; whereas straight 'calls to action' are better when delivered in person so perhaps you should go and talk to a colleague, pick up the phone or even make a presentation at the next management conference.

Example of the W-H-Y technique

You want staff not to use part of the car park next Wednesday as you are holding a customer seminar at the office and need to reserve spaces for an unusually high number of visitors. You know that this will be an unpopular message and that most people will bin an admin email that reads:

> Subject: Car Park Closed Wednesday 26th.
>
> Due to marketing running a seminar on Wednesday 26th January, the car park will have 30 spaces reserved for outside visitors. Please do not bring your car to work but, where possible, use alternative arrangements on the day.
>
> John Steel, Facilities Manager.

Instead, now apply the W-H-Y technique to create an effective email:

> *Subject: Win A Free Car Valet & Help Us Win New Clients*

WHAT

> *On Wednesday 26th January, 30 potential new clients are visiting us for a seminar on our leadership in new rapid prototyping techniques. The last seminar we ran led to £400k of new business and our winning the prestigious Ford account. These seminars take a lot of organising and investment to get right, and we know that making clients welcome with a personalised space leaves a strong first impression.*

HOOK

> *You can help us win our next large customer by giving up a space in the car park for just one day, on Wednesday. We will reimburse your*

parking costs and allow you extra time to get to and from work on the day. And your car will go into a draw for a free valet service, on the company.

YES!

Just email me with your offer of a car park space by noon today to be included in the draw and help us win that next client.

Yours truly,

John Steel

Facilities Management

34

Creating Meaningful Dialogue at Work

by Jacqui Hitt

> *Human beings think together and coordinate action through language. Conversation is real work.*
>
> Humbert Maturana, Evolutionary Biologist

In many ways conversations are the life blood of any organisation however large or small. Without some form of dialogue between the individuals and teams who work there very little can be achieved. It's part of what makes human beings, and the institutions they create, so successful: through talking and listening ideas are created, knowledge is shared, solutions are generated and issues are resolved.

Whether you're handling customers, designing new products or managing the back office, much of what happens in your area of the business will depend on the discussions you and your colleagues have around what you want to achieve and how you will make it happen. When these discussions are productive, and the thinking upon which they are based is constructive, teams can achieve high levels of performance and great results. All too often, however, such interactions lack focus, direction and energy. This can impact on the levels of engagement and commitment of those involved, and slow down the organisations ability to deliver its goals.

Harnessing the potential of these conversations presents a great opportunity for internal communication professionals. By helping to shape such interactions, whether formally or informally, they can be turned into meaningful and powerful forms of dialogue that move the organisation – and its people – forward.

Think back to the last conversation you had where a leader wanted to involve you in solving a problem or engage you on an important business issue. How was it? Did the process reinforce the status quo or open up new possibilities? Was is collaborative and inspiring? Did it change anything for the better and move things forward?

Take the typical town hall meetings that take place in many organisations. So many seem to follow the same formula and very few live up to their potential. In many cases what happens is that everyone in a particular area or office is invited to attend and, because the 'big boss' is in town, the venue is packed. For the next hour or so, the boss shares their carefully crafted view of the world and at the end answers a handful of questions. Few, if any, attendees are willing to ask the questions that are really on their minds for fear of limiting their careers. If you ask both the bosses and the people who attended such meetings how they found the event, their answers are usually similar: 'It was fine but we didn't really get chance to connect or talk about the real issues.' Well-organised and on-message these meetings may be but in this format, they are rarely a good use of people's time or the organisation's money.

Contrast this with a series of employee meetings held by an international law firm. Conscious that they were going through a huge amount of change, their executive team decided that they wanted to 'hear what our people really think about what's going on'. In pairs they visited key offices and held a number of open sessions with staff. Each session was structured around a series of powerful questions. The executive team member opened the session with candid and personal observations on the challenges that so much change presented to them personally and professionally and then they sat back to listen. Careful use of questioning encouraged people to share their thoughts, ideas and frustrations in a constructive way. At the end of the session both the executives and the participants felt they had a fruitful and constructive dialogue about the future that had 'helped to move us on'.

This last example illustrates the power of taking a dialogue-led approach. It results in a far more purposeful, involving and engaging experience that actively and constructively supports change.

Why Team Briefings are Very Rarely About Dialogue

When team briefings are initially introduced they have the potential to transform the conversations teams have around important business issues. Unfortunately, due to limited line manager training, they often become a process for 'information exchange' where the managers use the briefing document provided to simply update people – and if they are lucky their team gets the chance to ask some questions. It's a very far cry from creating real dialogue. To do that leaders have to bury their own agendas, encourage people to find their own answers and be willing to really listen to what others have to say. So what is dialogue?

> *Dialogue… is about a shared inquiry, a way of thinking and reflecting together. It is not something you do to another person. It is something you do with people.*
>
> William Issacs, *Dialogue and the Art of Thinking Together*

Dialogue often means different things to different people. One of the most common ways of thinking about it is as a *shared* exploration towards greater understanding, connection or possibility. In its most basic form, each person:

- talks about what's really important to them;
- really listens to others and sees how thoroughly they can understand other people's views and experience;
- says what's true for them without making another's view wrong;
- sees what they can learn together by exploring things together;
- avoids monopolising the conversation and makes sure everyone has a chance to speak.

What this means for individuals is that they need to be willing to:

- focus on what really matters;
- listen with their full attention;

- be open and honest about what they think;
- respect other people's point of view;
- focus on finding the best solution or way forward rather than the one they think is right;
- allow others to speak without interrupting.

These principles can be used to shape many different types of face-to-face communication – from team meetings to workshops, conferences and events.

The Difference Between Dialogue and Debate

It's important to recognise the difference between dialogue and debate because they both have their place. Debate is useful for making decisions and taking votes while dialogue is about new possibilities and ways forward. One of our challenges is that we live in a debate culture (or what Deborah Tannen calls an 'argument culture') where having the strength of your convictions is highly valued. While that's useful in some contexts, it actively works against finding new solutions to issues through increasing engagement, collaboration and innovation.

A Model for Creating 'Dynamic Dialogue'

One of the challenges with creating meaningful dialogue is how best to structure it so that it is purposeful. This involves getting the balance right between providing appropriate inputs to help shape the conversation and giving people the space they need to explore the issues and generate ideas. The Dynamic Dialogue model shown in Figure 34.1 is designed to achieve this balance by making sure that key employee interactions are grounded in real business issues, that they give people the space to explore what these mean and that an appropriate way forward is agreed.

The Factors that Help Encourage Meaningful Dialogue to Flourish

Successful dialogue involves nurturing a number of different factors within an organisation – many of which support and reinforce each other. Some are

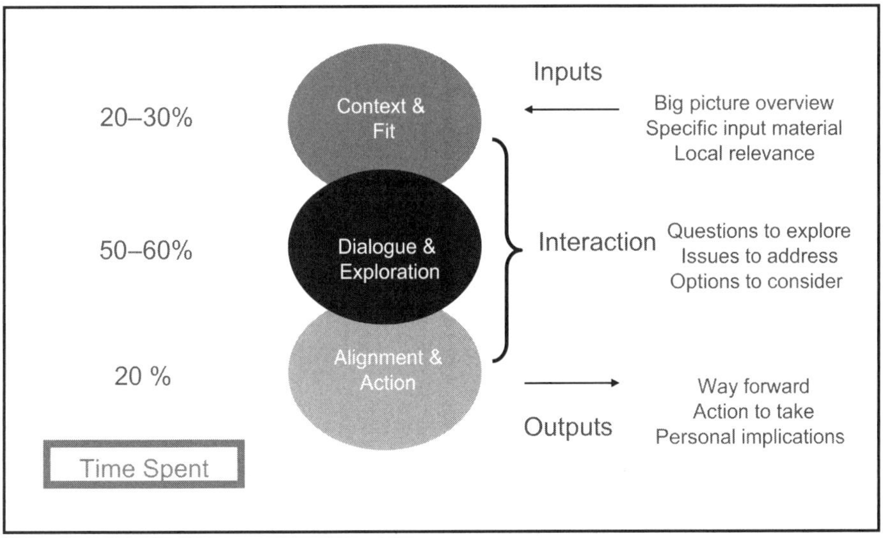

Figure 34.1 The Dynamic Dialogue Model

closely linked to leadership style and the type of internal climate and culture that exists within the organisation. Others revolve around respecting and valuing others.

- **Having leaders who are comfortable with helping others find their own answers to dilemmas** (rather than feeling they have to themselves) and really listen to what their employees have to say. This doesn't mean leaders do nothing: its means that they actively encourage and coach people to excel.

- **Allowing people to discuss the real issues facing the business** (rather than the ones that it is deemed safe to discuss) and take ownership for finding solutions. This can take courage, especially from leaders, because many prefer to focus on the positive rather than acknowledging that reality is filled with tensions and choices. Getting real on issues usually results in far greater levels of engagement.

- **Understanding the power of listening and actively encouraging different points of view.** The ability to listen well is still a rather illusive quality in leaders as is a willingness to accept that not everyone has to agree with your particular point of view.

- **The people taking part are willing to keep an open mind** (suspending their assumptions, putting aside their personal agendas and avoiding jumping to conclusions too soon) because they realised that what mattered was finding the best possible way forward rather than the one they think is right, easy or most obvious.

- **Being willing to share and build on ideas in a constructive and creative way.** One thing that will stop dialogue in its tracks is people keeping their ideas to themselves and a 'yes but' attitude.

- **Giving people time to consider and reflect on what could be rather than what is.** This involves challenging assumptions and being willing to consider alternatives and is an essential part of encouraging creativity and innovation.

- **Visibly showing people that their views are valued and respected.** This can be as simple as not interrupting others, concentrating on what is being said (rather than your own stream of thoughts) keeping your eyes on the person speaking and reflecting back what you've heard – all things that a remarkable number of people find very hard to do!

If you're interested in what sort of an environment is created when few if any of the above factors exist then the BBC TV series 'Can Gerry Robinson fix the NHS?' provides a very real example. During the series the business guru spent time at an NHS hospital in South Yorkshire trying to help them run more efficiently. By the end of the programme he was quite clearly in despair. Virtually every interaction that was filmed showed a total lack of dialogue between staff, consultants and management. The end result: an inflexible and inefficient environment for all.

HOW DIALOGUE CAN HELP PEOPLE ADAPT TO CHANGE

We are all familiar with the statistics on how often organisational change fails. One of the reasons is that there is too little real dialogue involved. People are simply expected to accept the changes that are imposed on them and rarely given the opportunity to influence the process or the time to adapt effectively. This can result in a whole range of responses: from denial to passive resistance or active blocking. Adopting a dialogue-based approach can help turn this into a far more constructive process. While it may seem more time consuming in the beginning, it can dramatically improve the likelihood of success as the following examples show.

EXAMPLE 1: INVOLVING THE RIGHT PEOPLE IN CREATING THE SOLUTION

When an energy company needed to move to a HR shared services model to reduce costs they decided to actively involve those affected in designing the new organisation. All the staff involved were invited to input their ideas and thinking to create a solution that would work for both the business and its people. While it took more time and effort initially to get the project off the ground, it quickly paid dividends. The final solution was highly innovative and adaptable to changing business needs. Through introducing new technology and more flexible ways of working, the company was able to retain most of its talented and experienced HR team. This helped keep disruption to HR services to a very minimum and sent a strong signal to the business about how best to handle change.

A large UK government department was aware that it had important issues to tackle if it was to reach the target level of customer service it had committed to deliver. As part of a wide programme of service improvement, the internal change team were looking for a way for over 1,000 people at six different venues to simultaneously share successes, best practices and ideas for delivering first-class service in a constructive and insightful way.

They were looking for a solution that would address the following issues:

- the people taking part were from different departments and offices and were unlikely to know each other;
- it was important that everyone felt able to share their thoughts and ideas right from the start;
- the process needed to actively encourage collaboration and cross-divisional working;
- it needed to allow senior managers to demonstrate a more engaging leadership style.

The solution they chose was to design two dialogue-based engagement activities as part of a 1-day conference. Using large discussion mats, groups were provided with information to stimulate their thinking and a series of activities to promote dialogue. Participants were encouraged to write down their thoughts and ideas on the discussion mats so that their input could be gathered and reviewed. Senior managers spread themselves throughout the room at each venue taking time to listen to the conversations taking place. Satellite connections were then used to share ideas and achievements between the venues, helping create a strong sense of collaboration and being part of one talented team.

EXAMPLE 2: BUILDING A PERSONAL COMMITMENT TO DRIVING SAFETY

A major oil company needed to get its employees to reduce the number of driving accidents and save lives. They realised that it is one thing to help people understand what driving safety means and quite another to help them truly live it on a day-to-day basis. In practical terms that meant making sure drivers always wore a seatbelt, switched off their mobile phones whilst their vehicles were in motion, that they didn't drive when tired and made sure any loads were secure. Success would depend upon convincing people to make the right choices when it came to driving safely and changing attitudes, assumptions and behaviours that were often habitual and engrained.

While from a policy point of view the company needed to introduce a new driving safety standard, they recognised that they needed to engage people in a meaningful dialogue around what driving safety means for them in their local environment. As a result the road safety team's engagement approach revolved around helping people discuss driving safety in a highly supportive, personal and compelling way.

This included interactive sessions where people could explore the issues for themselves, work out what actions to take and identify what they needed to do to improve. The end result: fewer accidents and no employee fatalities.

THE ROLES LEADERS PLAY IN CREATING DYNAMIC DIALOGUE

Leaders inevitably have a central role to play in modelling dialogue approaches in their day-to-day work. Some will find it is a natural evolution of their own leadership style while others will have to learn how to integrate its principles into their interactions with others. Training leaders in coaching skills is often a good place to start as the tools and techniques are often closely linked to the process of creating effective dialogue.

EXAMPLE: DIALOGUE MASQUERADING AS SOMETHING COMPLETELY DIFFERENT

A senior manager arranged to meet with their direct reports to discuss how best to restructure the department. The manager invited them to an away-day focusing on exploring how best to structure the team and said they were keen to have a 'dialogue' around the best way forward. However, rather than seeing it as an opportunity to get their team's input on what the options might be and their implications, they told the team what structure they were introducing and asked them for their reaction. This caused a huge and ugly debate because a number of important people decisions had been made without the full facts being known. At the end of the process the senior manager acknowledged that what turned out to be a very painful process could have been avoided if they had been willing to have a proper dialogue with their team right from the start.

EXAMPLE: CHANGING THE DYNAMIC, THE ROLE LEADERS CAN PLAY

Two teams within a government department needed to work more closely together to help improve what customers experienced. The two teams had very different views of the best approach to take and this was getting in the way of making progress. The director of one of the teams felt that a key problem was the conversations people were having with each other: they tended to be defensive, confrontational and focused on what was rather than what could be.

A workshop was created that allowed the two teams to come together to explore the issues they faced. A member of the board was asked to open the session. After careful consideration and with coaching, they opened the session in a novel but simple way. Rather than standing and making a speech at the front, they grabbed a chair, sat in the middle of the group and asked everyone to gather round. They then shared a story that highlighted why customer service had to change and explained how, working together, both teams could make a profound difference. They then invited other people to share their thoughts and ideas for the type of customer service that they wanted to see and how they could help make that happen. In less than 20 minutes, the whole tone shifted as the teams let go of unhelpful assumptions about each other and developed a new way of working together.

TOOLS AND TECHNIQUES YOU CAN USE TO CREATE MEANINGFUL DIALOGUE

Creating a culture where meaningful dialogue flourishes involves continually looking for ways to use and apply the principles that underpin dialogue. It is also an essential part of creating real engagement in organisations. A good starting point is to make sure that key interventions:

- focus on real business issues;
- allow people time and space to explore different options and solutions;
- encourage deep listening;
- respect different points of view;
- give everyone the chance to input and share their views;
- are built around powerful or insightful questions.

There are a variety of tools that can also be used to increase dialogue, some of the most useful of which include:

TAKING A WORLD CAFÉ TYPE APPROACH

This is an innovative approach to dialogue developed by Juanita Brown and David Issacs. The Café format[1] involves seating people in groups of four or five around small tables with paper covers and pens for writing and drawing. The group explores issues that matter in their current situation and they write their ideas and thoughts on the paper table cloths. After 30 minutes all but one member of the group, moves to join conversations on another table carrying their ideas, insights and questions into the next round of dialogue. After several rounds, the whole groups comes together to share their collective discoveries and insights helping to increase knowledge and identify real possibilities for

1 For more information see www.worldcafe.com.

action. The approach can be used for groups from as small as 12 people to over 1,000: it usually takes a minimum of 2 hours.

CREATING INTERACTIVE DISCUSSION MATS AND DIALOGUE SHEETS

These are usually A1 in size and highly visual. Some information or content is provided to help stimulate thinking and a series of question or enquiry points are also given to help frame the conversation. Some areas of the sheets are deliberately left blank for people to add their own ideas, thoughts and solutions.

A group of between four and eight people work on each discussion mat or dialogue sheet, each person having the chance to share their ideas and opinions.

SHARING STORIES TO STIMULATE IDEAS

Stories are a good way of helping frame an opportunity or challenge in a compelling way. Sharing stories opens up new possibilities and ideas, for example, if you are holding a dialogue around improving customer service, you can get the participants to share stories of when they have experienced great service and why it was so special. Similarly, if you want to encourage people to think differently, you can ask them to share a story where someone held a very different but equally valid point of view and how that changed their own thinking.

USING POWERFUL QUESTIONS EFFECTIVELY

The type of questions you ask can have a profound impact on the quality of the conversation and the thinking that takes place. In many ways the questions you ask determine the answers you get.

Powerful questions:

- generate curiosity and invite creativity;
- focus enquiry and stimulate conversations;
- are thought provoking and surface underlying assumptions;

- touch a deeper meaning and stay with participants;
- travel well and spread around the organization.

How you choose to construct a question can make a real difference to whether it opens minds or narrows the possibilities you are considering. The following continuum shows the way in which how you open a question influences the power it has:

More powerful							**Less powerful**
What if	What	How	Which	When	Who	Why	Yes/No Questions

Think carefully about the scope of your question as this can help broaden your domain of enquiry. If, for example, you want to explore how best to share information, your options will vary hugely depending on what level you are focusing on, for example, as a team, function or organisation.

Almost all questions, explicit or implicit have assumptions built into them:

- How can we better meet the needs of our customers?
- What is the best way of tackling retailers?
- What did we do wrong and who is responsible?
- What can we learn from what has happened and what are the possibilities now?
- How can we address the lack of collaboration between different project teams?
- What are all the possibilities for working effectively together going forward?

Think for a moment about which of these questions assume a solution? Which assume error or blame and could lead to narrow discussions or defensiveness? Which encourage reflection, creativity and or collaboration among those involved?

USEFUL EXAMPLES OF POWERFUL QUESTIONS TO HELP SHAPE DIALOGUE

Questions that provide focus	Questions that create connections and encourage insight
• What question if answered would make the most difference to the future of (your situation/issue)? • What's important to you/us about (this situation/issue) and why do you/we care? • What draws you/us to this topic/enquiry? • What's our intention here? • What opportunities can you see in (this situation or issue)? • What do we know so far/still need to learn about (this situation/issue)?	• What's taking shape? • What patterns are we seeing? • What's emerging here for you? • What connections are you making? • What really resonated for you from what you've heard? What surprised you? What challenged you? • What's missing from the picture that has emerged so far? • What is it we're not seeing? • What do we need more clarity about? • What's been your/our major learning, insight or discovery so far? • What additional thinking do we need to do? • If there was one thing that hasn't yet been mentioned that would provide further understanding/clarity, what would it be?
Questions that move you forward	**Questions that help check the truth behind assumptions**
• What would it take to create change on this issue? • What could happen that would enable you/us to feel fully engaged and energised about (this situation/issue)? • What's really possible here? • What needs our attention right now for us to move forward? • If our success was completely guaranteed, what courageous steps might we choose? • How can we support each other in taking the next steps? What role can we each play? • What challenges might come our way and how might we meet them? • What conversation, if begun today, would create new possibilities for the future of (this situation/issue)?	• What might we be assuming that is limiting our thinking on this issue? • If we knew that whatever we are assuming wasn't true, what ideas might we have? • How might other people (for example, CEO, customer, and so on) with different ways of thinking/beliefs view the situation? What would they do? • If things could be exactly right in this situation, what would we need to change? • If we had all the money/time/resources we needed, how would this change our thinking?

35

Advanced Employee Engagement

by Kevin Keohane

The aim of this chapter is to provide an overview of employee engagement through focusing on three key fundamentals:

1. engagement strategy;
2. stakeholder analysis;
3. engagement as a journey.

This chapter purposefully avoids deeply technical discussions, particularly about effectiveness measurement and this selection, development and management of particular communication channels and engagement techniques. Instead, it focuses on ensuring that the strategic thinking that lies behind the tactical delivery of engagement efforts is robust and will help practitioners deliver engagement that will make a difference to the organisation and its people.

What is Engagement Anyway?

Over the past decade, employee engagement has emerged as a term describing a range of organisational communication and development activities broadly related to internal communication, strategic human resource management and internal marketing – helping people share information and participate effectively in where the organisation is going.

There are many definitions of employee engagement, from the Chartered Insitute of Personnel and Development's (CIPD) 'a combination of commitment to the organisation and its values plus a willingness to help out colleagues (organisational citizenship)' to the Institute for Employment Studies' (IES) 'belief in the organisation; desire to work to make things better; understanding of business context and the "bigger picture"; respectful of, and helpful to, colleagues; willingness to "go the extra mile"; keeping up to date with developments in the field'. Best practice internal communication, HR 'people' activities are inherently 'engaging', yet the boundaries between and among practices are sometimes fuzzy. Because of this increasing overlap of responsibility and accountability for the 'people' side of the business, getting employee engagement right has presented significant operational challenges for organisations. And getting it right has major business benefits.

The problem with defining the term is that many of the definitions stray into a list of elements that demonstrate employee engagement and how to measure and enhance it rather than saying what it is. These lists are generally, and naturally, biased towards the perspective of those defining the term. Rather than descend into a lengthy discussion about the component elements that define employee engagement, it's probably a good start to say that employee engagement is broadly how much people care about, and are willing to do something extra for:

- their career;
- their company;
- their colleagues;
- their communities;
- their customers.

The foundation of the organisational business case for employee engagement is that the more people care about these things, the more effective they will be, the more effort they will make and the more they will enjoy delivering value with and to other stakeholders.

When it's working well, therefore, employee engagement is a good thing for everyone on the list. Employee engagement delivers commercial and cultural benefits to the organisation, and personal and professional benefits to the stakeholders involved.

Strategy: Where Do You Begin?

There are numerous angles from which different practitioners approach employee engagement. This generally ranges (Figure 35.1) from one extreme (highly rational) to the other (highly emotional).

From a process perspective, the most effective engagement efforts generally incorporate a range of approaches, rather than depending on a single approach. Many employee engagement efforts struggle at this fundamental level, since often there are a range of activities, processes and initiatives in operation across different functions at any given time within the organisation which may or may not be conscious 'engagement efforts'.

The reason this is important is that the approaches you select depend on your situation and your objectives. As obvious as that sounds, all too often engagement efforts get underway without explicit links to the organisation's strategy and a clear set of objectives.

Your employee engagement strategy is your answer to three simple, but big, questions that you should work with your leaders and colleagues to address:

- What are the problems facing your organisation, or what opportunities does the organisation want to capitalise on, that you believe are connected to involving people?

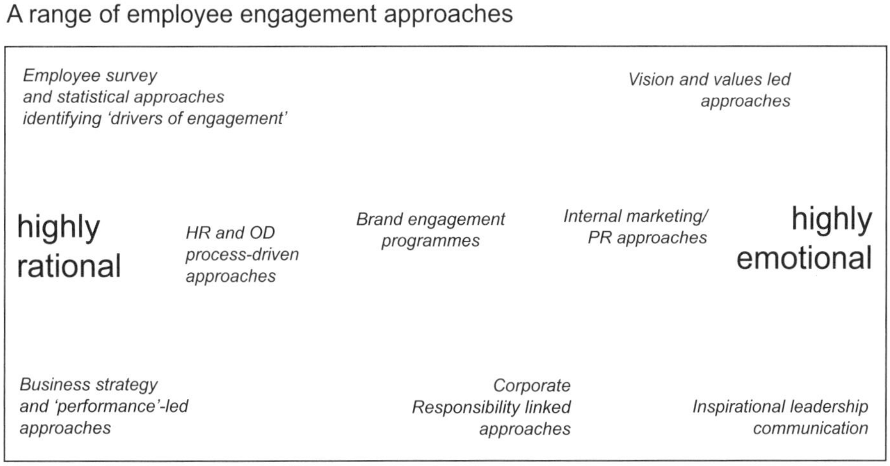

Figure 35.1 Employee engagement approaches

- To the maximum degree you can quantify this, what is the impact of these problems on: your people, their company, their colleagues, their communities and their customers?

- If you solve these problems or tackle these opportunities, what is the benefit for the organisation and its stakeholders – and what will this mean for their future?

Not only will this simple framework[1] help you define the issues and their impact on the business, it will also help you define the cost implications of the issues and the relative value of providing a solution. This helps you establish in relative terms:

- the relative business cost and the impact of the issues on the organization;

- who 'owns' the issues – and who they affect among stakeholders;

- the resources needed to deliver a solution.

One of the most important outcomes emerging from answering these questions is generally a realisation that no single part of the organisation actually 'owns' the engagement agenda – although many would like to believe that they do! This is why best engagement efforts generally involve a cross-functional team from across the business, so that the engagement agenda (and accountability for it) is shared across key functions – HR, internal communications, organisational development, information technology, marketing, corporate communications and the leadership/strategy team.

It's also why the reverse is true – where one function believes it is the sole owner of the employee engagement agenda, engagement efforts tend to be less effective because:

- efforts come from only one functional perspective, so they are not integrated and aligned and address only part of the issue;

- efforts have less buy-in and commitment from other parts of the organisation;

1 *Let's Get Real or Let's Not Play* by Mahan Khalsa, Banbury: Franklin Covey, 1999.

- efforts have less impact since they have fewer resources deployed from a single function;
- efforts are inefficient as different functions pursue different approaches and objectives.

Strategic Centre of Gravity

Once you have agreed the issues your employee engagement efforts are going to address, assessed their impact on the organisation and thus the size of the solution required, and aligned key functions behind the effort with a set of shared objectives, a key question arises: what actually sits at the centre of the engagement effort?

This is where it can all get quite complicated – and potentially political. There are a number of core drivers you can select to form the main focus of the effort. These include:

- your vision;
- your mission;
- your values;
- your commercial business strategy;
- your customers/clients;
- your people agenda;
- your leaderships' style;
- your corporate responsibility agenda;
- your brand;

... and many more.

Many employee engagement practitioners have a deep belief in the supremacy of one or more of these potential central drivers – again, naturally biased towards the perspective from which they view and approach engagement professionally. It's probable that HR professionals will see the natural centre of gravity in the human capital corner, while marketing may well believe it's all about living the brand, and IT believes it is about the user experience and improved functionality.

However, where to tie your engagement strategy depends a lot on your situation (of which, by now, you should have a pretty clear picture). Fundamentally, there are some issue-based guidelines you can consider:

- **Urgency**: burning platforms provide a context where commercial strategy and customer-centricity may be more appropriate than other drivers.

- **Complexity**: where numerous initiatives in the strategy and vision have been launched or tried before, it's best to go with the most simple and over-arching approach – often leading with vision (if lack of direction is a key issue) or values (if inconsistent behaviour and execution is a key issue).

- **Opportunity:** business strategy and brand-centric approaches can be powerful tools in moving an organisation into a new space.

- **Alignment**: in a people business or an organisation where the product or service has become homogenised, your brand can be a key driver, particularly when it is closely tied in to HR and OD processes.

While there is no single rule for which approach is best, the table shown in Figure 35.2 may be useful in considering your 'centre of gravity'.

This is a very broad guide to spur your thinking – you'll notice that some approaches appear in more than one place. The bottom line is that there is no 'one size fits all' approach to employee engagement – but it's important to know on what platform your approach is founded.

Why is a centre of gravity so important to an engagement strategy? Considering the increasingly wide range of stakeholders that engagement

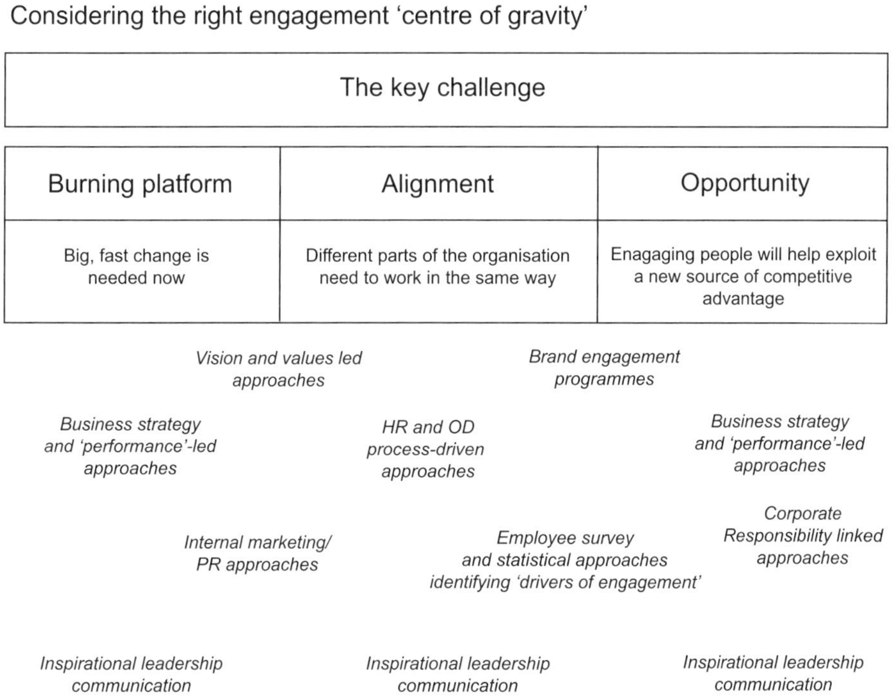

Figure 35.2 Engagement centre of gravity

efforts need to connect with, simplicity is not a 'nice to have'. Complexity kills engagement efforts – and, unfortunately, most change-related engagement efforts are fraught with masses of complexity and scores of work streams.

Looking at the list of possible employee engagement drivers above – vision, mission, values, strategy, customers/clients, people agenda, corporate responsibility, brand – chances are your organisation is already communicating about all of these, and more, and probably all at more or less the same time. It's no wonder employees can be confused.

As a stakeholder, there is a lot of information to process and try to make relevant to one's day-to-day role. While the difference between vision and mission, strategy and brand might seem very clear to a few enlightened people, the reality is that most people have a hard time understanding how they are different, and why the difference even matters. As Scott Adams says in *The Dilbert Principle*,[2] if you're not careful you can have people doing mission things when they should really be doing vision things, and vice versa.

---

2 *The Dilbert Principle* by Scott Adams, New York: Harper Collins, 1996.

Therefore, having one central organising thought, or centre of gravity, or big idea, to link your efforts to helps ensure that it's easy to understand and remember. While all of the corporate initiatives mentioned should be implicitly linked, a centre of gravity makes the links clear and explicit. It's an organising idea.

This is potentially the most challenging part of crafting an employee engagement strategy – working through the dizzying complexity of organisations, considering the objectives and gaining either consensus or a mandate to hang your hat on what some stakeholders will consider to be the 'wrong' strategic peg. This is where you'll need nerves of steel, tolerance for ambiguity, diplomacy skills and a single-minded determination that you will not allow the organisation to wallow – or revel – in its complexity.

A great example of this is Tesco, one of the world's most successful retailers. Retail is fast moving, fraught with complexity around supply chain, pricing and a myriad of other issues, but Tesco manages to ensure every employee from Board to Till is clear on a core set of ideas: Every little helps – Treat people how we like to be treated – No one tried harder for customers. Of course, there is a larger framework – but the basic core idea is indisputably clear.

Some Examples of Powerful 'Centres of Gravity'

Organisation	Internal centre of gravity	Drivers
Vodafone	Red, Rock Solid, Restless. The organisation's brand essence permeates every facet of organisational life, not just marketing. Translatable across geographies, cultures, job functions and goals, it's a great example of making values personal to the organisation and its people. Red is about passion. Rock Solid is about reliability. Restless is about challenging and never settling for good enough.	External market conditions – a need to be clearly differentiated in a fast moving, converging marketplace. Internal requirements – multiple operating companies around the world with different strengths and market conditions, all requiring a simple set of clear rules by which to evaluate their behaviours and activities.

BT	Being first for customer service means we all must share these values: Inspiring Straightforward Heart Trustworthy Helpful Inspiring.	Values can be shared in a very complex business with a wide range of different roles.
Apple	Think different. People before systems. Man is the true creator of change in this world. He should be above systems and structures, not subordinate to them.	For Apple, it is not about the technology. It's about people and the role technology plays in their lives.

Stakeholders

One powerful way to help focus your thinking and decisions in this area, and across the entire engagement effort, is to be very clear about your key stakeholders – who they are, what they need to do, what this will mean for the organisation and how you will involve them in the process. A stakeholder analysis is simply thinking through who are all the people that are affected by the employee engagement effort, how they are affected and what you want them to think, do, or do differently as a result.

Depending on your objectives, your stakeholders may not be limited to employees of your organisation. Often, engagement efforts need to take into account other stakeholders who may be affected by changes in the way people inside your organisation think and behave.

YOUR INTERNAL STAKEHOLDERS

While it is important to do a broader stakeholder analysis for the reasons noted, employee engagement is by definition about your employees. Like any internal communication and change effort, it is imperative that you know your audience. Although it is desirable to segment your employees as much as possible, using both quantitative and qualitative information, three key groups are critical to consider – leaders, line managers and all employees.

Leaders: it has become a truism that leaders must walk the talk – practise what they preach. What is equally important is that they buy into and not only understand, but actively demonstrate and champion, your engagement effort. If your leaders are saying one thing and doing another, your engagement effort will suffer.

Managers: most current communication research demonstrates time and again that the most important and trusted communicator to employees is the line manager. Engagement efforts should include this group not only as an audience to inform, but a group to equip and empower with the tools to ensure employees can make the engagement effort relevant to their part of the business and their day-to-day jobs.

All employees: much research in this field indicates that at any given time, only one-third of employees are actively 'engaged' in their jobs and their organisations. The remaining two-thirds are either not actively engaged, or worse, could even be actively disengaged. Making sure that the engagement effort provides a clear and compelling case is important, but equally important is making sure that employees understand what the effort means to the organisation, their part of the organisation, their team and their own role on a very real, day-to-day basis.

MESSAGING FRAMEWORKS

It's therefore a good idea for any engagement effort to make use of simple messaging frameworks. These are flexible frameworks, tied to the centre of gravity, consisting of:

- Key message – the one overarching idea that everybody needs to 'get'.
- Supporting messages – no more than three to five more specific supporting points.
- Evidence/Proof Points/Reasons to Believe – for each supporting message, what is the evidence that the message can be believed?

Such frameworks can be overarching, for the entire engagement effort, or smaller versions can be created for particular engagement situations. The key to their effective use is not that they are necessarily used word-for-word in a mechanistic manner, but rather that engagement and communication efforts align themselves to these ideas, rather than generating new and potentially inconsistent messages.

The Employee Engagement Journey

An area where employee engagement efforts fail is where leaders believe that change can be achieved through short-term programmes and initiatives. Such efforts are generally characterised by large, highly-visible launches including significant events, multimedia presentations and communication cascade efforts that run for a short period of time. If such efforts are not sustained and adequate 'follow-up' maintained, they tend to be treated with cynicism and ultimately disregarded by employees and managers alike.

Successful engagement efforts begin with the understanding that in order to succeed, change takes time – and is a journey. There are numerous models describing this journey, but most of it is based on social marketing theory – that is, that in order to influence behaviour, people must go through three stages of a 'K-A-B' model:

- **Knowledge:** stakeholders must become aware of what is happening, what the change or engagement effort is, and what they will see happening across the organisation, to and by whom, over what time period. This is the 'launch' part of most engagement programmes, and is also where much of the effort is focused – often to the detriment of the subsequent stages.

- **Attitude:** once stakeholders have internalised the knowledge, they need to form an attitude about what they know. Generally, this means they must see tangible, positive evidence that the organisation is serious about and committed to the programme. Evidence of behaviour change emerges in key leaders, managers and employees as, for example, processes begin to evolve and changes are made.

- **Behaviour:** once stakeholders have internalised the information and formed an attitude about the change and what it means to them, it is essential that they are given the tools, guidelines and support needed to change their behaviours. The organisation must recognise and reward the right behaviours, and must be visibly intolerant of behaviours that do not align with achieving the objectives behind the overall engagement efforts.

Some models break this journey into four, five, six, even seven or more distinct phases, but the idea is the same: sustain your effort and manage it differently through different stages.

CHANGE THE ORDER

An interesting thought to ponder regarding the so-called 'K-A-B' model is that is does not necessarily need to run in this order.

For example, it is possible to change Behaviours first, which then results in an Attitude which over time results in Knowledge. A perfect example of this is military training, where doing things in a certain, uniform way is drilled into recruits, who then grow to realise why it is important to do it this way, and eventually appreciate the strategic thinking behind doing it that way.

Similarly, many advertising and marketing approaches begin with attempting to create an Attitude about an idea, which then may result in either Knowledge (seeking more information about it) or Behaviour (trial and adoption of the product/service).

Depending on your objectives and situation, you may well want to consider the implications of this on your engagement strategy.

GIVING YOUR ENGAGEMENT EFFORT TEETH

The uncomfortable truth is that a properly developed and implemented engagement effort will inevitably not only reflect the business strategy and the organisation's operating model and processes – over time it should actually start to drive and change them. In particular, strategic human resource management should be affected, since behaviour change across different roles in different parts of the business will inevitably result in changing needs in performance planning, people and career development, recruiting processes, and indeed reward and recognition practices and policies.

For this reason it is critical to ensure that the effort remains cross-functional, so that engagement is managed as a business operational imperative – not just an internal marketing programme. Its internal key performance indicators (based on a combination of, for example, employee survey results and engagement drivers, as well as business performance metrics) should directly link to, and its success evaluated on the basis of, external key performance indicators such as customer satisfaction, loyalty, spend, share price performance, and so on.

THE EMPLOYEE JOURNEY

It's also important to think about the journey any employee makes in their overall relationship with the organisation. The reason this is important is that often employee engagement efforts only deal with one aspect of the employee journey, leaving critical personal experiences about the organisation to operational processes which may not reflect the engagement strategy and objectives.

Most frequently this is seen in three areas:

1. Where there is little alignment between the employer brand – and its expression in relation to the consumer/corporate brand (that is, reasons to join the organisation) – and the internal communication, HR processes and engagement efforts.

2. Where there is focus on employee engagement to improve employee satisfaction and effectiveness regarding career development and business operations, but without reference to the externalisation on the consumer/corporate brand. In other words, engagement efforts that are all about the employee experience (for example, I have a friend at work; pay and benefits are fair; my manager listens to me) and not about how each employee should be making an explicit contribution to delivering the brand.

3. Where little or no attention is paid to how the exit is handled, whether on good or less favourable terms, in creating an advocate for the organisation or a detractor.

THE TEN STAGES OF THE EMPLOYEE JOURNEY

In broad terms, thinking through how your engagement effort applies to people at each of the following stages of the employee journey can provide great insight into who needs to be involved and what actions need to be taken.

1. A person knows something about your organisation, or learns about it, through a variety of touch points. These may include your consumer/corporate brand, product and service experience, word of mouth, recruitment advertising or online experience.

2. At some stage, the person considers your organisation as a place to potentially work. They seek information about your organisation – again from a range of sources, most of which your organisation has no control over whatsoever.

3. The person decides to find out more about you, and to seek a job offer from your organisation.

4. The person experiences your attraction and recruitment process.

5. The person decides to join you or not join you.

6. The person is inducted into the organisation and experiences 'on boarding'.

7. The person experiences their initial time with your organisation, including initial perceptions, setting of initial goals, objectives and expectations, and forms a picture as to whether what you offered is what they receive.

8. The person continues to develop in their role (or not).

9. At some stage, the person considers looking for a different role of challenge – with your organisation or with another organisation. Or, the organisation considers finding a different role for the person with itself or another organisation!

10. The person leaves employment with your organisation – and may (or may not) consider rejoining at another stage, continuing to

advocate your organisation as an employer, and its products and services.

Summary and Conclusion

Through looking at three key considerations – Strategy, Stakeholders and the Employee Journey – this chapter provides a way of looking at developing and managing employee engagement. These four fundamentals are key to delivering a successful engagement effort.

- **Strategy**: because you need to be clear on where you are, where you are going, why you are going there and how you will get there.
- **Clear centre of gravity**: because complexity kills employee engagement.
- **Stakeholders**: because engagement an communication is ultimately about understanding and influencing the people involved.
- **The employee journey**: because engagement takes different shapes and approaches at different moments in the organisation's and the individual's lifecycle.

36

How to Create an Award-Winning Change Campaign

by Nicky Flook

> *It feels great to win awards. And winning an award for a change campaign feels particularly great, because you can't bluff it. The change either worked or it didn't – and, if it worked, that means you've overcome the odds and made a massive difference to your business. In terms of job satisfaction, that's off the Richter scale. So how do you make it happen?*

Well, the first piece of bad news is that, no matter what people might say, or how many theories you might read, there is no simple, ten-step formula for successful change campaigns. You have to find your own way, although there are some essential guiding principles, which you'll find in this chapter.

The second piece of bad news is that you may have to wait a while before you get the opportunity. Businesses go through change all the time, but it's quite rare to have change that is so fundamental, so urgent or on such a scale that it genuinely needs a dedicated campaign to communicate it.

When it does happen, it's even rarer to find a campaign that's executed with real vision and commitment – and that's the good news. If your business has a genuine need for change, and if you have the vision, energy, passion, clout and bloody-mindedness to go for it, then you'll find yourself in a very small and select group of competitors when the time comes for handing out the gongs.

So it's up to you. If you want that moment of shaking hands with Jonathan Ross on the stage of a fancy hotel and basking in the money-can't-buy-this feeling of a job well done, then it's yours for the taking. As long as you're prepared to stick your neck out, give up every waking moment and sell your mortal soul rather than settle for anything less than 'great'.

Still interested? Then let's start by considering the fundamental elements involved in successful campaigns:

- strong need;
- clear outcome;
- insightful research;
- great idea;
- brilliant execution;
- army of supporters;
- sustained delivery;
- robust measurement.

Did you find yourself flicking down that list, mentally ticking them off and thinking 'yep – got that covered'? Well, rewind a little.

This chapter isn't about read = done; it's about taking your time, challenging everything, then forging a bombproof plan. Every one of these elements is crucial to the success of your campaign and, if you slightly miss the mark on any one of them, you'll be playing perpetual catch-up – and you may as well blow the awards entry money down at the pub instead.

Strong Need

Before you do anything else, be absolutely 100 per cent sure your business really needs a big change campaign.

Change campaigns are typically needed where there is a fundamental change in an organisation's structure – a merger or repositioning – or where there has been a major and negative shift in an element of a company's operation that could dramatically affect its ongoing success.

Of course, 'need' is a subjective word. Change in big business is often driven as much by a political agenda as by a commercial one. When someone at the top is calling for improvements, it can generate knee-jerk momentum behind the wrong idea, as people scramble to protect themselves, rather than seeing the true opportunity.

As a communicator, it's your job to challenge the validity of a change campaign. Is it really necessary? Is it the right issue to focus on? What outcome will it deliver? Does it link with the overall strategy? Is it really what the people at the top want?

Here are a few examples of when a change campaign would be appropriate:

- Staff turnover: not just a blip, but a massive wholesale increase (say, 15 per cent year on year).
- Consistent negative press: where you're clearly falling down on a particular issue (such as customer service) and where that issue requires a large percentage of the workforce to resolve it.
- Complaints: again, not just the odd percentage increase, but a significant shift (the exponential increase in customers who choose not to use your company can damage your reputation and bottom line very fast).
- Cost of operating: whether it's shrinkage or margin, or another cost that can be influenced by most of your workforce, this is one that can truly benefit from a change in priority and attitude.
- Share price: for PLCs, a big drop in share price in a short amount of time is often the result of an issue coming to light, rather than a notion that the business is not doing well.

There are several reasons why it's important to be ruthless in deciding where change is really necessary. One of the biggest is 'campaign fatigue'. Too many campaigns lead to a cynical audience that is more resistant to change, making it harder to get your real priorities established.

You also need to be careful of your own success. A large, well-executed change campaign can inspire many people to produce their own campaigns, supporting smaller projects and departmental priorities. If this isn't controlled carefully and the sheer number strongly challenged, you'll end up with employees who are confused by too many messages and a blurring of priorities – and you'll find that, next time you try to launch a business-critical change campaign, it will have much less impact, however well executed.

THE ACID TEST: ARE THE RESOURCES THERE?

If you're being asked to carry out a change campaign and you want to know whether it's really necessary, there's one test that rarely fails. Do a quick summary of the time and resources that you'd have to devote to doing the job properly (including agency input, internal resources and what you'd have to stop doing in order to take it on) and give it to your boss. If there's no willingness to make the time and resources available, you should question how important the change really is.

Clear Outcome

The clearer the objective, the easier it is to know when you have an idea that will work – and the more chance you'll have of explaining it to your audience.

If you are being asked to create a campaign that will affect 15 different things, then my recommendation is to shut this book, pack your bag and go travelling, because you certainly won't make any difference to your business in the next 6 months.

Facetiousness aside, if you can distil the outcome down to one simple sentence, you'll have the best possible chance of achieving it.

Film-makers call it 'the big idea'. Your pitch needs to take the listener right into the middle of the campaign and paint a picture of what the world will look like after it. Bring it to life for them. Deal in emotion and action and, above all, make it concise. The simpler the premise, the easier it is to explain and deliver.

Build 'soft' and 'hard' outcomes, so that it challenges you and the leaders driving the change, and gives the audience a clear understanding of their role.

Link your outcomes to the bottom line in any way you can, and then start talking 'return on investment' *and* 'higher engagement'.

(If you're impatient to know more about measurement, fast-forward to the end of the chapter; otherwise, keep reading.)

Insightful Research

Having an idea is easy. Having an idea that's relevant to the need, makes sense to the audience and can be applied clearly and meaningfully to every part of the campaign is much harder. When you've got an idea that will do all those things without being stretched or squeezed, you've got a great idea.

So, where do you find one of those?

The starting point for having a truly great idea is to know your stuff. Before you sit down and start brainstorming, you should be 100 per cent clear about what you need to do, why you're doing it, who you need to talk to and what you want the outcome to be.

In other words, you need to do some legwork – and the diagram in Figure 36.1 is a good place to start.

Knowing your stuff does not mean that you have to be the ultimate authority on every aspect of what you're trying to affect. In fact, drowning in detail can often make it harder for you. Your job is to communicate, which means you have to understand the audience, identify the key messages and find a compelling way to explain them. You also need to be able to hold your ground in a debate and recognise the difference between a valid challenge and a distraction. But you don't need to get sucked into the detail – that's somebody else's job.

Great Idea

Well, here we are. You have the need, the knowledge and the desire; all you need now is the solution… so strap yourself in and hold tight because, if you can get yourself through this section without losing your single-minded desire to produce 'the best damn change campaign this business has ever seen', then you will be well and truly on the road to success.

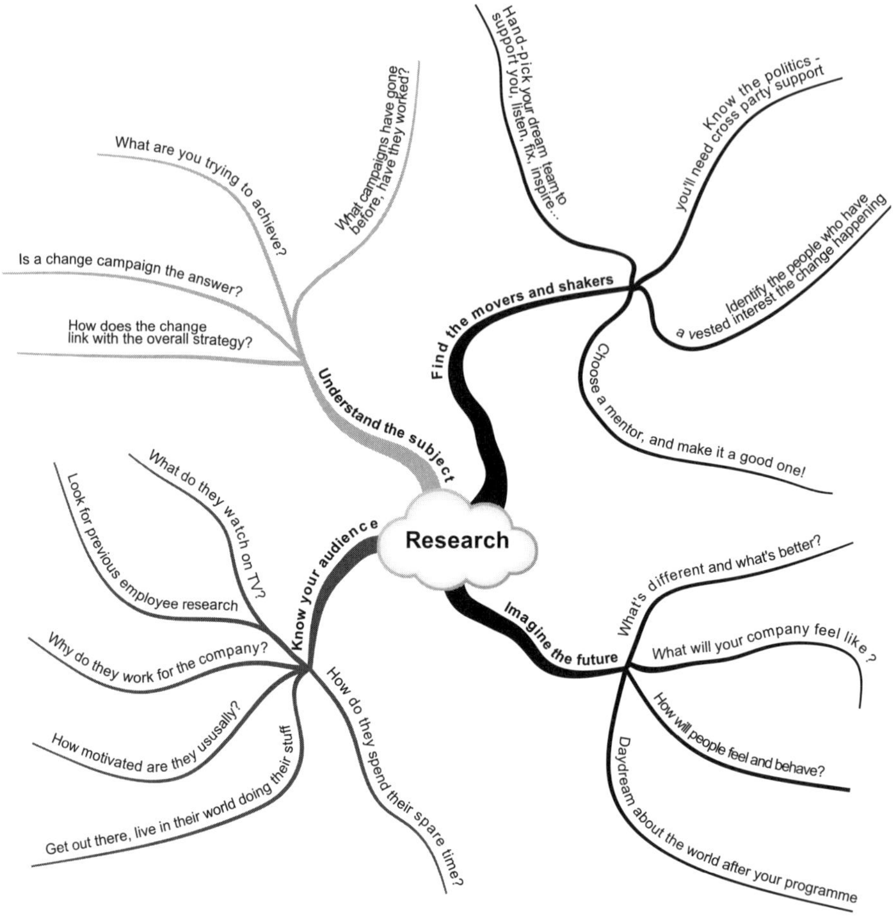

Figure 36.1 A starting point for research

Smile, it's play time.[1]

And your metaphorical tool to create a great idea – the Communication Colour Palette (Figure 36.2). Start with your primary colours, that is, your need, outcome and research discussed above. Then add the secondary colours that will help you paint the full picture, for example, your organisational culture, the overall business strategy or vision, the communication budget, timing and any other individual colours you believe are important to paint your picture.

1 For the purposes of this chapter, we are going to assume that your change does not involve large numbers of redundancies and that your audience, like most in the world, loves having fun. If, however, your change does involve significant job losses, you should be looking at a motivational campaign that builds confidence again, with a lighter note to it, but not with 'laugh out loud' fun.

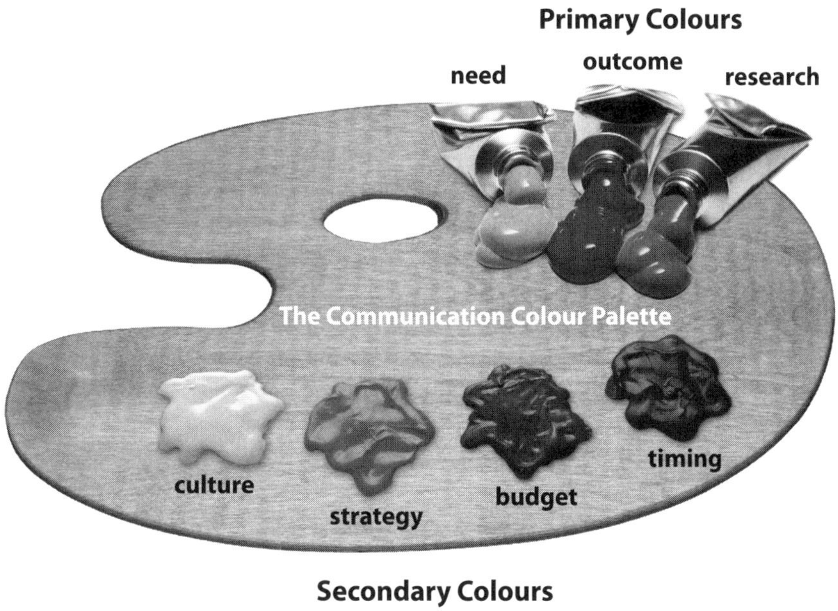

Figure 36.2 Colour palette

Now the creative bit – carefully mix your metaphorical colours on your colour palette to create your unique masterpiece. There are an unlimited number of ideas that can come from your colour palette, you just have to start with the right base colours and be creative.

Of course, the trick to creating great campaign ideas, or pictures if we're sticking with our colour palette metaphor, will be the weighting we put to one colour over another, how we blend our colours, and our choice of painting style. However, we also need the right environment to paint in, the right mindset to create a masterpiece, and the right people to inspire us.

There are some who say that innovation needs clear parameters, with minutes, representation from every department, a proper business environment, a deadline and no alcohol. And it's a safe bet you won't see many of them on the awards stage.

One of the hardest things in business is to find ways of being innovative. Your desk, computer, in-tray, emails, meetings and deadlines are all there to stop you thinking freely. What you really need is to grab your paints and go somewhere your mind can regress to being 8 years old without fear of judgement, although that doesn't mean it's okay to sneak off to a hotel lounge bar and spend the afternoon drinking cocktails and gossiping on the pretext that you're 'brainstorming' (sadly).

The next thing you need is the right mindset. This is why it's so important to get out of the office. You need to disengage your logical left brain and start using your right brain. Right brains are for feeling, images, philosophy, fantasy, risk-taking, imagination; all the things you need if you want to come up with an award-winning idea.

You also need to have the right people with you. These are likely to be the people you identified as the core team for delivering this campaign. If not, just be sure to have a relatively nutty creative person, a positive thinker, a leader and a doer. And make sure these people all feel comfortable enough to express themselves – use alcohol if necessary (just not copious amounts)! And expect the process to take more than one session.

Right: you've got the right people in the right place. How do you get started? Although I don't advocate a rigid structure, I would say that there are two musts at the start of any brainstorm:

1. Take the time to refresh yourself of the knowledge you've gained.

2. Step into the mind of your audience.

If you're having trouble with point two, try using that stage and screen favourite: method acting. Imagine yourself as that person, what you do, how you feel, who you hang out with and so on. Create yourself a character who represents the hundreds or thousands of people your change campaign is targeting (and if you find it hard to do this, then you need to do more research: spend some time getting to know your audience – if you don't, you'll fail).

The next thing to do is to start throwing the paint on the canvass.

Laugh, joke, doodle, play, find the 'anti' campaign, talk about the latest big things in your character's world, the outside influences and the team dynamics. *Don't* inform and educate; *do* excite and entertain. It's *your* job to ensure that the fun you create for your audience makes them do things that help establish the change you want.

Great ideas come from inspired moments. If your idea makes you excited, it might just make your audience excited. If you find yourself thinking 'that'll do', then it's not good enough.

It's also got to be an idea that's capable of feeling personal. You may be talking to thousands of people, but every one of them should feel you're speaking to them individually.

A WORD OF WARNING

You may have had a 'Eureka' moment – but you need to be absolutely sure you were in the mindset of your character/audience when you came up with it. Challenge it through their eyes: is it relevant and in their language; does it reflect the culture and stay within the boundaries of taste? You don't want to end up with one of those tumbleweed moments, where you totally misread your audience's sensibilities and humour (think Jim Davidson in a room with the annual Women's Lib Convention).

Brilliant Execution

Not to be confused with delivery, execution is about taking the idea and bringing it to life: giving it structure, rules and aims; linking it with existing communication and motivation tools; promoting it, protecting it, and getting the green light. Delivery is what happens after you've done all that.

Once you have the idea, it's worth using the people who have a wide knowledge of the company to help you with the structure of the campaign. You might have some guiding principles and thoughts about how it could run, but be prepared to listen at this point, because you are unlikely to be the person with the most detailed knowledge of the many daily and periodic activities directed at your audience.

If you can link the campaign into well-established competitions, bonus schemes and communication channels, this will help to make the change feel part of everyday life. Don't force it, and don't spread it too thinly but, if there is a clear opportunity to link with an existing part of the business, then do it.

With any change, people go through a transition in the way they perceive it, from a negative to a positive through a number of typical steps.

The process of change can be tedious and often painful, especially if a large number of people get stuck in the 'anger' part of the curve. So it's a safe bet that, if you could find some science-fiction way of getting straight through it – time travel or a light-speed vehicle big enough to fit your entire workforce – you'd happily write a very large cheque to do it.

Well, a great campaign can do exactly the same thing: getting people through the curve as quickly as possible – putting you where you want to be and saving you time, money and pain in the process.

An interesting point to make here is that a great campaign will usually cost exactly the same as a mediocre one – and it will generate much better results. In other words, if you allow your campaign to be mediocre (whether it's your decision or not), then it won't give your employers and shareholders the best return on their investment.

So the final point is that you need to be passionate about your idea – and you need to be prepared to fight for it. When you start to share it with people, you'll find that you're offered a lot of advice and opinions. It can be tempting to take some or all of these on board: after all, the odd change here or there won't make much difference and it'll keep your stakeholders on board without confrontation, won't it?

Possibly – but it's also a sure way to dilute the strength and simplicity of your initial idea (which, in turn, is a sure way to reduce the effectiveness of the campaign and the speed of return). Be firm: take suggestions on board but make no promises. Discuss the suggestions with your trusted team and, if they don't add anything, be ruthless about excluding them. Remember: your job is to communicate. Don't let anything get in the way of that.

BE HONEST WITH YOURSELF

It's essential to back your idea, but you also need to listen to feedback and be honest in assessing it. If the idea isn't translating as well as you'd hoped, or if people whose opinion you respect react badly (worse than the knee-jerk negativity you'd expect for any new idea), then stop immediately. Get your core team back together and assess the validity of the feedback. Don't be scared to scrap the idea and go with another – you've still got time, because you shouldn't yet be committed to anything. But be sure to reassess who should be involved at the creative stage, so that you can be certain your second idea will work: your credibility won't survive two false starts.

Once again, simple is best. If you can explain to someone in a minute what the campaign is, and how to get involved, then you're onto a winner.

Army of Supporters

Supporters are like a fan base. They buff up your confidence when 'the bad people' are picking away at your great idea. They spread the word about the campaign. They unknowingly lobby the people on the fence – and knowingly challenge people who are being obstructive. Mostly, they create that all-important 'buzz'.

It's all about momentum: you can't do it on your own, so get people on board.

Brief, involve and brief more. Tell everyone as early as possible. If you have consultation routes, use them, if you have senior management meetings, get into them and bring your mentor.

Be prepared to share the glory: people like humility; they're also far more likely to buy into your idea if it doesn't look like a massive ego-trip. It's not about you; it's about the business.

If you get it right, you'll start to see a wave of support building as you get closer to the launch date. People will be taking the idea and including it in their own briefings, plans and presentations. This is an incredibly exciting feeling – and it's also a sign that it's time to change your role. Your idea has taken on a life of its own, so you need to spend more time influencing and advising (making sure it's communicated consistently) and less time doing it yourself... at least for now.

Sustained Delivery

Delivery is all about the detail: hours of hard work behind the scenes, second-guessing everything and everyone.

Use your mentor to lead the way: keep them informed and get them to call in favours you don't have; use their influence to get people behind the campaign.

Cascading communication can work, especially if you attend as many of the senior communication sessions as possible yourself. Offer to guest speak, and make yourself as accessible as possible to other communicators in the business – try to infect them with your own passion and belief for the campaign.

Share the message in as many ways as possible (within reason). Make sure you know all the communication channels that are available, hand-pick a combination of channels that work most effectively, and use them throughout the campaign. Keep the messages coming: share the stories and successes, make it personal, have heroes and keep reminding people of the carrot and ultimate goal.

If there is a channel which would be ideal, but doesn't exist yet – then launch it. This is a perfect opportunity to test out new channels and you'll be in problem-solving mode by now, so no challenge is impossible!

Get out and see how the campaign is going. Chat to your audience, see where you could improve and see if there's anything you can grab hold of to increase the buzz even more. At the very least, you'll get great stories to take back to the board and fodder for the publications (but you should expect much more).

Regularly ring round to key communicators and senior managers to see how things are going. Keep in touch with your audience directly, through consultation groups, through their managers – any way you can find, in fact. It will keep you on the front foot: helping you spot any potential issues or flaws and fix them early. If things are going exceptionally well, the conversations will help you find the answer to 'what now?' when the campaign finishes.

And make sure you keep the stories. Throughout the campaign, you should be collecting anecdotal evidence of how the change is affecting people. Build a library of stories, pictures, film and hard measurement, and take the time to write up the case study when the campaign is over: it will be an invaluable resource for reports, presentations, articles and – let's not forget – award entries.

Robust Measurement

Although it's the final element we're discussing here, measurement is actually one of the first and most important things you need to put in place: the only way to know if your campaign has succeeded is to measure before, during and after.

The best advice is to see if you can use existing measurement for part, if not all, of the campaign. Make sure you have a way to capture both qualitative and quantitative results and get out there during the campaign to gather a robust library of anecdotal evidence.

It can be a tall order to create new and impartial ways of measuring success, especially with the one hundred and one other things on your list; chances are it's not your area of expertise either. But don't lose the will to live: the answer may be staring you in the face.

Use the same person you entrusted with the campaign integration, and enlist one person in the finance team and an expert in the area you are aiming to affect. Between them, they need to take ownership of the measures that everyone will be using and watching to understand how effective the change is. They should also be able to borrow or hack some of the existing ways the business measures, which will be much simpler, cheaper and quicker – and, ultimately, more effective than starting from scratch.

And Finally...

So that's it. You've planned the perfect campaign and executed it flawlessly. The business has embraced it, the results are great and you've got a bank of stories and images to illustrate it.

In other words: you've made a good start.

Where most change campaigns go wrong is in failing to translate short-term momentum into long-term change. What happens after the campaign should be a fundamental part of your planning – and, although you'll feel ready for a well-deserved break at the end of the campaign, it's your responsibility to make sure the momentum of your hard work isn't lost.

If you get that bit right, the only thing you'll have left to worry about is what you're going to wear to the awards dinner. Good luck!

PART VI

Social Media Inside the Enterprise

37

Social Media: An Introduction

by Euan Semple

Social computing tools and their emergence in the business world have been driven by the experience and behaviours of millions of people on the web who use similar technologies day in day out to ask questions, get answers and seek out like-minded individuals.

There are many benefits to this new informal, conversational online environment but it is unfamiliar and does challenge many of our current assumptions about the workplace. All of the tools that are covered in this chapter presuppose a world in which staff are encouraged to say what they think, openly and freely, and to seek connections and collaboration with other staff. There are still significant cultural hurdles to be crossed but establishing an online environment that spreads the possibility of this way of working is an important start.

The BBC has been a pioneer in implementing these tools since 2002 and this article takes a look at how they are already being used there to help people carry out their jobs on a day-to-day basis.

Forums

Sometimes called a bulletin board or newsgroup, an online forum is a place where people can post questions or statements and get answers or discussion from any of the other users in the system. Originally based on mailing lists and then Usenet, forums have been developed a lot recently and tools like Yahoo Groups and Google Groups have added in diary, file sharing, user profiles and so on to make them much richer collaborative environments.

talk.gateway is the BBC's online discussion board and with 6 years of activity and 27,000 users it represents a unique opportunity to understand how such tools affect behaviour in the workplace. The forums are primarily used as a means of asking questions and getting answers and anyone with access to a BBC desktop PC can ask a question on any topic which can then be answered by any one of the staff who can see it. Having started small with a very low cost solution and promoting its use simply by word of mouth, its use has now grown to reach most of the BBC's population.

Like many of these systems there was an early adopter group who were mostly younger and more technologically proficient but now contributors come from all parts of the BBC and the range of topics has become very varied. There are threads on the practical aspects of making programmes, producers looking for contributors or help with research for their programmes and even people suggesting new programme ideas. Posts to the system range from the trivial to the philosophical with everything else in between and fall into three broad groups:

PRACTICAL QUESTIONS

These questions such as 'How do I do...?' Where do I find...?' form the bulk of the activity in the system. They can have easy or complex answers and although some of them may seem trivial, dozens of such questions are asked and answered every week. The cumulative effect is to increase efficiency by saving time and effort and not only does the person asking the question get to benefit from the answer but so does everyone else who reads it. Visual feedback on activity is an important part of this ecosystem and the software shows how many times a topic has been read. Sometimes a question which may have had a simple answer and therefore only have, say, three responses, can have had thousands of views because although the answer was straightforward not many people knew it!

QUESTIONS RELATING TO HOW THE ORGANISATION GOES ABOUT ITS WORK

Large complex organisations are rarely straightforward when it comes to knowing how things should be done or what is expected in particular situations. Many staff don't know the formal position on policies and until they need to know there is little incentive to find out. Being able to ask a policy-related question in an online forum quickly gets access to people who know the answer and have faced the issues before. Very often there isn't a single straightforward answer and different bits of the organisation respond to problems differently.

The advent of online spaces, visible to the whole organisation, is arguably the first time that the collective learning so important to efficiency and consistency of activity can take place.

What becomes an issue is how you deal with difference and disagreement. If HR think they have a policy that is rigidly adhered to by the organisation, only to find out from an online forum that different parts of the business interpret it differently, how should they respond? Should they crack down on the dissenters and enforce their existing policy or should they listen to people telling them that it is inoperable in their part of the business and consider modifying the rules to reflect a more shared reality?

Unlike face-to-face conversations, the learning online is instantly distributed amongst a wide audience – with all the benefits and risks that that entails. Managers and staff need to learn the rules of this new game and learn to take joint responsibility for their new collaborative environment.

LARGER ISSUES AFFECTING STAFF

As with Internet forums, staff forums get used a lot for letting off steam about issues or comparing views about things that affect us in our workplace. This is a valuable way of establishing a sense of 'One BBC' – of being able to share problems and the emotions surrounding them.

As an example, the BBC broadcast 'Jerry Springer – The Opera' last year and by doing so provoked protests from Christian viewers. Inside the organisation there was a similar range of views expressed and this sparked off a thread of around 300 posts on talk.gateway. The thread exposed staff's reactions to the issue and developed into a really involved debate about the rights and wrongs of our actions and of religion more broadly. Threads like this represented the first time that there had been a pan-BBC platform on which to get our collective heads around large issues like this and it was a powerful learning experience for all involved.

Social Networking Tools

Within the last few years there has been a spate of tools developed for the web that build on the idea of yellow pages. Users upload information about themselves and their interests and can then form groups and associations with other users. These tools have been successful to various degrees but at their most simple they make it easy to surface and create informal communities and connections.

Connect, the social networking tool originally developed for BP and still in use there, was the one that the BBC chose to use in an attempt to increase the informal networks in the organisation and make them more visible.

At its simplest it is used as a way of adding colour and context to staff's interactions with each other. Many staff use Connect to look up people's phone numbers then as they are speaking to them on the phone they get to find out a little bit about them: their past, their interests – the sort of thing that makes conversation richer and more interesting.

The second use Connect is put to is to search for someone with specific skills either by probing the whole system or using the expertise topics to navigate to the right person to talk to. We have all had the experience of going outside the organisation to speak to an expert on a particular topic only to find out that the person who really knows what they are talking about works in the next office.

One of the most active areas of Connect are the interest groups of which the BBC has 250. These are used to identify users who have shared interests or expertise and to help communities to form around those groups.

The BBC recently combined Connect with its forum tool talk.gateway which now allows users to form interest groups in Connect and then create associated forums. For the first time these forums allow users to manage their membership (until this point all discussions on the whole system were open to all staff) and therefore have more specific conversations that may have been too challenging for totally open environments. The most important aspect of this change was that control was in the hands of the users and watching their use of the technology to meet their own work needs is the best way of understanding how this complex ecosystem works.

Weblogs

Weblogs are simply online journals but there are a number of things that make them special. Firstly they represent the first time that it has been trivially easy to publish into a web environment. Until now you have had to be geeky enough to write code or pay for dedicated applications. With a weblog (blog) you use your web browser to access free or cheap blogging tools, write your content, press 'save' and your content is published onto the web. Despite their deceptive simplicity blogs have had a significant impact on the web with 27 million of them currently in existence and power and influence being placed in the hands of ordinary individuals as never before.

One of the simple features of blogs that made them different was the permalink. With normal websites, pointing at content was a risky business as redesigns or changes of content could break those links. With a blog each post has a unique and persistent URL that makes that content linkable to for the life of the blog. This simple fact enables rich lines of thought to be built up between different blogs or within the same blog.

Another, and perhaps more significant, aspect of blogs, particularly in the early days of their development, was the blogroll. This is the list of other bloggers linked to from a particular blog. It reflects the selection of sources trusted by the blog's owner to deliver useful and trustworthy insight and information. As such a blogroll is an endorsement of those other bloggers and this networking effect of blogs is one of their most powerful consequences. Being linked to by highly-read and trusted bloggers is one of the main ways to surface in the network and equally being slated by trusted bloggers is the quickest way to have your sins found out!

Some time ago the BBC introduced a blogging tool for internal use and it is currently being used by around 200 staff. These blogs range from personal ones in which the writer reflects on incidents, events, other writing or conversations that affect their work and are of sufficient interest and relevance to capture and make public, to group blogs recording daily activity or research that affect the individuals in the group, or to operational blogs where people can record issues and share them amongst their teams.

A number of senior executives in the BBC now have internal weblogs including Richard Sambrook, Director, Global News & World Service. He started blogging partly as a way of understanding this phenomenon that was having such an impact on journalism and partly as a way of sharing his own learning as he took up a challenging role in the organisation. His blog has become a great example of the ease and directness of weblogs with around 6,000 staff accessing it each month. His ability to reflect in public on issues and challenges and to then engage in conversation, in his blog's comments, with others interested or involved in these issues is a real departure from previous internal communications methods. In the same way as blogs have started to affect power and influence in the wider web they will most certainly begin to do the same inside organisations.

Wikis

Wikis are basically collaboratively written online documents. They make it easy for groups to write, edit, link or delete pages in a way that enables collaborative working as never before. The word isn't an acronym, as many people assume, but in fact comes from the Hawaiian phrase 'wiki wiki' which means quickly. A number of features are common to most wiki tools. It is very easy to write and publish content. The history of each page's changes are tracked and can be seen by all users. Differences between versions are represented graphically and it is easy to revert to previous versions of each page.

The power of wiki technology is most clearly seen in Wikipedia where users have created and sustained nearly a million pages (that is just in English – Wikipedia also has versions in more than a hundred languages) to create an encyclopaedia to rival the Encyclopaedia Britannica in depth and accuracy.

The BBC installed a wiki tool in 2007 but the take-up has been faster for it than any of the other tools with around 5,000 staff currently using it. The use of BBC wikis falls into the following three main categories:

WEBSITE CREATION

Previously, establishing a website was a relatively complex business with most people having to buy the services of a designer and developer to build a static site which took considerable effort to change and keep up to date. With a wiki they are able to start publishing online content immediately and maintaining it is very easy.

RESEARCH

Being able to set up a blank wiki page and ask users to populate it with their own knowledge and understanding of a subject is a really quick and easy way to access their accumulated knowledge.

As an example, the BBC's librarians wanted to establish what directories existed out in the business, what they were used for and who owned them. To try to do this through conventional means using IT would have been a challenge and may not have surfaced all of the informal and unofficial stuff that goes on at the margins. With the wiki, users started populating it with really useful information very quickly. They established a style and format for the data collection and were able to see and potentially change each other's information as they wrote. The result has been the pulling together, possibly for the first time, of a huge amount of complex and valuable information freely offered by users and shared openly in an easy and speedy manner.

COLLABORATIVE DOCUMENT CREATION

Many of us have experienced frustration at having to write a document as a group. What normally happens is one person will kick off the document in Word and save it on a shared server somewhere. The trouble is that others, even if they can remember where the document is and find it again, tend to defer to this original copy and are reticent about changing it and it tends to end up mostly as the original writer intended. With a wiki this changes. There is no clear ownership from the start, anyone can read and change content at any time. Changes are tracked and easily visible and version control is in the hands of all users. It is usually possible with wiki software to be alerted to any changes made to the document more quickly and efficiently than is possible using the traditional document metaphor.

As an example we decided that we needed a policy for staff who have their own personal, external weblogs. Having identified our bloggers using Connect a colleague from Editorial Policy created a wiki page, wrote a 'straw man' policy and emailed the URL of the page to the bloggers. They then piled in changing, editing, improving and discussing their changes until they eventually arrived at a position of consensus and the wiki page stopped changing. At this point the 'document' was exported as a PDF and taken to the formal organisation for ratification. The power of this is that those affected by the policy were able to get directly, and very efficiently, involved in its creation and as such are much more likely to support and adhere to its guidelines.

Project Management

Wikis can be used to actually carry out work too. Project plans can be easily created and shared and, through comments threads on the wiki page itself, users can discuss, debate and agree changes and developments. Timelines are easy to create and share and the very open nature of wiki communication means that it easy to keep teams up to date, informed and engaged in projects as they happen.

An example of the potential for this came about through an activity that wasn't directly work related. In our forums a member of staff expressed frustration that they couldn't take part in BBC competitions and this prevented them from entering the Digital Britain photography competition. I responded to their plea of 'Why can't we have our own competition?' by setting up a blank wiki page called 'BBC Staff Photography Competition' and establishing a closed Flickr group for uploading and sharing the photos. That was all I did – no management, no direction no deadlines. Within a couple of days an enthusiastic group had joined in creating the wiki and had produced rules, criteria, tagging guidelines, judges, timetables and even plans for a physical exhibition of the winning photos! The result was around 400 photos entered by 250 or so staff and an undertaking to make it an annual event. Now OK this wasn't a work-related project but imagine this principle applied to 'real' work!

Really Simple Syndication, Tags and Folksonomies

RSS stands for 'Really Simple Syndication' and is a method for weblogs, wikis or forums to publish their content in a way that readers can then subscribe to it. This allows readers to select sites they value, subscribe to their content and be alerted in applications called aggregators when that content has changed. They can then read the various content from these diverse sources in their aggregator removing the need to visit lots of sources and try to keep track of what has changed since the last time they logged on.

RSS is fundamental to building a knowledge-sharing environment using these tools and brings about possibly the biggest shift in behaviour. Web content becomes streams and patterns of new and relevant stories rather than static unrelated content. Users who get expert at finding 'the good stuff' can share their RSS subscriptions with others and help them piggy back on their experience and valuable sources of news and information.

Tagging is the process of adding metadata to documents, photos or music and so on to make it easier to find in the future. Flickr was one of the web-based tools that first made the benefits of tagging apparent. Flickr allows users to upload photos to the web and in doing so tag them with words that describe their content. With thousands of photos being uploaded and tagged every day Flickr takes these tags and makes the patterns in their usage visible in powerful ways.

Del.icio.us came next doing the same thing for URLs. Instead of saving a bookmark to your bookmark file you save it to Del.icio.us and in doing so tag it with words that help you remember its significance. Again Del.icio.us takes these tags and makes patterns with them.

The word folksonomies has been coined to describe this bottom-up process of tagging and categorisation and it is increasingly being seen as an adjunct or possibly even a replacement for conventional top -down taxonomies.

Conclusion

In the past written communication in organisations was mostly one way and almost always done by a relatively small group of people. With the advent of social computing it is possible to move from the relatively static and increasingly unused world of documents to a much more conversational style of communication that is available to everyone. The effectiveness and creativity that this unleashes is previously unseen in the business world and its potential is enormous.

Once these tools, and more importantly the behaviours they encourage, become more commonplace in organisations they will start to shift the process of discovery, generation and movement of knowledge. Indeed the ability for staff to find each other and collaborate across organisational and geographical boundaries and the consequences of such activity in terms of power and influence are relatively unknown. The old adage that knowledge meant power usually meant holding on to it and acting as a gatekeeper. In this new networked environment it is more true to say that if you aren't taking part and being seen to be willing to share what you know then you are less useful to the organisation than those who do – and are seen to be such!

For those of you not attracted to the benefits and opportunities described in this article I would suggest that you don't have much choice. When the kids texting each other in the playground and instant massaging each other in the evenings start working for you the connectedness that we are only just beginning to understand will be second nature to them. They won't stand for much less and the ability to connect and communicate with fellow workers will be part of their decision as to where they work. Organisations who embrace this new environment, learn to get the best out of it and adjust to accommodate its potential will gain serious business advantage.

And those who don't...?

38

First Steps in Implementing Social Media

by Marc Wright

Falling for social media is a bit like falling in love with the boy or girl from the wrong side of town. You've had the first date, you've fallen in love and now you want to introduce your new passion to the people back home.

But guess what? They're not impressed.

As you present your proposals for blogging and employee forums you imagine the tumbling of communication hierarchies; they see management anarchy. You envision an interconnected workforce; they see a company dating agency. It's like introducing a pole dancer to your maiden aunt.

The trouble is that social media looks just too much like fun for it to be a serious business application. Sure we want conversations in the company, but only if they are on-brand and aligned to the business mission. Yes we want collaboration, but not on Facebook. The sad truth is that internal communications is the last bastion of feudalism in twenty-first century life. Today we can laugh in the face of politicians, ignore the strictures of bureaucrats, create and destroy celebrities with the push of a text, but we are still supposed to kow-tow to our employers like serfs at the annual hiring fair.

At a simply-communicate conference on social media in 2007 I asked the audience what were the top ten barriers to introducing social media into their organisations.

Top of the list was the lack of a demonstrable business case. Three-quarters of the audience felt that they could not justify the cost of implementing these new tools. Now where have we heard that one before? Oh yes, back in the 1970s when a few brave souls had the temerity to propose that PCs should be placed on every desk with a small printer round the corner. The centralists in the IT department soon put their digits in those cracks; only to have the dam crash around them when they were up to their necks in the demands of personalised computing power.

And PCs and printers were serious investments in corporate cash. With the relatively low costs of social media the barriers to entry have shrunk to barely ankle-high. Internal communication will fall to the pressures of Web 2.0 and social media will become the mainstream inside companies just as it is on the outside.

But it won't be an easy ride. The feudal barons of Compliance, Security and Legality are not going to loosen their grip too easily. But there's hope: I suggest that there are four Trojan Horses that you can use to get through the gates of Troy and bring down the walls of hierarchy, cascades and megaphone communication.

Staff Directories

Every company has them. Black and white columns in small type lists grudgingly reveal colleagues' titles, their location and a telephone and email address, which is usually a year out of date. And yet when each of those human beings was originally recruited they came brandishing a CV with full details of the mountains they've climbed, the books that changed their lives, the languages they've learnt and the awards they've won. All that colour and sense of brio now lies locked away in the HR archives, and in the staff directory they are now just Brian Smith, Mgr Claims in SB/Unit39. And yet just hop across the webfence to Facebook and there we can be seen in our full colourful personalities – telling the world our innermost thoughts and trumpeting our tastes to all and sundry from the towers of web 2.0.

Imagine that you want to set up a virtual team to work on a project; or you are looking for a mentor to help you in your new job; or you want to interview someone about your company's operations in Prague. You can stick a pin in the directory or you can harness the richness of information about people's personalities that social media trumpets on a thousand profile pages.

And the wonderful thing about social media directories is that they are as near to free as you can get in corporate communications. The coding has all been written for a thousand networks before yours, and of course it's always up to date because users care more about their own profile than any other of the deteriorating information sitting inside your corporation. When the forward-thinking, ever-flexible chaps in IT demur, just point out that 3,000 of the company's staff are already on Facebook and if the IT department doesn't revamp the directory it will only be a matter of time before the rest of the company joins them.

User Group Forums

Here's a second idea that will appeal to the sales and marketing functions. Good companies love to listen to customers, in fact they welcome criticism for what it truly is: free consultancy. When those customers are other large companies then they really listen: just think how much BP spends on airlines, or Accenture on hotels. So User Groups are really important to companies; they provide feedback on what is going right and what is going wrong with a company's services and products.

The trouble is that running user groups involves taking your clients to a hotel, arranging a conference, wining and dining them – only to hear their whinges and complaints. You can imagine how popular these events are with your senior executives. Who wants to be lambasted about problems they don't know about in a forum where they cannot be set right until you get back to the office?

But there is another irresistible benefit of social media gained by creating an online forum for your company's user groups. Suddenly they have somewhere they can blow off in real time and share opinions with other customers. If it's an unjustified complaint then other users will tell them so – in a way that is far more effective to anything you could say. The customer isn't always right – but it might take another customer to tell them so. And if there is a buzz growing around a faulty product or poor service then you can identify it earlier and act more quickly. That way the problem can be acknowledged, sorted and your brand improved before the next user group meeting. The technology is simple – it's just a forum. And if you don't start using them, then there are plenty of unofficial pressure groups who will fill the vacuum and set one up instead.

Video Library

Now this one really is a no-brainer. There are hundreds, if not thousands, of video programmes knocking around the average Fortune 500 company. Some are best left buried, but many explain issues or can inform debate, if only people knew where to find them. VHS tapes have long been confined to the rubbish skip of history while CD-ROMs and DVDs, thanks to their very slimness, have all long since disappeared behind drawers or been turned into coasters.

But video compression and the net were made for each other and now any video can be turned into a file and flashed into cyberspace. Which means they can always be found (provided you tag them correctly), and it won't be long before the videos themselves will become searchable. And not only is distribution cheap, the cost of video production has plummeted and the number of recording devices available in the average company means that there is usually a lens to catch that significant moment, when a target is broken or a customer gives praise.

So look at archiving all your videos on your company server – or find a reputable supplier who will do it for you. Remember that anything on video about your company is capable of ending up on YouTube anyway, so better to manage your media assets rather than let them languish. I predict a time when internal communications departments will run their own company web TV channels. Who knows, they might even run their own daily soaps to keep employees informed through entertainment, in the same way that the British radio soap The Archers was first created to keep farmers up to date with best practice.

Project Wikis

Thanks to Wikipedia we all know what a wiki is, but do you know just how useful this software can be for your company?

A wiki is simply a web page that anyone can edit. You can limit it to particular groups or teams, who have to log on using a password to make changes. Wikipedia now has restrictions about who can and cannot update its pages, but this has not stopped it becoming the most powerful encyclopaedia in the world.

Wikis make even more sense inside companies. Here users are far less likely to abuse a wiki by deliberately inserting inaccurate or misleading information. You trust your staff with the firm's resources, brand and customers; why should you treat them as a lunatic fringe just because they are dealing with you online? Instead a wiki allows you to collaborate with your colleagues in the most efficient manner known to man. You always have access to the very latest version of a document; if you spot errors you can correct them immediately and changes can be tracked to individuals so you know who wrote what.

In these days of virtual meetings over teleconference and instant messaging, wikis are becoming the only anchor point in a sea of ambiguity and change. They are cheap to set up and no one needs training to benefit from one. The only challenge is to encourage people to use them and this requires you to remove all other forms of written communication.

Indeed I used a wiki to create and edit the edition of *The Gower Handbook of Internal Communication* that you have between your hands. All contributors to the Handbook posted their chapters to the wiki where they could see my revisions and edits as the book progressed.

Return on Investment

Staff directories, user group forums, video libraries and project wikis are the four easiest ways to get social media into your organisation. Employee forums, better internal search engines, instant messaging, video enabled VOIP, folksonomies, RSS feeds and web-enabled widgets will all follow in time. As people feel the benefits of social media in their lives outside the organisation, the faster they will demand the same features inside.

As for making the business case, don't be too concerned. It's all just code and data and it's getting cheaper every day. Forget about making cases for the ROI. Just dive straight in; the investment is negligible, if not zero, while the benefits are limitless.

39

Blogs and Blogging

by Marc Wright

It is the hot new tool in corporate communications that none of us can ignore for much longer. This chapter looks at what a blog is and how you can set one up; why they work; the power of external blogs; how to use blogs internally; the legal ramifications; and the key do's and don'ts.

What is a Blog?

Blog is short for weblog – a log that anyone can write and publish online. The clever bit is that blogs are interactive. They invite others to respond and comment on what they have just read. It's like a cross between an email and a webpage – a medium for one person to talk to many, but with the many having the chance to answer back.

They are made possible by a simple piece of software that you can download from the web. A popular version is typepad or wordpress but there are numerous sources – and they are all very good value for money. You can be up and blogging in minutes for a monthly fee that's less than the cost of a good sandwich.

A blog is different to a message board or a chat room in that it is driven by the thoughts and writings of the blogger. Other people can then respond to the blog and post their own views online – but these are tributaries off the main stream; the reader will always return to the blogger's column.

But describing a blog through its technical capability is like describing *Pride and Prejudice* as a medium-sized book with stiff covers. The technology is irrelevant; what is important is what you do with your blog.

Why Do They Work?

Blogs work because they deliver the authentic voice of an individual. They circumvent the usual PR happy brochure speak that is the curse of corporate communication. They work because they are immediate and are associated with a human face in your company, They are like a note dashed off while waiting to board an airplane: all the embellishments of polite writing are stripped away – leaving just pure opinion, pithily expressed. It is this quality of authenticity that makes them so appealing to the reader – a good blog reads as if you are getting the news first hand.

Of course it all depends on the writer; a conscientious lawyer will probably make a poor blogger, checking their facts to the nth degree, covering their statements with caveats and get-out clauses and reviewing and revising a document to the point of insipid irrelevance. But if you – or a senior director – have strong opinions and a clear idea of what you want to say and can get to your laptop in a timely and regular fashion, then blogging is for you.

The Power of External Blogs

Journalists love blogs – it gives them online access to attributable sources inside your company. For better or for worse, they can circumvent the PR officer and get to your CEO's views (or at least they think they can). Blogs allow a direct feed from your senior directors' minds to the outside world, and appear to give an openness and honesty – particularly if the blog publishes criticism of your company in any posted replies.

Readers and consumers find these postings refreshing. Here at last is a company that is prepared to be honest in its own communication and is big enough to take negative comments. Journalists can copy and paste the thoughts of senior executives and track the views of others inside and outside the organisation through a blog conversation that keeps expanding. Sure, there is a risk that people will be critical but criticism of your company already exists on the web. Just type your company name into Google followed by the word 'sucks' and you will get an idea of what is out there.

Through a corporate blog, you can control the more extreme and illegal comments through a blog moderator, and you get all the kudos of a communication channel that makes you look transparent. Companies love blogs because they offer them free, word-of-mouth marketing for them and their products. Chris Barger is Vice President of Communications at General Motors, North America. He inherited and developed two very successful blogs for the car-maker. http://smallblock.gmblogs.com/ which is a highly focused blog on a particular range of GM engines, and http://fastlane.gmblogs.com/ which is a platform for Bob Lutz to talk about more general goings-on in the GM world. Lutz writes from the hip – usually without much concern for legal clearance; his blog gets an incredible 7,500 visits a day and generates 3,600 consumer responses.

Since each blog constitutes a web page, these can be searchable –which means that many users will be driven to your site via a blog. The blog run by Air Conditioning Contracts of America is second only to Google in driving traffic (and income) to their website as engineers log on to get answers to specific questions.

Using Blogs for Internal Communication

Because blogs are interactive, they are ideal for getting conversations going inside an organisation and they can be a litmus test for contentious issues that are bubbling under the surface. Equally a blog is an opportunity for a CEO to demonstrate what is most important to them at the time. If they are focused on a particular subject, then others will be as well. And if your CEO finds the time at the end of a busy schedule to write 300 words on the subject, then that is even more impactful.

GM monitor and censor any comments from the workforce that could be libellous or insulting but otherwise they let all comments through on to the blog. It is a self-managing system; if someone is unfair or unrepresentative in their comments, then others soon contribute to the blog to give a more rounded picture of the issue.

Your blog does not have to come from the top. Subject experts buried inside your organisation can become blogging stars if they are masters of their subject. There is no official blog in Microsoft – instead there are thousands of individuals blogging inside the company.

The Legal Bits

The downside of blogging is just too horrendous for the legal mind to contemplate – a combination of libel law, trademark infringement and the CEO unbridled all conjure up a nightmare for most companies' legal departments. That's why many communicators don't bother to get the lawyers involved until after the blog has been running for a while. By then the upsides are more obvious, the CEO will be converted and none of your staff have broken the law. It's all a question of being able to trust smart people – that's why you hired them in the first place.

Clearly, you have to take some basic precautions: a trained moderator who checks comments for libel before they are posted, and a cool head of communications who can spot trouble at 7 pm on a Friday evening when the CEO wants to use the corporate blog to settle scores with the Press.

Do's and Don'ts

Do:

- keep your blog down to a couple of paragraphs;
- use active language;
- encourage feedback;
- monitor the blogosphere – know what others are saying;
- stay focused and specialist;
- keep new weblog content coming – at least once a week.

Don't:

- ghost write your CEO's blog – you will be found out;
- get too diffuse – remember the blog is there to build the company's reputation and sell product;

- comment on your share price;
- criticise new blogs that spring up from other departments; it's the best way of killing them stone dead.

40

Blogging for the Finance Sector

by Yang-May Ooi

At The Housing Finance Corporation (THFC), we wanted a fresh, innovative way to engage with our clients and stakeholders after years of mailing out a PDF newsletter every quarter. The blogging platform was an obvious technology to use to create an interactive online presence for the business. But first, we had to consider some very real issues about reputation, brand and time-investment.

THFC is a specialist not-for-profit lender that makes loans to housing associations to provide affordable housing to tenants in housing need in the UK. Since 1987, we have lent nearly £2 billion to the social housing sector, funded through the issue of bonds to private investors and by borrowing from banks. In this context, our online presence needed to reflect the serious business of finance and our unique position in the market.

The first obvious thing to consider was what we were going to blog about. What would engage our readers and give them a reason to keep coming back to read our blog? There are already a number of weekly housing sector journals and magazines employing professional journalists to cover news and topical issues in the housing world. It would not make sense for our blog to try to be a housing news delivery portal. We wondered about commenting on sector news – but we would then be just an echo chamber for information that was already in the public domain. Piers Williamson, THFC's Chief Executive, a long-time follower of political blogs with bite, was very clear that he did not want an anaemic online newsletter that had nothing innovative or bold to offer.

What seemed to be missing in the market was a forum for housing finance insiders and leaders to come together at a specialist level to share their expertise on current issues affecting the sector. Using the Wordpress blogging platform, we launched THFC Space, the online discussion space for housing sector chief executives, finance directors, treasurers or equivalent. While the technology makes the site a blog, the content, focused as it is on housing finance- and treasury management-related issues, allows it to be approached by senior executives as a serious financial journal.

We also made the decision that THFC Space should be a private, members-only forum available on an invitation-only basis to CEOs and senior housing finance executives. Its articles deal with specific finance- and treasury-related topics requiring a high-level of sector knowledge and expertise for productive engagement by the readers. The 'invitation-only' basis of the blog puts us in a unique position in that we know each of our registered members personally and this helps us target the articles specifically to the interests and concerns of our audience. For Piers Williamson,

> *The joy of the blogosphere is its openness. However, the quality of around 90 per cent of blog posts is dubious. THFC Space is targeted at CEOs and CFOs who have limited time to trawl typical blogs. By keeping the site 'exclusive' we aim to keep the quality of posts and debate up. The flip side is it takes longer to build up a truly inter-active exchange of ideas.*

For a specialist blog with a limited readership like this, the priority then is high quality articles rather than a high rate of published posts. We aim to publish on average one article every other Wednesday and we have implemented an editorial process with regular team meetings, an editorial planner and schedule for the delivery of articles. As editor, my job is to encourage the corporate team to come up with ideas for articles – as well as making sure they write them in time. To minimise the time the team spends 'blogging', I manage the administrative aspects of the blog such as uploading posts and images, reviewing comments and managing subscribers – so all the team have to do is focus on the writing.

As well as articles from within the organisation, a hallmark of THFC Space is to offer views from industry leaders, especially those with an insider's specialist knowledge of topical issues. Piers Williamson's view is that:

> *THFC would by no means claim to come up with all the bright ideas. Equally, we think our customers are just as interested in listening to each other as they are to us and there is scope for leading ideas on a variety of finance and leadership issues to come from many sources.*

For example, as a key report on financial regulation was published in June 2007, we invited three leaders in the field – the Deputy Head of Policy for the

Council of Mortgage Lenders, the Chief Inspector of Housing and the Chief Executive of the National Housing Federation – to offer their reactions to the report. They were our first 'guest bloggers' but I don't think they or our readers would have thought of their contribution in that way!

Piers Williamson says, 'There are too many fence-sitters out there in corporate newsletter land so our brief to our bloggers and guest bloggers is for short and snappy articles that state an opinion.' We also use photos[1] from Flickr.com to illustrate the blog posts in a jokey but memorable way – these help to pull readers in. Social media tools have also been useful in interspersing the serious articles with an occasional light-hearted touch – such as an online poll to gauge views on the reasons for planning delays and a slideshow of photographs from our recent 20th anniversary celebration.

The main challenge week on week for us is the management of the process – contacting guest writers, making sure that articles are written, adding new members and uploading and formatting the posts and images. But as managing THFC Space becomes part of our weekly routine, the blog is ingraining itself into our transactional work – our executive team are finding opportunities to remind clients to visit the online forum and notice issues that would make good articles. Also, our clients are spread across the whole country and we've found that some of our most avid readers are those who are located in the most remote regions since our blog offers an easily accessible online forum without the constraints of geography.

By sharing expert views on our particular industry with our clients in this way, THFC Space has become another opportunity for us to add value to our stakeholders offline as well as online.

For corporations looking at blogging and social media as ways to extend their online presence, I would suggest that the keys to successful engagement lie in.

Knowing the Audience You Want to Engage With

Identify who are the influencers or decision makers you want to engage with. These may be your customers or clients or your internal staff – or other demographics that you may not currently be reaching through your

1 Licensed under the Creative Commons Licence.

communications strategies. Put yourself in their place and ask 'What would I be interested in? Why would I want to keep returning to this site?' THFC Space specifically targets the key decision makers that we are likely to do business with – finance directors and chief executives. The blog specifically offers them a high-level forum for sector leaders themselves to share ideas directly relevant to them, unmediated by the press, and this distinguishes it from other publications such as the housing journals and magazines. The content is focused on what our audience is interested in, not on THFC as such – so press release-style articles about THFC are out and thought-provoking discussion around topical housing finance issues are in.

Finding a USP (Unique Selling Point) for Your Blog/social Media Presence

It can be tempting to fill up your blog, podcast or video blog with everything and anything to do with your company, business or industry but having a clear 'mission statement' setting out what your blog or site is about helps to keep you focused on relevant content for your target audience and also tells your audience clearly what they can expect. In particular, in an increasingly crowded blogosphere, your blog's USP will distinguish it from your competitor's blog or other blogs on similar topics. Ideally, you should be able to sum up your USP in the strapline for your blog – the advantage of that is it is clear to everyone who lands on your site what they will find there. On THFC Space, we have preferred to favour fewer good quality articles over more regular 'space fillers' in order to avoid diluting the value of the site in the eyes of our busy senior executive audience.

If Calling it a Blog isn't Helpful, Call it Something Else

Sometimes people can't see beyond a name and all its associations, negative or otherwise. If setting up a 'blog' conjures up images of anarchy and the end of the civilised world as we know it for your board of directors, then you might propose setting up an easily updatable resource site for up-to-date articles, sortable by date and topic and annotatable by readers. A blog is nothing more than a hip name for a great content management system – and that functionality is what makes the platform a useful tool, not its name.

Setting Up a Proper Management/Editorial Process and the Specific Role of Blog/Social Media Manager

An organisational blog or social media project needs to be viewed as any other organisational project – and as such it is good practice to put in place appropriate project management policies. While the infrastructure of a blog can enable many different individuals to upload blog posts directly to the site, it makes sense to coordinate the content and timing of postings. This way you can avoid numerous posts on one topic all uploaded on one day with the blog empty for weeks on end afterwards. Some bloggers within your organisation may prefer to focus purely on content and leave the technical uploading to someone else. It also makes sense to ensure that all bloggers understand who their audience is and what the 'mission statement' of the site is. There are also various administrative tasks such as dealing with comments, spam and email queries that need to be managed daily. Social media optimisation also requires time and resourcing – for example, making links with other blogs, expanding the network and readership of the blog through submission to blog portals and so on. All these elements are most appropriately coordinated through a social media manager, who would have primary responsibility for the blog but who needs to be supported by an 'editorial' team so that the technical aspects, the social media marketing aspects and the content come together seamlessly.

Having an Engaged Blogging Team

Your staff are in a good position to help identify the audience for your blog and to develop its mission statement and USP. They are the people who know your customers and clients and their expertise about your business can add value to the blog content. Training will help them brainstorm ideas for posts in keeping with the blog's mission statement and also help them express themselves in a style that works for social media. Where staff are encouraged to blog, they need to be given time within their work day to do so and their input into the blog can be treated in a similar way to how other marketing activities are incorporated into their objectives and appraisals. For all staff, even those who do not actively blog, can be encouraged to 'spread the word' about the blog to clients and to suggest ideas for content. We have found that over time, all these activities around our blog mean that we are more actively engaged in reflecting on and discussing issues pertinent to our clients and our sector internally as well as externally, which is of course good for our business.

Finally, and Most Importantly, Leading from the Front, Preferably at Chief Executive or Other Senior Management Level

As with any organisational project, senior level support can contribute substantially to its success. Blogging works best in this setting as a team project so a style of leadership that sustains the team approach is more likely to help the blog flourish than a style that is more hierarchical. An engaged senior level executive can facilitate and encourage the blogging team to create the best content for what is essentially an online showcase for the organisation as well as for the bloggers. Content management in this context is closely allied with client or employee management – the best content is not necessarily the rosiest content and sometimes, being seen to grasp the nettle of a tricky issue can gain more respect from your stakeholders than being perceived as serving up the usual PR spin. Appropriate senior level engagement in the blog means that such issues can be debated and sensibly steered through the blogging process. The blog can also be leveraged for offline networking, serving as a useful conversation stimulator at meetings and conferences as well as a means of extending the business's real world connections if you invite a range of guest bloggers to take part on your blog.

41

Writing for the Web

by Fiona Robertson

The web is a curious beast. Unlike other forms of written information, material on the web is not read in the conventional sense; it is scanned. Perhaps it's the fact that it's harder to read from a VDU or maybe it's because the reader is absorbing information and searching new hyperlinks simultaneously? What we do know is that, either way, surfers rarely pore over an article which appears online.

Instead, they cast an eye over the page, trying to pick out key pieces of information or significant words and hyperlinks. This being the case, web pages and the material they contain are organised to facilitate scanning.

This chapter explains what that means in practical terms, covering how to set about structuring and styling your material for online publication as well as looking at the language usage, tone, references and links that deliver best practice web design.

Web Usability

In a study by Jakob Neilsen, 79 per cent of users scanned pages; only 16 per cent read word by word and users read from computer screens 25 per cent more slowly than from a printed page. So, before you create an online article, first consider how the end product will be used, and therefore how you can make it more user-friendly. Consider how you can make your page layout conducive to scanning by organising ideas or subjects into separate paragraphs. Also highlight key words, topics and links to related pages, make sentences short and to-the-point and use simple, clear language.

Page Layout

Structure your page like a newspaper column, restricting the number of words in a line to no more than 12. This has been shown to yield maximum readability since a viewer can take in a whole line at a glance. Use a Sans Serif typeface, with plain legible characters and make your text stand out by contrasting the colour of your type with a background. The default is always black text on a white background – but if you decide to change these colours, make sure the result is easy to read because some colour combinations make text virtually illegible.

Give meaning to your content through the use of titles, headings and subheadings. Use line and character spacing intelligently to separate articles, headings and paragraphs in order to give them obvious definition.

Content Structuring

Use the inverted pyramid principle adopted by journalists. Let your headline encapsulate your story or theme then give a brief explanation of your headline in the opening paragraph, using one or two sentences. Discuss the most important aspects of your article first, then expand on the subject a little more in each paragraph that follows. Reserve details and background information for the end of a piece.

This way, readers will get the gist of your article immediately; those that are interested will drill down into the details up to the point that their curiosity is answered. Organise your material into one topic per paragraph; it allows readers to skip through a subject quickly and efficiently, dipping into the areas that interest them and ignoring the rest.

Writing Style

Again, follow a journalistic approach to get straight to the heart of a subject. Answer the fundamental questions: *who, what, when, where, why* and *how* to give top-line information, whatever the subject. Make both sentences and paragraphs short and crisp, avoiding lengthy or convoluted subordinate clauses. If a subject requires more detail, cover it in as many short sentences as are needed; alternatively, use bulleted lists to summarise a series of points. Use active verbs rather than passive ones – they suggest immediacy and action, and their tone is more direct. Use only as many modifiers as are necessary – so no flowery prose; no unnecessary adjectives; no wordy descriptors.

In keeping with briefer sentences, sparer language and active verbs, also avoid jargon, foreign expressions and hackneyed sayings. They'll lead to clumsy phrasing and prevent you from saying what you actually mean.

Presentation Tips

For titles and headings to be efficient, always make them succinct and literal. Puns and wordplay may be ambiguous or misleading so always make your titles explicit. Use headings to label subject matter so that readers can identify the sections they want at a glance. Also bear in mind that, as headings can be identified by search engines, they will be used to direct readers to your content. It's therefore vital that the titles you give to a piece are an accurate reflection of their content. Headings also appear in indexes and teasers from other pages so spend some time crafting them until they're just right.

A parallel was drawn (above) between a web page and a newspaper column; the use of headings and titles is where the two media diverge. Newspaper titles can afford to capture the imagination with figurative or oblique statements because they're usually presented with imagery to give context. The web, however, relies solely on language; material is sourced using precise, literal word searches. Given the way the web is used, it's important to input information in line with this functionality; hence the crucial importance of using the correct wording online.

Best Practice Web Design

The information given so far could apply to most forms of written communication; however, writing for the web is unique because it contains embedded links to other areas of an article, to other web pages or to other sites altogether. This means an article is not a stand-alone document; it is yet another piece within a huge mirrored mosaic that reflects, and is reflected by, an infinite number of the other elements around it. As with titling and headings, linking is an important element of writing for the web and best practice as regards hyperlinks requires the following actions

Embed links at appropriate places in your text, ideally highlighting words that are significant or relevant to a link's destination. Label links correctly so that a reader understands where they are likely to be taken; State whether a link will take you to a different file type (for example, from a document file to a PDF). Program links to open in a new window so that, if a link isn't required, the reader can return to the original article immediately. Don't standardise your links; make each one individual. For example, don't create a hyperlink using meaningless or repeated text like, 'Click Here'; it tells your users nothing and can be misleading.

Create metadata for each article you post online, which means processing the relevant words and phrases that readers are likely to use in their searches of that subject. That way, you can steer other web users to your piece. By placing links strategically, you can help readers to scan your material since key words will be highlighted. Links that are appropriate (in terms of both related subject matter and placement within a piece) can prompt action: you can help to direct a reader's navigation of your site.

Finally, links allow you to provide additional information on your pages without reinventing the wheel each time; you can simply harness the resources that already exist online by placing links in your material to appropriate reference sources anywhere on the web.

42

Instant Messaging as a Communication Tool

by Joanna Goodrick

Instant Messaging (IM) is one of the communication tools that fall under the banner of social media – it's one of the new kids on the block and is often still viewed with suspicion by businesses. But it's also a close relative of email and therefore offers some interesting benefits for communications in a corporate environment.

What's the Big Deal with Instant Messaging?

In case you were thinking that IM is not going to knock on your workplace door anytime soon, let's take a look at some interesting trends: IM is estimated to be used already by some 65–75 per cent of employees. Projections vary, but it is widely held among technology strategists that IM will one day be as ubiquitous as email is currently; just think of what was first said about the future of email! As with other social media, IM is associated with a trend among youngsters and sits alongside blogs and wikis as tools whose usefulness in the workplace doesn't yet seem clear to many communicators and executives.

What Instant Messaging Does

IM is a way of 'pinging' messages directly to a contact who can reply directly in the form of a 'written conversation' rather than that of an 'electronic letter' (on which the term 'email' is of course originally based). The key difference is that an IM conversation takes place in real time, in contrast to asynchronous email exchanges. The most-cited advantages of IM are that it enables more spontaneous and therefore time-saving communication and that it facilitates human interaction with a much stronger experience of a natural-feeling conversation. Some even argue that IM can help promote innovation and creativity. What it definitely does is encourage communication that resembles a telephone chat – thanks to the rapidity of response and the ephemeral way the message trail disappears once the conversation is closed.

The 'disappearance' of 'conversations' can be light relief to people who fight to keep their email volume in check. IM offers an effective solution for communication that doesn't clog up the screen, overfill inboxes or demand management to keep it under control.

Industry research has found that email volume can be reduced by around 40 per cent following the introduction of IM.[1] Reducing the time spent sorting through email – estimated to take up hours of the typical information worker's week – is certainly an appealing feature of IM for many people and businesses. In addition to the ability to send messages, IM systems typically allow people to flag presence information so that contacts can quickly see their status and choose their communication method accordingly.

Is There a Catch?

While IM certainly has its advantages, in the business environment, it can appear to have disadvantages from the perspectives of IT, legal and regulatory or compliance areas. The downside of some of the well-known Internet-based versions of IM is that they don't run over the in-house IT infrastructure; this can raise concerns around the security and traceability of company data. Fortunately, being in a world where technology tends to provide solutions to its own problems, major software companies have developed enterprise versions of IM that can be custom-configured to meet the organisation's compliance and security requirements. For example, IM communities can be locked down to restrict them to users who share the corporate network or smaller subsets of these. Attachments to messages can be automatically excluded and 'conversations' can be stored in an archive – just as organisations already archive their email data.

There have also been some objections around the human side of IM: does presence information mean that 'Big Brother' is watching to see what employees

1 Gartner research.

are up to? Does having IM mean that people will waste time on non work-related chatter? This last concern should at least in part be allayed by the argument that there is an associated reduction in email; IM is not necessarily going to have an additional negative impact and people are probably communicating like this anyway – either over email or another means.

Other Advantages to Instant Messaging

Depending on the IT environment, enterprise packages can integrate with the standard company (computer!) desktop suite to offer the kind of presence and personal contact information described above. They also present the ability to attach links and files and to integrate with mobile devices, the intranet interface and so on. With the right product and infrastructure, further possibilities include web- and videoconferencing along with Voice-over IP (VoIP) telephony integration. Some of these features help to facilitate mobility and flexibility and may work in support of policies to allow homeworking.

Some tips for effective IM implementation include the following:

- Work closely with business areas such as IT and legal on all aspects of any new implementation – for example, consider whether there is a legal requirement to archive messages, as this will have implications for the IT infrastructure side.
- Ensure adequate information is provided to people about how to use IM effectively and its particular benefits.
- If necessary, update your company's email/e-communications acceptable-use policy to cover IM.

Create Some Buzz

Finally, it's a good idea to create interest around the launch of IM, including awareness information surrounding etiquette. Some employees will not be familiar with using IM and may not understand its purpose or benefits; therefore, try to point out its advantages: that it provides a useful alternative to longwinded or formal communication; its convenience factor where phone use may be an issue in open plan environments; and IMs potential to reduce email.

When educating employees on IM etiquette, be sure to remind them to:

- Maintain respectful language when writing IM messages (no matter how informal the tool).
- Keep it within sensible limits: IM may lighten your inbox, but if others feel bombarded by it, it can become just as intrusive and annoying as too much email!
- Remember that the e-communications (or equivalent), legal and other policies of the organisation still apply to use of IM.
- Use features appropriately: in a scenario where old IM message trails are not accessible from the computer desktop, people should avoid sending important business information that will subsequently be needed for collaboration. Unlike with email, the message will have disappeared!

For companies who choose to implement IM as a communications tool, be sure to recognise the need to work with IT, legal and other relevant business areas to ensure that functionality and criteria for use are well-understood. Of course, these IM etiquette guidelines will be most successful if developed and adapted to suit the particular organisation and culture in which they apply.

Index

Figures are indicated by **bold** page numbers, tables by *italic* numbers.

S

simply-**communicate**.com

www.simply-communicate.com is the first port of call for any professional working in internal communications. With over 1,200 separate articles of advice, toolkits and templates we cover every aspect of internal communication inside organisations. And each fortnight we publish fresh case studies and advice in our magazine simplyupdated.

We are passionate about our subject and travel around the world visiting the major conferences on communications and employee engagement to find the latest thinking and case studies that deliver real practical benefits to the large organisations.

We run monthly seminars featuring the world's leading practitioners such as Gerry McGovern on intranets, Steve Crescenzo on advanced writing and editing, Shel Holtz on Web 2.0 and Liam FitzPatrick – the UK's leading trainer on corporate communications.

Our editorial team is based in New York (Kelly Kass) and London (Marc Wright) and we have correspondents throughout Europe, Australia, India and Russia. You can read the simply team's blog at http://simply-blogging.typepad.com/weblog/

But we are not just observers; in the simplygroup we have teams of practitioners.

simplygoodadvice (www.simply-goodadvice.com) is a hands-on consultancy that works with multi-nationals like Maersk, Shell, BP and the University of Cambridge.

simplyexperience (www.simply-experience.com) is a full-services production company working in events, video for clients such as Tetra Pak and Vodafone.